VENEZUELA:
Oil and Politics

Rómulo Betancourt

VENEZUELA: Oil and Politics

TRANSLATED BY EVERETT BAUMAN

Foreword by Arthur M. Schlesinger, Jr.
Introduction by Franklin Tugwell

HOUGHTON MIFFLIN COMPANY BOSTON
1979

Library of Congress Cataloging in Publication Data

Betancourt, Rómulo, Pres. Venezuela, date
    Venezuela, oil and politics.

    Translation of Venezuela, política y petróleo.
    Includes bibliographical references and index.
      1.   Petroleum industry and trade—Venezuela.
2. Venezuela—Economic conditions—1918–
3. Venezuela—Politics and government—1935–
I. Title.
HD9574.V42B413 1978   338.2'7'2820987   78-26422
ISBN 0-395-27945-3

Printed in the United States of America

Q10 9 8 7 6 5 4 3 2 1

Contents

Foreword

This man and this book go to the heart of a tangle of problems that have agitated and transformed the modern world — the struggle for national independence against political and economic colonialism, the international consequences of oil, and the vision of democracy in developing countries.

These issues shaped Rómulo Betancourt's life. He left his mark on all of them. Nineteenth century Venezuela had hardly known democracy; and, when Betancourt was born in 1908, his country was still passing from one military dictator to another. Juan Vicente Gómez, who came to power the year after his birth, reigned in Caracas until 1935. In these years the oozing black sludge that Latin American Indians had called "the devil's excrement" was found to contain oil. The Gómez dictatorship enriched itself by selling the oil field rights to foreign corporations. As a young law student in the 1920s, Betancourt joined a rebellion against Gómez and was exiled.

From an early point he saw oil as the key to his country's independence and its future. Returning to Caracas in 1936 after Gómez's death, he pointed out that Venezuela's subsoil had been partitioned among the oil trusts and that 80 percent of Venezuela's exports consisted of petroleum, "an industry in which Venezuelan capital plays no part at all." The national problem, he said, was that of an economy "dominated by the most daring and aggressive sector of the international financial world, the oil companies." Driven underground in 1937, he began work on the book that grew into *Venezuela: Oil and Politics*.

The same year he founded the clandestine Partido Democrático Nacional, legalized in 1941 as Acción Democrática. In 1945 the authoritarian Medina regime was overthrown, and Betancourt became president of a provisional democratic government. Venezuela was now the world's leading oil exporter and second only to the United States as an oil producer. The first Betancourt government stopped the policy of granting new concessions to foreign companies, instituted the celebrated "fifty-fifty" division of oil revenues between the companies and the government and backed the labor unions which negotiated the first collective bargaining contract in the oil fields. It also organized a general election in which, for the first time in Venezuela's history, the people chose the President and the Congress through direct and universal vote. The new President, Rómulo Gallegos, the celebrated novelist, was overthrown by a military conspiracy nine months after his inauguration. Betancourt, driven into an exile that lasted ten years, took advantage of unaccustomed leisure to complete this book. It was published in Mexico in 1956.

Venezuela: Oil and Politics is a remarkable work—as analysis, as history and as advocacy. Betancourt has never concealed his passion about his nation. His prose has a personal pungency and bite unusual among Latin American political leaders, so many of whom are addicted to an endless flow of juridical abstractions. In his book he explains how the national life had come to hang on the thread of oil. But he perceived that, if oil was essential to Venezuela, it was also essential to the industrialized world. In the past the possession by weak countries of vital raw materials had been an irresistible invitation to imperialist expansion; but the dependence of world industry on cheap energy might now turn oil into a potent weapon against foreign masters. In any event, Venezuela could not pretend to be truly independent until it had regained control over its own natural resources. Betancourt saw oil as the key not only to authentic national independence but to national economic and social development as well. By plowing oil revenues back into Venezuelan society instead of remitting them to foreign investors, a progressive Venezuelan government, he contended, could build the country's infrastructure, encourage diversification and begin the institutional reforms necessary for balanced and sound economic growth.

Elected President in 1958 after the popular uprising against the crooked Pérez Jiménez regime, Betancourt began to carry his program into action. In 1960 the Libyan oil fields came into play. Irritated by Betancourt's policies and emboldened by the discovery of alternative sources of supply, the oil companies pushed down the price of Venezuelan oil. One result was the formation in 1960 of the Organization of Petroleum Exporting Countries (OPEC)—a Venezuelan initiative designed to protect oil prices. (In later years Venezuela became a moderating influence in OPEC, "totally rejecting," Betancourt wrote in 1977, "the idea that OPEC is entitled to use its very powerful economic weapon to exert political pressure and even in some cases to blackmail third parties.") The internal Acción Democrática program culminated in the nationalization of Venezuelan oil by President Carlos Andrés Pérez, with Betancourt's enthusiastic support, in 1976.

So far this program—the use of oil for national independence and economic development—might have been undertaken by any reasonably intelligent Latin American or Middle Eastern despot. But what distinguished Betancourt from the egotistical nationalists of his age was his profound and persevering conviction that oil could also serve as the basis for democratic institutions. His nation had suffered under one or another arbitrary regime for all but three of the first fifty years of his life. A brief association with a

Communist group while he was in exile in the 1930s had convinced him that authoritarianism was as odious on the left as on the right. He was persuaded that progressive democracy could strike roots in Latin America, and he was determined to make it succeed in Venezuela.

This determination embroiled him both with the oligarchic right and the totalitarian left. He had the honor of being regarded as the major target both by Trujillo of the Dominican Republic, whose bravos tried to murder him in 1960, and by Castro of Cuba, whose terrorists engaged in guerrilla warfare against his government in 1961 – 64. "If the Communists have been hostile to my regime," Betancourt said in 1963, "it is . . . because we are carrying out the type of social action that strips the Communists of support and followers."

President John F. Kennedy launched his *Alianza para el Progreso* in 1961 on the gamble that progressive democracy on the Betancourt model would prevail in Latin America. In 1963 Betancourt came to Washington. After a brisk private exchange between the two presidents over the import restrictions imposed on Venezuelan oil by the Eisenhower administration—an exchange recalled candidly on pages 389 – 391 of this work—Kennedy saluted Betancourt publicly. Betancourt's battle for democracy, Kennedy said, had made him "a symbol of what we wish for our own country and for our sister republics. . . . You represent all that we admire in a political leader."

In 1964 for the first time in Venezuela history one freely elected president peacefully succeeded another. After so many years as a cockpit for ambitious *caudillos*, Venezuela was on its way to becoming the most stable democracy in South America. This was an historic achievement. Yet in retrospect it would seem that the Kennedy administration had overrated the capacity of the democratic left, at least in the short run, to change things south of the border. In the years since, the younger generation in many Latin countries has turned to more fanatic creeds and more militant solutions. Even in Venezuela the democratic left has not attained its objectives. In later years Betancourt himself was a stern critic of the failure of progressive democracy to achieve more in his own country.

Venezuela, he wrote in 1977, "clearly faces the possibility of going rotten, or even disintegrating." He called the distribution of income—65 percent going to the richest 20 percent of the population, 7.9 percent to the poorest 40 percent—"quite simply revolting because it is so inequitable." He continued:

> The pretentious facade, which announces that this is the Latin American country with the highest per capita income, and one of the ten countries in the whole world with the largest holdings of strong currencies to support its own monetary system, conceals the dramatic fact that this is a poor rich nation.

The flow of oil money, Betancourt feared, threatened the moral integrity of Venezuelan society. "Our system of values has suffered a grave distortion."

A "crazy collective hysteria" had incited his countrymen to insensate consumer extravagance. Even worse was the spread of corruption and graft.

> The conspiracy of multimillion dollar rackets against the national interest is be-
> ginning to contaminate all levels of Venezuelan society. Venezuela has now de-
> veloped its own version of the Mexican 'mordida,' a cut taken by government offi-
> cials, who, though previously incorruptible in Venezuela, have now started to
> demand regular bribes and to sell small-scale favours. . . . There must be no delay
> in combating the shameful vice of administrative corruption until it is completely
> stamped out.

The old warrior at the age of seventy remained full of passion about his
country. If progressive democracy has a future in the southern half of the western hemisphere, it will owe much of its hope, élan and energy to the example
of Rómulo Betancourt, who has so nobly combined an indomitable dedication
to national independence and an analytical mastery of his nation's problems
with an iron conviction that these problems can be met within the framework
of a free and humane democracy.

New York, September 1978   Arthur Schlesinger, Jr.

Introduction

This book was written more than twenty years ago, while Rómulo Betancourt was living in exile in Puerto Rico, and it has undergone minor revisions twice, once in 1967 and again in preparation for its publication in English. If anything, however, the passage of time has enhanced its value as an historical document and as a lively and detailed description of a critical epoch in Venezuelan development.

Two themes shape the narrative: the founding and nourishment of democratic politics through the consolidation of strong party organization, and the taming and domestication of an outpost of the world's most powerful international industry. It will prove a useful resource both to those interested in Venezuela's distinctive pattern of economic and political development—a pattern that today stands in such marked contrast to the unstable authoritarianism that has seized so many developing nations—and to those seeking a different perspective on the long, and ongoing, struggle between developing nations and foreign corporations over the control of petroleum resources.

As a book, *Venezuela: Oil and Politics* is not objective in the scholarly, academic meaning of this term; on the contrary, it is a very personal and partial account of events, one intended to serve as both explanation and justification of Betancourt's, and his party's, actions and policies. Betancourt has strong opinions, and in writing often resorts to hyperbole and exaggeration in defending them. As he confessed in the prologue to the first edition: "I write as I think and feel. Venezuela is in my blood and bones. Its troubles hurt me. When I write of them I would be a hypocrite were I to pretend to be impartial." As he defends and attacks, explains and justifies, Betancourt also reveals a great deal about himself and about his distinctive leadership style, which is both egalitarian and *criollo* in character, reflecting his identification with, and genuine respect for, the ordinary citizens of Venezuela and their traditions and customs.

Betancourt himself grew up in a small town, in a family of modest means. His father was an immigrant from the Canary Islands, his mother a Venezuelan of mixed racial background. Although he studied at the well-known

Liceo Caracas—his father wanted him to become a lawyer—his political activities interrupted his formal education and he was forced to do without the university credentials that are so widely admired in Venezuela as a sign of success.

Betancourt's leadership style is evident in his manner of speaking, and in the ways he deals with his countrymen, as well as in his writing. Like so many skilled politicians, he is a gifted orator, able to stir his audience with ease. But he is also able to communicate with the poorest of his countrymen in a way few others can. He has a knack for expressing difficult ideas in a colloquial, often colorful, language. His appreciation of the customs and traditions of the various regions of his country is enormous, and surfaces quickly in conversation. Although his lifestyle is modest (by Venezuelan standards), he is an enthusiastic gastronome; he relishes the varieties of local fruits, cheeses, and dishes, and serves these with regularity at his own table. In contrast to many members of the political and economic elite, he communicates pride in his country's own traditions and respect for the average Venezuelan's ability, given the chance, to understand the most complicated issues of public policy.

Of all the problems he handled as a political leader, none has been more important, and occupied more of Rómulo Betancourt's time, than the formulation and implementation of petroleum policy. And though many have contributed to Venezuela's success in managing petroleum affairs—among them Gumersindo Torres, Nestor Luis Pérez and, of course, Juan Pablo Pérez Alfonzo—no Venezuelan has had more direct responsibility for the taming and control of this giant industry than Betancourt himself. If political activity has been closest to his heart, petroleum matters have been his central intellectual preoccupation. Indeed, using his approach to oil problems as a guide, we can gain insights into his role as a leader, a measure of his values, and a glimpse of the enormous abilities that have won him a place among the handful of great democratic nation builders in history.

Very early in his career Rómulo Betancourt realized that Venezuela simply could not achieve political stability with liberty, or balanced economic growth, without control of its petroleum resources. In one way or another, accordingly, he has been involved with petroleum policy issues ever since: while a young political activist, studying the industry and helping define the orientation of the fledgling opposition groups he helped form; while head of state, supervising the formulation of new policies; and while in exile or retirement, writing and speaking out in an effort to influence key decisions. His own career, in fact, has closely paralleled the lifetime of the privately controlled oil industry in Venezuela—development of oil began in earnest in the 1920s, and the industry was nationalized on New Year's Day 1976—and the successes of Venezuela's oil policy over long years of struggle and conflict with foreign companies must be attributed in large part to his concern and activity.

Betancourt's orientation toward petroleum policy questions has remained remarkably consistent. Most evident, of course, has been his uncompromising nationalism, reflecting his deep resentment of the longstanding superior/inferior relationship between representatives of the foreign companies and his own countrymen. As a member of a generation of young political leaders whose outlook was basically Marxist in character, he very early concluded that the concessionary system of oil development was intolerable as a long-term agreement. He also realized that it was the responsibility of the Venezuelan government to see beyond oil, to develop a strategy of transition which, in addition to domesticating the industry, would allow Venezuela to build a productive infrastructure capable of supporting the country when the oil reserves became depleted. As time passed, he became increasingly aware that this was not happening, and he decried the fact that Venezuela was, to use his own phrase, becoming a "petroleum factory."

Another fundamental tenet in Betancourt's approach to oil—and this is especially important because of his preoccupation with democratic institution-building—is that there tends to be a connection between oil and authoritarianism; that there is often a natural affinity between dictatorial governments and the managerial elites of the petroleum industry; and that, because it would bring greater controls and self-assertion on the part of the state, democratic government often tends to be opposed by oil companies. Belief in the power of this "unholy" alliance was an important reason for his advocacy, from the outset of his career, of a multiclass popular alliance, with a firm organizational base, as the only means of achieving the twin goals of enlarged popular participation and domestic control of natural resources. Oil, democracy, and political development were all related.

By his own account, Betancourt's interest in petroleum began during his first period of exile following the stillborn student protests of 1928. After remaining in hiding for a period, he made his way to Curaçao, where his interest was aroused when he saw tankers arriving laden with Venezuelan crude for the refineries of Standard Oil and Shell. Unable to find literature on the oil industry in Spanish, he purchased an English-Spanish dictionary and proceeded to translate Ludwell Denny's *We Fight for Oil*, word by word, sentence by sentence. As his English improved, he read on, beginning a lifelong habit of accumulating knowledge about petroleum and preserving much of what he learned in his voluminous notes. Always an avid and broad-ranging reader, he habitually took advantage of periods of exile to write and continue compiling documents and published material.

Upon his return to Caracas in 1936 he retained his interest in petroleum, writing critical dispatches on the subject for the pages of an opposition newspaper, and, after a second period of exile in Chile, helping establish petroleum policy as one of the main concerns of the newly founded Acción Democrática (AD) Party.*

---

*Many of these were subsequently published as a chapter in Betancourt's book *Problemas Venezolanos*, which appeared in Chile in 1940 during his period of exile.

Between 1941 and 1945 Betancourt dedicated himself to the enlargement of AD and to the forging of political ties between the party and nascent labor and rural movements in the country. He traveled throughout Venezuela during these years, speaking and organizing meetings. Although as a young man he had worked briefly for several small parties in Venezuela, it was in AD, a social democratic party he helped found, that Betancourt found the most satisfactory outlet for his enormous political energy.* Of all his accomplishments, in fact, he takes the greatest personal satisfaction from his role as founder and member of AD. "Even if I had not become president of my country," he recently confided, "I would feel satisfied in my career as a politician as a result of the work I have done in building the AD party."

Betancourt participated actively in the public debate over the revised petroleum code presented to Congress by President Medina Angarita in 1943, and in fact actually drafted the formal statements of objections to the new code made by Deputy Juan Pablo Pérez Alfonzo and by the unified opposition bloc.

Passed despite these objections, the code formed the legal basis for petroleum development for the next three decades. A retrospective review of the results of this important law reveals that the opposition was largely correct in its assessment of the mixture of costs and benefits to the nation that the agreement with the companies represented.

In essence, the reform was a compromise in which the companies agreed to pay Venezuela more, and to recognize an enlarged and consolidated state responsibility in petroleum matters, in return for the legitimization of past concessions, legal immunity for past misdeeds of many kinds, and a promise of new concessions. The companies favored the law—indeed had a hand in writing it—because they wanted to set the stage for expanded operations on a new, more secure footing.

When AD collaborated with a group of reformist officers to overthrow the government of Medina Angarita in 1945, Betancourt became president of the governing junta. As chief executive, he presided over the most far-reaching socioeconomic and political reforms in Venezuela's history—a process whose triumphs, and abrupt termination in 1948, are described in detail in the pages of this book.

During this period, he was able for the first time to take a direct hand in the design of oil policy. His first step was to call his friend Juan Pablo Pérez Alfonzo to the Ministry of Development (the entity in charge of oil affairs at that time). Together they mapped out a strategy for reordering the relationship between the foreign-owned industry and the Venezuelan state. Conceding that nationalization was impossible, Betancourt nevertheless suspended the granting of new concessions; levied a special tax designed to raise actual

---

*Betancourt also briefly allied himself with a tiny communist group in Costa Rica while in exile there, but he subsequently broke with it over the question of adherence to the Communist International.

state receipts from oil company profits to 50 percent; set up a commission to study the possibility of creating a state oil company; and, for the first time, offered the government's royalty oil (previously automatically resold to the companies) for sale on the open market, in search of higher prices. An additional achievement, one especially important to Betancourt, was the consolidation of the labor movement in the petroleum fields and the signing of the first collective contract—the *very first*, after nearly three decades of oil production in Venezuela—with the petroleum industry. The contract increased workers' benefits and opened the way for a rapid growth in organizational power that eventually made the petroleum unions the most successful, and oil workers the best paid, in the country. Finally, the government also began discussing the possibility of sending a delegation to visit other poor oil-producing countries to compare experiences in the handling of petroleum policy.

This forceful beginning in the redirection of national petroleum policy was cut short, along with many other political and economic reforms of the junta and of the freely elected government that replaced it, by the military regime that took control of the country in November 1948.

Betancourt's third, and longest, period of exile was a time of enormous frustration. In the prime of his life—for roughly the decade of his forties—he was forced into relative inactivity and obscurity. He traveled extensively, living in Cuba, Costa Rica, and Puerto Rico, and remained the leader of an opposition-in-exile to the Pérez Jiménez dictatorship. And, of course, he wrote *Venezuela: Oil and Politics*, an important part of his attempt to draw international attention to the accomplishments of the AD government and to the depredations of the dictatorship. A beach home outside of San Juan provided a quiet refuge for this work.

When Pérez Jiménez was finally deposed, Betancourt returned to Venezuela and quickly gathered the reins of the AD party. After forming a compact with the other major parties of the country (excluding the communists) to share the responsibility of government, he launched a successful campaign for the presidency. Upon assuming office in 1959, he again took up the struggle to refashion the institutional relationship between the government and the foreign-controlled industry.* It would be difficult to overemphasize the difficulties he faced when he took office. The economy almost immediately slumped into a serious recession, the combined result of mismanagement by the dictatorship and of the fiscal extravagance of the transitional junta. The government itself was saddled with heavy debts, making it even more dependent on the continued operations of the oil industry (which accounted for two-thirds of total state income), and insurgency remained a chronic problem as first military conspirators, and then terrorists on the left, sought to over-

---

*For a more detailed account of the petroleum policy of the Betancourt administration, an account upon which I have relied heavily here, see Franklin Tugwell, *The Politics of Oil in Venezuela* (Stanford, Ca.: Stanford University Press, 1975.)

throw the elected regime. And to make matters worse, Betancourt's carefully
assembled multiparty governing coalition suffered repeated defections—all
of this while an inexperienced group of administrators sought to accomplish a
wide range of social, economic, and administrative reforms. Only Copei, the
Social Christian party headed by Rafael Caldera, held out in its support of the
foundering democracy.

The international petroleum market posed obstacles of a different kind.
World oil prices, already low, were eroding in the face of a production glut
that followed the heavy investments by majors and new "independent" companies following the Suez Crisis of 1956. And the concessions system had
become more firmly established in Venezuela as a result of the new holdings
granted by Pérez Jiménez in the late 1950s. All together, it was hardly an
auspicious time to undertake, or even threaten, a reform of the regime of
petroleum exploitation.

Betancourt nevertheless moved ahead with determination. He recalled
Pérez Alfonzo to his post in charge of petroleum administration, and announced again that no more concessions would be granted in Venezuela.
Although he had stressed, in his campaign for president, the need for new
taxes on oil company earnings—he assembled a detailed account of company
profits for this purpose—he was spared the need to seek these because, after
the election but before the inauguration, the transitional junta headed by
Edgar Sanabria issued a decree which accomplished this objective. (The motives for this action remain a subject of controversy.) Betancourt did, however, fulfill another campaign pledge by quickly establishing the Corporación
Venezolana del Petróleo (CVP), Venezuela's first state oil corporation.

An urgent goal of the new government was to somehow slow the erosion of
prices and, thereby, the drop in income that Venezuela was receiving for the
sale of its oil. Accordingly, policymakers began to pressure the companies to
resist the price cutting trend, and to market Venezuelan oil at the highest
obtainable prices. A new agency, the Coordinating Commission for the Conservation and Commerce of Hydrocarbons, was created within the Ministry
of Mines to monitor company contracts and prevent company decisions from
exceeding broad guidelines set by the state.

Although the government did resort to sanctions against two small
operators who refused to comply with its requests, it quickly became clear
that price trends were basically international in character. Betancourt therefore gave his strong support to a series of diplomatic contacts and informal
agreements that led, within a short time, to the creation of the Organization
of Petroleum Exporting Countries (OPEC).

Venezuelan leaders hoped at first that OPEC could quickly take control of
both price and supply decisions affecting petroleum moving in international
trade. When the Second OPEC Conference opened in Caracas early in 1961,
Betancourt himself addressed the assembled delegates and urged them to
move ahead quickly and establish a full-fledged international oil prorationing
system. But it quickly became apparent that few of the producers in the

Middle East and North Africa were prepared to go this far. Indeed, it is uncertain whether OPEC was able in these early days to deter price cuts to a significant extent. Venezuela urged the other members to establish coordinating commissions of their own, press for price increases, and raise taxes on company profits. And during 1963 and 1964 a series of negotiations did take place in which the companies agreed to change the tax basis of royalties. But the main objective of forcing the companies to restore prices to the levels they had reached before the worldwide slump in 1960, was unattainable. However, thanks in considerable part to the initiatives of the Betancourt administration, the process of collective consultations and exchange of information between the producers was begun, and OPEC was prepared to take advantage of the more favorable conditions of the early 1970s.

Closer to home, the Betancourt administration also sought to work out an arrangement with the United States for the orderly control of the petroleum trade within the western hemisphere. Although it seemed for a while that the United States might be willing to cooperate with Venezuela to this end, the North American government instead chose an import control policy that discriminated against Venezuela, in favor of imports coming from Canada and Mexico. Repeated requests from Venezuela did little to change this situation.

The innovations of the Betancourt administration in oil policy did not go unchallenged. Within the AD party many felt that, given the fiscal plight of the government, more taxes should be levied against the companies. However, Betancourt was convinced that for the time being the state could not safely go further in this direction without a possible disruption of the production and sale of petroleum—the lifeline which made all his reforms possible. He therefore resisted these demands.

He also stood firm against a growing clamor for better treatment of the oil companies that was raised by the domestic private sector working in tacit alliance with the foreign companies themselves. The private sector in Venezuela had benefited enormously from the oil bonanza. This is true especially of those companies that responded to the growing purchasing power of the urban middle classes in the country—in activities such as construction, real estate development, food and drink, and automobiles—and many representatives of the private economy resented, and feared, that the government would go too far and permanently damage the fount of their prosperity. The oil companies were aware of these apprehensions, and did their best to mobilize influential private sector opinion in support of their industry. In well-funded publicity campaigns the companies deplored the deterioration in the climate of investment in Venezuela, and stressed that the petroleum of the Middle East and North Africa had become more competitive because of the harsh measures and strict controls of the Venezuelan state. At the same time, the companies brought pressure to bear by reducing their investments in exploration and drilling, and by drawing their increases in production from other areas under their control.

The issue of the competitiveness of Venezuelan petroleum is especially

interesting because it goes to the heart of the problem of dependence on
multinational enterprises. Careful studies completed in recent years have
shown that although Venezuelan oil was often more costly to produce, and
profits were more heavily taxed, a part of its cost differential was due to the
particular mix of crudes and products that the companies themselves chose to
produce. In addition, the relatively greater security of Venezuela as a source
of supply to key North American markets enhanced the value to the companies of offtake from there.*

But setting aside for a moment the technical issue of comparative cost,
there remains the much more serious problem of uncertainty which the Venezuelan government had to face. Given its position as the host of several
branches of an enormous vertically integrated industry, how could the Venezuelan government be sure that the companies were telling the truth and not
just punishing Venezuela for its nationalistic policies in order to prevent the
spread of this example to other poor producing countries? Put succinctly, the
answer is that the government could not be sure; that the companies were in
fact exaggerating their plight in order to pressure the government; and that
the uncertainty and insecurity revealed by posing the question in these terms
serves both to illustrate why the concessions system of development itself
would never be acceptable to Venezuelans, and to define the very severe
quandary in which the government found itself when confronting the protective measures adopted by the industry.

Betancourt's willingness to take a firm stand at this juncture was critically
important. Convinced by prior experience, and by his extensive reading of
the history of oil affairs, that the statements of the oil companies simply could
not be trusted in decisions about the public patrimony, he and his Minister of
Mines and Hydrocarbons, Juan Pablo Pérez Alfonzo, instead embarked on a
program of policy experimentation which in the end led Venezuela to one of
the most orderly and successful nationalizations in the long and conflict-
bound history of oil. The key to this policy, which I have elsewhere called
the policy of "assertive experimentation," was the willingness of the
president—the one ultimately responsible to the political process—to take
some risks, to live with uncertainty, and to trust his own judgment. "Assertive experimentation" refers to the disposition on the part of policy makers to
test the waters where uncertainly prevails, to formulate novel approaches and
move ahead with them, watching the results carefully to gain understanding
unobtainable by any other means. The Coordinating Commission for the
Conservation and Commerce of Hydrocarbons was a prime example of such
a policy experiment, as were the CVP, OPEC and many other initiatives.
Indeed, the assertive mode of policy innovation begun by Betancourt set the
pattern for the governments that followed. In retrospect there can be little

*See, among others, M. A. Adelman *The World Petroleum Market* (Baltimore, Md.: Johns
Hopkins University Press, 1972), pp. 69, 146; and the review of this topic in my own book
The Politics of Oil in Venezuela.

doubt that Venezuela was fortunate indeed to have a man like him at its helm during these critical early days. Only a committed reformer and master politician, a man with insight into just which risks must be taken, and willingness to support the innovative ideas of his subordinates, could succeed under the difficult circumstances Venezuela faced in the early 1960s.

As his term drew to a close, Betancourt's government came under increasing pressure from terrorists determined to prevent free elections from taking place. His unwavering belief in the primacy of democracy brought him into conflict with some in Venezuela, especially among students and the political left generally, who placed greater emphasis on economic equality and redistribution, and who advocated more rapid reforms to achieve these other ends. As president, this conviction led him to prolonged and bitter conflicts with Trujillo, the dictator of the Dominican Republic, and Fidel Castro, and to the promotion of what came to be known as the Betancourt Doctrine, which asserts the obligation of democratic governments to use unilateral and multilateral diplomatic means to prevent, and dislodge, authoritarian and tyrannical regimes in the western hemisphere and elsewhere. Since leaving office, he has continued to promote, and live by, this principle. He has avoided traveling to countries ruled by nonelected governments, and within his party has consistently opposed the establishment of friendly ties with regimes, such as the Cuban, which he feels are unacceptable. In this, of course, he has not succeeded; AD presidents have gradually abandoned the rigid application of the Betancourt Doctrine in order to more easily accomplish other policy objectives such as the promotion of regional economic and political cooperation.

His struggle to guarantee the survival of democratic institutions in Venezuela, however, won the support and deep respect of democratic governments everywhere. Indeed, few political events in the turbulent 1960s could rival the spectacle of the beleaguered Venezuelan president battling for the privilege, not to retain power, but to turn it over to a freely selected successor. More important, of course, it also won the support of the vast majority of Venezuelans.

At the end of his term as president, Betancourt left the country to avoid encumbering his successor. Following extensive travels in Asia and Europe, he took up residence first in Naples and then in Berne, Switzerland. He returned to Venezuela in 1973. Although he has declared that he will not again seek the presidency, he nevertheless remains active in national and AD party affairs. As might be expected, he has continued to read, and write, about oil. In retirement in Switzerland, and then later back in Venezuela, he has followed carefully the many changes taking place in the international petroleum market.*

In 1975, as the nation debated the final steps needed to nationalize the industry in its entirety, he made a lengthy address on petroleum policy be-

---

*In 1972 he published a long review of key developments in the magazine *Vision*.

fore the Senate. As an ex-president, he remains a lifetime member of that body. After reviewing with care the long history of oil in Venezuela, he tried to calm the fears many held about the possible dangers of the controversial Article Five of the nationalization law (which allows the option of foreign operational assistance to the industry). He noted that the provisions in this portion of the law assured a flexibility necessary to the government, while providing both legislative and administrative safeguards against unwarranted foreign influence.

In making this address, his main purpose was to unify and reassure: to express his support for this step of such enormous historical importance to himself and to the life of the country; to appeal to his compatriots to do the same; and, finally, to voice once again his sincere belief that democratic Venezuela would be able to handle new and greater challenges in the future. It was a characteristic gesture for him. And if it should turn out that he was right and Venezuela can take advantage of the difficult new responsibilities it has accepted, it will be in large measure due to its gifted leaders—to men like Rómulo Betancourt.

Franklin Tugwell

Pomona, California
October 1978

Prologue to the First Edition

The preparation of this book has been as hectic as the life of the author.

I wrote it first between the years 1937–39 while I was underground hiding from the police. It could not be published then because no Venezuelan publisher could dare risk printing a book written by one who was in such a compromising situation. It was not published later because during those turbulent times, when Acción Democrática was moving from opposition to power (1941–45), party work took all my time and attention. When we were leading the government (1945–48), it was more useful to the country and more in accord with my own temperament to spend my time implementing the program later described in these pages than to rewrite them for publication. The only typewritten copy was among my personal papers and it disappeared with them when a military patrol plundered the house I was living in when the constitutional goverment was overthrown on November 24, 1948. Thus, most of the material from the first draft was lost and could not be used for the book, except that included in a pamphlet published in 1937, *A Republic Up for Sale (Una República en Venta)*.

Venezuela: Oil and Politics was written amid all the difficulties inherent in the life of an exile—a nomadic exile, to boot. Papers, books to be consulted, and notes were taken with me from the United States to Cuba, from Cuba to Costa Rica, and from Costa Rica to Puerto Rico. I had to wait for months for the boxes in which they were shipped to arrive. I lacked documents which were to be found only in Venezuela. Furthermore, I had to combine this writing with the unpostponable tasks of one who dedicated his exile to unceasing political struggle, rather than contemplative retreat.

Despite these adverse circumstances, I have been able to document all the statements I have made in these pages. Many of my party associates have helped in this. Many American compatriots have read the manuscript and made valuable suggestions. So many persons have helped me that I would risk forgetting some were I to mention names. I remain in debt to them all.

I should warn the reader that he will not find these pages written in serenity. They are quite different from the elevated tone of scholarship. Friends urged me to write in a more unemotional and objective manner. Because I have been the chief of state, they felt I should be using the language of a statesman. I have not been able to do this. I write as I think and as I feel. Venezuela is in my blood and in my bones. Its sorrows pain me. When I write of them, I would be hypocritical were I to pretend to be impartial. So I confess to passion as I analyze the problems of my country. Some will say nothing is to be gained by this. I would answer them with the words of another great emotional writer, Miguel de Unamuno, who sorrowed so deeply for his Spain: "We are not seeking to gain anything, but simply by pouring out our souls to rouse those who may be asleep or even dead, that they may rise and live again, that they may kindle and burn. Without fire, there is no light."

I am frustrated to think that this book won't be read by companions and friends of mine—no longer living—who encouraged me to write. Leonardo Ruiz Pineda, at the climax of his dangerous life as leader of the underground resistance, urged me to finish the book. Alberto Carnevali worked on some of the chapters with me in Cuba. Antonio Pinto Salinas and Luis Troconis Guerrero, from their hiding places in Venezuela, sent me data and information which I had asked for. In my house in Havana, the great poet Andrés Eloy Blanco, and Castor Nieves Ríos and Victor Alvarado—two men of the people without university training—listened together while I read some of the pages. I discussed with Mario Vargas, the democratic and civilized military officer in exile in Washington, the role of an exclusively professional army in the service of democracy. From Quipue, where he spent his last days, Valmore Rodríguez sent me some observations on parts which I had asked him to read. All are dead now. Some died in exile, others in jail, others were cut down by the guns of the security police in Venezuela. All fell doing their duty as citizens, during this "time of hate" that began in Venezuela on November 24, 1948. In dedicating this book to them, I do so with full awareness of the obligation I thereby undertake. I will merit the repudiation of my fellow countrymen and the implacable judgment of history should I ever desert the ideals for which they fought and died.

I believe that "the dead command," although not in the sense that reactionaries have traditionally given the phrase. When they die they give the command for an ideal of human excellence, obliging those who survive to finish their work. It is the same interpretation of sacrifice for a just cause that José Martí had in mind when he wrote: "The death of chieftains, the death of the great teachers, is that death which moves our fingers to write the book of life." More recently, Nehru said: "Life is born again from death. Individuals and nations which do not know how to die do not know how to live. Only when there is a tomb can there be a resurrection."

I offer this book for discussion and analysis to those concerned with the social problems of our time, with the humility of one who does not believe in self-sufficiency and who rejects all forms of dogmatism.

R.B.

Manti, Mar Chiquita, Puerto Rico
December 1955.

Prologue to the Second Edition

The first edition of this book was published in 1956 by the Editorial Fondo de Cultura Económica in Mexico City. The author was then in exile. *Venezuela: Oil and Politics* was prohibited from circulating in Venezuela; only a few copies managed to get past the police into the country.

When I returned from exile in February 1958 after the overthrow of the dictatorship, I planned to publish a second edition immediately. I accepted an offer made by a Venezuelan publisher and even received an advance of Bs. 20,000 for author's rights.

The book had to be revised, but my intense political activity during these days when the Acción Democrática party (AD) was being reorganized after nine years of operating clandestinely kept me from getting on with the work. The editing I was able to do consisted mostly of adding passages rather than cutting anything out. There were only changes of wording—none of concepts—in the second edition. I do not believe it is ethical for one who wrote history in 1956 to make retractions in 1967. Despite the fact that I was in a difficult personal situation, persecuted by the dictatorship even in those countries where I sought exile, I had tried to give the original text the tone of thoughtful analysis rather than the aggressive vindictiveness of a pamphleteer. In our times the calm recital of facts and statistics is more persuasive than the exalted prose of earlier writers.

When I worked on this book in Caracas, I was not planning to be a candidate for the presidency. This is not the place to explain why I later changed my mind. I will do this in my *Memoirs*, now near completion. When later circumstances led me to accept the AD candidacy for president, I felt it was inopportune to republish *Venezuela: Oil and Politics*.

It was a controversial book that analyzed and evaluated the contemporary political history of the country. Although I was sure of winning the election, it did not seem appropriate to bring out such a polemical book at that time. Furthermore, it did not seem right for a chief of state—which I was convinced I would be—to use his high office as a propaganda vehicle for a book written by him. Once the decision was made to postpone publication, I obtained a bank loan and paid back the money advanced to me by the publisher.

This is the first time I have publicly explained why the second edition of this book, which had already been announced, did not appear earlier. My decision brought varied comments, especially from the followers of General Medina Angarita, who had been overthrown on October 18, 1945, and replaced by the revolutionary junta which I led. Those who lost out with Medina have been among the most prolific writers for newspapers and magazines, posthumously eulogizing the fallen government—perhaps with a desire to justify themselves for having served in a regime of such limited achievement. One of the principal figures of the Medina government, generally recognized as the power behind the throne at that time, Arturo Uslar Pietri, has challenged my silence during recent years regarding this period in the evolution of our country. His criticism of my attitude can be seen in his prologue to a posthumous book by General Medina, published in 1963, with the title *Four Years of Democracy*, in which Uslar Pietri wrote: "This was the government that was overthrown on an unhappy day in 1945, six months before it was due to leave office, *an event about which even its most immediate beneficiaries to this day try to maintain silence*." [My italics.]

This was not the case. We never have regretted our participation in that political episode of 1945. We believe that the period which followed will generally be seen as one of great progress, when a change for the better occurred, as the public demanded. This will be recognized widely when these events are judged from the perspective of history.

In a lengthy chapter of the book I analyze the circumstances which inevitably led to the violent events of October 18. Democracy was on the march internationally and autocracy was in crisis after the end of World War II. The right to elect governments was being exercised almost everywhere, but in Venezuela it was sought to retain the Gómez tradition of having the outgoing president select his successor. We opposed this system long before we had any knowledge of the conspiracy underway against the government among young military officers.

In the years following the events of October 18, 1945, there were historians, high officials in the Medina government, who, to a degree, have admitted the inevitability of what occurred even though they do not justify it. Mario Briceño Iragorri was president of Congress and a personal friend of President Medina. He has written of the crisis among the Medina forces caused by the strong movement favoring the return of General López Contreras to the presidency. Medina, he stated, had had to deal with a world of passions he could not handle and was under strong pressure to put another native of the state of Táchira in the presidency. The historian and novelist Ramón Díaz Sánchez, head of the government press office, wrote that Medina's stubbornness in wanting to continue to have a Táchira man in the presidency helped bring about his fall.

> Intent, on the one hand, upon this dangerous idea, and on the other, his desire to block a return of López Contreras to power, Medina first supported Diógenes Es-

calante, who became mentally incapacitated. Then he turned to Angel Biaggini, a distinguished lawyer who lacked political experience except as Secretary of the Presidency and Minister of Agriculture. It has been said that if Escalante had not fallen ill, the revolution would not have occurred. That is possible. However, it is doubtful that Biaggini would have been elected since López Contreras had a majority in Congress.[1]

Uslar Pietri, himself, told me in a chance encounter during those tense days which preceded the October revolution, "The situation is alarming. Biaggini will not last in the government. The sergeants will overthrow him." Uslar Pietri denies having said this, although he does not discard the possibility that he might have forgotten the exchange. I reaffirm that he did say it. I have kept diaries for many years to record important political events, and I noted his remarks as he had made them to me. I have dozens of these diaries in my archives. They are the basis for the autobiography I am writing.

It has been argued that the revolution of October 18, 1945, led to the counterrevolution of November 24, 1948, when the government of Rómulo Gallegos was overthrown. This view will not do. It would be like blaming those who staged the French Revolution for the takeover by Napoleon, or blaming the liberators of 1810 for the prolonged autocracies of Páez, the Monagas brothers, and Guzmán Blanco. National histories do not follow a straight line like modern thoroughfares. The evolutions of nations follow a zig-zag pattern, and there are also ups and downs. It is important to recognize whether a development is good or bad and then to learn from it. We should not return to a reactionary past when we have taken the direction of democracy and social progress.

This is a book recounting history. I believe it pertinent to explain how I see the task of the historian. No historian is impartial. It is nonsense to deny that he is not influenced by his own ideological convictions when writing about people and events. However, he cannot justify distorting facts or inventing situations that falsify a nation's history to justify his personal ideas. That is why I have tried to document every statement made regarding the behavior of individuals or the interpretation of events in this book, even though this has meant some sacrifice in readability. Someone has defined the historian as a man seated on the wall of a besieged city, dispassionately observing the besieged with the left eye and the besiegers with the right. Such impartiality is impossible. The historian's own feelings, his manner of interpreting social phenomena, his attitude toward the protagonists of the events he relates—all perceptibly influence him.

However, if the historian who writes for the world at large is given freedom to put much of himself, his own ideology, and his manner of evaluating the historial process of a country into his writing, the man who writes for educational purposes should not, for ethical reasons, report things according to his own viewpoint. Many of his readers will be young and unable to distinguish between truth and deceit. The Venezuelan historian, Guillermo

Moron, for example, has done this in the fourth edition of his manual on the history of Venezuela, written for students under the title *Venezuela*, and published in 1967. This book dedicates pages of bombastic propaganda to the government of General Medina Angarita. It is an unrestrained apology that borders on deification. On the other hand, he hardly gives three paragraphs to the government of Gallegos and to my own, and all are saturated with negative remarks.

> The measures of the new government were: establishment of an illegal enrichment tribunal, which rapidly sentenced the former presidents Medina and López Contreras for misappropriation of public funds—without any right of appeal; expulsion of the two former presidents, Dr. Arturo Uslar Pietri, and many other politicians; and the convocation of a Constituent Assembly which met December 17, 1946. After approving a new constitution and a new electoral statute, elections for president were held amid great public enthusiasm. On February 14, 1948, the presidency was turned over to the president-elect, Rómulo Gallegos.

Two additional paragraphs complete this brief and distorted report by Moron on the three-year period, 1945–48.

At that difficult moment in national life, it is true, a number of former public officials were accused of graft by the newly created Illegal Enrichment Tribunal, but they had the right to defend themselves with the help of lawyers, free from official pressure. The sentences of this special jury could be appealed to a special commission selected by the National Constituent Assembly, which included representation of the opposition parties. Quite a few of those accused were able to prove their innocence, and many others had their penalties reduced. It should also be noted that the right of appeal did not exist under the constitutional provision which applied to similar cases against officials of the governments of Gómez and Castro when Medina and López Contreras were in power. It might be argued that the provision was applied to very few individuals; this was not because of legal inhibitions but because of clan solidarity. Those who should have been accused of fraud had close ties with the prosecutors in their mutual service to the Castro and Gómez regimes, especially the latter.

The example of uncompromising morality in the handling of public funds by the government of 1945–48 was of infinitely greater importance than the punishment of those responsible for abuses in the past. It was the first government of the century in Venezuela which could not be accused, then or later, of private enrichment of its members as a result of holding power. During most of this period, I was president. When I turned over the presidential chair to Gallegos, I was as poor as when I entered Miraflores. This should not be considered as anything extraordinary but simply as strict compliance with ethical standards and the need for self-respect through honest conduct. Moreover, it was widely noted by foreign commentators who were well accustomed to the unbridled graft that traditionally existed in the Venezuelan government. *Fortune* magazine, New York, wrote in April 1949: "When Betancourt, in accordance with the legal requirement, accounted for his assets after two years as president of one of the richest small countries of the world, his capital amounted to only Bs. 1154. Such honesty is a miracle in Latin America." And the North American professor Austin F. MacDonald wrote in his book *Latin American Politics and Government*: "The president's salary was about $14,000 yearly, which is not enough for a country with living costs as high as Venezuela's. The law obliged the chiefs of state, on leaving office, to go before a judge and publicly account for their assets and debts. The former president, Betancourt, demonstrated that his total worth upon leaving office was $343." This same thing could have been written about the other members of the government that ruled from 1945 to 1948.

Extensive chapters of this book—perhaps too extensive—are dedicated to the administrative work during the three-year period of the 1945–48 government. So much has been said and written about the alleged inefficiency of those who governed then that it has been necessary to explain what was accomplished and what was programmed for the future. Hoping to tempt the reader a bit, let me note just a few facts regarding the economic and administrative accomplishments of this period.

The national budget grew from an average of Bs. 350 million in the period 1938–45 to Bs. 1315 million in 1947, a growth of almost 400 percent. This increase was provided by new revenues from the oil companies and prosperous national industries; simultaneously, there was a corresponding decrease in the cost of goods and services in general use. In the period 1938–45, oil provided the government with 40 percent of its income and other taxes provided the remaining 60 percent. The proportion changed substantially, and by 1947 the taxes on the oil companies and big national concerns provided 63 percent of government income and only 37 percent came from the rest of the population. In 1945, there were 252 labor unions; these increased to 1014 by 1948. Oil workers, for the first time in the nation's history and after more than twenty years of oil production, signed a collective contract which provided benefits of more than Bs. 100 million, according to the *New York Times*, June 1, 1946.

The creation of the Venezuelan Production Corporation (Corporación Venezolana de Fomento) made the industrialization of the country possible. It ceased to be a simple distribution agency for goods produced abroad which could have been manufactured in the country. Loans made by this organization increased rapidly. By 1947, they were Bs. 84 million, and by 1948 they had reached Bs. 109 million. Similar encouragement was given by the government to agriculture and cattle raising. The Economic Commission for Latin America (ECLA) in a monograph entitled "Facts and Trends of the Venezuelan Economy," published in 1950 by this agency of the United Nations, reported that official promotion of agriculture and cattle raising, previously negligible, was now conducted on a large scale. Before 1945, the state credits granted had never exceeded Bs. 10 million annually. In 1948, the last year of the three-year democracy, they exceeded Bs. 116 million.

The amount spent on education was tremendously increased. From the Bs. 38 million spent in 1945, the government increased expenditures to Bs. 119 million in 1948. In a period of thirty-six months, the number of students attending primary schools increased from 130,000 to 500,000. Expenditures for health increased fourfold, growing from Bs. 28 million in 1945 to Bs. 110 million in 1948.

The armed forces were reorganized, their equipment, as well as their training, was improved. The entire country was moving ahead in all respects.

Most important was the collective enjoyment of people freely electing those who were to govern them. This outdid all the material gains made during this three-year period. The North American magazine *Newsweek*, on December 9, 1947, reported on the stellar moment in Venezuelan history when the people had their first opportunity to cast a universal, secret, and direct vote:

> For the first time in their history, the people of Venezuela, men and women, rich and poor, literate and illiterate, without distinction of creed or color, were choosing directly their own president, senators, and deputies. The Sunday quiet of the sun-drenched city, the good-natured patience of the long lines of waiting voters, the speed and efficiency—and pride—with which the votes were cast: All these showed how far Venezuela had come . . . since the revolutionary junta took over. This was more than the fairest and most orderly election Venezuela had ever known. It could have served as a model for any country in the Western Hemisphere, not excluding many parts of the United States.

This book also tells the history of "the time of shame," the dark era of the dictatorship that began November 24, 1948, and was finally overthrown by the combined effort of the people and the armed forces on January 23, 1958. In the Epilogue, the new oil policy of February 1959 also is summarized. This nationalistic policy of defending our oil came with the elected democratic government.

As I finish this preface to a book which can now freely circulate in Venezuela, I hope that it will enable the new generations to understand the contemporary historical process of the nation. I will be well paid for the effort the book has taken if these pages awaken in the youth of my country—physically far away but always close to my heart—the desire and determination to investigate and to study in depth the causes of what occurs in our country. This is my wish as I labor in a library overstocked with books, magazines, and newspapers in a small house in Switzerland.

R.B.

Berne
October 18, 1967

PART ONE

A Republic for Sale

1

Castro and Gómez: Despotism, Asphalt, and Petroleum

The Peaceful Beginning

The first efforts at commercial oil production in Venezuela took place during the second half of the nineteenth century. In the 1870s, Dr. Carlos Gonzalez Bona pursued his professional activities in Táchira, "the Great State of the Andes." He traveled by muleback from village to village, using a green umbrella to protect his corpulent body from the summer sun and the winter rain.

On the road to Rubio, capital of the Junin district, Gonzalez Bona, "who was also an engineer and something of a chemist," noticed that various small streams had oily traces on their surfaces—a kind of tarry substance floated on the waters. One of the streams was actually called La Alquitrania (Tar Creek) by the natives of the region since there was a kind of natural tar spring bubbling near its source. The doctor persuaded the owner of the surrounding land, Antonio Pulido, his relative Pedro Rincones, and two others—a General Valdo and one J. R. Villafañe—to form a company to produce the mineral he had discovered. The group sent Pedro Rincones to Pennsylvania in the United States to study the new methods of drilling wells being developed there. Pennsylvania had become the Holy Land for oil seekers since the prospector Drake had drilled the first oil well there. At the same time, an audacious businessman, John D. Rockefeller, foresaw the future of this magic fountain of riches and laid the foundations of what would become the greatest industrial enterprise of modern times—the Standard Oil Company.

Pedro Rincones returned from the United States, where the god of pe-

3

troleum now had an extensive cult of worshipers. The modest new company received its first land titles from the government of the state in 1878, and by 1886 the Oil Mining Company of Táchira (Compañía Minera Petrolia del Táchira) began with rudimentary equipment to drill in search of the promising new wealth.

There was no official interest in this small company. Venezuela was sluggishly developing its economic life in terms of agriculture and cattle raising. The nation was still recovering from the wounds of the long and cruel Federal War. Guzmán Blanco was obtaining foreign loans with fat commissions for his own pocket; he offered railroad concessions in which the state guaranteed private investors a 7 percent return. He gave all public activities a European character—very Second Empire—and very slavishly copied all things foreign.

Without official support this Venezuelan company was barely able to exist with an initial production of a few dozen barrels of crude oil. Twenty-six years later, in 1912, its production was only sixty barrels daily and finally the company was dissolved. This was the idyllic beginning of an industry that in Venezuela, as everywhere else, had a history of violence, lawlessness, and financial shenanigans.

The New York and Bermudez Company, the Asphalt Trust, and the Midwifery of the State Department

Although beginning peacefully, the oil industry in Venezuela soon took on a dramatic character. The main actor in the first scene, however, was not oil but another bituminous product—asphalt. In 1883 the Venezuelan government gave a concession to a United States citizen—Horace Hamilton—to produce asphalt from the Guanoco Lake in the eastern part of the country. This was then the world's largest known deposit of the substance. Hamilton ceded his concession to the New York and Bermudez Company, with headquarters in Philadelphia. However, the Venezuelan government declared the concession expired in 1889 since the concessionaire had extracted asphalt but had not carried out any of its other contractual obligations, which included the dredging of the Colorado and Guarapiche rivers. For the next decade the concession, though theoretically at an end, continued under production by the company.

In 1889 General Cipriano Castro, leading a group of revolutionary horsemen from the Andes, took over the government. This despotic and truculent personality, who badly needed money to pay the extravagant expenses of his retinue, quarreled with the asphalt company. Rather than pay Castro what he wanted, the company provided financial support to an armed opposition movement. The leader of this movement was named Matos, a typical exponent of upper class society, lacking both ideals and scruples, who had close contact with the company directors. One of them, the manager himself, actually accompanied Matos to Europe where he bought the steamer *Ban-Righ* which was then used to ship war material to the Venezuelan coast. Matos received ample financial support from the Philadelphia Trust: there were two checks that alone amounted to $130,000; on the company books they were charged to an account with the suggestive name: "Government Relations."

In 1902 the so-called Liberation Revolution broke out. The people, especially the youth, rushed to shoulder arms distributed from the *Ban-Righ*. They were not aware how they had been purchased; they were simply anxious to overthrow a despot who had humiliated and dishonored the country. Military caudillos of the different regions rose with their own followers. It was a desperate effort by a regional coalition to resist the centralized impersonal system that Cipriano Castro had established and that would be carried to its ultimate extreme by his companion and successor, Juan Vicente Gómez.

The Liberation Revolution dominated much of the republic. The nation was in arms against a hated regime, and 14,000 rebels reached La Victoria, only a few hours from Caracas. There, however, they were repulsed by government troops. The rebel camp was divided by rivalries among the caudillos, and Matos, going around in slippers and a big hat, was more a manipulator than a leader who could impose order among the rival chieftains. Thousands of dead littered the hills surrounding La Victoria—a dramatic testimony to the desire for freedom among the people.

The rebellion ended in total failure, and Castro sought revenge against its financiers. Ambrose H. Carner, a faithless employee of the New York and Bermudez Company, provided the government with full documentation revealing the company's connections with Matos. The minister of the interior demanded from the company an indemnity of Bs. 50 million, which was refused. Suit was brought against the company; the courts seized the rich asphalt lake and turned it over to the trusteeship of this same Carner. Then dollar diplomacy took over. At this time the U.S. State Department was frankly and directly intervening in the political life of Latin America—a period later characterized by Sumner Welles as "a time when many American republics could not be called sovereign because their sovereignty was often violated by the U.S."

An aggressive defense of the asphalt trust was undertaken by Bowen, the United States Minister in Caracas, who used the domineering and tough language of a proconsul. Neither he, nor the "Big Stick" policies then in vogue in the White House of Theodore Roosevelt, who had boasted "I took Panama," was completely blameworthy. Castro himself, by his irresponsible conduct, invited insolent treatment and disrespect. A few months before, the delirious despot, between gradiloquent passages of oratory and gulps of French brandy, had happily heard from the lips of Bowen himself that the Yankee cruisers *Cincinnati* and *Topeka* were anchored at the port of La Guaira while the Germans and British were trying to blockade Venezuelan ports. After the two nations had bombarded Venezuelan ports—a joint aggression by the two European powers against a small nation, which is one of the most shameful episodes of international history—Castro had given Bowen full powers as minister plenipotentiary of Venezuela to deal with the aggressors.

Roosevelt did not conceal his opinion that Castro was a "villainous little monkey." Now, after replying to the piratical attacks by the English and German squadrons against La Guaira and Puerto Cabello with ridiculous and bombastic proclamations, Castro conferred on the minister from the White House, which detested him, the official representation of Venezuela.

The English and German subjects resident in the country had been arrested in immediate reprisal for the bombardment by the ships of Edward VII and Wilhelm II. They were freed under pressure from Bowen, who had assumed the joint diplomatic representation of Germany, Great Britain, and the United States. The people were told in boastful but false communiqués, typical of the despot, that Venezuela was making a magnanimous gesture instead of fighting as it should have. The people wanted to fight as national honor demanded, no matter how many or how strong were the aggressors. Castro and his clique, however, were only interested in taking advantage of the foreign aggression to consolidate their rapacious hold upon the country. General José Manuel Hernández was even released from jail—the "Mocho" Hernández (Hernandez the Maimed)—and that ingenuous and honorable caudillo now embraced "El Cabito" (the Little Corporal), a nickname given to Castro by his flatterers in an effort to compare him to Napoleon. Castro tried to present himself as the champion of national sovereignty, but all he did was make himself ridiculous to those who were strong and even to those not so strong. Even Italy sent two warships to Venezuela in this lively competition to demonstrate which European government could be most aggressive and violent in its attack upon the impoverished little country under the irresponsible rule of a government dominated by those who robbed the treasury and profited from monopolies, and which was plagued by avid profiteers who enriched themselves illicitly to pay for their extravagant and bacchanalian orgies.

The attitude taken by the United States government at this difficult moment for Venezuela has been objectively documented by the North American professor, Arthur P. Whitaker, in his book.* Whitaker pointed out how Venezuela played an important role at this time in the development of one aspect of Yankee imperialism—the Roosevelt Corollary of the Monroe Doctrine, which proclaimed the United States as "the international police power" with the right to intervene unilaterally in Latin America. Great Britain, its ally, and Germany had obtained the agreement of Roosevelt before they began their blockade of Venezuelan ports. (President Cleveland had reacted strongly some years before in the dispute between Venezuela and England.) The blockade led to bombardment, and Latin American public opinion be-

---

*Arthur P. Whitaker, *The United States and South America* (Cambridge, Mass.: Harvard University Press, 1948).

came enraged. Foreign Minister Drago of Argentina formulated his famous declaration condemning European intervention in America and the collection of international debts by force. The press and liberal sectors in the United States also condemned the cowardly aggression. Then came the mediation of Roosevelt and the dispute was referred to the Court of International Justice at The Hague. In 1904 this court aggravated the situation by a verdict against Venezuela. According to Whitaker, "this decision not only justified armed intervention but rewarded it." At this point the State Department issued what became known as the Roosevelt Corollary to the Monroe Doctrine. This doctrine "rejected European intervention in America but proclaimed the general right of the United States to do so."

The Castro dictatorship, seeking new funds to deposit in private bank accounts abroad for its reckless spending, brought suit against the New York and Bermudez Company. This was an irreproachable step, from the viewpoint of Venezuelan law and international justice, but it was taken by men who were repudiated by their fellow citizens and held in international contempt because of their vile behavior in government.

Washington understood the situation, which made it easy for it to conduct matters. Secretary of State Hay, faithful interpreter of the aggressive spirit of the first Roosevelt, cracked the whip. Acting like a spokesman for the asphalt trust, he told the Caracas government: "The U.S. government can properly take whatever measures are required to give the American company the protection it needs." Minister Bowen, Castro's former plenipotentiary, now urged the White House to use the Parker Plan, suggested by the military attaché of the U.S. legation in Caracas. It was simple and speedy: land the marines, capture Castro, take over customs collection, and establish a provisional government "made in the USA." But there were other opinions. Sectors of the United States press, loyal to Jeffersonian ideals, repudiated the use of force. Perhaps most effective of all was the intrigue mounted by the asphalt trust in New York against its rivals in Philadelphia, which operated the Guanoco concession and had supported armed intervention in Venezuela.

Instead of cruisers, Washington sent a White House commissioner, Judge Calhoun, to investigate things on the spot. His verdict was never published but it obviously did not favor the concessionaires. The Department of State toned down its aggressive attitude and talked of submitting the quarrel to arbitration. A suggested proposal was drafted in Washington by the company lawyer and sent to Caracas by Francis B. Loomis, acting Secretary of State during the illness of Hay. Caracas had accepted the idea that the arbitration cover all differences between the governments of Venezuela, the United States, and other nations. However, the proposal drawn up in Washington simply restored to the New York and Bermudez Company "its" Venezuelan lake. Caracas rejected the proposal. Bowen later published a book claiming that Castro had sent a confidential agent to Washington with a suitcase full of dollars to undermine the Hay position. The verbose diplomat accused Loomis of having received a check to support the Venezuelans.

Bowen was dismissed and on March 19, 1908, the *New York Herald* published an editorial with the magnanimous title: "There Is No Need to Send Warships to Venezuela"; in it, aspects of the smelly affair were mentioned:

> The Bowen-Loomis scandal and the statements reluctantly made by the asphalt trust indicate that the reports sent to Washington by its diplomatic agents were influenced by personal enmity and by the influence of the oil concessionaires. The government has tacitly confessed this by failing to publish Judge Calhoun's report submitted to the State Department after his return 2 1/2 years ago. However, since his return, a much more conciliatory attitude has been taken toward Venezuela.

The editorialist concluded with the observation that Uncle Sam had refrained from sending cruisers to Venezuela "not because of love of General Castro, but because Venezuela had a stronger case than the American company, whose hands were not clean."

Meanwhile the asphalt company had been condemned by the Venezuelan courts to pay an indemnity of nearly Bs. 25 million, and Castro repossessed the Guanoco. He toured the country in triumph, crossing the republic from one end to the other amid outpourings of fulsome oratory, passing under cardboard arches bearing mottoes in the same style and listening to the frenetic bars of the waltz "Castro Always Victorious." In Washington, Elihu Root, who succeeded Hay and Loomis as secretary of state, declared, "All measures in our power have been exhausted in trying to bring Castro to justice."

Diplomatic methods having failed, it did not seem opportune to use the "big stick." There were other subtle but efficient methods. Castro was going to be replaced by another leader, just as rapacious and despotic, but less difficult for the State Department. Castro was confident that the United States, invoking the Monroe Doctrine, would block any permanent occupation by a European power, so he engaged in constant provocations for domestic political reasons and to give himself the opportunity to sign grandiloquent proclamations. However, his thirst for money and his impossible megalomania led him to fight with the Yankees, his protector against the German-British blockade. His days as head of the government were numbered after he committed this stupidity.

Castro himself made possible what we shall call "operation root." Relations with the United States had been broken off in June 1908, and the U.S. Minister, Jacob Sleeper, was called home. Castro, without wishing to, cooperated in his own downfall. His chaotic, promiscuous life style finally ruined his kidneys. He was forced to seek the assistance of a famous surgeon in Germany and left the presidency in the hands of one who seemed utterly submissive and loyal to him, his trusted companion from the Andes, Juan Vicente Gómez. He forgot the many precedents for seizure of power when the leader's back is turned; besides, he did not know that a clique had formed around his lieutenant, vowing to displace him, and that its members had

already made contact with representatives of the big powers. In light of subsequent events, it may be stated with assurance that the most important of
these contacts were with agents of the United States government.

Everything happened as planned. Castro left the country on November 24,
1908. The conspiracy got underway almost before his ship *Guadalupe* disappeared on the horizon. During the first days of December, there were street
disturbances in Caracas—some spontaneous, others provoked by agents of
the palace plot—and on December 14, five days before the culmination of the
conspiracy, came the infamous request for foreign armed intervention. The
Foreign Minister, José de Jesús Paul, on instructions from the acting President, Juan Vicente Gómez, called on the minister of Brazil in Caracas, who
handled United States diplomatic representation, and in a shameful interview asked him to pass along a request for Washington to send warships to
Venezuelan ports. The transcript of the message which the Brazilian official
sent to Washington has been published, and includes the promise of acting
President Gómez to arrange all pending problems satisfactorily.

On December 19, there occurred what the sybilline language of the time
called "the evolution of the situation." Gómez took power, named a cabinet,
and the same persons who a few weeks earlier had placed Castro at the right
hand of God now heaped all kinds of insults upon him. "The revolution was
like a comic opera," the *New York Times* correspondent Samuel Hopkins
Adams reported. But, for the State Department, it had all the grandeur of a
hero of Wagner entering Valhalla after vanquishing the dragon. Forty-eight
hours after Gómez staged his tragic burlesque, the first U.S. battleship, the
Maine, left Hampton Roads to back Gómez with its guns and marines. Two
more, the *Des Moines* and the *North Carolina*, followed shortly thereafter. On
the latter was Rear Admiral W. I. Buchanan, who had been named special
commissioner for the United States to Venezuela. The admiral was advised
that his appointment was due to a dispatch the U.S. government had received through the Brazilian minister in Washington (the same dispatch cited
above). On the same day that Buchanan was given his credentials, December
21, 1908, the State Department sent a note to Caracas stating the the U.S.
government interpreted the offer of mediation to mean that "the new government intended to abrogate the policy of President Castro."

Events now unfolded like a film script. In his first week of power, Gómez
had various talks with the U.S. commissioner. The three great hulking warships of steel were at the La Guaira docks, their cannon shining in the sun,
and their marines drilling on deck daily, with the steady crackle of small arms
fire in target practice. These were healthy warnings for the "natives." If there
had been any national protest—and, of course, there was none because there
were no popular political parties—at the peaceful transfer of power from
Castro to the one who had been his accomplice and unconditional col-
laborator for ten years, it would have been put down by the troops of Uncle
Sam.

This virtual occupation by foreign troops lasted for three months. On February 13, 1909, the Buchanan-Gómez protocols were signed—the initial price to be paid to the State Department by the new government to obtain protection and the rank of a servant. The correct stand taken by the previous government with regard to the three claims by United States companies and persons against the Venezuelan state was now abandoned. These claims, resolved to the satisfaction of the U.S. government, were that of the United States and Venezuela (also known as the Grichfield claim); that of the Orinoco Corporation (known also as the Manoa claim); and that of the Orinoco Steamship Corporation.

The agreement provided for a compromise solution of the first two claims, while the third was referred to the International Court of Justice at The Hague. These claims had different origins. The first was the result of a capricious donation, by Castro to Grichfield, of an asphalt deposit in Maracaibo. The recipient had organized a company to engage in operations, but the Constituent Assembly, at the suggestion of Castro himself, annulled the Grichfield contract. Grichfield's company, however, went right ahead mining asphalt and appealed to the State Department for diplomatic support. Gómez agreed to indemnify the company, generously. The Manoa claim involved an old dispute between the government and three American companies—the Manoa Corporation, the Orinoco Company, and the George Turbull Company. They had obtained different concessions to exploit natural resources in the Orinoco delta and now complained that their concessions overlapped. By agreement between the two governments, joint Venezuelan-United States conciliation commissions were established in 1904 in an effort to reach friendly agreement. The Manoa claim was referred to the Venezuelan courts, but the claimant sought diplomatic assistance and the State Department became involved, supporting what was in effect a fictitious entity, the Orinoco Corporation. Gómez, however, paid an indemnity. Finally, in the case of the most absurd and unacceptable of the claims—that of the Orinoco Steamship Company—a U.S. citizen named Ellis Grell, who had been given a monopoly of transport, claimed that his rights had been affected when the government opened the Orinoco delta channels to free passage. The two governments could not agree on this claim and it was referred by common accord to the arbitration of Harry Barger, former governor of Curaçao. He ruled in favor of Venezuela. The company insisted, with the support of the State Department, that there be a second arbitration. This had been rejected by Venezuela, but now Gómez agreed to it. The Hague tribunal, with its pronounced sympathy for the strong over the weak, condemned Venezuela to pay an indemnity. Gómez told Congress in his message of 1911 that the sum would be paid "although it was unfair."

Nothing was said then, or later, about the most scandalous claim—that of the New York and Bermudez Company. It must have been a shameful arrangement behind the scenes, because nothing further was heard of the Bs.

24 million fine levied by the court against the company, which continued to enjoy unlimited production rights in Guanoco. We shall see later how this became a precedent for oil-concession hunters.

Everything went well until a cloud appeared on the horizon. Castro was released from the Berlin hospital and prepared to return to America. He packed his bags after proclaiming himself, with his inherent modesty, "the man of destiny"—recalling Napoleon as he did so without remembering that the Corsican had referred to himself in the same terms shortly before he was "destined" to permanent exile. The United States press reported the concern of the White House and Miraflores for this tropical version of Napoleon returning from the Isle of Elba. On March 13, 1909, the *New York Times* noted that Castro possessed much greater financial resources and personal following than when he had begun his successful adventure in 1899. But, the newspaper added, Gómez had strong support abroad, and this time the famous Andino would find the road to Caracas full of obstacles.

The New York newspaper was right. The State Department and the Casa Amarilla (Foreign Office) of Caracas worked in close collaboration to prevent Castro from landing in America. United States diplomats, following instructions received from Washington, took action with the governments of London, The Hague, and Paris to stop Castro from reaching their American possessions. Colombia, Panama, and the Nicaraguan dictatorship of Zelaya were also advised to deny asylum to the reprobate. Theodore Roosevelt's successor in the White House, President William Howard Taft, took up with his cabinet the question of blocking Castro's return and guaranteeing the stability of the Gómez regime. Secretary of State Knox did not hide his concern that some of the former aides of the caudillo might support him and cabled his worries to Russell, the new U.S. Minister in Caracas, on April 7, 1909: "There are disquieting rumors that Gómez may allow Castro to return to power. Is the government firmly decided to arrest him, in agreement with our understanding? Unless this is certain, it will be difficult for the Venezuelan government to exclude him from its territory."

Rear Admiral Buchanan suggested to Secretary Knox that "to guarantee peace and order" in Venezuela "we send one of our ships to anchor off La Guaira "and another to Port-of-Spain, Trinidad." The suggestion was unnecessary. Already, the *Montana* and the *North Carolina* were off the Venezuelan coast while the *Paducah* was anchored at La Guaira. The spiderweb spun by the Potomac diplomacy was very efficient. Castro could not land in Trinidad. He returned to Martinique only long enough to be forcibly transferred from the *Guadeloupe* to the *Antilles*, which was escorted by United States cruisers until definitely bound for Europe. Castro disappeared for years from the American scene. Thanks to the efficient aid and tutoring of North American mentors, Gómez now seized the reins of power and held them for the next twenty-seven years.

The historians J. Fred Ripply and Clyde E. Hewitt wrote in the *American*

Historical Review of October 1949 an article with the suggestive title, "Cipriano Castro, Man Without a Country." They detailed, with complete documentation from the archives of the State Department, the persecution that the despot in disgrace suffered from the new despot in the making. The article concludes with the ironic comment:

> This was another example of dollar diplomacy—less complicated and costly than that employed by the big powers against Castro in 1902–03, but highly effective. *Gómez became an even more rapacious and cruel tyrant than Castro, if that were possible, but he never became an international problem*. [My italics.]

The unpredictable tyrant had been replaced by one who was submissive. This satisfied the hopes of certain United States financial circles, as reflected in the *New York Times* editorial of December 15, 1908, which stated: "The best thing that could happen would be to have a Venezuelan Díaz come to power—sufficiently strong to maintain order and sufficiently wise to make the Venezuelans want to keep him in office . . ."

"Strong" he was—in the subjugation of all liberty; and "wise" he was—in auctioning off at a miserable price a good part of the subsoil wealth of the nation to the foreign investor. He was a worthy emulator of the Mexican Porfirio Díaz in his colonialism, cruelty, and thirst to keep power—this Juan Vicente Gómez who came to power because of the chaotic condition of the nation and the help of the U.S. State Department, the midwife and godmother of the creature!

Secretary of State Knox, who had replaced Elihu Root,* made an official visit to Venezuela in 1910 to solidify the entente between Washington and Caracas that would last for three decades. The Archbishop of Caracas issued a special absolution permitting meat to be consumed on Good Friday so that the important guest might enjoy an adequate culinary welcome. Perhaps this was the result of a subtle suggestion by a Catholic member of the U.S. legation staff—Jefferson Caffery—who was beginning his extensive diplomatic career which later included such important and controversial roles as United States "mediator" in the Cuba of Machado (1933) and in the downfall of the nationalistic Iranian regime of Mossadegh (1953).

Knox returned to Washington pleased and excited. An ideal man had been found to carry out "dollar diplomacy" in a country rich in minerals—despotic with his fellow citizens—but agreeable to the foreigner. With one hand he struck down public liberties; with the other he opened the door to commerce and investments from the United States. The dance of oil conces-

---

*Elihu Root is very well remembered. He is glorified on Pan-American days as one of the architects of the system. We Venezuelans would say other things about him. He denounced the existence of an "invisible government" by businessmen in his country—as reported by Harold J. Laski in his book *The Presidential System*—but he went on to act on behalf of this government insofar as Venezuela was concerned. He has stated emphatically in the Pan-American Conference of Rio de Janeiro that "the smallest and weakest nation deserved as much respect for its independence and its rights as the largest empire." But that did not stop him from sending Buchanan and his naval escort to Venezuela, in flagrant violation of its sovereignty, with instructions he himself had issued.

sions had already begun, and the government was showing itself apt at corruption and irresponsibility. Lest there be any doubt, Gómez read his annual message to Congress in 1911 in the stammering voice of a semiilliterate, with the following revealing paragraph written by some of his more learned secretaries:

> I understand that the Great American Nation desires to extend the already large place which its products have in our markets; I judge the aspiration to be natural. In my patriotism, I say with complete sincerity, there is not the slightest fear of the power of that nation because I see that its actions are in accord with its principles, and that it is the most complete and least imperfect democracy that humanity has ever seen.

The Dance of the Concessions

After the failure of the national Petrolia company and the stormy episode of asphalt mining, it was not until 1909 that the Venezuelan government issued the first contract for oil to a foreign company. In December 1909 a contract was signed with John Allen Tregelles, who represented the Venezuelan Development Company Ltd., for exploration and development of the enormous area covered by the states of Táchira, Trujillo, Mérida, Zulia, Lara, Falcón, Carabobo, Yaracuy, Anzoátegui, Sucre, Monagas, Nueva Esparta, and the Orinoco delta, with a few pieces of territory excepted. The contract had very generous conditions for the concessionaire: the royalty tax was only 5 percent on oil produced, and only half the import duty for kerosene and other refined products had to be paid. The concession was for thirty years and the holder agreed to deposit Bs. 120,000 in the Bank of Venezuela in bonds as a guarantee for any debts. This first company to seek "light oils" was not successful. It claimed various oil fields in the different states but never drilled a well; the Ministry of Production finally declared the contract void because of inaction by the concessionaire.

Meanwhile, during the first decade of the century, the government awarded various concessions to private persons who had close personal connections with the regime. These contracts still survive; they were granted in 1907. On February 28 of that year, Andres Jorge Vigas obtained a contract to produce oil in the Colón district of Zulia state. On the same date Antonio Aranguren—the same person imprisoned from 1950–53 for presumed complicity in the assassination of Delgado Chalbaud—obtained contracts for the Maracaibo and Bolívar districts of the same state. Various districts in Falcón and Lara states were "conceded" to Francisco Jiménez Arraiz and to Bernabe Plaza.

These concessions obtained by Venezuelans were turned over, years later, to foreigners. In the meantime, a United States company scouted with an expert eye the lands for which it was to make a big play. The Bermudez Company, an affiliate of General Asphalt, was set up to obtain oil concessions. The company was aware of public hostility toward it because of the publicity given to the machinations of its sister company, the New York and Bermudez Company. In order to avoid problems, it decided to ask for concessions in the name of Rafael Max Valladares. On July 14, 1910, he signed a contract for the rights to explore and develop the lands which had not been included in the Tregelles contract, including the Paria peninsula, Benitez district in Sucre state, Pedernales, and the nearby islands in the Orinoco delta. The conditions were the same as in the Tregelles contract, but the life of the contract was extended to forty-seven years. Four days later, Valladares transferred the contract to the Bermudez Company.

Two years later, Valladares signed a second contract with the government, on January 1, 1912, acquiring petroleum rights in the subsoil of Sucre, Monagas, Anzoátegui, Nueva Esparta, Trujillo, Mérida, Zulia, Lara, Falcón, Carabobo, and Yaracuy. This monstrous concession covered 27 million hectares (about 68 million acres). The stipulated conditions were payment of a surface tax of Bs. 1 per hectare, a royalty of Bs. 2 per ton of oil produced, and 50 percent of the import duty for any refined products. Two days after signing, Valladares transferred the contract to another affiliate of General Asphalt, the Caribbean Petroleum Company.

Valladares had obtained the concession by bribery and corruption; it was granted with blitzkrieg speed. Ten days were all that were needed for the application to become a contract. The objections formulated by the director of mines, J. M. Espindola, and by Leopoldo Baptista, a member of the so-called Federal Government Council, were brushed aside. The prediction made by the latter that the concession would wind up in foreign hands was fulfilled immediately.

The concession violated specific legal regulations. Under the mining law of 1910, then in effect, the maximum area that could be granted in concessions was 800 hectares. The Valladares contract covered 27 million hectares, and included national and private lands—anything that could be explored in the eleven-state area. The government's action exceeded anything that could have been dreamed up by the wildest and most anti-Venezuelan imagination.

Clearly this was one of the most scandalous holdups in the history of world petroleum. It evoked a wave of angry protest—not from the Venezuelans who did not know at that time of the wealth that was being thrown away by the most implacable dictator the nation had suffered up to then—but from the foreign competitors of the beneficiaries (also foreign) of this fabulous deal.

The protest was led by an Englishman, Erconswald Wostan Hodge, who, on February 16, 1917, filed a protest with the Ministry of Production demanding the annulment of the concessions transferred by Valladares to the Bermudez Company and the Caribbean Petroleum Company. The demand claimed the contracts were "unconstitutional and illegal" and modestly asked that part of them be transferred to this zealous defender of the violated legal system. The government held the protest was "without basis."

Some years later a United States citizen, Harry W. Schumacher, went to the Supreme Court and demanded annulment of the contract. The case proceeded slowly in violation of specific legal norms, and it was not until four years after it had begun, in 1932, that the high court rendered sentence. Avoiding a decision, it simply declared that the claimant had no right to sue. The case brought forth adverse opinions from the most eminent Venezuelan jurists of those days—Juan José Abreu, Juan José Mendoza, José Ramón Ayala, Celestino Ferrera, and others—as to the legality of the contracts.

This was not the end of this Venezuelan version of the Teapot Dome scandal, which so besmirched the Harding administration in the United States. In 1922, by means of a liberal distribution of checks among venal officials, the life of this concession was extended until 1943. This infamous case will come up again more than once during the history of the Venezuelan oil industry.

The English Take the Lead

The extraordinary pools of oil included in these concessions—which in a few years would produce torrents of petroleum and an astronomical profit to their holders—originally were controlled by North American interests. However, these were displaced. United States capitalism, as a whole, did not have a clear idea at that time of the future of oil. Its foreign investments were not placed, as they were after World War I, in Latin America. In Venezuela, as in other countries of our region, it was Royal Dutch Shell whose agents staked out claims early in the game, before the North Americans began to come in.

The advisers of Sir Henry Deterding "smelled" the enormous wealth contained in the concessions of the Caribbean Petroleum Company. This concern had profitably drilled in 1914 the first "commercial" well found in Venezuela: the Mene Grande. As a result, its shares went up 200 percent. Royal Dutch Shell then rushed to take over the vast rich concession, paid its titleholders $1.5 million when the contract was signed, and promised to pay a royalty of 8 percent of the total production of all wells drilled there in the future.

England wanted to take over this new source of precious fuel that had suddenly appeared in the world, but had learned to be cautious and waited to be sure it could proceed without legal entanglement. Thus it was that the attorney general of the republic introduced on June 19, 1912, a claim before the Supreme Court pointing out the conflict between Articles 8, 10, 40, and 42 of the Mining Code, the second guarantee in Article 20 of the national Constitution, and Articles 462 and 467 of the Civil Code. The High Court issued a judgment eight days later declaring Articles 40 and 42 of the Mining Code unconstitutional. These had given 33⅓ percent of the product produced from the subsoil to the owner of the surface rights. The Court's decision meant that the fortunate beneficiaries of the subsoil rights in this defenseless country would in the future have to negotiate with but one obliging partner—the dictatorial governing clique. They no longer had to share the oil wealth with private landowners, with the occupants of public lands, or with renters of municipal properties. All of these were eliminated with one stroke of the pen. Even though it is true that in the long run the nation was better served by the Supreme Court decision of June 27, 1912—because it is the nation as a whole that should benefit from oil and not private persons or individual corporations—it was still true that the concession seekers now had to use subtle influences to achieve their objective on only a single, venal, and complaisant partner.

Now that the road was open, hordes of bidders for the Venezuelan subsoil descended hungrily upon the country. In 1913, Royal Dutch Shell organized another affiliate, the Venezuelan Oil Concessions Ltd., which acquired from Bolívar Concessions Ltd. rights to explore and produce concessions in the Bolívar and Maracaibo districts of Zulia state. The contract gave the most "liberal" terms to the concessionaire for a period of fifty years from 1907, with an option for renewal at midcentury. Surface taxes amounted to less than Bs. 1 per hectare, while the royalty was Bs. 2 per metric ton. The concession covered more than 3000 square miles of an area which was so productive that for years the Venezuelan Oil Concessions Ltd., was the highest individual producer in the nation.

In the same year, 1913, Royal Dutch Shell organized one more affiliate in London, the Colón Development Company, which acquired from Andrés Jorge Vigas an extensive concession of 840,000 hectares southwest of Lake Maracaibo in the frontier area between Venezuela and Colombia. It included all of the Colón district of Zula state. Colón Development controlled 75 percent of the so-called Vigas concession, with the other 25 percent belonging to the Carib Syndicate, a company organized in 1915 by the well-known New York banker, J. Pierpont Morgan.

While powerful foreign interests were obtaining overwhelming control of the principal Venezuelan source of wealth, events were taking place that would determine the political course of the nation for many years. Elections were scheduled for the year 1914 and until then, Juan Vicente Gómez had not been able to eliminate all opposition to his autocratic plans. Many of the ambitious generals and politicians around him were still maneuvering for power. The imminence of the elections made him and his clique decide to usurp power once and for all.

The 1909 Constitution existing at that time prohibited the reelection of the president. A Federal Council of Government, composed of learned men and leaders of the civil wars, each with his own political following, seemed about to enforce the antireelection clause. A newspaper editor of civic virtue, Rafael Arévalo González, wrote an editorial in *El Pregonero* urging the candidacy of a lawyer, Felix Montes.

Gómez and his followers acted quickly and simultaneously on all fronts. The Federal Council was dissolved and its members sent into exile. A threat of foreign invasion by enemies of the government was drummed up. Gómez declared that "public peace was endangered" and took the field against an imaginary enemy. Editor Arévalo González was put in jail where he would languish for fifteen years with leg-irons of 100 pounds each on his feet. Montes began an exile that would last twenty-two years. Even the most timid signs of opposition were suffocated, and Venezuela fell under a savage oppression that lasted until 1935.

The conspiracy of Gómez against the country climaxed in 1914, at the time the first guns were being fired in World War I, by a so-called Congress of Plenipotentiaries. This was a unique constituent assembly, all of whose members were handpicked by Gómez. The assembly elected him chief of the army while Victorino Márquez Bustillos, a man of the Gómez clan, was named provisional president, after the necessary constitutional reform. Two years later, another Congress, also handpicked by Gómez, again celebrated elections by going to the trouble of calling for election boxes—so that a semblance of legality could be given his regime. Gómez was elected constitutional president for the period 1915–22. For many years thereafter, there existed a strange simulation of dual power—the real power was exercised by Gómez from his military stronghold in Maracay as president and commander-in-chief of the Army. The other power remained, as was traditional, in the Caracas palace of the chiefs of state, Miraflores, where the docile, moustached man of letters, Márquez Bustillos, received diplomatic credentials and handled the boring details of signing executive decrees.

Thus was born one of the most primitive despotisms that any people of Latin America has suffered. This despotism did nothing to inhibit the continuing dance of oil concessions. The British, who then had no competitor, had learned in the Middle East that the sheiks of Arabia and the shahs of Persia were more docile with the foreigner who enriched and favored them than they were with "natives" who opposed them. Proof of this was found in the fact that a state-controlled enterprise—the British Controlled Oilfields—followed the private companies into Venezuela. The British Admiralty had watched with pleasure as the trust of Sir Henry Deterding established a solid foothold in the country and obtained the advantage of low-priced oil. The strategic location of Venezuela near the Panama Canal was also noted by the Royal Navy, and so it was that the British Controlled Oilfields—directly under the British Crown—sought to combine economic and military advantage and control part of Venezuela's subsoil.

In 1918 the "Venezuelan" affiliate of the British Controlled Oilfields (BCO) was organized in Canada with capital assets of $27.5 million. Once installed in Venezuela, the company covered the country with a vast net of affiliates. Just as Hollywood had the "man of 1000 faces," so the BCO had many different fronts: Antonio Díaz Oilfield Ltd., Aragua Exploration Company Ltd., Bolívar Exploration Company Ltd., Lara Exploration Company Ltd., Pedernales Oilfield Ltd., Tucupita Oilfield Ltd., Central Area

Exploration Co. Ltd. (with 20 percent of the stock), and American British Company, in which it had a royalty interest.

The concessions of the British company covered 3000 square miles in the northwest coastal area of the country and some 15,000 square miles in the Orinoco delta—a zone that had been coveted by the imperial leaders for many years. This is the area where the Orinoco—one of the greatest rivers of America—enters the sea. It is the apex of the vast Amazon basin and close to British Guyana and the English island of Trinidad. Its commercial and military strategic importance need not be emphasized.

In the six years between 1912 and 1918 British imperialism sank its wells and reserved for itself the most strategic zones throughout the length and breadth of Venezuela.

Standard Oil: A Late Arrival

The world rival of Royal Dutch Shell arrived late to our shores after its competitor had been installed there for some years. This is difficult to understand as Venezuela was governed by a regime which had been so efficiently aided by the State Department. However, various factors explain the tardy appearance of United States capital in Venezuelan oil development. A truly national consciousness with respect to the vital importance of mineral fuels did not exist in the United States prior to the war of 1914–18. Also, United States capitalism had not developed to the stage of large-scale exports of capital prior to the war. Besides, the builders of the modern oil industry, John D. Rockefeller and Sir Henry Deterding, had widespread differences at the start regarding the structure of the industry. Rockefeller concentrated on the vast domestic United States market and sought to control the refineries, transportation systems, and sales outlets rather than the producing fields. Deterding, on the other hand, affirmed in 1920 that "the advantage of not concentrating production in any single country but in dispersing it throughout the world, has been clearly established." This concept of the astute Dutchman has become known in oil history as the "Straight Line Policy"—the theory of total horizontal and vertical integration of the oil industry and the organization of monopolies more complete than those found in any other production activity.

The Deterding thesis, applied across seas and continents by Royal Dutch Shell, coincided with the views of the British government, which gave diplomatic help in a systematic way to Deterding's efforts to monopolize oil wherever it could be found.

In contrast to the privileged position of its English rival, Standard Oil during the first decade of the twentieth century was under the crossfire of public criticism and official hostility. "Until the first World War," wrote Paul H. Frankel, "Standard Oil had nothing to expect from the government, which was personified for it in the tax-collector and in the Justice Department applying the Sherman Anti-Trust Law." In 1911, because of this law, Standard Oil had been forced to dismantle its monopolistic structure. Formally at least, the sentence was carried out, and Rockefeller's company had to stretch its imagination to continue as a monopoly without seeming to be one. But the outlook changed during the war.

Petroleum outdistanced all predictions of its importance as the conflict between the Allies and the Central Powers developed. Motorized warfare gradually became a substitute for infantry. Tanks, planes, transport vehicles, submarines, and warships all consumed crude oil, fuel oil, and gasoline in ever increasing quantities. The importance of finding and distributing these fuels, as well as the need of the belligerents to plan their use carefully, led to the appearance of ministers of petroleum in the governments of the entente. Finally, the Inter-Allied Council of Petroleum was formed to control the production and distribution of crude oil and products among all the Allied nations.

Germany was crippled for lack of oil (Ludendorff in his memoirs blames the defeat of the Central Powers on this lack) and resorted to the tactic of trying to prevent the Allies from fueling their motorized war machine. Its submarines tenaciously pursued oil tankers on all seas. England was forced to reduce the number of oil-burning ships in its fleet. The situation of France became critical as need of oil imports incessantly increased after 1914. The "oil hunger" felt by the French General Staff was brought out in the pathetic message from the chief of the French government to the president of the United States in 1917, now considered a classic: "Premier Clemenceau personally requests President Wilson to use his authority to send 100,000 tons [of oil] to French ports. If the Allies do not wish to lose the war, French troops, at this supreme hour of the great German attack, must have gasoline—as necessary as blood itself in the coming battles."

When the war on the battlefields had finished, another secret and just as desperate struggle continued to be fought in the ministries and international conferences. At the Geneva and Hague conferences a bitter struggle took place behind the scenes between Standard Oil and Royal Dutch Shell. Louis Fischer in his book *Oil Imperialism*, in recounting the incidents at this conference, concluded: "Diplomats today are no more than instruments of the gigantic oil companies." Dispute among the victors over sources of petroleum, as war booty, became so heated that those who had formerly fought the Boches side by side now seemed at the point of violent rupture. The division of the Mosul oil zone between France and England, behind the back of the United States, strained relations between the State Department and the Foreign Office. The San Remo Pact finally put an end to the differences.

Tempting offers were made to Moscow for the development of the Soviet nationalized oil fields at Baku at the same time that help was given to the czarist counterrevolutionary armies and threats were made of armed intervention in Russia by the European powers to rescue the oil "stolen from its rightful owners." The war had taught the victorious nations that the old Bismarckian formula of wars being won by blood and iron needed to be modernized to "blood and petroleum."

At the same time, some of these nations, especially the United States, began to realize how the intensive production of oil during the war within their own boundaries had greatly reduced their reserves. With this in mind, and taking to heart the poetic phrase of Lord Curzon that the victory had come to the Allies "flying on the wings of petroleum," the United States threw itself almost desperately into a search for new sources of oil. President Harding was so conscious of the need that he said at the inauguration of the Federal Oil Conservation Board: "The day quite possibly will come when world hegemony will belong to the nation that possesses most oil"

On April 28, 1920, the Senate authorized the secretary of the Navy to establish oil reserve zones in the United States, and six days later the U.S. Geological Service predicted that national reserves might soon be exhausted. It urged that "instead of producing our own reserves so rapidly, we should obtain more oil from foreign countries or reduce our consumption. Our sons surely will have to do both." Ironically, the "fathers" only adopted the first measure.

Faced with the threat of exhausted reserves, the United States employed all its powerful resources to procure petroleum wherever it might be found. Diplomacy began to mix with oil. Solidified with time, underground connections among the State Department, Standard Oil, and other oil companies go back to that period. The process has been underlined, with a certain irony, by P. H. Frankel:

> The activity of American oil firms abroad may not have interested Washington when it thought only of markets. However, after 1920, when the specter of oil poverty began to haunt the United States, a very effective cooperation began between the oil companies and the State Department. To believe this did not happen would be to underestimate the intelligence and responsibility of both parties. Protestations to the contrary only demonstrate that the North Americans now adopted the classic attitude of the British, who pretend that they conquered an empire . . . through carelessness.[1]

The most convenient area in which to establish the United States oil empire was the Caribbean. It was nearby; there was easy access to the principal United States consuming centers; and there was cheap manpower. Mexico logically should have been the immediate choice. It was an important oil producer at the time the United States petroleum crusade began; Venezuela was not. At this time, in 1921, Venezuelan wells produced scarcely 1 million barrels of crude yearly, while the Mexican fields accounted for 193 million. But high winds were disturbing the Aztec region. Porfirio Díaz, with his imperious patriarchal rule which blandly submitted to the foreigner, was no longer in charge. The Mexican Revolution was beginning. The subsoil had been nationalized, and rising hostility against the uncontrolled investment of foreign capital was evident.

In contrast, the outlook in Venezuela could not have been more favorable for easy conquest. The Gómez regime was more implacable by the day, but only with the local population. Its unlimited capacity to oppress and make exactions of the Venezuelans contrasted sharply to the submission and obsequiousness shown toward powerful foreigners.

At the same time that President Wilson was enunciating the Fourteen Points and praising universal democracy and Secretary of State Lansing was denouncing European tyrannies, Venezuelan despotism uncovered a civilian-military conspiracy to overthrow it. Jails were filled with political prisoners locked into medieval leg-irons weighing 100 pounds. The dictator's son himself supervised tortures taking place in Villa Zoila, where prisoners were hung by their feet or genitals and suffered straps tightened with a tourniquet around their heads until the eyes almost started from their sockets. Dozens of men were poisoned with arsenic behind the thick walls of the old colonial dungeons of La Rotunda.

But Venezuela was not only a country of tyranny, terror, and blood. It had oil—much oil. And the men of Wall Street turned greedily toward the country. The delegate sent by Gómez to the Pan-American Finance Conference in Washington on May 24, 1915, clearly extended an invitation to participate. Pedro M. Rincones spoke with an unmistakably hospitable accent when he said:

> This is the time for U.S. capital to take advantage of the great opportunities offered by the industrial development of the Latin American countries. The field has been wide open for the past fifteen years. The big question for those interested is how to handle the markets that have been for so long in the hands of European competitors. What plan can be followed to assure success there?

Once the war was over, the big United States oil firms remembered the invitation. It was not necessary to repeat it. They came hunting concessions with all the eagerness of those arriving late to the party. Gómez gained further admirers. He was genial, just as Porfirio Díaz in Mexico had been, generously handing out the natural resources of the nation to foreigners acting under the protection of different flags. "Just as Díaz had done," writes Ludwell Denny, "Gómez balanced the monopolistic power of one foreign group by giving concessions to a second, in this case North American."[2]

Fortune magazine, in its issue of April 1949, also told how thirty-five different United States companies with vast resources entered the field in Venezuela after becoming discouraged by declining production and the threat of expropriation in Mexico. Leading the march was Standard Oil, which sent various experts in intrigue and dozens of geologists. After a few years it had managed to concentrate in its hands various operating companies: Lago Petroleum Corporation, Creole Petroleum Company, Vacuum Oil Company, Standard Oil of Venezuela, Richmond Petroleum Company, and others.

Lago, Creole, and Standard Oil of Venezuela obtained the most favored concessions. Lago was organized in 1923. Ten years later, it controlled more than 3.5 million acres in the states of Monagas, Sucre, and Zulia. One of its best concessions included the entire Lake of Maracaibo, except for a border 1 kilometer wide along its shore.

Creole Petroleum Corporation (which at present concentrates all activities of Standard Oil in Venezuela) was organized in 1920. Originally, it developed the coastal strip just mentioned, but eventually it evolved into a holding company which owned all the shares of Standard Oil of Venezuela, 51 percent of those of Rio Palma Land & Timber Company, and 70.65 percent of Merida Oil Company. In accordance with the internal arrangements of the Standard Oil trust, Creole possessed 6.5 million acres of concessions which were later reduced as some were shown to be unproductive. As *Fortune* magazine wrote:

> The capstone of Creole's present operation is dated 1932, when Jersey, in what was proved to be the oil "steal" of the century, bought all Standard of Indiana's foreign properties from some $135 million. These included Lago Petroleum, then producing around 100,000 barrels a day in Maracaibo, and Lago Oil & Transport Company, which operated a large refinery at Aruba. It is safe to say that Lago's production in the Maracaibo fields has long since paid off the whole investment and that the reserves already proved on the Lago concessions could, and probably will, pay it off a good many times more.

> In 1943, Creole was transformed into an operating company and Lago and Standard of Venezuela were liquidated. Since then, Creole has been the leading oil producer of the world with nearly 1 million barrels of oil output daily. Its capital is only one-sixth of the total $3 billion of Standard Oil of New Jersey but accounts for half the annual earnings of the parent company. Its reserves total nearly 5 billion barrels. In 1949, Jersey Standard forecast that it would reinvest $1.2 billion in Venezuela by 1953 to expand the activities of its favorite affiliate.

Fortune concluded by pointing out that "although Jersey Standard could exist without Creole, it could not maintain its present level of earnings nor could it maintain its existence as a worldwide integrated empire of production, refining, and marketing, as it is today."[3]

Formerly, Standard Oil of Venezuela had concentrated its activities in eastern Venezuela where United States capital predominated and there was hardly any sign of the British. Oil production began in Monagas state in 1928 when the first two wells of Quiriquire were brought in. By 1936 Standard Oil of Venezuela (SOV) controlled 3.7 million hectares of concessions in eastern Venezuela. In 1923 the Mellon interests arrived. Venezuelan Gulf Oil Company (later the Mene Grande Oil Company) was the affiliate of the trust whose principal stockholder was Andrew Mellon, Secretary of the U.S. Treasury during the administrations of Presidents Harding, Coolidge, and Hoover. This company also acquired the Maracaibo Oil Company and other very productive concessions in the lake area. In the language of the oil companies, "the Big Three" referred to the three largest producers, of which Mene Grande was third, preceded by the giants of the industry—Standard Oil (Creole) and Royal Dutch (Shell).

The youthful and aggressive impetus of the United States companies enabled them to achieve their goal. They arrived late but they got what they wanted. Their British competitors fell back in the unequal battle between the rheumatic pound sterling and the agile dollar. The investments of the latter increased by leaps and bounds: $11 million in 1924; $72 million in 1925; $128 million in 1926; and $157 million in 1928. Venezuela became the prize jewel in the imperial oil crown of Uncle Sam.

The British and the North Americans conducted a bitter battle for Venezuelan oil. The lawyers' offices of Shell and Standard Oil were like enemy forts. All kinds of political intrigue and financial maneuvering went on. Dollars and pounds competed in the black market of influence-buying among the friends and relatives of Gómez. The investors of Wall Street and the City of London incited the struggle and, behind them, offering encouragement to those whose greed was despoiling the helpless, were the State Department and the Foreign Office. The methods they used showed no more integrity than those of the investor companies.

In a note to the State Department on November 21, 1919, Preston McGoodwin, U.S. Minister in Caracas, complained that the British oil companies were sending their U.S. employees, pretending to be employees of U.S. companies, to the U.S. legation for help and information. "American tactics were no more honorable," comments Edwin Lieuwen.[4] He recounts the occasion when Washington obtained information that the North Venezuelan Petroleum Company, holder of the Arraiz concession, was controlled by the Anglo-Iranian Oil Company. Anglo-Iranian was in turn owned by the British Crown and therefore could not legally operate in Venezuela since the old mining law and the oil law expressly prohibited concessions being given to foreign governments. The U.S. Assistant Secretary of State Adee instructed McGoodwin on March 23, 1921, to inquire of the Gómez government whether "activies of the Anglo-Persian Oil Company had been considered by Venezuelan authorities in connection with the oil laws." McGoodwin replied on June 14 that the Venezuelan government would annul the concessions as a result of the "advice" from the Potomac. However, the English were not without resource and evidently loosened their purse-strings. Anglo-Persian and British Controlled Oilfields, both owned by the London government, continued their activities in flagrant violation of all the mineral laws that had ever been promulgated in Venezuela.

It was after 1915 that diplomatic maneuvers of the British and North Americans became especially intense. An incident involving the Vigas concession became a long and prolonged affair, and revealed how the activities of the legations of Washington and London in Caracas were aggressively unrestrained on behalf of private companies from their respective countries. The Vigas concession had been granted by Castro in 1907 and then was transferred to the Colón Development Company, a Shell subsidiary. The legal termination date for the exploration rights was 1915, and the company should have returned to the state the land not selected for production. Despite the fact that it had selected only three parcels, Colón argued that it had the right to retain the rest of the vast territory of the Colón district of Zulia state for fifty years. It refused to pay taxes except for those parcels which had been selected—an amount of only Bs. 1200 annually instead of the

Bs. 3.8 million claimed by the Ministry of Production. The dispute dragged on until 1920 when the government insisted that Shell pay the amount claimed by the ministry retroactively from 1915. Furthermore, the government advised the eager North American companies—envious of the privileged position of the English—that the Vigas concession would be rescinded. United States companies hastened to make offers for the area. Minister McGoodwin reported on the outlook in notes to the State Department early in 1920. Without hesitation, he reported that one of the North American companies had already offered $1,350,000 for the exploration rights of the concession for one year—plus an equal amount to Gómez as a bribe.

The Venezuelan government took its dispute with Colón Development to the courts, and the attorney general of the nation sued the company before the Supreme Court. It turned out that the Carib Syndicate, a United States company headed by C. K. McFadden, owned one-fourth of the stock of the British concern. "Vital U.S. interests are threatened," cried McGoodwin to the State Department. His concern did not seem to cause much effect. Assistant Secretary Adee, in notes to McGoodwin (April 28) and to McFadden himself (May 29), clearly let it be understood that help would not be given to the English on behalf of minority United States interests. There was a much greater and more ambitious objective: to eliminate once and for all the overseas competitor from the rich petroleum area.

It seemed that the United States hope might be realized. On June 12, 1920, the Court voided the Vigas concession and left the Colón Company with just the three parcels that had been selected. This decision had transcendental implications. Other early concessions that had placed the petroleum bonanza in the hands of the English were in an identical situation to the Vigas concession: the Aranguren concession (controlled by Shell), the Planas concession (controlled by British Oilfields), and the Arraiz concession (controlled by North Venezuelan Petroleum). It seemed so certain that the initial Anglo-Dutch monopoly was going to be completely dismantled that Minister McGoodwin informed the State Department (note of June 11, 1920) that important United States companies were ready to distribute the spoils of the vanquished. They had made their offers and were sure the concessions would revert to the nation and then pass to their control as the puppet Congress of Gómez begain its session of 1920.

Then occurred an unexpected development—a "diplomatic blunder" of the U.S. government as Lieuwen describes it.[5] The State Department—which had previously decided to leave the Carib Syndicate to its own devices with the obvious purpose of making a small sacrifice so it could gain everything—now acted like St. Christopher and pulled McFadden's company onto its shoulders. McFadden's? It turned out that J. Pierpont Morgan, a magnate of tremendous influence in Washington, was the principal stockholder of the company. Perhaps that explains the note of one Davis of the State Department to Minister McGoodwin (June 24). The U.S. diplomat was instructed to take the note to Gómez and tell him that "the property interest involved in the Vigas concession should be recognized and all of its rights protected."

Gómez accepted what he took to be an order. Furthermore, what seemed like demands from North America cleared up the difficulties with the English. The British minister in Caracas also used the language of a proconsul. Access is not open to the records of the Foreign Office, which keeps its diplomatic papers secret, but quite a bit can be learned from the correspondence of the U.S. legation in Caracas with the State Department in Washington. A tone of violence and disrespect toward Gómez is evident on the part of the British at this time. J. C. White, an officer of the U.S. legation, wrote to the State Department on November 14, 1921: "The British Chargé d'Affaires took a very strong line, going so far as to verbally inform the Venezuelan Foreign Minister that the British government would not recognize a decision adverse to the Shell company by Venezuelan courts. He demanded that the matter be called to the personal attention of Gómez, in accordance with his instructions."

In addition to this abrupt diplomatic action, other maneuvers were carried out by Shell officials, led by W. T. Doyle, a North American who was then manager. He was personally acquainted with the intimacies of the Potomac diplomacy since he had been nothing less than former chief of the Latin American Division in the State Department. These maneuvers led to a solution of the Vigas concession problem, which left the United States oil men stupefied and indignant. On February 15, 1921, it was announced that the Gómez government had arrived at an extrajudicial settlement with Shell, annulling the Supreme Court decision voiding the concession. Similar arrangements were made with respect to other concessions awarded in 1907, since then in the hands of the British.

The State Department voiced the exasperated stupefaction of the United States oil companies. McGoodwin, in a note of March 22, 1922, sought to explain that Gómez continued to be subservient to Washington: "There is no doubt that the Venezuelan government reached its agreement with Shell thinking to protect the one-fourth American interest in the company."

These explanations did not seem to convince Washington. There was poorly disguised irritation in the State Department, and McGoodwin, despite his close connections with Gómez and his service to the United States companies in their struggles with the British, was recalled. Apparently he was considered inept in presenting his government's position in the case of the Vigas concession. The frustrated hopes of the State Department were expressed in a memorandum from a certain Murray of the Latin American Division in the State Department, dated April 27, 1924: "It has been particularly unfortunate that this vast British concession has been prolonged despite the efforts of our Minister, when it was the main purpose of our Department to get it cancelled."

The fight between the British and North Americans continued without quarter in later years until finally, in 1929, a truce was declared in Venezuela, as well as elsewhere, between the English and their first cousins on the other side of the ocean. That year the famous Achnacarry Agreement was reached. Under the pretext of hunting foxes, two human representatives of that biological species had met in an aristocratic castle in Scotland—Sir Henry W. A. Deterding of Royal Dutch Shell and Walter D. Teagle of Standard Oil of New Jersey. There they arranged a peace on a worldwide basis—the so-called "As Is" agreement. Each giant agreed to keep off the territory of the other.

Accommodating Legislation and Instant Concessions

"The petroleum laws of Venezuela are the best in the world for the companies," wrote Gumersindo Torres, a production minister of Gómez, in 1930. The statement was contained in a confidential memorandum to the companies, a kind of "letter of apology" that will be cited more than once.

Even the least alert observer would agree with this emphatic statement were he only to consider the scandalous total of profits received by the companies and the minimum participation of the government, the oil workers, and the entire nation in these profits. We will comment on this later, but for the moment let us make a rapid survey of Venezuelan oil legislation.

For some years after oil exploration by foreign companies was in full swing, Venezuela had no oil law. Relations between the government and concessionaire were regulated by the obsolete mining law of 1910, which had no specific arrangements regarding oil but only general rules covering subsoil development. A reform of this law in 1918 had only limited application, and two years later a new law was promulgated with regard to oil production.

This first law of 1920 was approved by a Congress—named by Gómez and picked from within the circle of his friends—with hardly any discussion of the draft sent by the executive. It had a few timid nationalistic provisions, and it might have been thought that the Venezuelan dictator had learned something from the recently ended war and was trying to obtain a greater share of the profits for the nation. Any such presumption would have been ingenuous. Its provisions were simply an alert to foreign investors—present and future—to warn them subtly to open more liberally their purses from which Gómez, his friends, his doctors, and his generals were anxious to extract a few more million.

All that preceded and followed the 1920 petroleum law justifies this thesis. Before its promulgation some of the most attractive concession contracts to individuals had been transferred to foreign companies. The Vigas, Aranguren, and Jiménez arraiz contracts were ceded to various British companies: the Colón Development Company, the Venezuelan Oil Concessions, the North Venezuelan Petroleum Company, and British Controlled Oilfields Ltd.

The promulgation of the first oil law was one of the judicial comedies so typical of the age when Venezuela was a "no man's land" in regard to the legal situation of these companies. At the time the legislation became effective, the concessionaire companies had selected only twelve parcels and the time allowed for new selections had run out. In consequence, they should only have been able to drill wells in the areas selected, and the rest of the immense area of the original contracts should have been recovered by the nation, with the right to award new concessions under the new legislation. This was the basis for the suit by the attorney general against the Colón Company and the Venezuelan Oil Concessions (VOC). However, there were no court proceedings, only a complete farce. Without waiting for a court decision, the affair was settled behind the scenes. VOC made a single payment to the nation of Bs. 10 million and other payments—nobody knows how much—to the officials of the dictatorship. For this the four British companies were allowed to select parcels in the areas included in their contracts during a period of five years, with five additional years allowed to begin drilling. Still more: the VOC contracts did not refer to oil, but to asphalt. The transaction purged the contract of its original shortcoming, and the company was given the privilege of exploring and producing any kind of combustible mineral.

Thus the first-born of Venezuelan oil laws died—asphyxiated in its cradle. It suffered from a grave defect: it did not please the foreign companies. Two years later it was changed.

The law of 1922—model for all subsequent legislation until 1936—did satisfy the companies. It should have; it was written by their own lawyers with all the care with which a Bond Street tailor would have pieced together a jacket for the wardrobe of Sir Henry Deterding.

It was an open secret in Venezuela that this had been done, and a reading of any part of the law makes clear whom it favored. But it was a North American journalist who years later, after interviewing the oil company managers, stated the matter specifically in that very capitalist publication, *Fortune* of New York (March 1939). Clarence Horn, in his report on the oil industry in Venezuela, indiscreetly told the story: "Gómez called the company managers together and told them: 'You know about oil. You write the laws. We are amateurs in this area.'" The rats were assembled to legislate regarding the cheese which was to be shared.

In *Petroleum in Venezuela*, Professor Lieuwen has summarized with objectivity and precision the process whereby the oil law of 1920 was replaced with that of 1922. His book recounts the shady maneuvers of the U.S. oil companies and of the U.S. Minister in Caracas, Preston McGoodwin, to get the law changed:

> Early in 1921, after a series of meetings between the U.S. oil companies and Minister McGoodwin to agree upon the changes desired in the oil law, they carried out a joint action to obtain them. While McGoodwin went to Maracay to present their case to the dictator, the company representatives presented complaints to the officials in Caracas. Pressures were also brought on the Venezuelan landholders who

had acquired exploration permits under article 28 of the 1920 law. They hoped to sell these contracts to the foreign companies but the oil men threatened them with boycott advising them that they would not buy until the law had been changed.[6]

They also demanded that Gumersindo Torres leave the cabinet where he had become known as a champion of an oil policy that would bring more benefits to the country. This pincer movement—the double diplomatic and financial squeeze—gave the desired results. Lieuwen tells in a few words what happened, confirming what Clarence Horn heard and reported: "Minister G. Torres was dismissed and the American Oil company representatives were called in to cooperate in writing a more acceptable law. One of the oil company lawyers, Raphael Hidalgo Hernández, was assigned by Gómez to write it."

The same Congress that approved this oil law "made in the USA" carried out another assignment. This was not to legislate but to elect—to elect Gómez president of the republic for the third time for the period of 1922–29. The serpent bit its tail: Gómez had placed the deputies and senators in their seats by an action of his imperious will; every seven years, seated in Congress, they placed him in the presidential chair. In addition, in this year 1922, as a revelation of how the nepotism of the governing clan had reached its climax, not only the dictator, but also his close relatives were selected for the highest executive posts. His brother, Juan Crisóstomo Gómez, was elected first vice president, and a son, José Vincente Gómez, was made second vice president. Three different persons, but a single barbaric government. And if anyone believes my concept to be exaggerated, let him recall that this gallows trilogy was abruptly ended when one of its members—Vice President Juan Crisóstomo—was cut to pieces in his bed at Miraflores Palace by assassins on the payroll of his own relatives.*

The jails continued to be filled with political prisoners who had neither been sentenced nor granted the right of defense. The university had been closed. Colonies of political exiles scattered throughout America grew without ceasing. The only press permitted to publish was that which eulogized the despot and his regime. But the dance of the oil concessions continued. Certain facts obtained from the testimony of persons, themselves involved, reveal how the concessions were distributed among the relatives and friends of Gómez so they might later negotiate them with representatives of international capital.

---

*Gómez finally realized that his exaggerated nepotism was encouraging palace crimes and even endangering his unipersonal system of government. This realization led him to remove his sons from their high political posts and to order his tame congress to suppress the vice presidencies of the republic. The document in which he set forth the opinion he had reached in this respect was not known by the country until it was published by ex-President López Contreras in 1955 in his book, *Proceso Politico-Social, 1928–1936.* The curious Gómez document faithfully portrays the man and his epoch. It said: "Maracay, April 1929. Gentlemen of the Congress: In view of the ingratitude prevalent in politics, I have decided that none of my sons should become politicians and I am giving the order to suppress the inspectorship of the army and the military academy. It is up to you to suppress the vice presidencies. Your friend, J. V. Gómez."

Juan Vicente Gómez, Jr., traveling in Europe in 1928, wrote his father from Paris on December 3; a paragraph from this letter thoroughly illustrates how the oil concessions were given out in the Gómez family as if it were a matter of private wealth: "I use this opportunity to urgently ask that you allow Dr. Pedro M. Reyes to stay here because, as you know, I am engaged in the sale of the petroleum that you, with your infinite goodness, gave your son. . . ."[7] What a poem of paternal generosity, of filial gratitude, and of governmental rapacity!

On April 20, 1926, a Caracas notary registered a petroleum document whereby Eloy Maria Pérez ceded to Josefina Revenga de Gómez, wife of José Vicente Gómez, the rights to a 5 percent royalty on the crude oil or gas production from the concessions granted to Charles E. Hermann which had been transferred to the Texas Petroleum Mining Company. The price was Bs. 7.28 million. In 1946, before Illegal Enrichment Tribunal established by the revolutionary junta, over which I presided, S. R. Pérez swore that he personally had not received any money from this transaction "carried out to find a European buyer for the concessions owned by the family of General José Vicente Gómez."

Lieuwen, in his book, writes that he was told by one of the veterans of the oil industry in Caracas, Leonard W. Henry of the Richmond Petroleum Corporation—a resident of Venezuela for more than thirty years—that the company operated in conjunction with the unscrupulous dealers in the wealth and economic destiny of the country, one of whom, the favorite son-in-law of Gómez, Julio F. Mendez, received seventeen concessions of 15,000 hectares each.

> Oil men quickly found out who was able and who was not able to obtain oil concessions; the most favored intermediaries became, practically, their agents. A company representative would approach one of the political favorites of Gómez and indicate to him the number of concessions desired; the Venezuelan would obtain them in his own name and transfer them to the companies. Often the intermediaries retained a large number of parcels without registering them, since registering meant payment of taxes. When a buyer was found, the intermediary would register the concession and immediately transfer it to the buyer, who would pay the taxes.[8]

All of this hanky-panky was closely related to gangsterism, the author concludes: "The law was a farce. It was used as a front whereby Gómez and his cronies obtained money from the companies and defrauded the public treasury. The 15,000-hectare concession parcels awarded under the law brought to their fortunate purveyors more than $30,000 per hectare."

The money obtained from this scandalous profiteering with the Venezuelan subsoil rapidly enriched the governing clique. The ostentatious display of ill-gotten gains contrasted with the misery, ignorance, and backwardness in which the people languished. It was not until the government which I headed established the Tribunal of Illegal Enrichment in 1946 that the facts as to how Venezuela had been plundered came to light. A few facts, selected at random from the five volumes of proceedings of the tribunal, will reveal how things were.

Santos Matute Gómez, relative and associate of Juan Vicente, fraudulently appropriated an oil-bearing strip along the coast of Lake Maracaibo and sold it to an oil company for Bs. 8 million.[9] Adolfo Bueno, physician to Gómez and his secretary for many years, solicited for himself and his associate, Gustavo Escobar, three concessions of national reserves in Lake Maracaibo on June 15, 1922. The following day they were granted. Six months later, he sold them to the British Equatorial Oil Company (which later sold them to Lago Petroleum), reserving a royalty of 5 percent, two-thirds of which was transferred to Adolfo Bueno. In 1938, Bueno sold his portion of the royalty to the Falcón Oil Corporation for Bs. 9,126,000 after having previously received Bs. 2 million in profits.[10] Vincencio Pérez Soto, when president of Zulia state, made more than Bs. 10 million selling oil lands to companies, using the names of third parties to obtain the property from public domain lands.[11]

The policy of the dictatorship was usually capricious and disorganized—it was only consistent in its repression—but there did appear sporadic nationalistic gestures by some functionary or other. This explains the resolution of November 27, 1917, which, had it been retained, would have been of extraordinary importance to the country. It reserved for the state the administration of oil fields located in Mérida, Trujillo, and Zulia states that were not rented or did not belong to private persons or companies. A year later, the administrator who issued this resolution was removed for "exceeding his authority."

The extensive zone that had been reserved for the government by the ephemeral decree covered rich oil land in the Maracaibo basin, with easy access to the sea. The reason for the annulment of the resolution, a year later, became clear when a few months later 3.7 million hectares in the area were opened for bids and concessions were issued in the name of various dummies, who immediately passed the contracts to the following companies: Mara Exploration Company, 75,000 hectares; Perija Exploration Company, 75,000 hectares; Páez Exploration, 73,680 hectares; Miranda Exploration Company, 90,000 hectares; and the Venezuelan Oilfield Ltd., 80,000 hectares. The total was 393,680 hectares.

This scramble for concessions using dummies was later replaced by another formula. After the oil law of 1922 was passed, Gómez decided not to continue to distribute oil lands among his relatives and friends so that they could take a cut when they transferred them to the foreign companies. He decided to take over this sale of national lands for himself. He founded the Compañía Venezolana de Petróleo (Venezuelan Petroleum Company) and placed three of his closest friends at its head: Lucio Baldo, as president; "Colonel" Roberto Ramirez, a celebrated bagman for Gómez, as vice president; and Pedro González Rincones. A United States geologist, Edwin B. Hopkin, was hired as sales agent and opened offices in New York and London.

In 1923, the New York office offered 100,000 hectares of national reserve lands in sale. There were no takers. The oil companies knew perfectly well that the concessions were of illicit origin and that in accordance with Venezuelan oil legislation that had been drawn up by their own lawyers, they might be annulled by any future government. But the promoters had cards up their sleeves and played them. Their financial agents abroad had connections with the German Stinnes, one of the biggest magnates under the Weimar republic. In February 1924 the North American companies learned that Stinnes and his group had obtained an option on 200,000 hectares of national reserves. The U.S. legation in Caracas transmitted the news to Washington and, in successive dispatches, recalled the Germanophile antecedents of Gómez and his well-known sympathy for the Central Powers during the war. The United States companies, for their part, asked for support from Washington and were not kept waiting. In a note on March 26, 1924, the State Department instructed the Caracas legation "to inform Venezuelan government officials that the U.S. government would view with alarm any measure which suggested confiscation, or any which excluded the interest of the United States from the opportunity to compete on the basis of equality with other foreign interests to obtain concessions for the future development of those zones which make up the national reserves." Foreign Minister Chacón Itriago must have been tremendously surprised when he received the accusation that a government so docile to Washington's tutelage had alleged "confiscation" plans affecting interests so fully supported by the State Department. On March 31, 1924, the Casa Amarilla replied to the legation note, affirming that "any suspicion of confiscation completely lacks any truth."

The "Stinnes Operation," however, produced the result Gómez wanted. The option to the Germans was for only one part of the enormous area included in the national reserves. Now, like animals released from a cage, the companies pounced on the vast remainder. Standard Oil of New Jersey was the first to begin to buy concessions from the Gómez company, Venezolana de Petróleo, "despite the questionable legality of these contracts," as Lieuwen remarks. He adds: "Standard reasoned that if it were eventually proved that Gómez was the real owner of these concessions, it would still be difficult to nullify them because of the doctrine of 'innocent purchaser,'"[12] Furthermore, since Gómez had honored the concessions given out by Castro in 1907, it was possible that the next government would accept the validity of the new titles. That opinion was transmitted to the State Department by the legation in Caracas in correspondence of April 15, 1924.

Gómez and his friends continued their maneuvers. To force higher prices for the reserve lands and bigger profits for themselves, they circulated the rumor that the concessions would all be given to Standard of New Jersey. The other North American companies became alarmed and again went to the State Department to complain. This presented a difficult problem. Could the same procedures used in the Stinnes case be revived when the possible monopoly was not by an outsider but by an unmistakably United States concern? This time, there was no diplomatic pressure. The companies discriminated against outdid each other, handing out gifts and bribes and paying the prices—then considered very high—fixed by Venezolana de Petróleo for its concessions. The prosperous company of Gómez sold not only national reserves but also ordinary concession properties for exploration and production. In 1926, from a total of 234 concession contracts, the Compañia Venezolana received 189.

The full history of this colossal rip-off was not disclosed until 1946, when it was investigated by the Illegal Enrichment Tribunal. Ramírez, the former vice president of the company, told the tribunal how the matter was organized. "I was the promoter," he explained. "I organized the company at the suggestion of General Juan Vicente Gómez, who called me and said that he would look with great pleasure on the formation of a wholly Venezuelan enterprise that would undertake oil negotiations and that it would be financed by Venezuelans." The company had a book capital of Bs. 5 million that was never paid in by its phantom stockholders. The Ministry of Production paid for the expenses of the office installation. Ramírez added: "General Gómez participated in the company, thanks to his power and the official protection he gave the company in the award of concessions." When asked how much Gómez got from this gangster traffic, he replied without hesitation: "He was paid large sums at different times." According to the audit of the company books, these sums totaled Bs. 20 million, or $4 million according to the exchange then prevalent.[13]*

One does not have to have to be a Venezuelan, nor take up a position in defense of its people's interests, to feel indignation when the rotten foundations of the oil industry are brought to light. Thus, Edwin Lieuwen drops his dispassionate scholarly tone for very outspoken opinions when he refers to the methods that have been discussed here:

> These were the methods by which concessions were given out in the days of Gómez. Fraud and deceit, trickery and double-dealing were the rules of the game. The companies which were best at adapting themselves to the corrupt government system took the lead; as accomplices in the crime they received the lion's share of oil lands. Three big U.S. companies (Standard of New Jersey, Standard of Indiana and Gulf) obtained their contracts in the corrupt manner of the Gómez era.[14]

The millions invested by the companies to bribe venal officials and line the pocket of Gómez were returned, many times over, by the oil wells. Their profits were typical of colonialism. The statement by Minister of Production Torres—"The oil laws of Venezuela are the best in the world for the companies"—was absolutely true. The lengthy period of the contracts, some

---

*The exchange rate between the bolivar and the dollar has changed several times since the 1930s as follows: 1937–41, 3.19 Bs. to $1; 1942–63, 3.35 Bs. to $1; 1964–70, 4.5 Bs. to $1; 1971–72, 4.4 Bs. to $1; and 1973 to present, 4.3 Bs. to $1. (Source: International Monetary Fund, *International Financial Statistics*, a monthly publication.) During most of the time period discussed in this book, the reader can use the ratio of 3 bolivars to 1 dollar as a rough measure of comparison.

of them lasting for half a century, extremely low royalties, absence of any supervision by the state over oil production, and complete lack of protection for the Venezuelan worker who, prevented from unionizing, was without any labor laws to protect him—these were the characteristics of the system by which Venezuelan oil was produced.

Among the many advantages which the oil companies had assigned to themselves when they wrote *their* law of 1922 was the exoneration of tariff duties for everything which they imported from abroad. Thus they carried out in succeeding decades a legal contraband of gigantic proportion through the ports of the nation. The national treasury lost a far greater amount through being unable to tax their imports than the amount which the companies paid altogether for the taxes affecting the industry.

In his secret memorandum to the companies in 1930, Minister of Production Torres corroborated the foregoing affirmation with figures—during the seven preceding years customs duty exonerations for the oil industry totaled Bs. 219 million, while during the same period oil taxes collected amounted to Bs. 187 million. Minister Torres complained: "It would have been better not to have imposed any taxes at all but to have charged import duties." He concludes with a tragic summary of the true relationship between the government and the companies under Gómez and for some years after: "The companies take away the oil and the Venezuelan government pays them to do so."

What happened to the price of gasoline and other oil products illustrates the same irritating reality. By 1931, Venezuela was a first-ranking oil-producing country. Despite the "gentlemen's agreement" among the big oil companies to reduce production because of the great economic crisis that was then shaking the capitalist system to its foundations, Venezuelan wells produced 120 million barrels. Nonetheless, the nation did not even enjoy the minimum advantage an oil country should have had: cheap fuel. On the contrary, it was a nation in which gasoline and other oil products were sold at exorbitant prices. Gasoline prices were from 45 céntimos per liter (about $.54 per gallon at the exchange then) in the most favored areas to Bs. 1 ($1.21 per gallon) in Encontrados, a region within the Zulia oil basin.

Minister Torres, with the timidity before foreign capital so characteristic of officials of regimes without popular support, requested a decrease in the price of gasoline. He pointed out to the companies that gasoline made of Venezuelan oil could be imported from the United States or Trinidad into Venezuela and sold at a profit. "It cannot be justified that gasoline here— where there is a tax of only 3.5 céntimos per liter ($.04 per gallon)—costs more than in countries where the tax is greater."[15]

The companies (West India Oil Company, Lago Petroleum Corporation, and the Caribbean Petroleum Corporation) replied to this request with a disdainful reduction of 5 céntimos per liter ($.06 per gallon). The "Memoria del Ministerio de Fomento al Congreso" (1932) shows how this reduction bore little relation to the low production costs and the high profits the companies were making on their domestic monopoly of gasoline sales. The companies produced gasoline at 7 céntimos per liter ($.08 per gallon), the sales of which gave them an annual profit of Bs. 32.4 million ($9.8 million). Surplus gasoline was not sold in the country but was exported at dumping prices to foreign markets where its price was so low that it provoked boycotts of locally refined products in Mexico.

These timid protests of the colonial treatment received from the oil barons reflected world events which were then dominating attention. In faraway Persia, Reza Shah, a monarch of nationalist tendencies, had annulled the D'Arcy concession. Awarded originally to a Dutchman, this grant had become the possession of His Britannic Majesty. The Anglo-Persian Oil Company, favorite of the English Crown and star pupil of the Admiralty, exploited Persia and humiliated its people for decades. The nation's tolerance reached its limit and on November 27, 1932, Minister of Finance Teqizadeh notified the company that its concession was annulled. A great uproar followed. The then youthful but always well-dressed Captain Anthony Eden, undersecretary of foreign affairs, spoke in the Commons like an angered Jupiter: "Great Britain will not tolerate interference by the Persian government in the Anglo-Persian Oil Company." The English minister in Teheran called on the shah and threatened punitive action by the troops of the king of Afghanistan. Cruisers were dispatched to the Persian Gulf. Two destroyers anchored three miles off Abadan. Tribes on the Indian frontier armed by English agents revolted against the Teheran government. The British press, including the liberal *Manchester Guardian*, orchestrated an aggressive campaign against the faraway country that dared to stand up to imperial Albion. Some newspapers even reproduced the arrogant poetry of Rudyard Kipling from the Boer War. Lansbury, head of the opposition, spoke in Parliament—not to defend the just cause of the Persians—but only to ask that the government not begin military action in the Middle East without consulting the House of Commons.

In Teheran, meanwhile, the Majlis, or Parliament, voted unanimously to support the shah and the cancellation of the D'Arcy contract. The Persian press ventilated in retaliation the stored-up resentment of the people. Finally, the dispute was taken to the Council of the League of Nations. Terrified by the display of military force and the psychological pressure, the Iranian government took a timid and fearful stance in the Geneva debate. Sir John Simon, the British representative, spoke in haughty tones with an unmistakable Victorian accent. Davar, the Persian, took an almost apologetic stand. The shah capitulated, following an interview with Sir John Cadman, the British Minister in Teheran, from whom he received the vivid impression that his nationalistic venture was risking his throne. The affair ended with a new contract for the Anglo-Persian Oil Company, extending the life of its concession to 1993. This "arrangement" was ratified by a rubber-stamp Majlis, picked by the government and not chosen by the people. All of this was explained before the United Nations Security Council in 1951 by the great old man, Mossadegh. After exhibiting official telegrams which had determined the action of this Parliament, he said, between tears and sobs, in his peculiar style of a lamenting prophet: "You have seen how these deputies who prolonged the concession for another thirty years were men who did not represent the nation. The Minister who signed the law did not do so freely. The Shah was under great pressure and refusal would have cost him the throne. . . . A concession given under those conditions is not valid . . . ."*

Venezuelan Oil Refined Outside the Country

There are still many innumerable favors that Gómez granted the oil companies to be recounted. Few of these had more unfavorable echoes in the country than the tolerance with which the companies were allowed to export crude oil to be refined in plants built outside the national territory. Against the most elemental sense of economic nationalism, the Gómez regime permitted almost all Venezuelan oil to be refined in Curaçao, Aruba, or New Jersey. Most of the workers in the refineries of the Dutch Antilles islands were Venezuelans, forced into exile by the misery of their homeland. Both Curaçao and Aruba, once arid and thinly populated, were transformed into active economic centers, thanks to the economic prosperity provided by the refining industry installed there.

In 1936, twenty-two years after commercial production of Venezuelan oil had begun, 22.3 million metric tons of the 23.9 million that were produced here were exported. Of this amount, only 1 million tons—equivalent to 5 percent—were refined in the small plants installed in Venezuela. In contrast, Royal Dutch Shell and Standard Oil had constructed gigantic refineries in Curaçao and Aruba. The Anglo-Dutch consortium, built on the first of these islands, was at one time the largest refinery in the world with a capacity of 165,000 barrels daily. There were other refineries in Aruba. The Eagle Petroleum Company, a Shell affiliate, had a small plant with a capacity of 20,000 barrels daily while the Lago Petroleum Corporation, a subsidiary of Standard Oil, had a plant which could refine 110,000 barrels per day.[16]

After the death of Gómez, defenders on the payroll of the companies tried to justify their policy of refining outside the country. The version in the press was that it was the dictator himself who had opposed refinery installations in the country. This was absolutely false. The dictatorship sought—even though it spoke the language of those who feel themselves without moral

*Nasrollah Saifpour Fatemi, *Oil Diplomacy* (New York: Wittier Books, Inc., 1954), pp. 151–83. The author was professor at Princeton University, and brother of the Foreign Minister of the Mossadegh government, an ardent nationalist who was shot in November 1954, amid gunpowder smoke and the fumes of "Western" gasoline, falling dead on Iranian soil, but over subsoil belonging to foreigners. The book was dramatized when its author suffered a heart attack upon hearing over the radio that his courageous brother had been killed. It is of general knowledge that the overthrow of the Mossadegh government, which had nationalized Iranian oil, was promoted and organized by the Central Intelligence Agency (CIA) of the United States.

authority or the backing of public opinion—to have the companies refine in
Venezuela the oil they produced there. But the companies never agreed to do
so. Their reason was fairly obvious and was set forth by Ludwell Denny
when he wrote:

> Fearful that a radical government would come to power when Gómez died, the
> British and American companies hesitated to invest in refineries within Venezuela
> and had only small plants there. Sir Henry selected the neighboring island of
> Curaçao and the Shell refinery there processed most of the crude from its com-
> panies in Venezuela. Dutch Shell in 1928 built another refinery at Orangestaadt on
> Aruba while Standard of Indiana also built a large refinery on this same island in
> 1929.[17]

The same author tells how the dictatorship fruitlessly tried to get Standard
Oil to build in Venezuela the refinery which was constructed in Aruba in
1928. The Minister of Interior, Arcaya, in a message to Congress in 1927,
promised special measures in favor of any company that would build refineries in the country. A law in 1928 exonerated refineries from the payment
of a tax equivalent to 2 percent of their gross profits as established by the laws
of 1922 and 1925. The same 1928 law exonerated refineries from paying
another tax on the transport of oil refined in the country.

However, these incentives did not change the decision of the executives of
Standard Oil, despite the fact that they were encountering much resistance
from the Dutch colonial authorities concerning the construction of a refinery
on Aruba. It may have been through communication channels that Sir Henry
Deterding had with The Hague government that the Rockefeller company
request for a permit to build a refinery in Aruba was delayed. In any case,
Standard Oil preferred to deal with the Dutch resistance rather than install
refineries in a nation whose government was taken advantage of by all the oil
companies and which they knew was detested by the people. If we may
believe the writers Frank Hanighen and Anton Zischka, all kinds of tricks
were resorted to by the Rockefeller trust to "persuade" the stubborn Dutch
authorities. It was suddenly "discovered" that the Dutch Antilles were the
center of operations for bootleggers from the United States, which then had
the famous "dry laws"; the loyal subjects of Queen Wilhelmina were contra-
vening the laws prohibiting the introduction of rum and other alcoholic bev-
erages into the United States. Immigration authorities placed obstacles in
the way of entry of Dutch subjects into the United States. All obstacles
disappeared when Holland took a reasonable attitude regarding the request of
Standard Oil. When the first shipload of steel arrived at Aruba docks for the
refinery construction, the rubicund Dutchmen were free of all suspicion of
engaging in bootlegging.[18] By 1938 the three Antilles refineries had a total
capacity of 450,000 barrels of oil per day.

Another timid pressure brought by the dictatorship on the companies to
induce them to build refineries in Venezuela was the tax on crude oil which

the tanker fleet carried from Lake Maracaibo to Aruba, Curaçao, and the United States. A law promulgated in 1928 established a tax of Bs. 2 per metric ton on tankers that passed over the Maracaibo bar, the narrow entry at the mouth of the lake through which passed the tanker caravans carrying abroad the crude oil as it was taken from the wells. The companies offered bitter underground resistance to the law. When it was approved, they decided to violate it with the complicity of the local authorities, as well as thinking up all kinds of other tricks. They persuaded the government to agree that the customs authorities should recognize as a ship's capacity the figure that was certified in the ship's port of registry. This meant that most of the tankers—whose registered capacity was far less than what they actually could carry—paid a duty "calculated on approximately one-fourth their capacity," Minister Torres complained in his 1930 memorandum.

The law also specified that the tax would be reduced by 50 percent when the ship carried, along with "crude," agricultural or cattle products. Therefore the companies customarily shipped some crates of bananas or a half-dozen goats on deck with their thousands of tons of oil below, thereby reducing by half the bar tax. Another way of evading the tax was to take advantage of provisions in the law exempting ships engaged in coastal traffic from part of the tax. The companies then registered their ships in Las Piedras, on the peninsula of Paraguana, and routed them to that port when they came out of Lake Maracaibo, before going on to the Dutch West Indies, thus paying the lower bar tax.

Maximum Benefits for the Companies; Minimum for Venezuela

During the Gómez years and after the death of the dictator, Venezuela was the land of promise for the international oil companies. During the twenty-seven years of tyranny there was no public debate of the petroleum issue, nor of any other subject of general interest for that matter. Government offices had only rudimentary organization; there were no departments to investigate production costs. The Venezuelan people could not know then how badly they had been plundered or how their mineral wealth had provided exaggerated profits for the foreign investor and minimum income for the government and the country.

Publications referring to this matter appeared outside Venezuela, but national public opinion did not have access to them. A kind of Chinese wall isolated the country from outside ideas. Beyond the national boundaries there was general knowledge of how Venezuela was being victimized. Ludwell Denny reported on the exorbitant earnings of the oil companies; how the Shell subsidiary, Venezuelan Oil Concessions, had net earnings of $3.4 million on an investment of $10 million in 1927; and Lago Petroleum Corporation, a subsidiary of Standard Oil, obtained $8 million with a working capital of $3.5 million. Denny reported that the value of the stock in the United States and English companies increased 600 percent from 1924 to 1927.[19]

Oil company profits continued to rise in geometric progression, as revealed by a Congressional investigation early in 1931 in the United States. According to the *New York Times*, February 8, 1931, the Tariff Commission had informed the Senate that "Venezuelan crude oil can be laid down at Atlantic ports at half the cost of oil from the [U.S.] Middle West." At this time the respective committee of the Senate approved a bill proposed by Senator Capper to restrict importation of crude and oil products from Venezuelan oil fields. This was the culmination of a movement begun in June 1930 when Senator Thomas of Oklahoma—"spokesman for the western oil producers"—proposed a congressional investigation of the production and transportation costs of domestic oil in comparison with petroleum from Venezuela. This investigation reported that the cost of a barrel of United States crude oil laid down at the Atlantic seaboard was $1.98. A barrel of oil from the Maracaibo basin cost only $.89 at the same place, of which $.69 were production costs and the rest were transportation and other costs. In other words, the "cheap oil" from Venezuela—as it was called in the market—cost the companies $1.09 less per barrel in the United States than domestic oil.

Actually, the truth regarding the scandalous profits which the oil companies were obtaining from their Venezuelan oil wells was fully known by the professionals in the Gómez government. Gumersindo Torres, minister of production, whose memorandum to the oil companies has been sited above, cautiously reproached the oil companies in 1930: "The market for these products [referring to the crude oil and gasoline] is in the USA, where production from Lake Maracaibo competes favorably with similar U.S. production because it is possible to place our oil at a lower cost in the market—so much lower, as a matter of fact, that today the idea of taxing Venezuelan petroleum is again being discussed in the USA."

Gumersindo Torres presented this memorandum to the oil companies and wished he could do more to defend his country's interest. In all justice it should be recalled that he was the only minister of production during this shameful period of Venezuelan history who showed any patriotic concern. On August 1, 1930, he issued regulations for an oil law designed to give the government more control over the industry. Moreover, when the U.S. Congress investigated the prices of foreign oil, the companies operating in Venezuela submitted figures on the cost of transportation per barrel completely different from those they had given Venezuelan authorities. Standard of Indiana, for example, claimed in Venezuela that the transportation cost was $.68 per barrel, but told the tariff committee of the U.S. Senate that it was only $.33. Torres then made the easy calculation that in four years Standard Oil had defrauded the Venezuelan treasury of Bs. 26 million and Gulf Oil Company, of Bs. 30 million. These companies were then sued by the attorney general for these amounts owed to the nation. The companies brought pressure on Gómez. Gumersindo Torres was removed from office for the second time. Nobody heard anything more about the suits that had been introduced in the Venezuelan court.*

As might have been expected, the dictatorship became alarmed. If these United States restrictions had been put into effect, they would have meant the bankruptcy of public finances and of the economic life of Venezuela, which was now revolving more and more around petroleum. The news agencies in those days reported the constant visits of the Gómez minister in Washington—Pedro Manuel Arcaya—to Secretary of State Henry Stimson. At the same time, the oil companies operating in Venezuela mobilized their friends in Congress. The pressure on the Senate brought about the desired result—the Capper bill was tabled, and all that the independent producers could do was to make a fuss in the press because of their defeat.

They returned to the attack, however, some time later, and although they did not attain what Senator Capper had proposed, they did get an import tax of $.005 per gallon for crude and fuel oil, $.025 per gallon for gasoline, and $.04 per gallon for lubricants. The Venezuelan dictatorship, foreseeing a drop in income because of these measures, reduced its 1932 budget to Bs. 144.8 million from Bs. 200 million the previous year.

The national share of this oil wealth which offered such exceptional earnings to non-Venezuelan oil companies was scandalously low. An official document issued shortly after the death of Gómez gives an impressive numerical summary of the situation:

> From July 1919 to June 1936 inclusive, the national treasury received from the oil companies a total of Bs. 612 million. Since 1262 million barrels of oil were produced during this same period, the country received 48 céntimos per barrel. During this same time, the average price per barrel was $1.37 which, calculated at Bs. 5 per dollar, meant a total income to the oil companies of Bs. 8644 million. The amount paid in taxes by them to the treasury represented only 7 percent of this total.[20]

Fiscal Prosperity, Economic Distortion, and National Poverty

Despite the fact that the Venezuelan tax system was so favorable to the foreign investor, the treasury income increased progressively along with the violent jumps in production. This assured income enabled the dictatorship to regularly pay the cost of the praetorian guard of Gómez—which was the Venezuelan army at that time—pay the salaries of the untrained officials of a

---

*Gumersindo Torres died during the three-year period 1945–48 when I was president of the revolutionary junta government. I went to his funeral. Most of the people present there were survivors of the Gómez period. It came as a great surprise that the head of a government seeking to eradicate the last roots of the Gómez despotism would attend the funeral of a person whom he did not even know. My gesture was meant as a testimony of recognition by the country represented by me, as the head of the executive power, of an official who had tried to defend the interests of his country at a time when the subsoil of Venezuela was auctioned off under the worst possible conditions to the members of the international oil cartel.

rudimentary government, construct some hundreds of kilometers of bad roads, and cancel the foreign debt.

In 1928 the petroleum boom reached a spectacular stage: the year's exports of oil reached 100 million barrels. Just six years earlier, on December 14, 1922, the blow-out of the well Barroso No. 2, located in Zulia state and belonging to Shell, had revealed to the world the prodigious oil reserve accumulated in the Venezuelan subsoil. The well inundated its surroundings for nine days with 100,000 barrels of oil. Since then, production and exportation had increased upward in parallel lines. Tax income in 1928 was Bs. 230 million. Customs duties ceased to be the principal source of revenue; their place was taken by the various petroleum taxes. These jumped from .09 percent of total income in 1921–22 to 26.2 percent in 1929–30.

Petroleum also became the leading export product. In the five-year period 1918–23 the total exports of the country were Bs. 945 million, of which only Bs. 56 million, or 5.5 percent came from petroleum. In the period 1928–36 the total value of exports was Bs. 6.16 billion, with Bs. 5.26 billion, or 85 percent, coming from petroleum. Thus, during two decades the economy had been warped and the treasury had become dependent upon oil to an alarming extent. Instead of being an important exporter of coffee, Venezuela dropped to seventh or eighth place as a world supplier, below the European colonies in Africa. During the time of the colony and much of the republic, the country had been a great cacao producer but now its production dropped to a minimum harvest, scarcely 3 percent of the world's total production. Only memories remained of the time when the llanos were a great cattle emporium.

The country generally became impoverished. Loan offices and banks foreclosed mortgages on haciendas and ranches. Gómez and his people monopolized all the land they could and became landholders on the scale of medieval feudal lords. A survey carried out in 1932 revealed that about 84 percent of the arable area was in the hands of big landholders. The peasant without land became a nomad, and two-thirds of the population in rural Venezuela was uprooted and tended to wander away from the land. Internal migrations took on an unprecedented intensity. At that time the thesis was propounded that oil was the only factor responsible for this distortion of the Venezuelan economy. This argument was particularly used by the shameless defenders of the Gómez period. The truth is otherwise. A chronic structural crisis existed in Venezuela and was accentuated under Gómez due to the system of agricultural production—the persistence of large landholdings, the improvised methods of cultivation, and the lack of artificial irrigation in a country poorly treated by nature—all of which evoked the pathetic concern of William Vogt: "In few parts of the hemisphere have the land and the natural resources been so badly treated as in Venezuela: the waters, the plains, the animals and the plants."

If only the income from petroleum had been used to prime the pump, this industry would have led to the development of a prosperous rural economy.

It is also false that many workers were taken from agriculture to work in the oil fields. Not even one-half of 1 percent of the total working population found employment there. What happened was that an avalanche of dollars and pounds sterling rolled down upon a little country that had not democratized or modernized its system of production. It was using eighteenth-century methods to produce in the twentieth-century and was governed by a coarse and rapacious tyranny incapable of carrying out economic reforms or of using the oil income—even the inadequate share then received—as a springboard for collective progress.

The overwhelming presence of oil did act, indirectly, to deform the economy and national life. Privileged sectors of the population began to acquire the mining mentality of newly rich spendthrifts. The uninterrupted flow of dollars encouraged imports and expanded commerce to such a degree that the nation became primarily a consumer of foreign products. We began to appear too much like that chaotic California—the paradise of adventurers and thieves—during the days of the gold rush.

These theoretical considerations did not concern the people during the Gómez era, not even the majority of the population which did not share the prosperity with the tribe that had seized power. The people were ruined and without recourse; they suffered the rigors of a regime which respected no law. There were no political parties, unions, or visible public opinion. Such sporadic outbreaks of rebellion as occurred—more on the style of old tribal warfare—were easily put down by machine guns imported from England and the United States, along with dollars and the pound sterling. The worker was defenseless, illiterate, humiliated, and ill with malaria or syphilis; he was like a serf on the haciendas or a salaried slave in the mining camps. Meanwhile, the only press that could be read in the country—regimented by the dictatorship—reproduced the eulogies showered upon Gómez and his administration by statesmen and writers in periodicals from many nations and in many tongues. Those men, who because of their education and intelligence should have led an underground wave of resistance to the despotism, did not do so because they had entered its service. Venezuela can also talk about a "lost generation." Intellectuals, professionals, writers, and scientists of the 1900s, with occasional exceptions, filled the ministries, the diplomatic posts, and the editorial rooms of the official newspapers. They were well-paid galley slaves on the dictatorial ship of state.

The Rebellion of '28

The combination of factors, domestic and international, which favored tyranny in Venezuela created a rarefied climate of oppression and general anxiety. This was the atmosphere in which the generation of 1928 went into action; it was in their ranks that I fought the first political skirmishes of my public life, which from its beginning has been militant and hazardous.

Through cracks in the Chinese wall that surrounded the country, we heard whispers of the winds of change that were buffeting the world, caused by the Russian Revolution of 1917 and social changes taking place in western Europe after World War I. News of the Mexican Revolution—then resounding throughout America—was a powerful stimulus to us. In some chance magazine, we would read—our youthful eyes shining with the emotion of one who suddenly surveys an unknown world—of the student fights in Córdova, Argentina; of the street demonstrations in Lima, Peru; and of the battle beginning in Cuba against the *machadato*—the dictatorship of Machado. Moved by the growing insurgence of youth throughout America, we organized the "Week of the Student." There was a carnival-like atmosphere, with the election of a queen. The affair deceptively seemed to be just another harmless game with flowers, so our activities were permitted. We took advantage of the moment, however, to speak forth. The throng filled with astonishment at our boldness. We made daring revolutionary orations with repeated references to that forbidden word—liberty.

Repression followed. Those of us who had figured most prominently in the demonstration were thrown into prison, where two pairs of leg-irons *(grillos)* were placed on our ankles (the classic type, called *sesentones* weighed sixty pounds; others, smaller, were called bumpers). They called us "the first martyrs of El Cuño" among the students, in reference to the jail in which we were held and to our role as the first among many who would later pack the prisons. It was in this penitentiary cell that I celebrated my twentieth birthday on February 22, 1928. There were four of us in a tiny stuffy cell, without a single opening to give air or light from the outside. Of the four, two died, victims of the Gómez terror. Pío Tamayo, the poet, was dragged from the cell, dying, after seven years in leg-irons and solitary confinement; and Guillermo Prince Lara, a medical student, died of galloping tuberculosis contracted while fighting as a guerrilla in 1929. Only Jóvito Villalba and I survived.

The students of 1928 answered the imprisonment of the four of us with energetic solidarity. Hundreds of students were thrown into jail. Then, much to our surprise—we did not know about the laws of social dynamics and had little confidence in the people—the general public spontaneously rose against the dictatorship. There was a revolutionary general strike. It took place where there was not a single union organization. Barricades were improvised in the streets of La Guaira and Caracas, and the unarmed populace defended themselves with stones against the guns of the despot. In Maracaibo, the capital of the oil Canaan of Zulia, intellectual youth and common people also engaged in an outbreak against the dictator.

This popular uprising opened the jail doors for us. We went out into the streets to conspire. The popular revulsion for Gómez was also manifest among various young officers of the armed forces. One night, April 7, 1928, in combination with them we took the presidential palace of Miraflores (Gómez never lived there, but occupied a fortress in Maracay) and tried to assault the barracks of San Carlos, where there was a large arms deposit. We failed in our bold attempt, and I suffered for many days thereafter from the bruises on my left shoulder caused by my inexperience in firing a rifle—a pain which added to the bitterness of defeat.

Prolonged prison was the fate of some. Others of us, hunted by the police, managed to escape the country to an exile that would last for eight years. Meanwhile, another wave of students confronted the dictatorship. Hundreds of them were put to forced labor, building roads through malaria-infested regions. Gómez cynically declared to the newspaper *Nuevo Diario*, an official organ; "Since they don't want to study, I am teaching them how to work . . ."

Those of us in prison and those of us in exile were a fervently romantic group of youth, devoid of any doctrinaire training. *Sachka Yegulev*, the nihilist book of Leonidas Andreiev, was our Bible. We believed we were historically obliged to sacrifice ourselves for the liberation of our nation, but we had not had access to modern social doctrines. We were but a group of idealistic young people in a world in which political currents were rapidly dividing into two irreconcilable fronts: that of antihistorical reaction and that of social revolution.

While our comrades dragged heavy leg-irons or cleared the way through jungles for roads, those of us who had managed to get out of the country dedicated all our energy at first to organizing armed invasions from abroad, Garibaldi-style. We sought to unite with the expedition led by General Román Delgado Chalbaud on the steamship *Falke* and embarked one hot summer night in 1929 from the docks of Santo Domingo aboard *La Gisela*, a sailing ship used in coastwise traffic. Our group included Simón Betancourt, a romantically courageous guerrilla who had participated in previous uprisings; Raúl Leoni, Hernando Castro, and Carlos Julio Ponte—who would die later in another attempted invasion—Atilano Carnevali, and others totaling some twenty men. Our "armament" consisted of some old rifles and a number of pistols. Once at sea, we opened the sealed envelope containing our instructions and found that we were supposed to meet the others at the island of La Blanquilla, off the eastern coast of Venezuela, in a number of days. *La Gisela* was not in shape to make this voyage and began to leak as soon as we put to sea. We finally had to put in at the Dominican port of Barahona, discouraged by our utter failure.

We did not understand then the ineffectiveness of revolutionary action that was not backed by a popular organization within the country. Neither were we aware then, although we rapidly learned, that the police agencies of the big powers would follow us to protect the regime which furnished them with cheap petroleum and was completely submissive to them.

However, we were beginning to develop an ideology. First came the realization that Gómez was something more than a local despot: he was the instrument of foreign control of the Venezuelan economy, the ally and servant of powerful outside interests. We began to lose our faith in an armed struggle against the dictatorship that was not the result of a definite political-social program, of precise ideological objectives, and of an organization and discipline much more mature than simple man-to-man loyalty characteristic of the leadership of caudillos.

We dedicated ourselves to an impassioned study of different political doctrines. We devoured, rather than read, texts on history, economics, and social sciences. As was common among most American youth of the 1930s, most of the exiled students—with the fervor of neophytes—delved deeply into the classics of socialism. For a brief time, at least, we believed that Russia was developing a social system that would have universal application. We even dreamed of a Bolshevik-type revolution with our czar of Maracay being shot at dawn. However, none of us who later founded the Acción Democrática party, even during our first exile, ever became active members in political groups subordinate to the Third International. Although we were very young—a majority of us were still in our twenties—we resisted the temptation to submit our political independence to Soviet leadership, even though that was so attractive at that time to young people everywhere. As we drew near the communist position, the deeply felt Venezuelan and American loyalties of our group received a heavy blow. We began to understand that this political party was under foreign influence, was deaf and blind to the vital needs of our peoples, and was only a cult of worship which gave blind obeisance to the imperious orders of the Comintern. The small group of our countrymen, who at this time organized the group which would later become the Communist party of Venezuela, dedicated themselves to widening the breach between our groups by conducting a campaign of insults against us—which they continue to do with extraordinary tenacity forty years later.

We did not remain idle when we rejected the imported doctrines as a means by which to confront the reality of Venezuela and of Latin America in an effort to change and reconstruct it. On the contrary, we began to develop our own system of ideas and to devise plans for the solution of Venezuela's basic problems. We proclaimed ourselves defenders of economic nationalism, of agrarian democracy, and of social justice, ardently searching for the best means whereby our country might recover its public liberties. We felt this must be the first step before we took our nationalistic revolutionary message to the people.

Gómez, A World Personality, and Venezuela, "Model of a Well-Governed Country"

While students, professionals, some old-time military chieftains, and both city and country workers spent years behind bars or in exile—where they suffered material want and struggled to find an acceptable ideology—Gómez consolidated his power. The dictatorship was shaken by the turbulence of 1928, but it had bayonets, money, foreign protection, and all the advantages of power. The student opposition lacked both a truly revolutionary doctrine and the solid support of influential social sectors. The despotism emerged from the crisis more arrogant than ever.

At the time when it was disconcerted by the rebellion of students and masses, the government did announce several measures to placate discontent: a labor law, a bank to finance low-cost housing, and another bank to assist with agriculture and cattle production, which were in ruins. However, the Agriculture and Cattle Bank (BAP) and the Workers' Bank only distributed additional millions to the political clients of the regime. The labor law, even with its few provisions, was inoperative; there were no unions to insist that it be applied, and its framers forgot to include any punishment for violations. In any case, it was not worth insisting on. Its antiworker orientation was demonstrated by the fact that it provided for a nine-hour workday for workers in cities and mining camps and no hourly limitation for rural workers.

The labor law was approved by Congress in 1928, the same year that it elected Gómez to a third term. Surprisingly, he refused the office. It seems that he felt he had sacrificed too much for the country. All of the congressmen rushed to Maracay. The rural despot, usually so laconic, was loquacious on this occasion and made a speech which has been preserved for posterity. Its publication was mandatory by the press. Among others, he coined the following priceless phrases:

> I don't want you to come here to beg me, because I am not accustomed to beg or to be begged. . . . I do not accept the presidency, but I would like you to name me general-in-chief of the army. . . . Then you should pick a man [for the presidency] who will agree with me in everything and for everything. . . . If you want me to, I will look around for a candidate and will pick him so that he will be in agreement with me.

Yes, yes, was the unanimous reply of the flock of sheep. This Congress became known as "the super-rubber-stamp" *("sisiista")* body, and Venezuela once again had a marionette as head of state, Juan Bautista Pérez, picked and operated by the puppet-master of Maracay. He lasted until 1931, when Gómez had himself elected again for the fourth time. First he staged a comedy: a congressman angrily accused the hapless Pérez of not having managed the national economy as well as Gómez had, and of not having been sufficiently energetic in defense of the country against certain dastardly but nameless enemies.

At this time Gómez not only had his jails, his bayonets, his oil income, and international help; he was also intellectually supported by a political philosophy, hand-tailored to suit him. In 1929, a handsome official edition of *Cesarismo Democrático (Democratic Cesarism)*, writted by Vallenilla Lanz, a cynical and intelligent sycophant, was widely circulated. Citing fragments from Bolívar and data from reactionary historians and sociologists, Vallenilla improvised his thesis. Gómez was a unique natural phenomenon, the product of a torrid physical environment, of mixed and primitive races, and of a backward pastoral economy. He was a "benevolent tyrant," the ultimate expression of "the need of strong governments to protect society, to reestablish order, to support the home and fatherland against demagogues, revolutionaries, anarchists, bolsheviks."

Sometime in an unspecified future, wrote the court ideologue, destiny might be more benevolent with Venezuela. To help along the inexorable laws of history, he suggested the only practical way: "European and North American immigration [white blood] and money, much money, to develop our wealth." Put in simple language, his theory presented Gómez as the only possibility at the time—"the necessary gendarme"—whose "penetrating eye and harsh hand, inspired terror by his deeds and through the use of terror brought peace," according to a phrase of Taine, cited by Vallenilla. Also, perhaps in preparation for a different future, foreign investments were allowed to come in without any condition, to accelerate the colonization of a nation supposedly incapable of ruling its own economy. The torrents of Caucasian blood would allow the arrogant British of Shell and the Texans of Standard, with their racial prejudice, to feel more at home in a country where all traces of mixed blood had disappeared from the skin of the natives. . . .

As if to confirm Vallenilla's argument that the creole masses had a fatal tendency for disorder, the workers and students of Caracas took to the streets on December 17, 1930, the centenary of the death of Bolívar—of their Bolívar—without leaders or plans, led only by the Venezuelan flag, in a suicidal effort to free the political prisoners from the cells in La Rotunda. Dozens of victims lay scattered over the ground, cut down by the fire of the Gómez soldiery, new sacrifices to the undying passion for liberty among the people.

It was an uneducated people, but one anxious to acquire culture and to live in dignity. This general ignorance had been the seedbed for *gómecismo*. Some despotisms have highly valued intellectuals. But not Gómez. He was a tyrannical brute of the most primitive sort. From the years 1908–09 to 1925–26, those being educated in schools varied from 3.3 percent (1925–26) to 6.3 percent (1933–34) of the population. In the only normal school in the entire country, the graduating class of 1932 had a tragically memorable number: only one. The figure of 80 percent illiterate among the adult population is the most eloquent testimony to this somber stage of national life—so devastating to the population of the country.

The income level of the workers was as low as that of the inhabitants of the European colonies in the Caribbean. This cannot be expressed in statistics because no statistics were kept until 1936, after Gómez. But the average daily salary in 1937 was Bs. 3.28 and Bs. 2.90 for the farm worker and cowhand, respectively. Since there had already been an increase in the daily wage, one can deduce that during the three decades of the despotism, the average salary for most of the working population averaged around $.50 in U.S. currency daily.

While Venezuela was being thus humiliated, oppressed, and betrayed, it gained fame as an important country, thanks to the fabulous riches of its subsoil; and Juan Vicente Gómez became something of a world personality. Venezuela was the Mecca of world petroleum. For the international press, President Gómez became something of a superman—worthy of bronze effigies, biographies, and panegyrics—who handed out oil concessions left and right. "Until fourteen years ago," wrote *Fortune* magazine in 1949, "all the oil industry required was a personal understanding with Juan Vicente Gómez, the astute but cruel and voracious dictator who had governed the country with a hand of iron since 1908."

Newspapers of the most important world cities took an interest in Venezuela. The leading oil producer of Latin America, which would soon become second in importance in the entire world, was the subject of printed commentaries in many languages. Maracay, the habitual residence of the dictator, became the center of a unique tourism. Princes of the blood, financial magnates, marshals, and politicians alternated with cowboy ballad singers and Spanish bullfighters to pay court to this dissolute dictator.

French personalities took the lead. The adversary of Germany forgot the pro-German feelings of Gómez during World War I and sent its school ship, *Jeanne d'Arc* to Venezuelan ports so the cadets of France could render homage to the celebrated President. The Legion of Honor, of the highest rank, decorated the chest of the despot. The French marshal, Franchet D'Esperey, "victor over von Kluck and hero of the World War," made a trip to Maracay to present his respects to the illustrious ruler. This flirting, so typically Parisian, between Marianne and Gómez, created a favorable climate for the development of the activities of the Societé Française de Recherches au Venezuela. This company had been organized in France with a capital of F.F. 40 million and began to produce oil in the Maracaibo basin. Its name was a variation of that of the parent company—La Compagnie Française des Pétroles. Its formation was due to the efforts of Raymond Poincaré and was a joint enterprise, with the state holding 35 percent of the stock. France, in matters dealing with mineral fuels, followed the rule of Aristid-Briand: "In our days petroleum makes foreign policy."

Spain, the monarchical Spain of Alphonse XIII, sent a prince to do honor to General Gómez. Ferdinand of Bavaria and Bourbon arrived one day at our coast followed by an impressive entourage. He brought a trunk full of eulogies for the "genial statesman" and the Grand Cross of Isabel the Catholic for his collection of baubles. It should surpise no one that the eulogies, the decoration, and the visit all ended with the inscription of the Compañia Española de Petróleo, S.A., in the Venezuelan registry of commerce. It acquired oil concessions in eastern and western Venezuela and a 5 percent share in the total production of Lago Petroleum.

The friendship between General Gómez and Queen Wilhelmina of Holland became proverbial. The Grand Cross of the Netherlands Lion was draped about the neck of the "good and great friend" of almost all the European royal families. Royal Dutch swam in a sea of concessions. In Holland a ship armed by the enemies of Gómez was seized and the leaders of the expedition, with heads shaved and in the striped clothing of common prisoners, were interned in a penal colony. Curaçao was an outpost of the Gómez police. José Ignacio Cárdenas, a kind of semiliterate Fouché of the sort the dictator used for his espionage abroad, kept watch over it from his post of influence in The Hague. In a letter to Gómez, Cárdenas revealed, despite his poor grammar, the great influence he had with the Dutch government, so closely linked to Royal Dutch Shell. It is an historical document, worth more than any theoretical speculation about the intimacies between Gómez and the powerful states connected with the international oil consortium. Cárdenas wrote: "Send a person of your complete confidence to Curaçao to be in touch with the governor there so that he may find out what is going on and what may have repercussions in Venezuela. I will recommend this person secretly to the government here in The Hague and to the governor."

Belgium also fell into line. The Cordon of Albert I was draped around the neck of the honored personality. Moving messages where the statesmanlike "gifts" of the "general" are to be found in every line were sent from Brussels to Caracas. As a result the Belgian Venezuelan Oil Corporation begin drilling in Sucre district of Zulia.

The close cooperation and aid of the governments of His British Majesty and the United States were even more pronounced with the Gómez dictatorship. The intelligence services of both powers kept the dictator closely advised of any threat to the stability of his regime. The homages of famous personages from the Anglo-Saxon nations to Gómez were continuous and of worldwide interest. Such was that of the five-star general, John J. Pershing, who, with the laurels of the European war still fresh on his brow, gave his campaign pistols to Gómez as proof of his deep admiration.

However, the later and more recent history of the country reveals that out of this vortex of administrative corruption, political backwardness, and venal complicity with the foreigner, there emerged—as an antithesis—a liberating movement. From the very entrails of the Gómez-oil combination, the result of the alliance of the military caudillo with colonizing imperialism—as its consequence and dialectical negation—sprang a group of men who were going to provide the Venezuelan people with the political tools and the repertoire of ideas with which our mineral patrimony might be slowly rescued, along with our national sovereignty, from the grasp of monopolistic capitalism. The nation would be redeemed from its institutional backwardness and its chronic despotism.

PART TWO

The Trustees of the Dictatorship

2

López Contreras, Offspring of Gómez, Inherits the Presidency

Death of Gómez and Survival of the Gómez System

Juan Vicente Gómez died in Maracay on a December day in 1935. The rigidity of death accentuated the Mongolian features of the dictator.

Those who viewed his corpse in its catafalque worthy of a pharaoh testified that his face had never been so expressive of cruelty and cunning as when he lay in the coffin carried on a gun carriage.

Behind the bier, marched the grief-stricken, faithful palace courtiers. In a photo taken at the time, the most prominent mourners are seen to be those who would be the recipients of the Gómez inheritance—General Eleazar López Contreras and Isaías Medina Angarita—the two chiefs of state in the post-Gómez decade (1935–45).

Following an intense period of intrigue worthy of an imperial court, including the assassination of the family member who was the presumed heir to Gómez, General Eleazar López Contreras reached the presidency. He had been minister of war and navy at the time the dictator died. His mentality and his governing style were shaped during "The Rehabilitation," the name which he gave to the Gómez cause. Neither his political upbringing nor the environment surrounding his ascent to power provided him with the capabilities of decisively changing the political course of the republic, as history demanded.

I have written elsewhere that the personality of López Contreras and his tendency to compromise in governmental affairs were matters for psychological study but did not result in historical change. His government led the

51

country through a turbulent period of transition, but it had come to power without any revolutionary shakeup of the autocratic state structure.

With Gómez dead, the disorganized people—without the guidance of any political party—gave vent to their feelings merely by burning the special edition of the newspaper *El Nuevo Diario* dedicated to the memory of the despot, and by getting themselves killed in front of the Governor's palace in Caracas as they demanded liberty for political prisoners. The police smothered spontaneous protest and López Contreras made it his first order of business to restore the old order. In Miraflores, there reappeared as his secretary the perennial Márquez Bustillos, who twenty years earlier had been the puppet president under Gómez. Public mourning was decreed because of the "immense national tragedy" overwhelming Venezuela with the death of Gómez. The new president, in speeches made at the various garrisons, professed his *gómecista* faith, dashing the hopes of the group of democratically minded officers. He avoided coming to grips with public opinion and retained the same group in key official posts who had been there for the previous twenty-seven years.

Nobody should have been surprised. López Contreras had been picked to succeed Gómez by the ministers of Gómez, in accordance with the formula set forth in the Constitution prepared by the scribes who translated Gómez' will into juridical language. The Constitution had been unanimously approved without amendment by senators and deputies, all named by Gómez. This confabulation clearly signified that the post-Gómez era was autocratically imposed. The people of Venezuela were not consulted in any way.

One night in January 1936, I was meditating on these matters as a deck passenger aboard a fruitboat as it sailed from Puerto Limón, Costa Rica, back to my own country. The name of the successor to the despot brought back memories from the days of my student struggles. It was López Contreras—dressed in campaign uniform—who had supervised, one cold morning in 1928, the transfer of the student prisoners in Caracas from the El Cuño prison to the colonial dungeons of the "Libertador" fortress of Puerto Cabello. There were cheers for Gómez and for General López Contreras from the soldiers, answered by obscene phrases from the students, who had failed in their attempted insurrection under the fire of sentries at San Carlos barracks on April 7 of this same year.

The People Awaken

But the confident belief that the dictatorship would be able to perpetuate itself with the same regularity that the old monarchies were able to pass along their crowns to the heirs of dead kings rapidly disappeared. Venezuela no longer was a simple agricultural and pastoral country. In the cities, and especially in the oil camps, a new class had appeared: the workers.

Two groups were returning from exile, the emigrés of petrified mentality who, like the Bourbons of the restoration, "forgot nothing and learned nothing"; but also, youthful leaders who had been nurtured on the social problems of the day.

An encounter occurred between the people and their future leaders and organizers—men who like that Argentine generation of the 1850s had whiled away the interminable hours of exile and prison studying new social doctrines. The general desire for a truly democratic society triggered a demand to "liquidate *gómecismo.*" The democratic political parties, the labor unions, the student federations, and the teacher organizations took up this cry as they became active.

The new generation of politicians used every means of communication possible to expose the dramatic national reality. They sought to inaugurate an ideological crusade, and had much new economic information to work with. Irrefutable statistics showed how little the nation received from its oil production, how backward its agriculture and industry, and how poor its people. The myth of Venezuelan prosperity spread by the Gómez people was now exposed as fiction.

My first speech, made after eight years of exile, is an example of how we sought to awaken the country to its dependence upon oil. It was delivered before the first public political meeting to be held in the country since the beginning of the twentieth century at the Nuevo Circo in Caracas on March 1, 1939:

> It is true that the country has no foreign debt, but its economy is controlled by the most bold and aggressive group of international financiers—the oil men. We may not have any foreign creditors, but our subsoil has been turned over to the oil consortium. Some 80 percent of the nation's exports are oil, an industry controlled by foreign capital. The government gets 45 percent of its income from this industry, so its independence is only a sham. The truth is that we are at the mercy of these big foreign interests.[1]

The people were not aware of the magnitude of the problem. They suffered its effects without knowing their origin. For decades, there had not been a free press; not even fraudulent elections were held in the country. Congressional activity was a mockery, and so were political parties and labor unions.

This explains the universal ignorance regarding the petroleum question. The new government officials, trained in the schools of the dictatorship, were the last ones to be interested in informing the nation on the subject. The statement made by Juan Paris, the first Minister of Production in the government, is very revealing. On taking charge, he found that everything in his ministry "was beautifully organized."

The oil companies had a group of national supporters, made up of government officials, lawyers, and writers with a company mentality. Another group took a pessimistic view of the oil question. Little or nothing could be done, according to this group, to change the relations between the state and an industry so solidly based on what was called "the national reality." Furthermore, this industry was backed by the flag and cannon of powers which dominated the world. These defeatists often acted like mystical poets and described the oil wells from which the black gold flowed as the "veins of the devil." They were the forerunners of economists and essayists who later on would deal with the oil problem with similar superficiality. They referred to the oil industry as a "minotaur," or, in more plebeian language, as "excrement of the devil."

As soon as we returned from exile or emerged from prison—early in 1930—our political movement confronted these colonial mentalities, these defeatists, these hapless phrase-makers. We went about the task of orienting public opinion regarding oil in a systematic and perseverant way. From public tribunal and meetings, and from the pages of the press and in pamphlets, we sought to bring home to the public the political implications of the oil industry. We tried to bring the oil problem to the people in down-to-earth language and to remove the mantle of mystery, sometimes approaching the satanic, with which it had been protected by the crafty or the ingenious. We proclaimed that oil was not the product of medieval alchemy but was the best fuel to power a nation toward a higher destiny. In modern times, we affirmed, there was no comparable source of easy wealth. However, it was necessary that the people who controlled the oil act with honesty and nationalistic vision—virtues that the venal men of the Gómez era did not possess. We urged the government to rectify the indescribable policy followed up to that time in the relations of the companies with the state and with the workers; to review the terms of the concessions which had been granted; to readjust the tax system; in brief, to inaugurate a completely new deal that would lead eventually to the complete control of the industry by the nation.

It would only be possible to reclaim our national patrimony if the reserves of resistance could be organized and a national conscience awakened regarding our dependence on international financial capital and the uncontrolled exploitation of our principal source of wealth by foreign investors. To do this, we had to incorporate in our political parties and labor unions people who had no training whatsoever in this type of activity since they had been isolated from the mainstream of world events for three decades.

We threw ourselves into this task with encouraging immediate results. The Venezuelan has an almost plastic receptive capacity and an innate desire to get ahead in the most rapid way—typical of formerly downtrodden people when suddenly brought into the life of modern society. They assimilated our message with eagerness. Political parties and labor unions were filled with new members, eager for action.

The Historic Day of February 14

The neo-Gómez forces in power, together with their foreign associates, were alarmed by the newly awakened civic consciousness. They decided, early in

1936, to contain the wave of popular discontent. The recently granted freedom of the press was revoked by executive degree.

This governmental action gave birth to the first violent confrontation between the forces of the status quo in the government and widespread public groups desiring progress. On February 14, a general strike of obvious political origin broke out. Its announced goal of national democracy was supported by all social classes of the population. The government replied with gunfire. In the countryside small farmers also attempted revolutionary actions. The hatred accumulated against landowers during decades of oppression broke out in primitive but spontaneous acts of violence. Looting and destruction became the order of the day. In Caracas, the ostentatious mansions of the generals and henchmen of the dictatorship were burned, while in the countryside cattle, fences, and pasture land belonging to the Gómez supporters were destroyed.

The impressive outbreak of collective wrath appalled the government. It felt obliged to make concessions in the makeup of the government and in its policies. Gómez henchmen of more odious reputation fled the country. Some of the generals and intellectuals who had broken with Gómez but now had returned to Venezuela were brought into the government to give it a new look. The chief of state made promises to liberalize his regime and transform the national economy in what was called "the February Program."

But only a few months had passed before all these promises were gone with the wind. The government's program was later known as "the Five-Year Deception." The Congress, with but a few exceptions, was made up of the same men whom the patriarchal Gómez had once selected—in a patriarchal act worthy of this Charlemagne of the tropics—under the same historic saman tree of Guere where Bolívar was alleged to have rested. It now began to debate a so-called Law of Social Defense, modeled upon the repressive code of Italian fascism. These were the days of the Spanish Civil War and the heyday of Mussolini and Hitler. It was fashionable to condemn as "communist" anyone who fought for social justice and liberty.

From the Movement of June to the Oil Workers Strike

The government was now better prepared to deal with the new demonstration of popular wrath. The popular movement was strengthened by the mystique of vast sectors of the population, but it was weak in its lack of experience and well-defined political objectives. The dictatorial forces, on the other hand, were accustomed to rule. The law of inertia, which exists in the political as in the physical world, was in their favor. The June movement accomplished only a few of its objectives. The attorney general of the nation provided a formula which made it possible to confiscate the inheritance of Gómez. The discussion of a new constitution was accelerated. A Labor Law and Oil Law were approved, improving upon previous jurisprudence.

We leaders of the June movement meanwhile renewed contact with people and places well known to us—"the preventive guards" of the jails, and the locks and bars of cells. However, the movement had been so strong in its initial stages that the government did not dare to keep us locked up for more than a few weeks. It was to be expected that the political parties would be declared illegal and the labor movement persecuted. The government sought to take advantage of the weakness caused by our partial defeat in June.

The opportunity to launch a wave of repression came in the same year with the strike of the workers in the oil camps of Zulia and Falcón states. They had shown themselves to be a combative group ever since the death of Gómez. At first, they behaved in the most brutal fashion; following the dictator's death various police and company watchmen were burned alive using fire from the gas flares of the oil wells. These primitive retaliations were soon ended; the workers organized themselves in unions to press their claims after fifteen years of helplessness. Their living and working conditions were indescribable. According to an official observer, men, women, and children lived in complete promiscuity in houses resembling "somewhat advanced matchboxes"—one-room homes without hygiene facilities where a person could barely stand under a zinc roof. The workers were treated with arrogance by their foreign bosses; they not only felt themselves exploited but wounded in their pride as men.

Once organized in unions, the workers insisted on change. They presented a list of demands on November 30, 1936—a timid document with modest aspirations, which was handed to the labor inspector of the state without a threat of any strike. The workers asked that their unions be recognized by the companies, which up to now had refused despite the fact that they were legally organized; that there be a minimum daily wage of Bs. 10 (a little more than $3 at that time); equality of salaries for equal work between foreigner and national employees; a 25 percent wage increase for workers who did not have company housing; exemption from paying rent for company-owned housing; and obligatory Sunday rest.

The companies were intransigent from the start. In retrospect, it would seem almost as though they were not concerned with the economic aspects but were eager to have a strike in order to give the new-Gómez regime a chance to crack down on the now democratic political movement. They rejected all of the worker demands outright, and a strike broke out on November 11. The president of the republic made a public call for "conciliation" and invoked the memory of Bolívar, so beloved by all Venezuelans, for his political purposes when he designated December 17, anniversary of the Liberator's death, as the date for signing a pact of conciliation between the companies and the workers.

If the government had really been faithful to the Bolivarian tradition, it would have proceeded with the same energy against the arrogant oil companies as Bolívar did against the Bourbon invaders a century before. Instead, it sent the head of the National Labor Office, Tito Gutiérrez Alfaro, on a goodwill mission to the oil camps. He talked with both sides in the conflict but finally gave up his attempt at mediation. In an interview with the newspaper *Panorama* of Maracaibo, however, he blamed the oil companies for their intransigence and said that they had received instructions from their home offices not to make concessions, whereas the workers had shown a flexible attitude.

The course of this oil strike differed from traditional worker-company conflicts. It was the touchstone which revealed how Venezuela quickly understood that the strike was the first skirmish in a great national crusade to win our independence from foreign tutelage. A great patriotic movement developed overnight in support of the oil workers. Industrialists and businessmen from all over the nation united with intellectuals, students, and workers in collective solidarity with the oil workers of Zulia and Falcón. The sons of the galley slaves of petroleum slept on linen sheets in rich men's homes when hundreds of them were brought to the capital city for care during the difficult economic times in the oil camps.

This virtual national plebiscite backing the oil workers, however, did not favor their cause. Before such popular fervor the government had the same "horror" of a vacuum that medieval theologians wrote about. Furthermore, it had to remain faithful to the Gómez tradition of obsequiousness to the English and North American companies. On January 22, 1937—74 days after the strike began—it ordered the workers to return to their jobs. None of the modest demands of the workers was granted in full by the government decree. There was an increase of Bs. 1 daily (hardly $.30) for those workers who made less than Bs. 9 daily. An additional Bs. 1 was given as a housing allowance for those who did not have company homes. Finally, the companies were obliged to provide cold drinking water in their work centers.

Thus the working and living conditions of the oil workers did not improve much. Two years after the government had broken the strike which the workers had staged in protest for being treated like coolies, a United States journalist wrote about their terrible living conditions. Clarence Horn, writing in *Fortune* magazine, described conditions which need no additional comment:

> The oil companies use 20,500 Venezuelans as staff employees and workers. About 17,000 of them work in the prolific oil zone of Maracaibo, where a heavy scum of oil on the lake waters discourages their bathing to refresh themselves from the heat. The rest work in the oil camps of Quirguire and Caripito, carved out of the jungle. The Labor Law obliges the companies to give housing to the workers, with a space of 4.5 square meters per family member. Also, they must supply water, sanitary facilities, and light. Compared with what the ordinary peon has in Venezuela, this may seem like heaven. However, *in terms of civilized living conditions, it is nothing. The minimum oil wage is Bs. 8 ($2.25) daily, plus housing and services. But the cost of living is so high in Venezuela that this scarcely provides for food, clothing, and entertainment. If the worker prefers to pay for his own housing, he will get Bs. 9 daily as minimum. In Lagunillas, in the Lake Maracaibo area, this means that he will live in a shack built out over the lake waters, into which he is likely to fall when drunk. To bathe, he will have the lake, if he takes care to first scrape off the scum of oil on its waters. He must buy water to drink. His food*

*consists of corn, bananas, brown sugar, and black beans and rice for which he must pay Bs. 5
or 6 daily. The rent will cost more or less Bs. 12 for a room. He will have no money left by the
end of the month when he is likely to have contracted a venereal disease. The company doctor
will treat him for this without charge.* [My italics.][2]

Repression and Definition of Ideologies

The oil strike was ended, as described, in January 1937. This first post-
Gómez period was ironically called by the people "the democratic honeymoon." The 1936 Constitution had come into effect. Austin Macdonald
characterized it as "a notable document—notable for the fidelity to the
past—despite the alleged democratic sentiments of its authors." It continued
previous provisions for the election of the president of the republic by the
Congress, and the selection of the senators by the state legislatures and the
deputies by the municipal council. Thus, the people remained excluded from
direct participation in the government just as much as they had been under
Gómez.[3]

Actually, from the electoral viewpoint, the new Constitution was a step
backward from the previous ones of Gómez. Theoretically, the right of universal suffrage had been kept in the Constitutions since 1864; the new one
now restricted the vote to literate males over 21 years of age in a country in
which half of the population could not read or write. And, as Macdonald
observed, it left intact the indirect election of members of Congress at two
steps removed and of the president of the republic at three.

The absolutist character of the 1936 Constitution was worse than its pre-
decessors. Part VI and article 32 gave the president of the republic an up-to-
date version of those *lettres de cachet* so much abused by the monarchs of
France. The executive could imprison or deport, at will, those citizens whom
he might designate as communist, anarchist, or terrorist.

Notwithstanding these deficiencies in the new Constitution, the opposition prepared in 1937 to participate in the elections for state legislatures and
municipal councils. By a vigorous campaign to arouse public opinion, it succeeded in electing various leaders of opposition parties as deputies and
senators, even though the electors all had been nominated by the presidency.
This was intolerable for a government still tied by its umbilical cord to the
dictatorship. The chief of state made some virulent speeches against the
popular political parties and the labor and student organizations. The semiofficial press, with the new paper *La Esfera* in the vanguard, made all kinds of
threats against the opposition—threats exuding the odor of petroleum. After
the threats came outright repression. The opposition parties were ordered dissolved. Forty-seven political and labor leaders were expelled from the country in chains, like common criminals, as they were taken from jail to the ship
Flandre which carried them to exile. The Federal Court of Appeals, under the
control of the presidency, annulled the election of some of the opposition

leaders, who learned of their sentence after they were in jail or exile without having had any right to defend themselves. A few of us who were ordered expelled succeeded in going underground and continued the fight of the Venezuelan people for these great goals: political democracy, social justice, and the economic independence of the nation.

This repression, given the complicated dialectic of social phenomenon, had both negative and positive aspects. On the one hand, it weakened the people's ability to act by eliminating the legal agencies of political and labor struggle. On the other hand, it unmasked the repressive tendencies of the Gómez heirs and put an end to the illusion that the popular frontism which the progressive political forces had been using could be effective. (Remember that this was the time of the Spanish Civil War and of popular front tactics in France and other countries among the various ideological currents of the left.) In Venezuela, there now took place a crisis of clarification, a process of defining political objectives and ideologies, which was healthy for the political future of the nation.

The president had his own unique political apparatus—the so-called Bolívarian Civic Groups, composed of the most reactionary groups of Venezuelan society, ranging from the Gómez clique to the vast clientele of the oil companies.

PART THREE

Five Years of Frustration

3

Medina Angarita: Autocracy with a Liberal Face

General Isaías Medina Angarita came to the presidency at the height of the war between the totalitarian Axis and the Allies. Hitler had conquered more than half of Europe, and his opponents were relying—even more than on the production of North American factories—upon the doctrine and practice of democracy as their decisive weapon. Franklin D. Roosevelt was promising in his radio speeches, that "totalitarianism would be eliminated from the furthest corner of the earth."

In such an international climate, it was difficult for the new president to follow the policies of his predecessor. He also needed to have popular support to resist the insistent tutelage of López Contreras. He therefore sought to change the political direction of the country with more respect for public liberties and a less repressive attitude toward opposition political forces.

A Party Is Born—with Program, Doctrine, and Vocation of Power

The National Democratic party, which had been so active and labored so effectively during the five years of López Contreras now took the name of Democratic Action (Acción Democrática, or AD). It was difficult to legalize the party because the government continued to view opposition forces with ill-disguised apprehension. Our party had requested legal status in accord with the public order law, then in effect. The official who, as governor of the Federal District, would make the ruling on the party was Luis Gerónimo Pietri. His decision was based on our answers to an inquisitorial questionnaire. To obtain permission to hold public meetings, we had to demonstrate that we

His decision was based on our answers to an inquisitorial questionnaire. To obtain permission to hold public meetings, we had to demonstrate that we were fervent defenders of private property in its most authoritarian state; watchdogs of the most medieval concept of the family; and Saint George himself, going out to fight against modern ideas of social justice adopted long ago by other countries but believed by officialdom in the Venezuela of 1941 to be subversive and anarchistic.

To pass this gauntlet on, the Acción Democrática program had to be watered down to a vague set of general principles, rather than remain a strong revolutionary statement on the nation's problems and their possible solutions. This retreat was offset by the frank and forthright manner in which we addressed the national problems in our speeches and party literature. Undoubtedly, however, there was a discrepancy between our cautious official platform and the analysis of Venezuelan problems that we popularized as an opposition party and which we followed when we came to power. This was the result of the circumstances under which the party was legalized.

There was relative public tranquillity during the Medina government. People were discontented with administrative corruption and inefficiency, widespread poverty, and the institutional insincerity of the regime. However, due to the moderate attitude taken by Acción Democrática, the only organized opposition party, there was no large-scale strike or any riots. We were too conscious of the external threats against our country, the principal supplier of oil to the Allies, and we took care that our internal differences did not get out of control.

The military threat against us became evident when on February 15, 1942, Nazi submarines sank the Venezuelan tanker *Monagas* in our territorial waters. The following day, the Nazis shelled Standard Oil installations on the Dutch island of Aruba, off our northwest coast. And on April 19, the Axis submarines bombarded Royal Dutch Shell facilities in the harbor of Curaçao.

We were opposed to Germany and its allies because of our geography, economy, and, even more, our ideological beliefs. However, the attitude of the Venezuelan government was hesitant and contradictory. Nothing was done to unify or defend the country against these attacks. There was official inertia regarding the propaganda and espionage being carried out in the country. However, a minority congressional bloc under AD leadership, the so-called Unified Minority, presented a formal denunciation to Congress on July 15, documented with lists of names of agents for the German Nazis, Italian fascists, and Spanish Falangists in the country, and their activities.

Our moderation as an opposition also derived from the fact that we had not yet been able to get through with our ideological message to all the democratic elements of the country, nor to all its regions. Before making a serious effort to gain power, it was necessary to organize the party on a national scale. We set as our goal: "Not a single district, not a single town without its party organization." This was an immensely difficult and ambitious task. The nation's population was scattered thinly over 1 million square kilometers. We had no money except the dues of our membership—most of them from the working or middle class. The job, nevertheless, got done, thanks to the unquenchable faith of a movement destined to transform a nation.

These four years (1941–45) were unforgettable for me. I had always wanted to know our country, town by town, village by village, and to be able to speak directly with the men and women of the mountain country, of the plains, of the east, and of Guyana. I was able to fulfill this dream and learn much more about the country than I ever could have from my own studies. I traveled the Orinoco in a precarious homemade launch. I navigated Lake Maracaibo in a hollowed-out log canoe, and the Tuy River on a log raft. I slept in primitive huts on the vast plains of Guarico and along the Apure River. I heard about the lives and work of the common people while I drowsed in a palm-fiber hammock. I dwelt with the Andinos on their high mountain moor; with the oil workers in Cabimas, Quiriquire, and El Tigre; with fishermen in the Gulf of Cariaco; with the sisal farmers in Lara, the laborers on plantations in Aragua and Miranda, and the cacao growers of Barlovento.

I confirmed, through my direct contact with people of all the different social strata of the country, what the statistics and figures regarding national income had led me to believe—that the prosperity of the urban Venezuela of Caracas and its surroundings is superimposed upon another Venezuela of underproduction, technical backwardness, and general poverty. I sensed the frustration and general discontent resulting from the coexistence of these two countries—a well-to-do minority and an infinitely more numerous group without the advantages of civilized life. I heard this same sentiment expressed in all the different regions of the nation in tones bordering on anger. There was a general feeling that a revolutionary change was necessary since the peaceful road to change by vote was blocked. One of the prerequisites to the easy subversion of a political regime was spreading in the collective subconscious: the incompatibility of all our social classes with the existing order.

We founded a newspaper. It was a daring step to take. Although there was freedom of the press, it was necessary to operate under the suffocating and efficient pressures of a strong government. Any business or bank that aided an opposition newspaper, even just to give it credit, was exposed to reprisals—some very indirect. We had to use the classical method of capitalism and mobilize individual resources by offering shares in the enterprise. These were sold to friends and members of the party. Caracas boasted some millionaire newspapers with ultramodern rotary presses. We printed our combative eight pages on an ancient duplex with an historic past. It had been sacked twice during the overthrow of tyrants since it had been used to print the official newspapers of both the Castro and Gómez regimes.

History will confirm that AD acted in a measured, responsible manner during the Second World War. In speeches before and in public meetings, doctrinal discourses in the pages of *El País* and other party papers, we outlined our program. It is worth reviewing this program since it formed the basis of what we did later in the government.

We demanded the return of sovereignty to the people. The return of power from an autocratic clique to the nation would require a radical reform of the electoral system and voting practices.

We demanded direct elections of the president and all congressmen by a universal secret vote. We energetically fought the various forms of fraud and pressure used by the government in the elections for municipal councilmen and state legislators, the only offices that required a popular vote according to the Constitution then in force. Fraud was possible because all electoral machinery was in the hands of the government. A helplessly small minority represented the opposition in Congress. Various complicated tricks were employed to block greater representation. Thus, there was very little difference between the National Congress of Venezuela and the "corporative" parliaments of Franco and Mussolini or the Reichstag of Hitler. Such complete subordination of Congress to the head of state enabled him to pick his own successor. The republic thus was converted into a sort of elected monarchy, with the outgoing president choosing his successor.

In administrative matters, we objected to the lack of modern state agencies and fought against that worst plague of public administration in Venezuela—graft. This traditional vice became increasingly worse as the oil income grew and, in one form or another, was practiced by all the successors of Gómez who governed from 1935 to 1945.

Finally, we demanded a greater participation by the nation in the income from the subsoil whose riches were produced by foreign companies. We wanted to invest the increased income to diversify the Venezuelan economy and to improve the lot of the populace. This was the demand we pressed most vigorously during the days of World War II. We did not want to interrupt the flow of Venezuelan oil to the nations combating the Nazi-fascist Axis. However, we insisted that the oil policy carried out by governments oblivious to the national interest be rectified, taking advantage of the fact that oil was in such demand and that the oil companies were making exceptional profits. Any newspaper reader could easily find proof that the oil companies were making much money from their operations.

Continued Official Toleration of Huge Oil Company Earnings Despite Criticism from Acción Democrática

The newspaper *El Heraldo* of Caracas (February 25, 1942) published a report by the Royal Dutch Shell president, R. G. A. Van der Wonde, declaring that his company, 40 percent of whose production came from Venezuela, had achieved a net income in 1941 of $17.3 million compared with $15.6 million the previous year. He also revealed that the company had paid $9 million in taxes to the United States for the year, against $3.2 million the previous year.

An article by Henry E. Rose in the magazine *World Petroleum* (July 1942) revealed how the companies were skimming off the cream on behalf of their shareholders as a result of the situation created by the war. During 1941, the oil companies had averaged a 16 percent increase in their profits over the preceding year. In April 1941, the price of crude oil increased $.16 per barrel, followed by a 10 percent increase two months later. W. S. Farish, president of the Standard Oil Company of New Jersey, estimated early that year that his company's first-quarter earnings would be $75–80 million. Creole Petroleum Corporation, the Venezuelan affiliate of Standard, accounted for about half of the company's income.

Increased profits were directly related to the increase in oil prices. While the companies had been making the most out of the war in their harvest of dollars and sterling for their fortunate stockholders, Venezuela continued producing the oil at a low cost despite a fiscal deficit and the harm caused to its economy.

During 1941, when Venezuela produced oil at a record rate, the following figures from the Ministry of Production's annual report to Congress —comparing the participation of the nation and the companies in oil income—demonstrate how government officials failed to protect the national interest.

Value of oil produced	Bs. 691,093,935
Total taxes paid	85,279,158
Difference for the companies	Bs. 605,814,777

Even after production and other costs were subtracted, the concessionaire companies obtained three times more profit than the country received.

This situation did not seem to embarrass the government. On the contrary, the colonial-like treatment was accepted almost as an honor. For instance, an official economic mission which went to the United States in late 1941, led by the president of the Central Bank, stressed that the concessionaire companies obtained our oil "at a lower price than that paid by similar companies producing in other countries."

Submarine warfare was at its peak in the Caribbean during this tense period. Our ports were virtually blockaded. Merchant vessels arrived only sporadically. Our people suffered a great scarcity of many articles or paid exorbitant prices for those which could be obtained. The moment was opportune to promote local manufacture.

The official reaction, however, to this opportunity to promote national industry could not have been more discouraging. During 1941, the total amount of credit granted by the government to industry was scandalously low—Bs. 325,000. This amount, according to the Ministry of Production in its annual report, could not be any greater "due to budgetary limitations imposed by the drop in public income."

The loss of income and the unbalanced budget could have been easily corrected by an increase in oil taxes. Instead, measures were taken which did not affect the powerful foreign interests but burdened the domestic consumer and Venezuelan production. Government salaries were lowered; new taxes were placed on gasoline and matches. Budget allocations for the promotion of industrial production were drastically cut. The government resorted to loans.

The president of the republic, in his annual message to Congress, announced that he would utilize public credit instead of higher taxes on the oil companies to increase government income. In June 1942, the executive branch sought authorization to contract for a loan for Bs. 68 million.

Our party, which had always been devoted to the service of the country, then fought one of the hardest nationalistic battles of its life. The Acción Democrática party spoke for the most deeply held beliefs of the nation. Our congressmen, with the aid of some independent deputies, demonstrated that during its first year the administration of Medina Angarita had continued to permit Venezuela to be used as a factory to produce wealth for others from its oil riches. Their formal presentation showed that, in 1941, the oil produced was valued at Bs. 690 million, while the nation received only Bs. 85 million, or 12.3 percent. Furthermore, the nation's income per ton of production was reduced from Bs. 3.07 in 1940 to Bs. 2.25 in 1941. The oil companies for their part had invested Bs. 21 million less in the country than in the previous year. They concluded: "With greater production and with a lower cost, the nation has received an income from oil remarkably less than that of the year 1940."

"Article 21"—A National Slogan

The agitation in Congress was synchronized with efforts that our party was making in public meetings, the press, and in other political action. In the first national AD convention, held in Caracas, June 6, 1942, it was resolved "to continue stubbornly insisting on the need for a change in the relationship between the state and the oil companies so the nation might have a greater income from its first source of wealth." As a result of action by our representatives, the Caracas Municipal Council on June 15 voted to petition the federal executive, asking that article 21 of the customs law be applied to the oil companies. This provided for a 10 percent *ad valorem* tax on the value of mineral exports.

On July 4, the AD congressional group brought up this matter in the Chamber of Deputies. The ensuing debate had an extraordinary impact. At first, government supporters said that article 21 was unconstitutional, but Alfonso Espinoza, who had always been a leading spokesman in fiscal matters for the government, stated categorically that the article was legal. Then a well-known industrialist, Navarro Mendez, came to the support of the AD position and noted that "only in Venezuela has oil investment received such high return." Luis Felipe Hernández, legal adviser to business groups, also backed us. He countered with statistics the shameful argument advanced by the stubborn defenders of the outrageous profits of the oil trusts—that an increase in taxes would put Venezuelan petroleum at a competitive disadvantage in the market by demonstrating how low taxes were in Venezuela, even lower than in Mexico before nationalization. There, in 1938, the companies had paid $.38 per barrel to the nation, while in Venezuela, in 1941, they were paying scarcely $.10.

The presidency showed no sign of any favorable response to this debate, despite the clear fact that majority opinion favored our viewpoint. Even progovernmental newspapers began to support our thesis. The National Congress of Lawyers came out in favor of applying article 21. It was clear that the thesis of our party was receiving national support.

One of our younger leaders, Luis Augusto Dubuc, calculated that if the government had applied article 21 when the law was approved in 1937, the national treasury would have received Bs. 330 million additional taxes.

While our party was carrying on this fervent crusade in defense of the national interest, the Communist party was devoting itself to organizing some picturesque "victory fairs." Russia had now been invaded by the Nazis; and the communists, who a few months earlier had been dedicated pacifists, were now converted into the most passionate partisans of Mars, the god of war. They sought to collect money from the oil workers, promising that it would be sent to Moscow, London, and Washington to help finance the war against the Axis. When Luis B. Prieto and I questioned collections of such dubious use in a tour we made of the western oil fields, the communists attacked us with their heaviest broadside of insults. In an article published in the communist periodical *Aqui Está* (April 16, 1942), they compared the two of us with Charles A. Lindbergh and Senator Wheeler, the leaders of North American isolationism. Also, they held us guilty of a heinous crime because we stated before the crowds of workers that while Venezuela should send its oil without interruption to the war fronts and guard against fifth columnists, the workers should get a greater share of the profits the oil companies were making. The zig-zagging Stalinists were also scandalized when we said that Venezuela's interests should take priority above all others. When they attacked us in their periodical for our zealous nationalism, we seized their verbal darts, applied the Indian poison "curare," and returned their fire.

> We affirm that Venezuela comes first, because before everything and first of all, the problems of our own country affect us and worry us. Nobody should be surprised at this because we are Venezuelans, not English, North Americans, or Russians.[1]

Still another skirmish with the communists occurred as a result of my statement made to UPI in the name of our party regarding the widely publicized (by Moscow) dissolution of the Third International. My laconic statement said:

> Insufficient evidence exists to evaluate this latest turn of an organization which has been so contradictory in its procedures. In any case, this will not affect in any way the political line of AD, a party of the left with strictly American inspiration, not connected in any way with European internationals. We will continue to fight for

an effective and fruitful American democracy, free of mistakes and inconsistencies; for the decisive defeat of the Axis, the most dangerous enemy of human progress; and for true peace among peoples, without a new Versailles.

The communists replied with indignation. At the top of their voices, they proclaimed that Moscow would not be the tutor of parties yoked to its chariot but that, with the dissolution of the Comintern, each party would regain its organizational and tactical autonomy. They described my discreet, although somewhat deliberate, statement as "a new maneuver carried out in bad faith to obtain certain immediate results."[2] Later events confirmed once again that we were right and the communists were not. Some years later, when the Comintern was replaced by the Cominform, the Venezuelan Communist party returned, with ever increasing docility, to its old role as a propaganda agency for Russian foreign policy.

At this time, when the Venezuelan people were demanding a change in oil taxation, Mexico won an important battle with the international petroleum cartel. On April 19, 1942, the decision of the mixed Mexican-North American Commission, studying various issues resulting from the Cárdenas nationalization decree, was published. Its conclusions were basically favorable to the Mexican position. The sum of $25 million was fixed as the compensation Mexico should pay for the value of the nationalized oil properties, instead of the $250 million asked by the companies. The same decision recognized the moral and judicial legality of the Cárdenas decree taking over all the assets of the concessionary companies. Along with this decision, it was revealed that the Mexican government had obtained some important additional advantages from the United States government. President Roosevelt's administration opened a credit of $40 million to the government of President Avila Camacho to help stabilize the Mexican currency. The United States also agreed to buy, each year, 6 million ounces of Mexican silver, and the Export-Import Bank loaned Mexico $30 million for public works projects. Commenting on these developments, our official weekly publication once more insisted upon our party's nationalist thesis:

> See what Mexico has obtained and Bolivia, which is much less strong and politically important. On the other hand, Venezuela continues with contracts signed under General Gómez, drawn up according to laws which were written by lawyers of the oil companies. . . . We are not asking for the immediate nationalization of the oil industry but for measures which will strengthen our economy and our fiscal position. We ask, simply, for an increase of our part of the oil income to the degree that justice and equity indicate.[3]

The Government Agrees to the Oil Reform—Only to Water It Down

The national clamor for revision of the oil status quo now increased. The colonialists were on the defensive, without adequate arguments to defend a situation increasingly repudiated by the country as a whole. The national treasury was empty, public works projects were paralyzed, and the economic downturn was affecting the public. The government resorted to all kinds of maneuvers, short-term bond issues, extrajudicial settlements of cases against oil companies, and the sale of ships confiscated from the Axis powers to procure money to pay the bureaucracy and the military.

These factors contributed to the pressure on the government to tax oil industry as the only source of new money to meet its needs. The clever advisers of the oil companies foresaw the impending tax reform. They knew that public opinion was hostile to the continuance of contracts inherited from the Gómez period, vitiated by juridical and moral flaws. At the same time, they wanted to increase their existing concessions but not under the 1938 law. They perceived that they might reconcile the fiscal needs of the government with their own secret desires by proposing a minor tax increase as the price to be paid for achieving their own objectives.

These are my serene reflections, now without any political passion, as I look back on the oil reform process of 1943. When it was announced, as Venezuelans and as politicians who had fought for this reform, we greeted the news with great enthusiasm. It seemed justified, since the government which so long had turned a deaf ear to our vehement demands for reform in relations between the state and the oil industry now suddenly emerged as the champion of this idea. In a speech made at Miraflores Palace on July 17, 1942, to the commission announcing the closing of the ordinary session of Congress, the president of the republic said that "the government would work to change in accordance with our laws and in a search for equity—a situation that has to be changed in favor of the Venezuelan nation."

This gibberish was clarified in another more concrete paragraph of his statement when he asked that "Venezuela obtain from the production of its natural wealth that part which should correspond to it in all justice, and that the industries which are the logical consequence of the production of these resources have their location, movement, and expansion in Venezuela."

Everything seemed to favor the adoption of an energetic attitude on the oil question, but we were ingenuous in the enthusiasm with which we greeted the government's promise. A regime that had refused to alter its autocratic nature was historically incapable of really facing up to the oil problem. It lacked the kind of audacity and moral authority that is only truly derived from majority public support.

The government knew that the oil companies were aware of the weakness of an administration that did not have honest elections, that did not manage its fiscal affairs honestly, and that did not look after public needs fully. That is why it did not dare to carry out a true basic reform in its relations with the oil industry. It lost a splendid opportunity—with the world at war and thirsty for fuel oil—and with a President Roosevelt in the White House, a leader who had taken a moderate position when faced with the radical measures proposed by Mexico in a situation similar to that of Venezuela.

Soon we had reason to suspect that the heralded oil reform was only going to turn out to be a prearranged deal with the companies, favoring their interests. Any doubts on this score vanished when Gustavo Manrique Pacanins, who had previously arranged a giveaway deal with the Mene Grande Oil Company, traveled to the United States in August 1942 on what the press described as a "vacation trip." A little later, we learned of his visit to the White House, accompanied by the Venezuelan Ambassador, for an interview of more than an hour with President Roosevelt. This confirmed what we feared—that this great national problem was not going to be resolutely faced; rather that there would be another chapter written in the history of Venezuela's frustrations with regard to its petroleum in the post-Gómez era.

Soon there was proof that the companies still believed they were treading on the soil of a conquered land. With irritating arrogance, in September 1942, Standard Oil Company brought suit against the nation on behalf of two affiliates—the Compañia de Petróleo Lago and the Lago Petroleum Corporation for Bs. 1.5 million. It was an old dispute relating to the oil law of 1936. Our party's weekly bitterly criticized this suit, brought at such an inopportune moment against a bankrupt national treasury.

> The treasury is in crisis, with salary cuts for government employees and the manager of the Venezuelan division of Standard Oil, Mr. Henry Linam, has stated in *El Universal* that oil exports have gone down abruptly, with the consequent reduction in tax income. It is at this time, with government finance in a state of near collapse, that the company of Rockefeller comes along with its preemptory demand for payment. It is difficult not to compare this attitude with that of fascist Italy when it declared war on France, attacking it from the rear, when the German troops were at the door of Paris.[4]

The arrogance of the companies, the official secrecy regarding the oil reform, and indications that the latter was being negotiated with the United States by a person who did not enjoy public confidence—such factors justified pessimism. However, our party did not take a negative, defeatist position. We continued to struggle to get what Venezuela deserved, based on justice and law.

The "Marriage of Convenience" between the Government and Communists

In this task we encountered still another obstacle—the latest switch in policy of the Communist party. It now abandoned its widely proclaimed anti-imperialism to join the government as an ally and became its most enthusiastic mouthpiece. In Moscow, they had given a turn to the dialectical switch and now the Latin American sections of the Third International were giving their allegiance to all established governments, regardless of their origin, conduct, or social policies. The "new line" coincided with the tour made by the Mexican leftist, Lombardo Toledano, throughout Latin America. Anastasio Somoza and the contradictory Aztec leader now appeared side by side on the same platform before the Nicaraguan people. The Peruvian communists allied themselves with Prado Ugartache. The "Brazilian Knight of Hope" (the communist leader Luis Prestes) was released from prison for a spectacular reconciliation with Getulio Vargas, whose government had kept him locked up for years. In Cuba, the communists lined up with Batista, with Lazaro Peña bringing the Workers' Confederation into the Batista camp, and Juan Marinello emerging as a minister in the Batista cabinet. A similar bizarre alliance took place in Costa Rica with the government of Calderón Guardia. Meanwhile, in Venezuela, crying "With Medina Against the Reaction," the communists became the unconditional servants of the regime. Among other dirty jobs they performed were the attacks carried out on those who dared to dissent from official opinion. The most benevolent adjectives they used against those who offered opposition were "reactionaries," "fifth columnists" and "Nazi agents."

Gonzalo Barrios, member of the political command of AD, made a penetrating analysis of the series of shifts which had brought Venezuelan communists and those of all of Latin America into a series of alliances with dictators and oligarchical governments. He wrote:

> Before Hitler had attacked Russia, when the famous German-Soviet pact still existed, the Union Popular [communists] insisted that France and England were fighting an imperialist war. It was America's duty to stay neutral and to urge peace—even a Nazi peace. Hitler was exalted and blessed by some of them much as medieval heretics saw in the devil an agent of goodness. We know now how Hitler has carried out his plans for conquest. All Latin American governments have broken ties with Germany and are associated in the fight against Nazism and therefore in defense of the Soviet Union. It is now deduced that there were no reactionary governments in America and the reactionaries are those who oppose any of those governments.[5]

Out of this strange alliance of communists and governments, there emerged the idea of staging a public homage to President Medina as a kind of advance testimony of public gratitude. The idea was to portray the chief of state as the hero who had achieved the economic liberation of the nation, thanks to the oil reform whose terms were not even yet known.

Acción Democrática was invited to the mass meeting and decided to attend. This was a wonderful opportunity to get our viewpoint across by the national radio network in a country where, as an opposition party, we were denied use of the radio. The disciplined and self-confident AD members went to the meeting, identified by their own slogans and their own political line. The government-communist coalition carried huge banners with their stereotyped slogan: "With Medina Against the Reaction." Our banners all referred to national goals such as the just participation of the country in the oil income; refining in Venezuela the greatest possible amount of our oil; freedom to unionize, collective contracts, and better living standards for the oil workers; low prices for oil products consumed by the public; and efficient investment of the new income to be received by the state from the oil tax reform.

On January 17, 1943, the "Concentration of Los Caobos" took place in the plaza of that name in Caracas. I spoke for Acción Democrática. My speech did not attack or flatter the government in any way. Rather, it stated frankly our party's position. One of its paragraphs summarized our position on oil reform:

> An increase to the limit required by strict justice in the nation's participation in oil income; the transfer to Venezuela of the refineries which operate with the crude taken from our soil; a reduction of the absurd exemption from customs duties for the concessionaires; and guarantees for the economic and social improvements of all those who work for the companies—these are the bases for a new and significant oil policy.

I also made it clear that we would not support oil reform without knowing what it curtailed, and said:

> We are eagerly waiting with the entire populace of the country for the new oil law which is being prepared. We will analyze this project with a sense of responsibility and a desire to cooperate. At the proper time we will make public our observations and criticisms so the law which is finally approved will truly be a step forward on the road toward our complete economic independence.[6]

A National Issue Decided Behind the Back of the People

There was no word at all, official or extra-official, as to what was going on in the negotiations with the oil companies. "The nation ought to be able to vote on the oil question" was the title of an editorial in *Acción Democrática*.

> It is known that there are many important persons from the Anglo-American world of high finance here in Venezuela on behalf of their governments or the oil companies and that urgent conversations are taking place with the Venezuelan government. Among the visitors are Herbert Hoover, Jr., son of the former U.S. President, and Max Thornburg—both advisers of the State Department. For the companies, there have come such prominent officials as Wallace Pratt, vice president of Standard Oil of New Jersey, and Harry Sinclair, well-known Wall Street magnate, who heads the Consolidated Petroleum Corporation and who was linked with one of the most sensational oil scandals in Mexico. Conversations with these people take place behind closed doors. There is a heavy veil of mystery over the talks.[7]

The wait neared its end. An extraordinary session of Congress was called on February 18, 1943, to discuss the proposed new oil law. The bill was not distributed to the members of Congress until the day they met, perhaps for fear that the few opposition members might divulge its contents. In contrast with the ignorance in which the Venezuelan public was left, interested parties in the United States and England had the draft well enough in advance to study its most minute details. Our periodical *Acción Democrática* pointed out that news dispatches from New York and London were reporting the reactions of financial circles there to the new draft long before we got to see it.

Despite our criticism of the way the draft had been prepared, we made a last desperate effort to get across our nationalistic views to the solid bloc in

Congress which was obedient to the government. An editorial urged the government majority to take a "really patriotic" attitude. The historic debate should not be rushed, it urged, but should be carried out in such careful fashion that the goal set by President Medina "to obtain what legitimately belongs to the nation from its oil" may be reached.[8]

The "Negotiated Law"—Frustration of the Public

From the moment the special session began, however, it was evident that no amendments would be permitted to the government's bill, which disappointed those who hoped for a truly "new deal" in oil matters. The official spokesman in Congress came up with a new theory—that the bill, the result of a negotiation, could not be modified in any of its parts without destroying it entirely. In other words, Congress was asked to rubber-stamp an agreement that had been negotiated in secret between the government and the oil companies, advised by experts from the State Department.

It was not easy, however, for the government majority to carry this off. Our deputies failed in their efforts to get the draft modified, but they were able to use the debate to reach the public and convince the nation that it was being defrauded under the new law. Congressman J. P. Pérez Alfonzo summarized our views in a reasoned negative vote, one of the most impressive documents in Venezuelan history. He dealt with two advantageous aspects of the bill—technical and economic. Among the former the most important was the consolidation and clarification of state-concessionaire relations, involving the acceptance of a more precisely defined state intervention in the operation of the industry. Among the economic benefits were the emphasis on increasing the taxes paid to the nation despite the elimination of some the industry had paid before; the recognition that exemption from customs duties was up to the government; the obligation of the companies to keep their full accounts in Venezuela; the elimination of unjustified differentials in concessions payments because some parcels were underwater; and the agreements on refining that were to be made along with the law.

However, Congressman Pérez Alfonzo objected strongly to two fundamental aspects of the proposed law. The first related to "wiping out" of all claims against the industry. If the bill was not to be modified before becoming law, the nation would be obligated to drop innumerable claims which it had against the companies for faulty concession titles, underpayments to the treasury, and nonjustified profits during the period of some twenty years when oil operations had taken place.

Pérez Alfonzo insisted that wiping out all claims based on the past was "a pretense that cannot be carried out" due to the situation created in Venezuela by the oil companies. He stated:

> It is public and notorious how the companies exploited the wealth of the Venezuelan people, even though they knew how urgent these needs were. They have

taken advantage of the weakness of those who represented the nation. They have made illegitimate profits and caused damage which cannot be repaired by a simple phrase of the law. There is no juridical way in which injustice can be turned into law.

In round figures, the industry has produced in Venezuela up to now 2500 million barrels of oil and obtained an average price of $1 per barrel or $2500 million. If the production cost figure is $.50 per barrel, as indicated by the Minister of Production, Manuel Egaña, in his report to Congress last year, which includes taxes paid, depreciation and interest payments, we see that the profits of the companies were truly exorbitant. They were around $1250 million, a figure which is more than the capital employed in all the industry of the country—agriculture, industry, mining, and the oil industry itself. It is not reasonable to expect that public opinion will accept this, nor pardon it after the fact.

Pérez Alfonzo observed that various companies had, since 1935, made substantial special payments to the nation for various reasons. He suggested that greater amounts might be required from them as "a truly just reparation." On the other hand, he recognized that the increase in surface taxes and the return to the nation of many idle concessions was favorable to the nation. He noted, also, the important increase in the production tax to one-sixth per barrel produced or 16⅔ percent. However, he questioned whether this increase would really guarantee for the nation more than 50 percent of the income from the oil business. Was there, then, real reason to believe the optimistic preamble to the law: "this law finally defines the way the oil industry should function"?

He went on to point out that a just income to the state from the oil industry could not be determined without knowing what was the total capital investment of the companies, or what was the unit cost per barrel of oil produced. He asserted that the Ministry of Production had not made a thorough investigation to determine these facts and that there were many errors in the figures that had been presented. For example, a cost of $.40 per barrel had been accepted as an accurate figure, yet this included amounts that were completely unacceptable, such as the $6 million annually obtained by the companies for the domestic sale of oil products in the country. How could this income be accepted as part of the investment made in order to produce oil? Eliminating just this one figure reduced the cost per barrel by $.03. Other exaggerated amounts were included, such as the $10 million for payment of salaries to foreign employees, $20 million for interest, and the alleged $400 million in capital investment. None of these figures had been audited.

The $.40 per barrel cost figure was dubious enough, but, accepting it, there was an even greater flaw in the calculation of what the share of the nation should be. This flaw was the arbitrary fixing of the price received per barrel at $.81, based on an average of three years selected at random by the ministry's technicians—1937, 1938, and 1939. According to the presentation made by Luongo Cabello to the government congressional bloc, the $.81 was distributed as follows:

Production Cost	1.40
Government share	.245
Industry profits	.165
	$.81

It was on the basis of figures thus capriciously selected that the prologue of the draft law claimed Venezuela would receive more than 50 percent of the future income of the oil industry.

When more reliable figures were used, however, other results were obtained. The oil price in 1941 was $.92 per barrel. In 1942 and 1943, it averaged around $1 per barrel. If prices increased at this rate in the future, the distribution by which the nation was to receive the greater share of earnings would disappear as if by magic.

Take the year 1942 as an example: the estimated result under the proposed oil tax law would be Bs. 113,328,527 for the Venezuelan government, while the companies would obtain Bs. 163,665,597. Congressman Pérez Alfonzo pointed out that this division was diametrically opposed to the proportion of 24.14 (for the government) and 16.12 (for the companies) as proposed in the law—a relationship much more consonant to the national interest.

It should not be forgotten that this exaggerated prospect rested upon the vague premises that the companies would invest $400 million and that the production cost per barrel was $.40. However, all these objections and our motions formulated during the debate went unheeded. With only slight modifications of style, the bill passed just as prepared by the government.

The deputies of Acción Democrática refused to vote in favor of the bill and made a reasoned exposition of their objections to the law. They opposed "the complete wiping out of any previous legal defect" in the concessions and the renunciation by the government of the right to enter any past claim against the concessionaires. They said:

> We do not believe that the juridical concept of "conversion" can eliminate the defects or illegalities which characterize most of the operating concessions; nor compensate the government for the taxes which the companies have avoided paying; nor justify the exaggerated profits made by the foreign investors at great cost to a nation whose basic economy has not been stimulated by the oil boom.

The nation was generally aware of these defects and the government possessed even more convincing data. As Lieuwen wrote about the matter:

> President Medina had instructed a congressional committee to study the legality of the old concessions and to recommend that those of dubious legality be annulled. Without much difficulty the committee found sufficient evidence to upset the companies. The Valladares concessions could expire January 2, 1944. Shell could not claim its extension beyond that date based upon a payment of Bs. 10 million in 1923 for thirty more years, since this was not in accordance with proper legal procedures. Also, the committee discovered that the agreement between Gómez

and Standard of Indiana for new titles to Lake Maracaibo concessions had not been legally executed; therefore Standard Oil of New Jersey concessions—purchased from Standard of Indiana—were not valid. The committee also had evidence that various titles of the Mene Grande Oil to parcels along the Lake Maracaibo coast were questionable.[9]

The document also referred to the estimate of Pérez Alfonzo in Congress—which was never refuted anywhere—that during the years that the oil cartel had been sucking out the subsoil wealth of the nation (1918–43), it had amortized its investment many times over with profits of Bs. 3800 million.

The dissident deputies cited various examples from the past to prove that it would have been possible to obtain large sums from the industry in return for wiping the slate clean. They complained that the new income to be received under the law would not permit the government to initiate a program of "economic redemption" of the country. The official estimates, themselves, only anticipated an additional income of Bs. 3.5 million monthly. This amount, it was admitted, would only make up the chronic deficit of the government, not permit it to undertake an ambitious program of economic recovery.

The document also reviewed the failures of the efforts to introduce amendments which would have improved the proposed law. For instance, it was absurd that one of the world's leading oil producers should have gasoline and other oil products sold within its borders at such high prices. The Congress had rejected an amendment that would have given the government power to fix prices of oil products and thus "put an end to the intolerable abuse of a Venezuela, the world's leading oil exporter, where gasoline was sold at a price three times higher than in Persia, for example."

These and other amendments were voted down on grounds that the law being debated had to be taken as a whole, that it could not be touched because it was an "agreed upon law"! Such a thesis should have been completely rejected. The Congress would lose its dignity as a republican institution and a constitutional power if it were asked to legislate upon laws which had been agreed upon beforehand.

The high point of the debate came when Pérez Alfonzo presented a juridical thesis which events soon dramatically highlighted, and which we had the opportunity to implement when we, AD, gained power in 1945. This thesis was that the law—from the viewpoint of modern administration and in questions of public utility—was not unchanging dogma but a series of norms to be applied according to the national interest. This was stated in unequivocal fashion for the future:

> In truth, the law is an instrument that can be manipulated effectively to rescue the legitimate rights of the nation. This is true if the government is backed by public opinion and seeks sincerely to promote the general welfare and improve the living conditions of the people.

In justice to historical truth, it must be stated that there were some individuals who raised their voices in agreement with the criticisms our party made of the new oil law. Among them, the former Minister of Production, Néstor Luis Pérez, should be mentioned. He noted that none of the three points which the oil companies had so fiercely opposed in the oil law of 1938 appeared in the new law. These suppressed articles referred to the possibility of joint ventures by the state and the companies in operating the oil concessions; the provision for establishing a refinery of Venezuelan ownership which might, in the future, give us a monopoly in the sale of oil products; and the obligation for the companies to pay their taxes in gold, when deemed convenient by the government.

For its part, the Communist party of Venezuela used all of its dialectical resources to justify and defend this monstrous legislation. Despite the absence of public enthusiasm, the new law was passed by both chambers of Congress. Shortly thereafter, the outbreak of a major oil scandal in the United States revealed why the new legislation did not reflect the true will of our nation. Late in 1943, it came to light that the U.S. Navy had given Standard Oil the Elk Hill concessions under conditions that were considered flagrant by the Roosevelt administration. Following an investigation ordered by the president, the attorney general of the United States declared the deal was "a typical one-sided contract, exactly the kind of contract that this company liked to sign." At this time, columnist Drew Pearson revealed that among the people in the U.S. government who helped Standard Oil get this contract was none other than Max Thornburg, adviser to the State Department on petroleum, who had given similar services to the Venezuelan government in drawing up its new oil law. There was no immediate reaction to this revelation but the facts were fully admitted when Cordell Hull, Roosevelt's Secretary of State, later published his memoirs. Hull wrote that "when we became aware that Thornburg was connected with an American oil company, his immediate resignation was called for."[10]

The story of the 1943 oil law is now history, briefly summarized here. Persons far removed from Venezuelan political controversy have confirmed the judgment of our party at that time, based upon their independent studies of the facts. Edwin Lieuwen gives opinions coinciding with ours. He explains the reasons which the companies had for rapidly converting their old concessions into new ones under the 1943 law, despite the fact that their taxes would be higher.

> First, the government agreed to drop its investigation of questionable legal titles; second, the government promised to end its claims regarding company imports. Finally, and this was most important, conversion meant that the life of the concessions—many of which would have ended in 1960—would be extended.

This historian also describes, in terms that confirm those we used, the peculiar negotiation of the "agreement-law" by which the government made definite commitments to the oil cartel before the country or the Congress knew a single thing about it. Lieuwen says:

> The proposed law, which had been agreed upon down to its last detail by Medina

and the oil companies, was presented to Congress for rubber-stamp approval. The president ordered the law approved by both chambers, allowing only insignificant changes and a minimum time for debate. In the Chamber of Deputies, the minority opposition of the Acción Democrática party made helpless protest that the law really did not protect the national interest. In the Senate, there was not even a discussion. The law was approved March 12, 1943.[11]

A Party "Of the Government" Is Organized by Telegram

With the oil law out of the way, President Medina, on April 15, 1943, sent a circular telegram to all state presidents to which much publicity was deliberately given. It called for the organization of a party by supporters of the government and even provided the name to be given the new creature, whose birth was to be accomplished by administrative action similar to that of decreeing the construction of a new hospital. The self-sacrificing citizens who accepted the invitation to sup at the table provided from public funds were to be called "Partisans of the Policy of the Government." Thus the PPG was founded, but it was later rebaptized with a more phonetic name, the Democratic Venezuelan party. (Partido Democrática Venezolano—PDV). Some men of good faith entered this party—professionals and intellectuals without any previous political experience—taken in by the idea that social reform could be initiated from "on high." The majority of its members, however, were professional job seekers and political adventurers, most of them straight from the ranks of the supporters of the dictator Gómez.

Good reasons were apparent for the hurried organization of this official party. Municipal and state assembly elections were to be held in eleven states during the year. These organizations would later select most of the congressmen who, in 1946, would elect the successor to President Medina Angarita. By now everyone was aware of Medina's fight with ex-President López Contreras. President Medina Angarita needed a solid majority in the next Congress to block the return to power of the ambitious general of Queniquea (a village in the Andean state of Táchira). Also, Medina wished to be able to pick his own successor.

But there were hidden reasons behind this political maneuver. These became known after the revolution of 1945 when the secret archives of the deposed government were opened and a memorandum was found from Franco Quijado (the theorist and electoral strategist of the regime), dated March 1, 1943, in which he urged the formation of a party because "the enemy [Acción Democrática, precisely] is wielding power superior to ours. Our people lack faith, are disorganized and are out of touch with the government." There were suggestions on how to control at least 66 percent of the 109,000 registered voters through official groups. Other correspondence in the files demonstrated that Kodaks were sent in a steady stream to the interior, paid for by the government, to "facilitate" registration in the official party.

The "Oil Reform" in Figures

Meanwhile, Congress received the budget for 1943–44. The inexorable eloquence of its figures revealed the truth of what we had predicted about the modest increase in income from the new oil taxes. The oil income for the first year after the reform was estimated at Bs. 106 million, scarcely Bs. 40 million more than before the new law. Furthermore, the total figure included Bs. 19 million in taxes which were one-time payments.

Our party organ, *Acción Democrática* published a convincing analysis on May 7, 1943, showing that the increase in income was even less than this.

Income from oil (budget estimate)	Bs. 106,480,128
Less one-time payment production tax	19,133,256
Official estimate of permanent income	87,346,872
The same income in the year 1942	63,540,735
Increase in strictly oil income	23,806,137
Less loss of tax on light and buoys (eliminated in the reform)	6,300,182
Real increase in oil income during the first year of oil reform	Bs. 17,505,955

With this squalid increase there could be little substantial addition to the new budget for social welfare. No new funds were allocated to education. No new schools were planned. The education budget of Bs. 38 million allocated for 1944–45, the last year of the administration, was scarcely 7 percent of the total budget. Only 281,000 children were enrolled in the public and private primary schools of the country, merely 28 percent of the total 800,000 eligible for schooling. According to the 1941 census, 44.9 percent of the children not attending school had no school to go to. According to statistics of the Ministry of Education itself, only Bs. 1 million—little more than 3 percent of the ministry's budget—were spent for rural education in a country where 78.6 percent of the population lived outside urban areas.[12] At this rate, the percentage of illiterate adults—56 out of every 100 Venezuelans—was increasing. It was already higher in some regions, such as Portuguesa state, where 77 out of every 100 were unable to read or write, according to the 1941 census.

Secondary education was no better. Scarcely 2.5 percent of the Venezuelan population went to high school; while the comparative figure in Colombia, Chile, and the United States were 10, 19.2, and 94.2 percent, respectively. In the Federal District of Venezuela, the privileged area where the capital is located, only 10.3 percent of the adolescents attended high school. In some states, such as Barinas and Cojedes, there were no high schools at all, and there 11,000 youths had to do without secondary education or leave home to get it.

A small percentage of our young people graduated from high school and went to the university. According to the 1945 report of the Ministry of Education, of the 11,598 high school students in the country, 1337 were in the fourth year and only 929 in the fifth and last year. Our country needed doctors, engineers, laboratory workers, dentists, and other professionals by the hundreds, but how was the university to produce them if the state could not provide public primary and secondary education?

Seventy percent of the grade school teachers and many high school professors did not have teaching certificates. Little was done to make the teaching profession attractive. There were but five normal schools in all the nation. The base salary for teachers with certificates was only $100 monthly and for those without certificates it was around $75. The teachers were kept in a humiliating situation by being deprived of the right to any political activity. The single rural normal school graduated only 132 teachers during the entire eight-year period, 1938–45. Few teachers finished their training. Of the 226 enrolled in the National Pedagogical School, only 37 were enrolled for the last year in 1944. Vocational education was also in a sad state. The Practical School of Agriculture at Maracay, the only one in the country, had 118 students. The Technical Institute of Caracas, with 300 students, was barely able to exist and was put to shame by the fact that the Chamber of Industries—a private business group—had created a similar school with adequate staff and equipment. Only two universities in the country were in operation—those of Caracas and Merida. The budget of the University of Caracas, the main seat of higher learning in Venezuela, was a meager Bs. 2 million.

Although higher education was thus improverished, the Medina government decreed two monumental educational construction projects—the University City of Caracas and the Agricultura School of Maracay—at a cost of Bs. 80 million. They were showy projects, but the content of the education remained unchanged.

The 1943–44 budget provided barely Bs. 450,000 for industrial promotion credits while the funds destined for agricultural and cattle loans were but only Bs. 4 million. However, the secret budget of the Ministry of the Interior, used to finance elections and to buy off self-proclaimed generals, colonels without troops, and obedient scribes, was Bs. 3.5 million.

More Wealth for the Wealthy and More Poverty for the Poor

The oil workers of the nation held their first national convention on June 9, 1943. Luis Tovar, a labor leader of AD, who was emerging as one of the principal oil labor leaders declared: "It is clear that we have a long way to go before the oil workers get what they have coming to them." There was no support from the government, however. When the workers organized their first union, the companies fired or transferred its leaders. The government insisted that wages be frozen even though the real amounts received were now at prewar levels due to inflation. While the workers continued to receive only Bs. 11 daily through 1943, the price of pork went up 53 percent; rice, 123 percent; potatoes, 133 percent; and flour, 183 percent.

Workers in other industries without the fringe benefits of the oil companies were even worse off. Although the world press termed Venezuela "the small millionaire country of America," the people suffered real hunger aggravated by scarcity and high prices brought on by war and speculation. Congressman Pérez Salinas revealed that the average nonoil company daily wage was Bs. 6.99 in the Federal District, Bs. 5.85 in Zulia state; and Bs. 3.30 in Táchira state. These salaries had reached a higher level in 1937 but the government crushed the unions in that year and wages were reduced by 10 percent.[13]

It was incredible that worker income should be so low in a country whose oil was helping to determine the outcome of a world war on other continents.

The Venezuelan agency, similar to Roosevelt's Office of Price Administration (OPA) behaved like Pilate and washed its hands of responsibility for rampant speculation and the black market. When it did undertake some timid action to benefit the consumer, powerful private interest groups pressured the government to obtain decisions in their favor. For instance, there was the public scandal of electric energy rates. The Fox Mission in 1941, made up of officials of the United States government and technical experts, pointed out that Venezuelan electricity rates were three times higher than in Washington. In this same year, 422 units of electrical energy which cost Bs. 26 in Baranquilla, Colombia, cost Bs. 115.40 in Caracas, or four times more. The Venezuelan Price Regulating Agency ordered a symbolic reduction of just 5 percent in electric rates. The companies, fairly sure of what would happen, indicated on their bills to clients that the reduction was "provisional." Sure enough, on March 17, 1942, the *Gaceta Oficial* published a resolution of the Ministry of Production annulling this small decrease. The most absurd aspect of the affair was that the Ministry, in effect, contradicted itself in its annual report when it stated that: "The electricity rates are very high and prevent many industries from obtaining energy at normal costs."[14]

Low wages and public services at enormous prices, unrestricted speculation—these were the factors that made the Venezuelan people suffer economic anguish during the war comparable to those nations crushed by the boots of Japanese or Nazi soldiers. One might have thought that the government would seek to compensate the workers for their inadequate income with an energetic program of social welfare, but investigation of the facts reveals this was not the case.

The Social Security Service was not set up until 1943, three years after being authorized by law, and was then restricted to the Federal District. It was evident from its inception that this system would quickly become insolvent because of inadequate government contributions—only nine-tenths of 1 percent, while employers gave 5 percent and workers 2 percent.

The public health situation was truly dramatic. Endemic diseases undermined the health of many workers, especially the less skilled, as the following pathetic statistics illustrate. There were an average of 1 million malaria cases per year with 5000 fatalities. Arnoldo Gabaldón, the eminent chief of the Anti-Malaria Division in the Ministry of Health and Sanitation, estimated that the nation lost Bs. 200 million annually from work hours lost because of malaria. He urged that the disease be declared "a national calamity" and dealt with as such. The ravages of tuberculosis were devastating. According to the *Pan-American Health Office Bulletin* (September 1941), of 75,993 examinations in 16 different localities, the following results were found: 20 percent of those up to age 4 were infected; 51 percent of those from 5 to 14 years of age, and 82 percent of those over 14 years. There was a shortage of 8000 beds for tuberculosis patients and the mortality rate was 243 for every 100,000 people. In comparison, the United States rate was 44 deaths for every 100,000 people affected. A 1940 study by Berarroch and Hill (*Anquilistomiasis and Malaria in Venezuela*), reported on a joint study of the Rockefeller Foundation and the National Sanitary Department. The conclusions were that 99 percent of Venezuela's population suffered from intestinal parasites; 69 percent were victims of that tropical malady, malaria.

The International Labor Office had calculated that intestinal parasites reduce an individual's work capacity by 50 percent. This explains the apathy and lack of initiative among our rural population which has so often been stigmatized as laziness.

The hospital capacity of the nation was completely insufficient. There were 10,000 hospital beds in all the country in 1942 or 2.8 beds for every 1000 people. Chile, at this time, had 4.4 and Uruguay 7.1 beds for each 1000 inhabitants. Our country had only 1049 doctors but needed 4000, according to Rafael Risquez Iribarren, chief of the Rural Health Department, who also noted that at the rate the universities were producing doctors, it would take forty years to make up the deficiencies.

The health problem was at its worst in the rural areas, where 40,000 Venezuelans died each year of undiagnosed illnesses. There were not even cemeteries for the cadavers of these unfortunate victims of official negligence.

The ignorant country people buried their dead on corners of their farms after they received the charms or drank the potions of the local witch doctors. They suffered silently and they did not complain. The Venezuelan is tough and resilient, his stoicism reflected in the irony of his poetry and song. One song long popular in the countryside expresses the popular feeling toward epidemics:

> Measles, they are knocking at the door,
> Chicken pox, go see who it is,
> If it is my good friend Smallpox,
> Tell her to come back later.

This was the fatalistic reaction to the unhealthy conditions in the country. What did the government do about it? It assigned Bs. 28 million, only 6 percent of the national budget, to the Ministry of Health. There were good people there, but with such limited resources, they were powerless to deal with the epidemics that decimated our people.

The deficiencies of the popular diet made the Venezuelan easy prey to disease. In 1943, the Ministry of Health published impressive figures on the lack of meat and milk in the national diet. The annual average consumption of meat was only 35 grams per person; milk consumption was 83 cubic centimeters per person—not even one full glass. One month before President Medina was overthrown, the official Student Hygiene Service revealed that 63 percent of the 15,000 students examined in Caracas were threatened by tuberculosis because of dietary deficiencies.

All of these negative factors—low wages, stingy government expenditures for education and health, and the absence of any kind of social policy—alienated the public from the government.

Not only the lower and middle classes reacted against the government, but also businessmen and industrialists. Only those financial circles that were connected directly with the government and received benefits from it were satisfied. The Federation of Chambers of Commerce and Industry had repeatedly petitioned in vain that the government establish a National Economic Council. This body was authorized by the national Constitution and was supposed to give opinions regarding administrative economic measures. Outraged by the indifference of the government, the directors of the federation sent one last communication to the Ministry of Production: "Since it is ordered by the Constitution, there is no possible way you can avoid acting upon the matter."[15]

The government was dominated by a self-satisfied and complacent bureaucracy. At a time when, because of the war, most governments were trying to broaden their base and popular support, the Venezuelan regime continued to be partisan, myopically arrogant, and isolationist. Because of public pressure, it had, in 1943, created a commission composed of seven cabinet ministers and four other high government officials to study postwar problems, but it was completely inactive.

There was cautious criticism in the press, suggesting that the commission be widened to include other political sectors and business representatives, but this only brought Jupiterlike thunderbolts from the government against those who questioned official infallibility. The Ministry of Production replied to such a suggestion from the Chamber of Agriculture: "The government will make all decisions according to the power it has and in accordance with its own criteria and not in accordance with what this Chamber or any other unofficial agency may want."

President Medina received a thunderous ovation when he made his inaugural address before Congress, May 5, 1941, and declared: "Graft will not exist in Venezuela because I will apply the full weight of the law against those who practice this reprehensible activity."

This promise was never carried out, either by supporting legislation or in administrative policy. The congressional majority of the government, with an avalanche of raised hands, denied approval to the bill which proposed punishment for this sort of crime. It had been presented to the Senate by Jóvito Villalba and was warmly supported by Acción Democrática. In a mass meeting at the Nuevo Circo of Caracas in June 1944, AD Congressman Andrés Eloy Blanco urged that provisions be added to the law which would require officeholders to declare their assets publicly before a notary upon taking office and upon leaving it.

The official congressional majority rejected this bill, however, and sought to eliminate from the Constitution the clause confiscating the assets of anyone who used public office to enrich himself illegally. It was argued that this idea of reprisal had been put into the Constitution because of "temporary circumstances" and that it did not now belong there. Our party, again expressing the deep-seated desire of the public, countered with a plea to clean up public administration.

Another major problem about which nothing was done was land reform. The president had announced unspecified government plans in April 1943, but it was not until the following year that a study commission was created. A bill was discussed in 1945 and was finally signed by the president just a month before his overthrow.

During World War II, the cultivated area of the country decreased by 9.1 percent while the population increased 21.6 percent. According to the Economic Commission for Latin America (ECLA), the amount of land used to grow fruit decreased from 1,048,373 hectares to 954,300, while the amount in corn went down from 262,852 hectares to 200,000. This decrease in production, aggravated by smaller imports because of wartime difficulties, resulted in a serious gap between supply and demand during these critical years. This factual analysis demonstrates that those who governed during these five frustrating years were not exactly characterized by creative ability or their efficiency in solving the basic problems of the country.

The New Round of Concessions

The true character of that government was revealed by the haste with which it proceeded to grant new oil concessions without awaiting the results of the Oil Law of 1943. The craze of selling the subsoil rights was so great that in twenty-four months, the international oil cartel obtained more Venezuelan land than it had in all thirty-two years under the governments of Gómez and López Contreras. In the early days of the oil industry, it had been possible to argue that the risk factor was extremely high because the oil potential was unknown, but for those who governed in 1944–45 there was no possible excuse. Millions and millions of hectares were carelessly turned over to the international companies and with an irresponsible throwaway impulse, since Venezuela now knew the tremendous value of its oil wealth and was fully aware that it had been taken advantage of by the same companies to which it now gave new concessions.

The veil of secrecy with which the government sought to hide these negotiations of such importance to the country was also aggravating. Nothing was said in the congressional debate or any place else regarding what was going on between the government and the companies. The Venezuelans only became aware of all this a few months later when an economic takeover of the country occurred—as great as that in the decades of the Gómez-López Contreras governments. Extraordinary editions of the *Gaceta Oficial* published a series of contracts signed between the Ministry of Production and managers of the oil trusts.

The following figures are an indictment of the shameless conduct of the government which prejudiced the true interests of the nation.

New Concessions (in Hectares)	Awarded in 1944	Awarded in 1945	Totals
Exploration and production	3,755,025	1,367,449	5,122,474
Production	652,045	787,250	1,439,295
Total	4,407,070	2,154,699	6,561,769

Source: Annual Report of the Ministry of Production, 1945, p. 10.

The new concessions, together with those that had been handed over by previous governments, meant that by December 31, 1945, most of the area of the nation with petroleum potential—11,746,768 hectares—was in foreign hands.

What was worse, this irresponsible oil policy was carried out at precisely the time when oil was being eagerly sought by the great powers, by the statesmen of the hour, and by the international financial oligarchies. Toward the end of 1943, an editorial in the *Oil and Gas Journal* commented:

It is well-known that the conferences of Moscow, Cairo and Teheran dealing with the postwar organization have been devoted in good part to the development of petroleum production and distribution. The leading statesmen of the United Nations seemed fully convinced that petroleum, so indispensable in war, is also a basic element of a just and lasting peace.

Months later, at the beginning of 1944, Harold I. Ickes, Secretary of the Interior under Roosevelt and the so-called oil czar of the United States, said "Tell me what kind of agreement the United Nations reaches with regard to oil resources after the war and I will tell you what kind of peace there will be."

Audacious nationalistic steps by the small oil producers were propitious because of the extraordinary importance petroleum had acquired during the war. The open conflict at that time between Roosevelt's administration and the oil cartel also encouraged them. *Time* magazine, December 27, 1943, used a Hollywood movie title as the headline of its report: "The Honeymoon Is Over." The story was not a comedy about a platinum blonde but dealt with the fight between pugnacious Harold Ickes and the big oil companies. The story was a good lesson for the small nations which produced the prize fuel.

Ickes had, some months before, named a commission, headed by Orville Harden, vice president of Standard Oil of New Jersey, to study the principal postwar oil problems. The commission's report was kept secret until the *New York Times* broke the story and Ickes—whom the gossips of Washington called "Mr. Temper"—reacted hotly. He published the full report which revealed basic disagreement between the study commission and the government. The viewpoint of the companies dominated the commission, whose report opposed all state intervention in the oil industry and asked only for "full diplomatic support abroad." The secretary of the interior, on the other hand, favored government ownership of a part of the stock of the big companies and, in certain cases, complete government ownership.

Despite these divergences, both sides agreed publicly on three points: (1) that the United States was rapidly consuming its oil reserves and was in danger of dependence in the future upon imported oil; (2) that most of the capital investment in oil was flowing toward the Middle East; and (3) that the United States should undertake an aggressive commercial policy in the Middle East and immediately formulate a postwar oil policy.

The column which I wrote for the newspaper *El País* reflected the anguish resulting from seeing how impotent the official circles of Venezuela were at a time when oil was major preoccupation of the big powers:

> The most interesting aspect of the Ickes vs. Companies quarrel is their lack of concern for the small countries which produce oil. Both sides are thinking only from their own national viewpoint, a far cry from the beautiful promises contained in the Atlantic Charter. In reality, these debates are of tremendous importance to us. Our destiny and the future of Venezuela is at stake. It almost makes one despair to see how we continue to play children's games with our heads in the sand, while the future of Venezuela, for generations to come, is being decided in other latitudes.[16]

Press reports of the growing interest of the United States government in Middle Eastern oil were confirmed early in 1944 when the acting Secretary of State, Edward Stettinius, announced that an Anglo-North American Oil Conference would take place and a vast program of oil development would be undertaken in which the Reconstruction Finance Corporation would invest $400 million. As a corollary of these statements, the UPI reported from Washington on March 12: "A high official source said that the United States and Great Britain plan to control world petroleum and through it, the future peace."

Faced with the prospect that the world oil industry was going to be under the command of Washington and London, we increased our clamor in Venezuela at the lack of official interest in the conference. We even suggested that as the world's leading crude oil exporter and the principal supplier of the Allies during the final years of the war, our own country be represented at the conference. Because of its insolence and evident timidity before the Allies, our government did not follow this reasonable suggestion. Fortunately, the Anglo-American Oil Conference did not accomplish much. The agreement signed by the two nations on September 24, 1945, was a vague and elastic document of which someone said: "It is a Japanese kimono which covers everything but touches nothing."

Perhaps it was also due to timidity that Venezuela had never declared war upon the Axis. A difficult situation resulted early in 1945. The United States let it be known officially that those countries that had merely broken diplomatic relations with the Axis powers would not be able to attend the peace conference. Diógenes Escalante, Venezuela's Ambassador to Washington, returned to Caracas at that time, met with me, and with complete frankness informed me that the Soviet Union was responsible for this decision regarding the peace conference. The only solution was for the countries that had not declared war to hasten to do so. President Medina hesitated to take this step, and Escalante told me that the President's hesitation was due, in large part, to his fear that AD would criticize the government for its lack of a more energetic foreign policy and for placing Venezuela in the embarrassing position of declaring war on Hitler when the Russian and North American armies were already in the streets of Berlin. I assured this extraofficial emissary of the government that AD party directors were Venezuelans before anything else and would react as such with regard to foreign policy problems. Our National Executive Committee then publicly urged the government to declare war on the Axis. Furthermore, in a series of press articles, leaders of the party strongly criticized the idea of excluding Venezuelan representatives from the peace conference since we had contributed so much to the Allied victory with the unlimited flow of oil supplies. On February 15, 1945, the government declared that Venezuela was in "a state of belligerency" with Germany and Japan. This was just an elegant way of avoiding use of the term "war" when the fighting was practically over.

Thus, Venezuela was eligible to attend the conferences which were given unmerited importance by the nations of America. Here again, AD leadership had demonstrated its willingness to rise above domestic political controversy and to act in the supreme national interest.

A Great Opportunity Lost Because of Electoral Maneuvers

It became increasingly evident that the competition from low-priced, high-volume oil production from the Middle East was a grave threat to Venezuela. There was still, however, a tremendous need for petroleum for the remaining mobilized armies and war industries. Domestic discord between the United States government and the oil companies and the differences of the two great Anglo-Saxon powers regarding the oil wealth of the Middle East also militated in our favor. Then there was the conjectural Soviet control of the oil in central Europe and the diplomatic offense that Moscow was launching toward the oil reserves of the Persian Gulf. Finally, the United States and British governments, paying little heed to the protests of the private companies, were intervening aggressively in the oil business.

This would have been just the right time for Venezuela to have insisted upon an effective partnership in the production of oil and to have gotten a fair share of the profits as well as a voice in the operations of the industry. It would also have been the appropriate moment for Venezuelan oil workers to have obtained the kind of wages and benefits organized labor received in the United States, even though employers probably would have protested it was antipatriotic to make those demands during the war.

However, there is no evidence that the government of Venezuela at that time was aware of the opportunities and dangers confronting the national oil industry. The only administrative action was the overhasty delivery of concessions to the foreign companies—historical evidence of the lack of lucidity and foresight by the statesmen who then guided the destinies of our republic.

Provincial politics seemed to occupy all of Venezuelan official attention. Venezuela and its oil were on the lips of Roosevelt, Churchill, and Stalin, but the people in Miraflores Palace were only concerned that in the oil zone of Zulia state, Acción Democrática had gained control of the municipal council. As a result, when the votes of the October 1944 elections were counted, the poll-watchers of the opposition parties were excluded and candidates of the official party, Partido Democrático Venezolano, were proclaimed victors. The oil workers went on strike and filled the streets of Cabinas and Lagunillas. The government was forced to order a recount in the presence of the opposition poll-watchers. An overwhelming victory for the AD candidates had been achieved.

The loss of this electoral skirmish by the government, which would have been accepted in democratic countries, brought consternation to Venezuelan officials. On December 4, 1944, the Zulia state President, Benito Roncajolo wrote President Medina Angarita stating that the opposition triumph in the Maracaibo zone was "a very black cloud on the horizon." He had arranged for a petition to nullify these elections to be presented to the Supreme Court and concluded with a paragraph revealing that the judicial power was then a docile appendix of the autocratic, semitotalitarian government: "and I would like to suggest, furthermore, that you confidentially explain to the Court what you would like to have them do—either to declare the election null or to reject the petition so this matter may have the proper political character for your loyal friends."

Since the state of Zulia is important as the principal center of oil production, these elections were very revealing. They showed that despite official pressures and fraud, AD, with candidates in only four out of the nine districts, had obtained 34 percent of the vote. The official PDV party, with the open support of the government, got 54 percent of the vote while the Communist party, using the name of Union Popular, obtained only 4 percent. These results exploded the myth of communist influence among the proletariat of Venezuela.

Although the 1944 elections were only for municipal councilmen and state legislatures, they had a special political importance. It became particularly evident in Caracas that conflict between the people and the government was reaching its climax. The public meetings of AD attracted thousands of people from all social levels. The Communist party, acting as shock troops for the government, injected an element of street violence into the elections. The North American writer, Austin F. Macdonald, described this conflict as the forerunner of the stormy political days ahead:

> This election was of much greater importance than the offices in dispute. The political campaign acquired proportions hitherto unknown in Venezuela. The official PDV party bought foodstuffs in the agricultural areas and sold them at low prices in the poor zones of the capital. Airplanes distributed political literature in a spectacular fashion. The communists lacked sufficient support to present their own candidates and therefore supported those of the government. Some of Medina's closest advisers urged him to reject communist support but were not heeded. AD carried on a vigorous campaign but when the votes were counted the forces of Medina had a comfortable majority. No one could doubt that the President would be able to name his own successor with very limited opposition in Congress.[17]

Only an obstinate determination to suppress opposition could explain the government's activity. Even before the elections, there was no possibility that the solid majority provided to the president in both houses could be changed. Despite the electoral reform, Congress, and not the people, elected the President. Instead of having a universal ballot, voting rights were reserved for those citizens 21 years of age or older who could read and write. The immoral compatibility between the legislature and the president was maintained by the docility of a Congress made up public employees. Only two mediocre achievements were attained by the reform: women could vote in municipal elections, and deputies for the lower house of Congress were elected by direct vote. But even these two reforms were not put into effect until after the next presidential election.

A Tropical Fight for Power

Toward the middle of 1945, the Venezuelan political scene became highly charged. The official political party (PDV), which had been organized and promoted on direct orders of the president, engaged in feverish activity.

The Caracas populace with its mischievous humor labeled the PDV party the "trolley" because its energy all came from on high. The tolerance of the people for political organization, born in the presidential palace and nurtured liberally with public funds, was exhausted when this party formed an alliance with the unpopular Communist party. Prepared to confront the government, former President López Contreras organized his own faction and the scarcely dissimulated fight between the divided groups of the governing circle was the subject of press reports, the topic of comment in the halls of Congress, in the city's coffee shops, and in military barrack conversations.

The news that a faction of the military was supporting López instead of Medina reached the streets, and the civilian population waited anxiously. It was feared that this fight between the two generals for control of the government might mean civil war. History had taught the Venezuelans that their generals rarely settled their differences by civilized debate but rather by resort to arms.

I have written elsewhere of how AD boldly moved into this breach in the hitherto solid wall of *gómecismo*, behind which the country was still being governed, ten years after the death of the dictator.

We urged free elections, administrative honesty, and economic nationalism and were aided by the extraordinary events taking place in international life. In the postwar period, there was great political unrest and people everywhere were asking for freedom—with votes or with guns. In England, Winston Churchill and the Tories were replaced by Laborite candidates. In France and Italy, the first elections after the war were won by parties of the left. In Latin America, in Peru, Cuba, Guatemala, and El Salvador, the military was replaced by civilians and governmental oligarchies by democratic forces.

Questions for Acción Democrática

The situation of the leaders of Acción Democrática now became very difficult, even painful, because of the seriousness of the national crisis. We could tell in our daily and direct contact with the people that there were two main, although somewhat contradictory, currents of opinion. On the one hand, there was an aggressive anger because of the disdainful way in which two different men set themselves up as lords over the destiny of Venezuela. On the other hand, there was the fearful presentiment that this rivalry between the two heirs of the old *gómecista* tradition, which held that the people had nothing to say regarding the selection of their government, would inevitably conclude with an armed struggle.

We had tried to encourage among the people faith in democracy and confidence in themselves and in their immense power. In this critical hour the Venezuelan people turned their eyes toward us as if demanding that we find a rational and democratic solution to the impasse. Our party responded by intensifying its work of organization and indoctrination and attacked both *medinismo* and *lópecismo*.

In an effort to dignify the popular movement and to win allies from other sectors, we abruptly broke with the communists in the labor movement. The communists had always used organized labor unscrupulously as a chess piece to be moved about according to their political play of the moment. We now sought to associate with other social forces not connected with the government, such as the Federation of Chambers of Commerce and Industry. This group had recently been organized by a spirited group of businessmen who immediately incurred the wrath of the government because they were not subservient to official influence.

The country, however, was, ruled by a government with a balanced budget, thanks to the petroleum windfall. The government was apparently backed by a powerful army and was determined to deny its citizens free access to the voting booth. It really seemed ingenuous to hope that the civic resistance of the people alone would be enought to prevent these rival oligarchic cliques from settling the problem of power through resort to armed force.

Our efforts, whether they were oral or written, were addressed exclusively to the people. We did not go in for conspiracy. We had full confidence that our campaign to establish the democracy desired by the nation would, in the long run, be rewarded.

Without our having planned or proposed it, our political activity was bringing us toward the point of encounter with the discontent existing among the younger military officers. Already the voices from the streets had penetrated the walls of the barracks.

A Glandular Specialist—Contact with the Military Conspiracy

The first news we had of the unsuspected discontent which the government policies were causing among young army officers came to us in a surprising and disconcerting way. One day in June 1945, Edmundo Fernández came to my house. We had been friends as students in the university together. We both played the forward position on the championship soccer team then but had seen little of each other since; I had gone into public life while he had been busy with his professional career. He was a doctor of fine reputation, a specialist in glandular disorders.

Fernández, without preamble, gave the surprising news that a group of army officers who were unhappy with the present situation wanted to talk with me. My reaction was not that of a political adventurer but of one who measured his responsibility as a leader of a great popular movement.

Let Fernández describe my reaction in his own words:

> Rómulo was momentarily surprised by the officers' request because he had not had any contact with the armed forces. He was skeptical and suspicious, and my arguments did not seem to convince him. He really thought that any military uprising would basically hide some fascist intention and that his party—which had always kept its faith in the people—would be used as a front for some antidemocratic maneuver in government sustained by bayonets.

I could not act upon this news alone since teamwork and mutual trust always characterized the conduct of the leaders of AD. One hour after the interview with Fernández, I met the leader of our party to discuss what to do about this unexpected development. After much talk, we decided to listen to the officers but to be extremely cautious about making any commitments. I asked that another member of our leadership accompany me to the interview and the choice fell upon Raúl Leoni—a man respected and beloved by all in our organization. The interview took place on the night of July 6. The account which Lieutenant Colonel Carlos Marales gave of this meeting, which was to have so much importance for the future of the country, is worth repeating:

> The date was at 11 P.M. at the home of Edmundo Fernández. We met at 9 P.M. in the Carabobo Park and went in the automobile of Lieutenaut Horacio López Conde. . . . The question which would determine our success or failure was: Would we be able to convince Betancourt to go along with us ? . . . We arrived at the hour agreed upon. Major Marcos Pérez Jiménez and Lieutenants Martin Márquez Añez, Francisco A. Gutiérrez, Horacio López Conde, and myself. Fernández awaited us at the door and took us to a small sitting room where two civilians were waiting. Which one of them was Betancourt? They were introduced, Rómulo Betancourt and Raúl Leoni.[18]

As the highest ranking officer, Major Marcos Pérez Jiménez spoke for the military group. At that time, he was a minor official in the old Ministry of War and Navy. Now [1955] he has usurped presidential power.

I observed him carefully while he talked. He was dressed as a civilian with heavy tortoiseshell glasses. He stuttered often, did not know what to do with his hands while he shifted his short legs, and did not give a very martial impression but seemed more like a bookkeeper from the provinces. It was immediately clear that although he had an introverted personality, he was very loquacious, abundant in words rather than in ideas, and often confused by his own vagueness. "A man who ties himself up in knots," is the way in which he would have been described by one of our astute plainsmen. All of his wordiness finally came down to two concrete ideas: the young army officials were against both López and Medina and they wanted to overthrow the government. "And you, Señor Betancourt, are the person that we believe should take over the government," was the final sentence of this voluble introduction.

My reply was simple: Leoni and I were there representing our political party. We could not go beyond the instructions we had received, which were to listen to the officers with the interest they merited as members of a sector of the Venezuelan community.

Fernández said later, recalling this event, "I remember these words were repeated various times: 'We cannot act on our own but only as a party.'" Major Carlos Morales, referring to this first contact, said, "Betancourt promised to consult with his fellow party members and to give us their reaction in another meeting."[19]

Once the ice was broken—and after the echoes of the windy speech by Pérez Jiménez had died down—we obtained more precise details. Some of the other officers described the situation in the army. Even superficial changes introduced by the civil administration after 1936 had not been implemented. Arbitrary methods dating back to the time of Gómez were still used to run the military and select the officers. The young officers had organized themselves as the Patriotic Military Union (Unión Patriótica Militar) and had defined their objectives in a document they signed which stated: "It is time to put an end to the incompetence, the dishonesty and the bad faith which characterize our government." They invoked "the historic responsibility which this time places upon youth of the world," and they expressed their faith in democracy, declaring emphatically that they did not seek to defend personal or class interests but that they proposed "to have a government based on the universal and direct vote of the Venezuelan citizenry, a constitutional reform which would truly represent the national will, and the establishment of a truly professional army."[20]

History is not a succession of calm decisions of a puritan character. Rather it is rough interplay of actions and reactions. It is filled with complex situations such as the one which leaders of AD now had to confront. We were firm believers in civilian government. On the basis of our deeply held doctrine, we were against any kind of intervention by the army in a nation's political life, but the dynamic military development was a result of our own enunciation of political goals passionately received by the people. This had brought us into contact with a sizable group of the military, a contact not sought by ourselves. Rather, we were surprised because we would never have imagined that the armed forces' support for a government led by general-presidents was so weak.

We would have been mediocre political leaders, indeed, had we closed the doors of our party when military officials from all the services came to repeat what we were daily insisting upon in public—that the continuation of a personalist regime which had usurped popular sovereignty and denied Venezuelans the right to freely select their own government was inconsistent with the dignity of the nation.

As a result of various interviews, we concluded that the military group included men of true democratic belief who did not want the army itself to take over power as a result of the change in government. There were other men who showed themselves from the start to be wildly ambitious. However, it was clear to us that all of them were ready to take violent action, with or without us as they had strong pretexts for action because of the mishandling of the armed forces by the government.

During one of the nocturnal interviews, when I was accompanied by Gonzalo Barrios, another leading AD figure, we had contact for the first time with Captain Mario Ricardo Vargas, who had been one of the most active organizers of the conspiracy. He impressed us greatly. The pallor of the implacable lung illness which killed him four years later was hardly to be seen. His features were illuminated by the burning intensity of his eyes, so characteristic of those who are consumed by the ambition for glory. He was the key man of the conspiracy, and to this first meeting with us he brought lists with the names of hundreds of officers located in key posts who were pledged to the vast plot.

It was not only Captain Vargas who inspired us with confidence in our lengthy talks with the officers, many of which went on for hours, We dis-

covered not only the adventurous traits of some, but the widespread convictions among many others that it was necessary to destroy the vicious military
tradition of the general-president elected by rubber-stamp congresses, so
that the nation might democratically elect a civilian government. So it was
that the officers, some with sincerity and some with secret discontent,
agreed with us. We insisted AD was a revolutionary popular party, which
meant to govern; not a club of anemic theorizers. We would never allow
ourselves to be brought like poor relatives, secretly, into Miraflores Palace by
the servants' door. We would only assume power if free elections could be
held and a program of bold social reform initiated. In other words, we insisted upon control of any de facto regime, should it finally become necessary
to overthrow the government, but only until the nation could express its true
desire through free elections.

The Escalante Solution

The conditional expression—"If we should reach the point of revolution"—
reflected our state of mind at that time. We wished to avoid violence up to the
last moment. Now that we knew what was going on behind the scenes among
the military, we tried with greater boldness and more aggressively than before to work out an electoral solution to the political crisis. This was not
because of any formal allegiance to the evolutionary theories of democratic
socialism, nor was it because we had a horror of revolutionary violence. We
knew well that the latter has been the midwife of great historical events. Our
own conduct was determined, above all, by our conviction that we would
inevitably come to power, through natural gravity, if the people were allowed to vote.

   Thus we concluded—and we shared our conviction with the leaders of the
Unión Patriótica Militar—that we should try to convince Diógenes Escalante, a governmental figure who had modern political ideas and democratic beliefs, to accept the presidential candidacy. Raúl Leoni and I traveled to
the United States to interview Escalante who was then ambassador to
Washington. We made this trip without any previous contact or agreement
with the government of President Medina.

   It was a humid summer afternoon in Washington. Seated in the Hotel
Statler lobby, without having opened our luggage, we dramatically described
the situation in Venezuela for Escalante. We frankly told him that if the
government did not come up with a candidate who would reform the Constitution to give direct universal and secret vote to Venezuela, the outbreak of
a civil-military revolution was inevitable. Before voicing his agreement to
become a candidate on terms which would restore honor to the government,
Escalante sat there and looked at us in silence for a long time—maybe ten or
twenty minutes. It was the disconcerting stare of a man whose nervous system was already disintegrating for reasons that we wre not to know until two

months later, when he had to retire abruptly from the political arena because of a nervous breakdown.

This is not a facile retrospective explanation of what happened, as some suspicious person might imagine. It is the same one I gave to the National Constituent Assembly on January 20, 1947.

In my message as president of the revolutionary junta, I stated:

> It should be recalled what the party's attitude was when its cooperation was sought by the Unión Patriótica Militar. Like any other political party. Acción Democrática sought power. Its men and women were not anarchists. Their aim was not only to destroy that which they considered prejudicial to them; they wanted to build a new order based on effective democracy, economic nationalism, and social justice. The proposal of the Unión Patriótica Militar was very tempting to the party leadership, especially after evidence had been prepared that the officers could effectively control all of the armed forces. . . . However, the leaders of Accion Democrática were not political adventurers nor were they overwhelmed by their thirst for power. In cordial discussions with the military officers, it was unanimously decided that a peaceful solution should be found and that was when we went to talk with Diógenes Escalante in Washington. We promised him that we would not oppose his candidacy if he gave the nation concrete evidence of his promise to guarantee freedom of the vote, honesty in the management of public funds, and the determination to modernize our national institutions, including the army.[21]

The "National Candidacy" of Biaggini

Following the elimination of the Escalante candicacy, the AD leadership proposed a new formula: to agree upon some eminent citizen to assume the presidency—someone who had no political affiliation—with the pledge to hold general elections within one year. There would have to be some constitutional changes, but this proposal would be quite possible to carry out within the existing legal system.

This conciliatory proposal was put to President Medina personally by Rómulo Gallegos, who recalled the effort later in a speech he made in Mexico on September 13, 1949:

> There was already an understanding with the military conspirators. However, without betraying their confidence, we made one last effort to avoid the interruption of normal life in the country and to give President Medina an opportunity to occupy an honored place in history. According to my proposal, it would have been due to his initiative that the formula be adopted. However, he replied to us intemperately. We now could no longer avoid the October coup.

Medina Angarita was true to his autocratic tradition. He would accept no other solution than that of picking his own successor and imposing him upon the nation. To make his choice, the president retired to his Mt. Sinai—in this case, the country residence of El Junquito—and he returned early in September with his "graven tablets" of the law. On September 12, a spokesman in the Miraflores Palace grandiosely told the newsmen there: "Papa habemos" ("We have a new pope"). The divine dove had come to rest on the head of Angel Biaggini, the Minister of Agriculture. He was an official without national stature or political base. He would have been a simple puppet of his predecessor.

Foreign students of our political life, who cannot be accused of partiality, agree with this opinion. "The new candidate was a colorless figure, distinguished only for his loyalty when he occupied earlier secondary government posts. As president, he would have been only a tool of Medina's," wrote Austin F. Macdonald.[22]

Another U.S. writer, the well-known international commentator, Donald Marquand Dozer, had the same opinion:

> Inasmuch as the Venezuelan constitution prohibited the immediate reelection of a president, Medina selected as his successor his relatively little-known Minister of Agriculture, Angel Biaggini. This was interpreted as evidence of Medina's policy of *continuismo*, which violated the spirit of the constitution and was unpalatable to the opposition. The rightists immediately responded by nominating ex-President Eleázar López Contreras, who in the popular mind was identified closely with the remnants of the hated old dictatorial régime of Juan Vicente Gómez. Certain leftist opposition leaders, confronted by what they regarded as only a choice of evils and possessing no means of influencing the outcome of the election in the National Congress, readied themselves for revolutionary change.[23]

Venezuelans will remember clearly the outcry of opposition that the announcement of this candidacy provoked. This outcry in turn brought more active promotion of the López Contreras candidacy by his supporters and at the same time accelerated the pace of conspiratorial activity in the military. I was amazed when Arturo Uslar Pietri, the Secretary of the Presidency and a man having the utmost confidence of President Medina, also known as a militant opponent of AD, said to me at the time: "the political situation is most alarming. Biaggini cannot last in the government. The sergeants will overthrow him."

The optimistic speeches and public documents of the government were in great contrast with the anarchy that really existed in the government. There was a new proof of governmental duplicity when AD issued a public letter to all the other political parties and groups explaining its proposal of a "national candidate." Published October 14, this letter referred to the recent free elections in Guatemala, Cuba, and Peru, which had enabled the people to carry out a revolutionary process by defeating military and oligarchic governments at the polls. We asked for the same chance and concluded the document with words of prophetic significance: "Our conscience is clear before history. Future generations will not be able to say that we did not make every effort to reach a peaceful solution and avoid violence amid one of the most dramatic political crises in the history of the republic."

The official Partido Democrático Venezolano answered immediately, with complacency and arrogant confidence, expressing surprise at our claim that the nation was in crisis. "The only thing that is happening and thank God that it is so—is that a new first magistrate is going to be elected by the existing constitutional means." Nothing extraordinary was seen in the fact that a people, aware of its own desire and conscious of how the representative system worked for other nations, should be excluded from any say in the selection of its government. The PDV leadership professed to be astonished because of the unprecedented haste and impatience with which we wanted "*by means of a peaceful coup d'état* [my italics] to change the existing system."

Once again, it was proved that God blinds those whom he wishes to destroy. On the day following this publication, which referred to a "peaceful coup d'état," the government was overthrown by a violent revolution.

On the Eve of the Insurrection

The only solution now for a democratic Venezuela was through armed force. There had to be haste in acting because General López Contreras was also stepping up his plans for an armed coup. The country knew what he had in mind when he came out in a speech made October 14 against "the threat of institutional retrogression that looms over the country." With implied threat, he added that he had his uniform of general-in-chief at home; "and it is not hanging in the closet."

Now the contacts between the Unión Patriótica Militar and Acción Democrática took place daily. Luis Beltrán Prieto, in his bookstore, received messages from the barracks. The military messengers, to identify themselves, were supposed to acquire a copy of the book, *China in Arms*. There was such a run on this book that Prieto called me on the phone and said: "Either we finish off this business or you choose another book. I do not have any more copies left."

The last meeting, when the decision was taken to go ahead with the coup, was held October 16. Captain Horacio López Conde later wrote about it:

> It was held at the house of Delgado Chalbaud's mother in El Paraiso. Those in attendance were Major Delgado Chalbaud, Captain Mario Vargas, Lieutenants Edito Ramírez and Francisco Gutiérrez, and myself. We had to deal with the fact that our conspiracy had been discovered. I hurriedly left in search of Rómulo Betancourt and I found him at 9 P.M. at the Municipal Council and took him to our meeting. . . .
>
> Rómulo had been against the idea of a "revolution" since the beginning. He believed that "armed coups" breed quarrels and future uprisings, but that night we were all in agreement. The urgency for action was clear. We had to take action this same week and then "the die was cast."[24]

We went ahead with our commitments. Acción Democrática called a mass meeting on the night of October 17 at the Nuevo Circo of Caracas. Thousands of persons filled this bullring, the largest gathering place of the republic. The atmosphere was charged, filled with apprehension. Rómulo Gallegos made the first speech, an energetic call for democracy. It was my job to give the last speech to the electrified assembly and summarize the presentation already made. Never have I felt as I did that night, not as an orator voicing his own words, but interpreting the collective state of mind— an instrument carrying the feelings of the multitude.

I spoke for more than an hour. Later, my wife, who had been ill and unable to attend, asked me what I had said. I could not remember.

I must have spoken clearly enough, perhaps too clearly, in hinting what was about to happen because, when I left the meeting, I heard a man of the people say—slowly, dragging out his syllables as our people do when they wish to be dramatic: "Now it is ready, I smell gunpowder."

General Medina Angarita must have smelled it too, because there was found on his desk a report of my speech published by *El País* on October 18, underlined with red pencil. This was the date when the army and people rose against the government.

In this speech, it was clearly indicated that there might be a violent ending to the national impasse. The following paragraph, for instance, left room for little doubt:

> It is said that our proposal—for a national candidate—is the same as a peaceful coup d'état or, in other words, that we are trying to promote an evolutionary solution to the complex political situation. However, this evolutionary hope will be frustrated if the government continues in its attitude of insolent disdain toward public opinion.*

The Revolution Becomes the Government

The shooting began in the middle of the morning of October 18. Early that morning, someone had given President Medina the names involved and the details of the conspiracy. He had ordered the arrest of various officers and troops placed in readiness for combat. It was too late. Under the command of the imperturbable Mario Vargas, the revolutionaries took over the military academy without firing a shot and installed their command there. Then, the Miraflores garrison fell to the insurgents. The quiet city still was not aware of what was happening. The first indication that there was something extraordinary going on came when intense rifle and machine-gun fire was heard from behind the walls of the San Carlos garrison. There the revolutionaries and government defenders engaged in fierce hand-to-hand combat, one of the bloodiest incidents of the day.

The job of our party, outside in the streets, was to bring volunteers to the garrisons where they could get arms, and also, to explain to the public what was going on, mobilizing opinion on behalf of this crusade against an anach-

*El País, Caracas, January 6, 1946, published a stenographic text of the speech.

ronistic government which denied our people the right to vote and treated the nation as the personal property of the governing clique.

The fighting was fast and furious. This is not the place to detail what happened, but it should be said that both sides fought with the courage worthy of the Venezuelan warrior tradition. The blood of more than 400 military men and civilians was shed in the fierce fighting. Thirty-six hours after the fighting had begun, the revolutionary junta government was established in Miraflores Palace.

The government fell so rapidly that there was not nearly as much popular action as we had foreseen. The AD party members fought side by side with the military only in several isolated skirmishes in the city and in the hills around the military academy. Thus, we were not propelled to power on an overwhelming wave of popular arms. The revolutionary government was a typical result of a military coup rather than a heroic popular insurgency. It hardly needs to be underlined that this was an unfortunate circumstance.

Whatever its origin, we were determined that the provisional government give a revolutionary turn to the country with utmost urgency. It was a color-for scene, at nine or ten P.M. on October 19. The presidential palace was without electricity so it was illuminated by gasoline lanterns.

Intermittent shots fired by hostile marksmen still slammed into the walls of the old palace. The document establishing the revolutionary junta was signed by a mixed civilian and military group, all of us still tense from the battle. I presided over the junta which also included Raúl Leoni, Luis B. Prieto, and Gonzalo Barrios, all from Acción Democrática; and Major Delgado Chalbaud, Captain Mario Vargas, and Edmundo Fernández.

It is interesting to note how the well-known Colombian historian, Germán Arciniegas, a sworn enemy of military dictatorships, coincided to a degree with the Venezuelan editor, Ramón David León, an apologist for military governments, in stressing the fact that the revolutionary junta was presided over by a civilian and had a majority of civilian members. Arciniegas said that the "military did not dare to occupy all of the positions" and "presidency of the junta was turned over to Betancourt."[25] Ramón David León affirmed that the military "turned over power to civilians because of an excess of unselfishness."[26]

The idea that the military protagonists of the 1945 coup ceded their power to civilians as a result of malice or innocence or at least as a favor should be immediately corrected. The 1945 revolution was not a traditional military early morning coup similar to Batista's in Cuba in 1952 and the many previous ones in unstable Latin America. Rather, it was characterized by a revolutionary process in the streets with the active participation of the masses. It had been directed, for more than a decade, by the political leadership of AD. We had a clear idea of what we were doing and would never have agreed, either publicly or in the secret meetings of the army officers, to be simply a civilian front for military government.

On the eve of the revolution, in my speech before the great meeting at the
Nuevo Circo on October 17, I stated categorically:

> Acción Democrática will never enter the government like a poor relative entering
> by the servants' door and accepting two or three so-called "technical ministries."
> We are not a party made up of literary dilettantes or romantic adventurers. We
> have been organized to give the people power. We will govern with the people. The
> key positions where the political, economic, and social policies of the nation are
> determined, must be in our hands. We are not interested in just having ministries.
> We want to put a program of national salvation into effect.[27]

We made good on these words when the October revolution triumphed.
We governed for better or for worse, trying always to make it better. The
political and administrative record of the revolutionary government bore our
imprint and was the result of our personal style. A political adversary, Rafael
Caldera, has admitted this fact and it cannot be disputed. His conclusions are
right, although not his reasons, for he has attributed to intrigue and trickery
what was really a decision by a key army sector to have Venezuela governed
by men who did not wear uniforms and who would enforce respect for the
civilian authority. Having made this observation, I quote Caldera:

> Acción Democrática reached power capitalizing on the military coup. The fact that
> power was passed from the men who had seized it to the civilian leaders was so
> unprecedented that it gained widespread sympathy for the new regime. . . . Its
> leaders felt that the junta should have a president, and it was logical that the presi-
> dent be a civilian to dissipate suspicion of the military men. The president prom-
> ised to be a *primus inter pares* [first among equals] and encouraged his fellow mem-
> bers of the junta to function from the ministry buildings rather than Miraflores.
> The junta president announced that he would take over the Ministry of Interior
> himself; however, after the others had left, "he saw the need" of staying on in
> Mirafores "to hold audiences and transmit information." Later, he added to his
> functions by receiving "reports" from the other members of the junta who were
> thus converted into his "ministers." Then he was no longer called "president of the
> junta" but, instead, "president." Thus he remained with the tremendous political
> advantage of sitting in Miraflores Palace, for it was a national habit to obey the
> visible chief of the government.[28]

The way in which the revolutionary junta was named is most interesting
and had unsuspected future implications. In the name of the party, I stated
that, as previously agreed, there should be seven members of the plural
government—four of AD, two military officials, and one independent civilian. Major Delgado Chalbaud then spoke and revealed his complex, contradictory psychology. On the one hand, he was of a vacillating nature, seemingly with little decision and faith in himself. On the other hand, on certain
occasions, he was capable of taking the most abrupt positions. He had entered the conspiracy just a few weeks before the fighting and had few connections with the officer corps because he was an engineer, brought into the
army, rather than a military man by profession. Nevertheless, he had the

decisive voice in the Unión Patriótica Militar. He insisted that this group would honor the commitments to AD, limiting to two the military members of the government, and said more or less the following:

> Within the barracks, this has largely been a movement of captains and lower officials, with a few majors also involved. We should be represented in the junta mostly by officers of lower rank. Captain Mario Vargas is a very qualified person for one of the posts. The higher officials ought to be represented by Major Julio Cesar Vargas who is present here. As it would not be ethical or desirable to have two brothers in the junta, however, the other candidate of the armed forces is myself.

By common accord, Edmundo Fernández was elected as the independent civilian member; and both military men, Vargas and Delgado Chalbaud, said there was no need to discuss who was to preside over the junta as everyone was in agreement on this point.

The name of the then Major Marcos Pérez Jiménez was never mentioned as a possible member of the government. He had been arrested early in the morning October 18 as the Medina government sought to prevent the outbreak. He remained in a cell in the Ambrosio Plaza artillery barracks during all of the violent events of October 18 and 19. When the junta was organized, he was in the military academy where Delgado Chalbaud, the Vargas brothers and other officials had left him shortly before. For some time later, at least, it seems that he blamed me, rather than his army companions, for having passed him over in naming the junta. He complained of an alleged lack of gratitude on my part—an initial attitude of resentment which later events transformed into a bitter hate. It would seem that he considered me to be obligated to him because he had been the military spokesman in our first interview and had expressed the desire of the officers that I should head the government.

The truth is that at that moment our opinions were highly tentative. We hardly had time to evaluate the character and thinking of the leaders of the military group. Furthermore, they themselves had suggested Delgado Chalbaud and Mario Vargas as their candidates for the government. We had no objections since both obviously possessed intelligence and ability. My explanation should be recognized as completely sincere, since I should like to be able to say today that we had indeed maneuvered to exclude Pérez Jiménez, having immediately detected his cruelty and greed.

We got down to work immediately. The civilian members in the new government busied themselves writing its first decree. Major Vargas and I coordinated instructions to the military garrisons of the interior and to the party headquarters, seeking to stabilize the situation throughout the country. Vargas had gotten out of bed, suffering from one of the recurrent crises of his terrible illness, to take part in the October 18 action. He went two days without sleeping or eating; his ravaged body underwent terrible strain, but he was animated by the fervor of a crusader. Those forty-eight hours together, tense with hurried decisions, one after another, linked us together with a mutual esteem and affection that in later years, first in government and then in exile, turned into real brotherhood. Some of the orders given then had to be changed before they were fully executed. I remember one official whom I sent with utmost urgency to stop a battalion of the armored corps from assaulting the newspaper *El Nacional* where it was said that a group of snipers were still active. This newspaper had been aggressively hostile to Acción Democrática, and I had engaged in bitter debates in the press with its proprietor, Miguel Otero Silva. However, it was inadmissible that a government formed for "the exercise of justice rather than reprisal," should act as if it were inspired by revenge.

While Miraflores was boiling with excitement, Delgado Chalbaud fell sound asleep, slumped on a couch with a cup of coffee spilled on his uniform and his mouth hanging open. There he lay, motionless, for hours. That night he showed himself to be a man who did not stand up well under pressure. He lacked spiritual will power.

The Next Task: To Stabilize the Revolution

The following twenty-four hours were extremely tense. The atmosphere in Miraflores was charged with danger. A throng of people, civilian and military, milled around the presidential offices. Pockets of resisting police and some civilians, including communists, still sustained violent skirmishes with army patrols and groups of AD volunteers. In the western part of the country, in the most heavily populated states of Venezuela, some garrisons still resisted, and last-ditch defenders of the fallen regime even planned to invade the center of the country. A constant stream of telegrams flowed out of Miraflores Palace with energetic messages—the air force threatened to strafe the troops of the old Gómez chieftain, General Jurado, if he did not surrender within an hour. He did so. Then a warship of the navy sailed to take the port of Guiria where the garrison still held out. Another message warned those who were entrenched in the governor's palace in Maracaibo not to risk the "fire of our tanks." Those who were trying to encourage resistance there used epic tones like a Rommel giving instructions to the Afrika Korps. We sent instructions to guarantee the lives of those who did not offer resistance to the revolution.

That night, I understood why two men of such disparate ideologies as Leon Trotsky and Winston Churchill had been so intrigued by the planning of military movements. It causes extraordinary emotion to move great masses of armed men with a message of only three lines and then to follow their movements afterward on a map. It was an unforgettable experience.

That same night, the start of a new historical period for Venezuela, the first "communiqué" of the provisional government was broadcast by radio. It was a straightforward statement, edited without any heroic flamboyance or aggressive threats. Later, in a message read to the National Constituent Assembly, I recalled the manner in which we had acted from the very beginning, "not as improvised demagogues but as men with a doctrine and faith and an overwhelming commitment to Venezuelan and American democracy.

This initial statement of the revolutionary objectives affirmed that the provisional government would have "as its immediate goal, the convocation of elections in the country so that by a direct, universal and secret vote, the Venezuelans could elect their representatives, choose the constitution that they desired and elect the future president of the republic." It was announced that the ex-presidents López Contreras and Medina Angarita, both of whom had been arrested with some of their closest political and military associates, had not suffered nor would suffer "any injury or disrespect of any kind." It was also promised that measures would be adopted to clean up public administration, "to reduce the cost of living and to improve the economic and social conditions in which the people lived." The statesmen concluded: "In this hour, the new Venezuela affirms its determination to make history."

Attitudes Toward the Revolution

It was not exaggeration to say that the overwhelming majority of Venezuelans of all social levels jubilantly greeted the events of October. Representatives of all the business organizations and the workers' unions filed through Miraflores Palace to offer their warm support. Students, teachers, professionals, farmers, and workers exuberantly celebrated the victory in the streets.

The amount of violence against persons and properties of the fallen government was unusually low. Drastic measures were adopted against pillaging. The coordination of the troops with the AD volunteers and the unions to establish public order gave efficient results. By October 21, Venezuela's government was in control of the entire country. Civilians, many without AD affiliation, were placed in administrative positions, with the exception of the ministries of Defense and Communications which went to Major Delgado Chalbaud and Captain Mario Vargas.

The reaction of the foreign press varied, except for those newspapers under the control of Latin dictators or communists. Generally speaking, the liberal and democratic press greeted with hope the possibility that Venezuela would have a truly popular government. The newspapers of the dictators, Trujillo and Somoza, orchestrated the overture of what would be a constant symphony of aggression in print against the democratic regime in Venezuela. *Diario de la Marina* in Cuba and other periodicals that admired the Franco government did not hide their alarm at our coming to power.

The communist and procommunist press was uniformly hostile to our revolution. They synchronized with their fellow believers of Caracas, who, in a manifesto issued October 18, fruitlessly urged the people to "smash the insurgents" whose "subversive plans" were announced "just thirty hours ago in the Nuevo Circo" and "to back the government headed by General Isaías

Medina Angarita." The mouthpiece of Moscow throughout America continued with similar speeches for days after the provisional government was installed. *El Popular*, voice of Lombardo Toledano in Mexico, wrote on October 26: "The Venezuela counterrevolution gives power to the profascists and the conservative forces of the country."

This regimented reaction of the communists was not the result of political stupidity or resentment at the support our party had gained from the people. The word had come from Mecca itself and was dogmatically imparted to the faithful believers. November 8, 1945, UPI reported from Moscow on a significant article published by *Nuevos Tiempos*, which reflected the thinking of the Stalinists' inner sanctum.

"All that has happened in Venezuela stinks of petroleum" was the expressive title of this commentary: "From 1943, the Medina government had tried to oblige the foreign companies to modify the terms of the concessions in the contracts which were clearly unfavorable to Venezuela," the article reported. Without saying so expressly, the Soviet periodical was trying to make connections between the October 18 coup and the oil policy of the overthrown government. It tried to make us out as nothing more than instruments of the oil cartel and, of course, we never would have been able to "represent a more democratic tendency than that of the previous government."

Foreign offices around the world took an expectant attitude. In Washington and London, the economic capitals of the Venezuela of oil, the unexpected news of the revolution meant that those responsible for the Latin American area lost more than an hour of their bureaucratic repose. The democratic governments in Latin America hastened to offer us their support. Twelve days after October 18, most of the governments throughout the world had reestablished relations with Venezuela, recognizing one after another that public opinion supported the new regime.

The foregoing pages should serve to demonstrate that the Venezuelan revolution of October 18, 1945, was the culmination of a historic process that could not be detained. Even without our bold decision to lead and channel the revolution, it would have taken place; however, it would have been simply one more mutiny from the barracks. This is the reply that should be given to those questions that have been asked regarding the conduct of the men of Acción Democrática who participated in the preparation of October 18. The explanation is urgently required because there are people in America of democratic convictions who have asked and continue to ask whether it would not have been possible to avoid the reactionary counterrevolution of November 24, 1948, overthrowing the constitutional government of Rómulo Gallegos, if we had taken a waiting attitude and stood aside from the violent events of October 1945.

Even if the origins of the October coup d'état are considered controversial, the debate would seem to be academic—even theological—at this point in view of the accomplishments of the government formed then: the organization of democratic institutions, the effective purging of administrative practices, and the creation of an energetic, nationalistic petroleum policy.

PART FOUR

Time of Construction

4

Free Elections and the War on Dishonesty: A Government Born in Violence Behaves With Tolerance

History has proved that authentically revolutionary social movements, whatever their ideology may be, always conduct themselves, at the start, with great tolerance toward the vanquished. Robespierre began to use the guillotine only after the "emigré" nobility began to constitute a serious danger for republican France. Bolívar's terrible decree "Spaniards and Canarians, you will surely die even though you are neutral! . . ." was issued only after the cavalry of the armies of Ferdinand VII had disemboweled the leaders of the First Republic. The Bolsheviks allowed General Kornilov to go home when he promised not to fight against the revolution, but in a few days, he was leading the White armies. Francisco Franco, a monarchist and a belligerent reactionary, was given back his command in Morocco after perfidiously swearing allegiance to the Spanish republic.

It is fatal not to learn from the experience of others. In Venezuela, the leaders of the popular democratic revolution of 1945 committed the same error which historical experience has repeatedly warned against. Former Presidents López and Medina and some twenty of their closest collaborators were expelled from the country. The rest of the supporters of the old order were given complete freedom of movement in the country, which many of them used for bitter continued subversion against a government prejudicial to their personal interests. Newspapers which had prospered under the Gómez regime and were connected with the economic and political interests of those removed from power had full freedom to attack the new order.

The people did not understand these chivalrous gestures and manifested their discontent when it was announced that the leaders of the post-Gómez era had been allowed to leave the country without being taken to court. The Minister of Interior, Valmore Rodríguez, had to explain on a national radio network that the government had acted in this way out of strength, rather than weakness. I also did not want to seem to be influenced by motives of personal vengeance. We were anxious to get going with a series of concrete political and administrative ideas which had matured in three years of study. We plunged into this work as soon as we arrived at Miraflores.

Miraflores, "The Decree Machine"

This is what some of the newspapers began to call the new government and they were right. The junta issued one law after another in the form of decrees published in the *Gaceta Oficial*. The revolution created its own legal system with some haste because, for all we knew, our time in the government would leave only a collection of laws for those who would come in the future. This had been the classical tendency of all revolutions, even though their proponents would have wished otherwise. When Bolívar conversed in Bucaramanga with Perú De la Croix in 1826, he recalled his legislative efforts in Angostura in 1819 as a way of convincing the world that an organized republic now existed, even though royalist troops controlled almost all of Venezuelan territory. The leaders of the Paris commune in 1871 feverishly passed laws when the cannons of the counterrevolution were already destroying their barricades. Leon Trotsky told how Lenin wrote decrees even at the dining table because of his fear that czarism would reconquer the Winter Palace and no trace would remain of the Bolsheviks in power.

The decrees of the junta are compiled in two thick volumes, and I will comment now on those related to voting procedures and administrative honesty. Those which dealt with the economic and fiscal transformation of the country, with the determined and successful effort to provide the people with sufficient food, with culture and social justice, will be dealt with in later chapters.

The Junta Members Commit Hara-Kiri as Presidential Candidates

A highly significant political decree was promulgated October 22, just three days after the junta was formed, by which its members eliminated themselves as candidates for the presidency. I wrote this decree myself. Many people do not understand why I urged this decision when I was the most directly affected. I would have had a better chance than any of the other junta members as a presidential candidate. Others have believed that this decree was a Machiavellian maneuver to block the possible presidential ambitions of the two military members of the junta. People who think in this manner do not understand that for men of true democratic political conviction, politics is something more than decorating a cake.

I issued this decree, not because I was hesitant to accept the responsibilities of government or to maneuver against the other members of the plural executive, but simply because I was convinced that the next president would be a candidate of Acción Democrática and that he would be Rómulo Gallegos. There was no doubt that AD had the support of the majority in the republic, and that the party had been supporting the candidacy of the famous novelist since 1941. I deemed it my duty to facilitate the people's free choice.

The various legislative bodies, none of which had been freely elected, were dissolved by a decree. November 17, scarcely one month after the revolution, a commission was named to draw up a new electoral statute and the draft of a new constitution. Only one of the members of this commission was from AD—Andrés Eloy Blanco, one of our most eminent national intellectuals and a symbol of civic responsibility. With him were various independent legal experts, as well as distinguished members of opposition parties such as Lorenzo Fernández of the Copei party and Luis Hernández Solis of the Unión Republicana Democrática. Other members were Jesús Enrique Lossada, with one of the best reputations of all the public men in the country; Nicomedas Zuloaga, a prestigious lawyer; Germán Suárez Flamerich, a university professor who was then considered a person of democratic conviction but who, years later, played a tragic role as a civilian puppet of the Pérez Jiménez military dictatorship. There were three other distinguished jurists: Martín Pérez Guevara, Ambrosio Oropeza, and Luis Eduardo Monsanto.

The Most Democratic Electoral Statute of America

On March 15, 1946, the revolutionary junta decreed the enactment of the draft prepared by this commission without substantial changes. This electoral statute can be considered without exaggeration as the most democratic ever promulgated up to that time in all of America. Its second article gave voting rights to all Venezuelans, 18 years of age and older, without distinction as to sex, and excepting only those serving prison sentences. Its third article declared all Venezuelans 21 years of age and older eligible for public office.

The decree gave to the Supreme Electoral Council, made up of representatives of all the political parties, the majority from the opposition, such ample powers that I was correct when I described it as a "fourth estate," as Bolívar himself had suggested. The only connection the administration would have with the electoral process was to provide sufficient funds to the Supreme Electoral Council. Immediately following the publication of this decree, an electoral campaign "of an intensity without precedence in the history of the country" was begun as it was well described by a special committee of the

International Labor Office which visited Venezuela at this time. In a few months thirteen political parties were legalized, and the air was filled with the voices of their orators in thousands of public meetings. Political propaganda covered every inch of free wall space, while printing presses worked overtime to popularize political programs and promote candidacies.

An Opposition Without a Constructive Program

Three parties took the lead in a violent attack against our popular and democratic government: Copei (Independent Committee for Elections), Unión Republicana Democrática, and the Communist party of Venezuela.

Copei had been formed in the mid-1930s as a militant Catholic group and had collaborated with the government of ex-President López Contreras. During the presidency of Medina Angarita, this group had little activity, and its leader, Rafael Caldera, dedicated himself to professional activities and to teaching sociology in the Central University after a brief time in Congress.

During the early months of the revolutionary government, he had the important post of national attorney general, but he left this post to head one of the most belligerent opposition movements. His party was a complex mixture in which Social Christians, who invoked the liberal *Rerum Novarum* of Pope Leo XIII, mingled with reactionary followers of Gómez. There were also adventurers who were not really interested in elections but only in trying to stir up trouble in the army and disrupting the democratic process by armed violence.

In some parts of the country, especially the Andean regions, this party tended toward religious intolerance, due to the influence of the Spanish priests who ressembled the Carlists of the old country so well described in the masterpiece of Valle Inclán.

Unión Republicana Democrática (URD), organized by Jóvito Villalba, also had a heterodox character. It included the remaining followers of President Medina. Its leader had never tried to organize a party during those years when Acción Democrática was fighting so hard for liberty in the streets and was organizing itself throughout the republic. During this time, Villalba was taking potshots as an independent in the Senate. When the October movement occurred, he hastily organized a party calling for "a government of national concentration" to preside over new elections. This idea had no logical base because—except for Acción Democrática in the opposition and the official Partido Democrática Venezolano supporting the government—there were no other parties at the time the junta was formed. Years later, Vallalba admitted in a congressional speech that AD would have triumphed in any election even if held according to the suggestion of his party. Like Copei, URD included persons really working for democracy as well as reactionary plotters who were implacable enemies of freedom.

Thus, Copei and URD were both parties which had contradictory elements. There were those who had differences with AD regarding program and policy but still believed, along with our party, that matters should be decided in civic discussion through electoral channels. On the other hand, there were others who wanted a new coup, a reactionary counterrevolution, and the installation of dictatorial government.

Finally, there was the Communist party. It was divided into two factions which opposed each other but which coincided in their hatred of the popular revolution. They took the lead in opposing the democratization of the economy and the government, carried out to the degree possible within the historic conditions prevailing in Latin America and Venezuela. According to them, our revolutionary effort had two capital defects: it lacked the apostolic benediction of the Stalinist Sanhedrin; and it was led by a political party that was truly Venezuelan and American in its outlook, opposed to political slogans imported from elsewhere.

Acción Democrática confronted its political adversaries, old and new, with its traditional enthusiasm. Party members did not become bureaucrats, with the exception of those who entered ministries or governorships. The leaders of the workers gave an especially good example of their own in refusing to take government jobs, because party members did not go after the government jobs as spoils of war in the traditional manner. One year after the revolution, of the 7000 government employees in the Federal District, only 300 were AD party members.

One and One-half Million Venezuelans Go to the Polls

All the parties ceased their contention to witness how 1.5 million Venezuelans filed into the polling places with almost religious fervor on October 27, 1946. Never before had more than 5 percent of the population voted. This time 36 percent cast ballots. Ninety-two out of every hundred registered persons went to vote, and there was not a single act of violence reported anywhere throughout our vast country. The returns gave the following results: Acción Democrática, 1,100,000; Copei, 180,000; URD, 54,000; Communist, 51,000. The rest of the votes were distributed among eleven other political groups. The voters elected delegates to the National Constituent Assembly:

Acción Democrática	137
Copei	19
Unión Republicana Democrática	2
Partido Communista	2

There were many workers and women among our delegates and the Congress which, for the first time, was no longer the complete preserve of males with university titles. There was overwhelming recognition that the elections were honestly carried out although a few isolated voices challenged the election results and the elements of the former government tried to stir up trouble on this account among the military. They were energetically rejected by the leaders of the armed forces because the army had supervised the elections following the precedent established in democratic Chile. In doing the same in Venezuela, we wished to underline the apolitical character of the military and exclude it from party strife. Our military forces not only underwrote the honesty of the elections but also drew up a testimonial document signed by all officers on active service. This was brought to the Capitol building for presentation to the Assembly by three lieutenant colonels dressed in their gala uniforms: Carlos Delgado Chalbaud, Marcos Pérez Jiménez, and Luis Felipe Llovera Páez. Two years later, these same three were going to usurp power and ignore the popular will expressed in the elections they themselves had supervised.

The Constituent Assembly and the Election of Rómulo Gallegos

The National Constituent Assembly concentrated its activities on the elections of the provisional government, the preparation of a democratic Constitution, and the review of the annual reports presented by the revolutionary junta and its ministers. The opposition was so aggressive that, in the last, it was as if they were using a laboratory microscope.

The Constituent Assembly legalized the de facto powers which the revolutionary government junta had taken under my presidency. The Acción Democrática party had favored the designation of a provisional president to hold office until one could be elected under the new Constitution and went on record as favoring me for this position. However, in my message to the Constituent Assembly on January 20, 1947, I insisted that it was better to ratify the mandate of the junta as constituted since the elections were not far off. There were comments at the time that I was yielding to pressure from the military so in this same message, I took the bull by the horns:

> The country knows that I do not lie. Let me say that the chiefs of the armed forces have never put any pressure on me with regard to any political or administrative question. Furthermore, I never would have accepted it. Since I became president of the junta, I have demonstrated how a civilian can be president without subject-in himself to those who have command in the barracks.[1]

The new Constitution was proclaimed on July 5, 1947. Jovito Vallalba, who openly opposed our party which had so much to do with the contents of the Constitution, said at that time: "We have a Constitution that is without any doubt—and I want to be completely impartial on this—one of the most advanced and of the best of the American continent."

In addition to the most modern principles of representation and individual guarantees (including that of *habeus corpus*) found for the first time in a Venezuelan Constitution, there was also included a bill of economic and social rights consecrating the right of each citizen to have a life free of fear and of need.

Professor Austin F. Macdonald of the University of California, whose book described the new constituion as "the most democratic document in the history of the Venezuelan nation" was particularly impressed by the 400 words used there to set forth the social guarantees for the individual and the society. Some of these were:

> Work is a right and a duty, every citizen should contribute to society by means of work (Article 61).
>
> Workers are guaranteed the right to organize and to strike (except by essential public services determined by the law) and also to vacation and Sunday pay, pensions, termination indemnities, and profit-sharing. There should be no discrimination by sex, nationality, or race in payment of wages (Article 63).
>
> An efficient system of security must be maintained and the construction of low-cost housing should be provided for the workers; [also, the inhabitants of the republic are entitled to health protection, and] the state should establish the necessary services for the prevention and treatment of disease (Articles 53–57).
>
> Special protection by the nation is given to maternity cases, "irrespective of the civil state of the mother" (Article 47).[2]

Seven words sufficed to set forth the guarantees given to private property, but seven hundred were needed to list the restriction in its use, according to Macdonald.

The Constitution also stated that "he who works the land has the right to it" and other principles which later would serve as the basis for a special law on agrarian reform. Also, after extensive debates, the AD majority succeeded in introducing a new wording for the traditional article in Venezuelan constitutions regarding the relations between the state and the Catholic Church. This reform opened the possibility that there be a new modus vivendi between the Vatican and the Venezuelan government to replace the law of ecclesiastical patronage, which went back to 1824. This was consistent with the doctrinaire position of AD on religion. We were never like the Voltairian iconoclasts of the eighteenth century but were twentieth-century revolutionists who never made a problem of the religious beliefs of the party's membership. This was considered a question of individual conscience. Our attitude toward relations between the state and the Catholic Church—the religion professed by the majority of Venezuelans—was the traditional one in Venezuela since the time of Bolívar. It can be summarized as: (a) freedom of religion without a state church; (b) recognition of the fact that since the majority of the population was Catholic, government officials should behave in such a way as not to offend popular sentiment, regardless of their own attitude on religion, whether agnostic or believers; (c) a realistic attitude which would admit the revision of the century-old laws governing state-church relationships; (d) rejection of the tradition in the Spanish church that it, rather than the state, should exercise ideological control over public schools; and (e) prohibition of the use of the pulpit for political proselytizing.

Generally speaking, the Venezuelan clergy, including its highest hierarachy, respected the sincerity of this position. Only a few foreign priests or those under foreign influence sought to oppose our conduct in these matters, which was consistent with that of the republic's founding fathers.

The most controversial part of the new Constitution was Article 77, which the opposition called "the Alfaro Ucero clause" after the congressman who submitted it. This clause was similar to but weaker than one in the Colombian Constitution under liberal governments, but the united front of the opposition and the press fought furiously against this measure. Even some of our party leaders became alarmed at the thought that a party which had fought for public liberty so long would seem to be limiting its exercise.

Let me reveal an interesting historical episode regarding this matter. I thought that eighty congressmen should listen to the opinion of the military, and so I had a meeting at my house where Commander Delgado Chalbaud—with the precision of thought derived from his French education—gave a very persuasive argument. He predicted that the constitutional government would have to confront just as many subversive disturbances as those which we were having during the de facto period. Commander Mario Vargas seconded his arguments and stressed that a democratic government should have sufficient power to defend its stability.

Article 77 authorized the president with his cabinet to decide when "there existed sufficient evidence of plans or activities seeking to overthrow the established authorities." There could be preventive arrest of the persons against whom there were "serious reasons to consider them engaged in such plans or activities." These measures would have to be submitted within ten days to the Congress or the permanent commission that acted during its recess. After having been approved, and if continued for seventy days more, they would have to be submitted to the Supreme Court "which would decide whether they should be continued or suspended."

This article was approved and I decided that I should speak frankly to the country about it when the new Constitution was proclaimed in the Salón Elíptico of the Federal Palace on July 5, 1947:

> It would be easy to just emphasize those aspects of the Constitution which have merited almost unanimous approval and to maintain a cautious silence regarding those which have raised a storm of opposition, but we must be responsible as Venezuelans before our country and before history. Therefore, we should say here— we men of unbreakable democratic faith—that even though we had unlimited power during the many months of de facto government, we never took advantage of it. However, we are in full accord with the need to provide a democratic regime with sufficient energetic elements of defense. There exists in Venezuela today, and it will exist tomorrow for who knows how long, a fanatic opposition ready to engage in seditious plots.
>
> Despite our historic evolution, remnants of feudalism exist. These have been conquered, but not eliminated from the political arena. Despite the legal sanctions against that part of their wealth that had been robbed from the nation, they still

dispose of abundant economic resources both inside and outside the country to finance insurgent enterprises. It will be against this kind of criminal activity—and only against this kind—that we will use the preventive instrument placed in our hands. There is no reason to believe that the president soon to be elected by a free vote will use it otherwise.[3]

However, as a result of much reflection after my experience in government, I would say now that the 1947 Constitution had one great drawback. It did not face up to the logical consequences of the nation's political organization. During the period of the junta, we established the custom of annual conventions for the president and his cabinet with the governors of the twenty states and two federal territories in an effort to overcome overly dispersed administration. In these reunions, we tried to effect national coordination of the various administrative activities which should be administered from an overall national viewpoint, such as education, public health, communication, and electrification.

The new Constitution also made a start in this direction and required the executive branch to prepare for the Congress, at the start of each presidential period, a five-year national plan outlining its basic program of administration. In other words, the Constitution implicitly laid down the principal of political centralism, all the more so since the regional governors could be replaced at any time by the chief of state. However, the Constitution did maintain the principles of administrative decentralization although these did not prevent overall national planning. The national government was required each year to distribute to the state governments one-fourth of its regular income. This meant that the state governments would have adequate resources for the first time, even though their formal autonomy was reduced by the recognition of the need for national planning. However, the framers of the Constitution timidly shied away from ending the federalist tradition of a bicameral Congress; also, they continued the state legislative assemblies, which really had no useful function at all.

These errors were due to the lack of clear thinking by our party regarding the problem of political organization. The truth is that federalism is a fiction in Venezuela. Ours is a homogeneous people, without national minority groups such as exist in Russia or Yugoslavia. Neither is our situation the same as in the United States, where federalism exists as a result of successive agreements between what were once autonomous colonies. Furthermore, the economic problems of a country with only 5 million people scattered over an immense territory are of such magnitude that they could only really be managed from a national viewpoint and with overall national resources. This means that the most reasonable formula for our political organization is that of a centralized government which firmly holds the reins of power, which coordinates national planning, and which orients and supervises the execution of policy by the state governments coordinated by the president of the republic.

This centralized system can be tempered somewhat by the government's relationship with the communities. The municipal councils, if adequately financed, could become efficient collaborators on a local administrative level with the national government. But the country must be seen as a whole, not as an aggregate of regional entities. This kind of political administration does not conflict at all with a democratic system. It is old-fashioned to equate federalism with liberty. Two American nations, Chile and Costa Rica, had eliminated the federal system at a time when their public liberties were at their peak.

The Constituent Assembly also reformed the labor law in an effort to achieve greater job stability and to guarantee the right to organize unions. The right to termination pay was also established in all those cases when the worker was dismissed without just cause or retired because of cause (but never to exceed eight months' salary). Sunday and holiday pay and overtime were also provided. And those workers who legally had expressed their desire to organize were placed under the protection of the state, which meant that no worker could be terminated or transferred or have his working conditions changed until the union was formed or during a period no longer than ninety days.

On December 14, 1947, the election for the presidency of the republic was held under the new Constitution and Rómulo Gallegos of AD received an overwhelming majority with 870,000 votes while his rivals Rafael Caldera of Copei got 273,000 votes, and Gustavo Machado of the Communist party got 37,000 votes.

When I deposited my vote, just like any citizen of Venezuela, I felt the deepest emotion of my political life. Destiny had given me the priceless opportunity to contribute to the dramatically definite defeat of that thesis propounded by the sociologists who served the dictators—that our people, for reasons of geography, race, and history, were incapable of exercising and enjoying the democratic system of electing governments.

Further elections were held May 9, 1948, to elect the municipal councils in all of the states. It is interesting to note that the electoral support for Acción Democrática never fell below 70 percent, although there were some areas— such as the states of Táchira and Merida—where we lost. When the opposition had the votes, it won. There was a marked tendency for the voters to polarize their sympathies, whether for Acción Democrática or for the Copei party, and it could be foreseen that the Venezuelan electorate was not going to become fragmented but rather would follow the two-party system. The melancholy third place, which the Communist party presidential candidate got with scarcely 3 percent of the votes, revealed how this party had gone downhill. Under the situation preceding the revolutionary government, the communists possessed widespread support and it seemed that they had considerable public support. However, the democratic and social policies followed after 1945 by a government which stood in ideological opposition to communism attracted most of the clientele away from the communists. They were reduced to being a noisy and ineffective minority and did not even enjoy the prestige of having martyrs or suffering under repressive campaigns.

Many foreign correspondents came to witness our presidential elections, to describe their honesty and the enthusiasm of the people, and to analyze the political process which had taken place. One of the best commentaries was printed by the *Washington Post* in an editorial which read:

> It is especially significant that the latest flowering of democracy should take place in Venezuela, birthplace of Bolívar, especially when it is recalled how the iron control of Gómez and other dictators prevented this country from enjoying the liberty for which Bolívar fought. The change is largely due to the policy followed by the government of Betancourt since the revolutionary junta assumed power in 1945. There are some who have believed that the labor orientation of Betancourt's government meant that it was inspired by communism. The best reply is to note what has been accomplished. With the added oil income much has been done to raise the standard of living and to overcome illiteracy, both of which measures are an antidote to communism. The climax of the process was to give the people the right to vote, previously denied them. This explains why, in a nation of only 4 million people, more than 1 million went to the polls.[4]

Cleaning Up the Administration

At the same time that the revolutionary government brought in democratic government, it proceeded with great determination to restore honesty to public administration. As in other Latin American countries, graft in government was deeply rooted. It was inherited from colonial days when the viceroys, the captain-generals, and the governors resorted to various devices to avoid "residence audits" and to pocket a good part of the income which should have gone to the royal treasury. The founders of the republic tried to do something about this indecorous practice. When Greater Colombia—Venezuela, Colombia, and Ecuador—was under the presidency of Simón Bolívar in 1823, a decree was issued which condemned any treasury employees caught in fraud to the death penalty. During the early years, when a conservative oligarchy ruled the republic, administrative morality was at a high level, but it contrasted with an insensitivity to social problems and a virtual caste system of the government.

As the republic slipped into dictatorship, however, things became worse. Under the nepotism of Monagas, there began that practice of considering the public treasury and the private purse of the "chief" and his intimates as one and the same. When this corrupt regime was overthrown in 1858, the illustrious republican, Fermín Toro, wrote a decree, establishing punishment for "abuses, frauds and thievery" of public funds, which was promulgated, but never enforced.

The Federal Revolution triumphed and an agreement was immediately made between Pedro José Rojas and Guzmán Blanco to share hundreds of thousands of pounds sterling which used up the loan that the dictator Páez had negotiated with Baring Brothers of London. Marshal Falcón, who emerged as president after the Federal War, inaugurated the system of issuing drafts against the national treasury on behalf of his friends, written on fragments of paper. Later presidents continued the tradition. When someone proposed to President Alcántara a business deal, he replied: "Why should I get into this when I have the best business of all?"

Castro and Gómez considered public funds as their private property. Administrative dishonesty carried on into the post-Gómez decade. Thus, the tradition of honesty that Bolívar had tried to instill by his personal example of sacrificing everything he had for the nation—including the inheritance he received from his parents—was lost. It could no longer be said, as it was of another of our founding fathers, General Rafael Urdaneta, that "he had no wealth other than his honor."

This peculiar manner of administering public funds became even more scandalous when Venezuela became an oil producer. The dollar and the pound introduced new possibilities of corruption. It became the highest expression of native cleverness to accumulate fortunes while holding public office. Administrative corruption reached its climax under the long dictatorship of Juan Vicente Gómez. Upon his death, outraged public opinion demanded reform and a restoration of the stolen funds, but this went no further than the confiscation of Gómez' own assets. The fortunes of those who collaborated with him during his twenty-seven-year rule and continued to enrich themselves illegally thereafter went untouched. Our 1945 revolution sought to right these wrongs.

Justice, Not Vengeance

The tribunal of civil and administrative responsibility was directed to act as a sort of jury in accordance with the dictates of conscience. It had wide public representation, including lawyers, professionals, labor leaders, two military officers, and an illustrious Catholic priest, who presumably served with the authorization of his superiors. It proceeded according to the specific norms set forth in the decree, which were much fairer than those used against Gómez in the 1936 decree issued by López Contreras and ratified by Medina, then minister of war. Now the lawyers and supporters of these two former presidents claimed that the junta was motivated by vengeance when it confiscated their wealth according to decisions of the tribunal, forgetting that the same thing had been done by them to Gómez. However, we used court procedures and did not refer these decisions to the Congress and state assemblies, as had been done in 1936. Also, the accused were given the right of defense.

Acting with complete independence from the government, the tribunal condemned or absolved persons from a list of more than 100 former public officials. Its sentences have been collected in five volumes, which form an invaluable precedent in Venezuelan history, revealing as they do a great variety of methods used to divert public assets of private use. As a result, more than Bs. 400 million were restored to the nation. A special committee of the National Constituent Assembly reviewed all the sentences, and those affected thus had a second chance to present evidence. Almost all of the sentences were approved.

Two observations should be made regarding this procedure, which has been and continues to be a source of great public controversy. First, we were fully aware that this drastic cleansing of the administration would bring down upon us eternal hate and fierce resistance. We had read that reflection of Machiavelli that "men forget the death of their father before the loss of their wealth," but we had undertaken a public commitment to the people, in years of fighting against corruption, and it was impossible for us to just "wipe the slate clean" after assuming power. We had to keep our promise, but we were not motivated by resentment against anyone. We were fighting against administrative evils and not against persons.

Second, the action of the revolutionary government was more or less the same as what had been done in other Latin American countries against strong men who had accumulated wealth through misuse of power. Special decrees had been applied against their assets in Guatemala, El Salvador, and Ecuador. In Costa Rica, as a result of the popular revolution headed by José Figueres in 1948, special tribunals had also been set up to apply sanctions to figures from the deposed government.

Legal Base for Honest Administration

These prophylactic measures would have been incomplete unless we had established new formulas against administrative corruption for the future. We knew very well that many political and social reform movements in America had been unable to resist the temptation of easy money and had lost their moral authority. We wanted to protect ourselves against this possibility, and we succeeded in doing so.

First of all, we put an end to the infamous secret fund of the Ministry of Interior, which the president managed according to his own judgment. Now, the controller general of the nation was authorized to review all the funds spent on security matters which, for obvious reasons, could not be subject to congressional review.

Also, all high government officials were required by law to make a sworn declaration of their assets, both upon entering office and upon leaving it. This statement was available for public inspection. In my last presidential message to Congress on February 12, 1948, it was categorically requested that our administrative conduct be rigorously reviewed:

> On the eve of leaving power, we can face the country with a clean conscience after having administered the largest national budget in the history of the country. Our private fortune has not been increased; on the contrary, some of us have accumulated debts. With stern pride we demand that our contemporary detractors reveal a single instance in which any of us has obtained financial advantage as a result of high position.

On February 20, 1948, six days after leaving the government, I went before the same magistrate before whom, two years earlier, I had sworn that my only possessions amounted to Bs. 6000 in the shares of the company which edited the newspaper *El País;* an old automobile worth Bs. 3000, while I had debts of Bs. 2000. Upon leaving the presidency, my assets were one share in the Los Cortijos Club, valued at Bs. 2500 and instead of the old Dodge, I had a new 1948 Mercury bought on installments. My personal debts amounted to Bs. 15,000.

In the same presidential message cited above, it was admitted that "more than one lower official has taken funds from the state" and others were suspected of having "received commissions from merchants, both Venezuelan and foreign, who are accustomed to competing in a market where influence-peddling has been rampant."

It was also pointed out that simply suspending unscrupulous public employees was often not a sufficient sanction because of loopholes in the penal code or because the same judges have elastic consciences; therefore, the message urged Congress to pass a "special law, establishing the responsibility of public officials, sufficiently agile in procedures and drastic in punishments, to prevent public employees or private persons from inflicting material loss on the treasury and shameful deterioration of administrative morale." Such a law was prepared and approved by the AD majority in Congress, and the opposition deputies helped by tightening up some of its provisions. President Gallegos signed the law on October 18, 1948, on the third anniversary of the advent of the only political movement in modern Venezuela which had dared to carry out—to its last consequences without any fear or weakness—the purging of administrative morality.

The new Law against the Illegal Enrichment of Public Officials, as it was called, applied to all government employees inside or outside the country. All were required to make public sworn declarations of their assets upon entering and leaving office. Their conduct could be investigated by a special commission which included representatives of the presidency, Congress, the Supreme Court, and each of the political parties. If found guilty of wrongdoing, their assets were subject to confiscation and they were declared ineligible for public office for a period of one to five years, in addition to which they were subject to penal judgment. By this law, Acción Democrática left proof of its firm intention to restore the prestige of public service. However, the memory we left in the minds of Venezuelans of administrative honesty without precedent in the last fifty years of national life was more convincing than any law.

Was This Enough?

If we had not been men of revolutionary mentality, aware of the needs of our time, we would have applied the biblical injunction of resting on the seventh day. We had provided the first democratic elections in national history and we had energetically cauterized the purulent infection of dishonesty. These accomplishments would have been sufficient to satisfy any government of plutocratic origin which wanted to appear as democratic and liberal—but not one which came from the people and professed a modern political ideology. Therefore, we undertook more ambitious tasks and moved on vigorously toward the future. We undertook a radical transformation of the national economy and the government tax structure in an effort to do something effective about the poverty-stricken masses, about "the forgotten man."

First of all, we had to have a new oil policy. We had to finance long-range plans, and to do this, we had to look to that source of funds we had been long insisting should be taxed more—the oil industry. Also, we had to restore the nation's confidence in itself and its faith in its own possibilities by a new oil policy. We urgently needed greater national income from oil. We also had to prove to the Venezuelans that the overwhelming influence of this industry on the economic life of the nation need not constitute an obstacle to state control on behalf of the entire nation, the true owner of the oil fields.

5

A Responsible, Energetic Nationalistic Oil Policy

The Modern Myth of "El Dorado"

In their feverish greed, the Spanish conquistadors imagined that there was a fabulous city constructed of pure gold somewhere in the Venezuelan basin of the Orinoco River. The legend of "El Dorado" has persisted in the subconscious of many people, both in Venezuela and abroad. Many persons actually took the words of Cecilio Acosta around the middle of the last century as truth: "In Venezuela the seas are paved with pearls, the wild beasts walk on gold and everything that the hand touches is bread." This golden legend took on the character of dogmatic truth when Venezuela became in 1928 one of the largest oil-producing countries in the world.

The Gómez dictatorship and the psuedodemocratic governments which followed sought to propagate this version of Venezuela as a modern Eden. Venezuela "smells of gold," as a certain baron—Baron Rothschild—of Royal Dutch Shell would say. Our country appeared to be a notable exception amid the rest of the other Latin American nations with their inadequate public finances and their slow economic development. We had no external debt. The internal debt was small. Each year there was a surplus over the budget and everybody enjoyed a delightful, happy life.

Nothing could have been further from the truth. Venezuela was one of the most backward nations of America in technical matters, and its population was mired in misery, ignorance, and abandon. Intelligent writers from abroad who visited the country helped our political generation reveal the true

124

facts behind the myth. For instance, in 1939 the North American writer Clarence Horn, one of the editors of *Fortune*, asked in the March issue:

> But where has the oil money gone? What of the millions that the government took in between 1922—the year in which El Barroso No. 2 erupted and gushed its heavy crude petroleum for nine days sixty feet into the air—and 1938? Where are the roads, the public works, the subsidized agricultural holdings, the government-fostered mining concessions, the hospitals, the social-security programs—all of those many valuable things that these millions of dollars might reasonably have created at no cost to Juan Bimba? Why is the poor peon so often lethargic with malaria, infected with syphilis, even sometimes touched with leprosy? Why is he still using the fans of the moriche palm for his insect-infested roof? Why is he wearing those ragged trousers patched with pieces from an old cement sack?

With evident irony, Horn noted that the national oil income bore little relation to the amount of oil produced. It did not disappear as do fairy gifts of the salaries of Hollywood stars, he concluded, but "it has gone into the pockets of Gómez and his followers."[1]

There were also foreign technical experts who supported our position. Such was the case of the economic mission headed by Manuel A. Fox, which the Roosevelt administration sent at the request of the Venezuelan government. Its report was given such little circulation by the government of Medina Angarita that we published it ourselves with my prologue.

The government did not want to distribute this report because its objective conclusions were terribly damaging to the government. For instance, it reported that the living standards of 70 percent of the Venezuelan population were "notably poor." And in reference to the unjust tax system, the Fox mission foreshadowed the 1949 revolution when it stated: "The existing tax system will last only while the masses are not informed about it. Once they are aware of the facts, there could be a profound undesirable crisis. The tax system of a modern state inhabited by an informed citizenry cannot resemble a colonial dependency."[2]

The Social Drama of Venezuela in Figures

The 1941 census figures reveal the depressing drama taking place in Venezuela. Of the 2 million citizens older than 15 years of age, 1.3 million—75 percent of the adult population—were illiterate. Of a potential student population of 780,000 children, only 264,000, or 35 percent, attended school. Of the 678,000 homes in the country, more than 400,000, or 60 percent, were constructed of thatch and adobe brick, with dirt floors. Only 2.8 percent of the populace had pure running water in their homes, with 36.8 percent using well water in their homes and 29.8 percent getting water from the rivers. Only 32.2 percent of the population were actively employed—a figure considerably lower than in other Latin American countries.

This panorama had not changed appreciably when we came to power, although we would falsify history if we denied that in the decade after Gómez, certain positive changes had been introduced by the government. Progress was timid and hesitant, without a creative plan, since the governments of the time only took action because of some crisis or because of bureaucratic convenience. When we took over the government, the decades of inaction had left a climate of pessimism. The reactionary sociologists had gained credibility with their thesis that Venezuela was "a subtropical country with a torrid climate inhabited by a race so mixed that it could not assimilate modern civilization or make the most of its immense territory." They repeated the thesis of the Spanish philosopher Ortega y Gasset, who said that if there is an excess of land, geography will determine what the people are like. There was much defeatism since Venezuela had one of the lowest population densities in South America, barely 4.8 persons per square kilometer. The pessimists proclaimed the lack of any possible progress in a nation which could have easily held the population of both France and Italy, but whose actual population density was less than that of South Dakota, with most of its population strung along a narrow coastline and its Amazonic inland accessible only by plane.

But we accepted this geographic and social challenge. We had faith in the creative capacity of our people. We knew that history can be made by men and that they need not suffer as impotent spectators ruled by inexorable social law. With resolute spirit, we undertook to forge a modern state, governed in liberty and with its economy brought up-to-date and humanized. The outcome of this creative task would depend in large part on how we tackled the economic dependence of the state and the nation on the oil industry, which was manipulated by powerful foreign interests.

The Oil Policy of Acción Democrática

If there was any area in which we of Acción Democrática did not have to improvise when we took power, it was that of oil policy. We had studied the problem. We had concrete ideas about how to deal with it and the firm purpose of changing, once and for all, the weak and submissive policy which Venezuelan governments had always followed with the oil companies.

However, we were not demagogues but men with a desire to succeed in government. We knew how to reverse the policy which had been followed with the oil industry. We had made hundreds of speeches and written mountains of paper demanding changes in the relationship between the state and this basic sector of the Venezuelan economy. Now that we were in government, we had to stop speaking and writing in a polemic manner about oil and to begin taking action.

We were realistic in our "action." We had never flirted with the idea of decreeing the nationalization of the industry. No one should accuse us of going back on our word because we recognized the validity of the petroleum law passed under Medina and the concessions granted under it. Our leaders had been categorical in this respect. In a speech in Maracaibo in 1941, when he was a presidential candidate, Rómulo Gallegos said: "We must frankly state that the idea of an immediate oil nationalization such as that of Mexico should not be considered at this time in Venezuela." Three years later, I wrote: "Nationalization of the oil industry should not be considered now in Venezuela. We lack the technical capacity and we do not have a diversified economy which would allow us to follow such a bold nationalistic policy such as that which is the main claim to glory of the Mexican government of Lazaro Cardenas."[3] It is interesting to note also that in the congressional debate over the AD oil policy, no political party, not even the communists, advocated immediate nationalization of the oil industry.

We did not follow the Mexican lead in oil nationalization because substantial differences existed between the situation of the Aztec country and our own. Oil was and is an important element in the Mexican economy but there are other important factors. This enabled Mexico to survive without serious difficulty the boycott of its nationalized oil production declared by the international oil cartel and the governments supporting it. However, almost all the Venezuelan economy depended on oil, and 31 percent of its fiscal income came from oil taxes. Venezuela paid for 92 percent of all of its imports in 1944 with oil income: of the $326 million entering the country in that year, $300 million came from oil. In view of these realities, it would have been a suicidal gesture to have nationalized.

But what we did undertake immediately was obtaining the maximum possible income from a source of wealth which previously had not been adequately taxed by the nation. The policies followed can be simply outlined:

1. The increase of taxes to what was then considered reasonable under the capitalist system and the market economy.

2. The entrance of Venezuela itself into the international oil market to sell its own royalty oil.

3. Immediate cessation of the granting of new concessions to private companies; the organization of a state enterprise with authority to develop national oil reserves either itself or by contract with third parties.

4. Refining of most of Venezuela's oil production within the country and the establishment of a national oil refinery financed with government capital or as a joint venture with private capital.

5. Adequate measures to conserve our oil wealth, a nonrenewable natural resource; the utilization of gas produced with the oil, wasted in the past.

6. Reinvestment by the concessionary companies of part of their earnings to develop the agriculture in the country.

7. Substantial improvement in the wages, benefits, and living and working conditions of the Venezuelan workers and employees in the oil industry.

8. Investment of a large percentage of the additional income obtained from

new oil taxes to create a diversified economy under Venezuelan ownership.

The way in which the democratic government went about implementing these policies is one more proof that between 1945 and 1948 men governed the country who were not only capable of planning but of carrying out what was planned. In all justice, it should be recognized that the man who guided the oil policy at this time was a capable and honorable Venezuelan exceptionally gifted for this task—Juan Pablo Pérez Alfonzo, minister of production.

Larger National Income from Oil

Once we were in the government, with direct access to the sources of information, we were able to demonstrate how the former government had arbitrarily manipulated statistics on oil income in trying to justify the oil tax reform of 1943.

The annual report of the minister of production for 1943 had stated that oil royalties increased by 88 percent—more than the estimate of 80.5 percent made during the congressional debate. This was a completely misleading statement. The official income, in 1942, was Bs. 3.75 per cubic meter whereas it was Bs. 5.12 in 1943. In other words, the law which, according to its apologists, guaranteed the maximum income for Venezuela, only increased our income by 37 percent.

The situation in 1944 continued to be unfavorable for the country. The ministry's annual report claimed that the total oil taxes of Bs. 196.2 million was three times greater than the tax income in 1942. But these figures, presented in such an optimistic manner, concealed the fact that Venezuela was not applying the doctrine which had been formulated officially, both within and outside the Congress, when the 1943 oil law was discussed. An increase in oil income was not the basic question. This was produced by price increases for the crude exported and by the increase in production. Much more important was that Venezuela should, as had been predicted, receive *at least* an amount equal to half the net earnings of the industry.

Furthermore, in accord with the correct interpretation of the law, the tax income of the state might even reach a total half again as much as the industry's earnings. But not even the 50/50 proportion was reached in 1944. The income from the various oil taxes reached Bs. 223.1 million that year, it is true. However, despite this greatly increased tax income of the nation, the companies' net earnings were Bs. 323.1, or Bs. 100 million more than what the nation got.

These millions of excess earnings by the companies belonged to Venezuela. The government urgently needed them to meet community needs which could not be postponed. It was necessary to claim them for the treasury, even if it meant running obvious risks, for by this time, international market conditions and relations between the government and the oil industry had changed significantly.

By 1945, the foreboding situation of the nation and the industry had been somewhat improved by the new oil law. The war had ended, and, with it, the urgent haste of the belligerents to obtain fuel for their war machines.

The Middle East emerged after the war as a large producer of oil. Its competition with other producing areas was on unequal terms, since its tax systems were primitive and the workers received miserable wages. More than 1 million barrels daily of crude oil produced at very low cost flooded the market. These other countries were often virtual colonies as their governments were so much under the influence of the big powers and their crude costs were scandalously low compared with Venezuela. In 1946, the first year of our rule, production costs were more than $.50 a barrel. In Saudi Arabia and Bahrein, they were $.406 and $.25, respectively. The cost was $.27 per barrel in Kuwait. Such lower costs were largely due to incredibly low taxes and to the privileged conditions which the companies enjoyed—almost as if they were the conquerors of the country.

Furthermore, there had been a major national and international propaganda campaign to present the oil reform of 1943 as a great achievement on the part of the Venezuelans. Many important opinion leaders were taken in by this thesis. The idea was circulated that if we tried to get more from the powerful oil consortium, it would respond by diminishing or even paralyzing oil production in Venezuela. This threatening possibility was widely publicized by the press.

Prominent play was given to the impressive production figures from the Middle East, and the implication was clear that the oil trusts would increase their production even more in that area if Venezuela increased its taxes. Even learned professors contributed to spreading this idea in university classes. For instance, Professor Lester Charles Uren of the University of California, in a book about the international oil industry, extolled the golden age when "free enterprise" ruled in Venezuela; he blamed "socialism" for an unfavorable change in that idyllic panorama wherein three large oil companies had behaved as though the Venezuelan subsoil belonged to them.[4]

We were not intimidated by such hints of reprisal, and we carried out our commitments to the nation. Although we were still insecure in the government and threatened by military conspiracies, the revolutionary government decreed an extraordinary tax on December 31, 1945. The decree affected taxpayers of that year with an income of more than Bs. 800,000. It affected 75 persons or business entities of the 20,000 in the country which paid income tax. Additional tax funds of Bs. 93,381,775 were collected, of which 98.5 percent came from the oil companies.

Thus, for the first time in the oil industry of Venezuela, the income of the nation from oil was appreciably greater than that of the industry. According to the annual report of the Ministry of Production, the total government income after the special tax decree was now Bs. 7.41 per cubic meter.

We had reasonable precedents for this decree. It was a bold measure, but it was based on solid arguments. In the report of the North American experts, Curtice and Hoover, at the time of the 1943 oil bill, it was promised that

Venezuela would receive an amount equal to half the industry's earnings. This same argument was put forward, using fictitious figures, by one of the ministry of production officials. Edumendo Luongo Cabello, in a presentation to congressmen, and also put out in pamphlet form by the National Press Office in 1943.

However, the facts prove that the critics of the reform, not its apologists, were right. In 1944, the government's income (before income tax) was Bs. 4.41 per cubic meter when Luongo had promised that the state would get Bs. 6 and the companies Bs. 4.47.

The direct unitary taxes received during the first two years of the new oil law, 1943 and 1944, were Bs. 5.46 and Bs. 5.12 per cubic meter, while the income in previous years had been Bs. 3.75 in 1942 and Bs. 3.72 in 1938. The 1943 oil reform, so extolled by the spokesman of the government, actually meant that an income of scarcely 36 percent more was received instead of the 70 percent promised. The situation would have been even more unfavorable in 1945 and the following year if Acción Democrática had not come to power, because the prices of crude oil rose sharply along with the production of the country during the postwar years. This would have accentuated the disproportion in the incomes of the industry and government.

Production increased steadily during our three years of government. In 1938, 180 million barrels of crude oil had been produced. In 1942, this figure fell to 152 million barrels because of German submarine warfare in the Caribbean. This was about equal to the 1935 production, and it was a level that could have been considered satisfactory under the new taxation rates. It would have been possible with our income to promote economic development at a steady pace and without violent jumps. However, the reconstruction of the war zones in Europe and Asia required increasing amounts of fuel, and we could not slow down the rate of our oil production. We knew that the people's welfare was a basic condition for international peace and that energy was required for the reorganization of industry in many countries.

On the other hand, we felt that it was not in our own best interests or those of the American continent to rapidly deplete our petroleum reserves. We made our views known to the companies and warned them that once the postwar reconstruction era was finished, reasonable limits would be fixed for Venezuelan production, which during those years was increasing by leaps and bounds.

In 1945, Venezuela produced 323 million barrels—as increase of 72 percent over 1938. In 1946, we doubled the 1938 production with 388 million barrels. In 1947, our production was 131 percent that of 1938 with 435 million barrels. In 1948, it went up 22 percent more and reached 475 million barrels, so that our production was one and one-half times greater than in 1938.

Taxes increased along with the production. While we did not deny the oil from our subsoil to the world, we were determined to obtain a fair price. Venezuela would not continue as a producer of low-priced petroleum, nor was her oil wealth to be paid out as dividends to foreign investors. It was to be used to finance the development of an independent economy and for the general welfare of its population.

After the special tax decree at the end of 1945, Decree 212 was prepared by the junta and submitted to the National Constituent Assembly in 1947, where it was approved by unanimous vote. This law increased the maximum income tax from a rate of 9.5 percent to 26 percent on incomes of more than Bs. 28 million.

Only the oil companies had this kind of income in Venezuela. The tax was applicable at a progressive rate of income greater than Bs. 380,000. The maximum rates applied to the extractive industries and were reduced for national capital investment or individual income. Our objective was not only social justice. We also wanted to use the opportunity to encourage national capital investment. Since the oil taxes covered most of the public expense, it was desirable to reduce taxes on employees and small business, the weaker sectors of the economy, and to eliminate a number of indirect taxes. Although the opposition press tried to make out that the increase in oil tax income came exclusively as a result of higher prices and production increases, it can be easily proved that our tax reform was the primary factor in increasing government oil income. The 1947 production was 130.9 percent higher than the 1938 base but the tax income was 621.2 percent higher. If the same tax structure had been applied as in 1944 (one year after the earlier tax reform), the government's income would have been only 392 percent higher, including in both cases a 166.9 percent increase due to higher prices. In other words, the nation would not have received Bs. 814.5 in 1947 but Bs. 554.9 million, if the earlier tax system had been in effect, in spite of the price increases. Consequently, our new tax measures, after 1945, increased the 1947 national income by Bs. 259.6 million.[5]

It will be easier to understand this extraordinary income if it is reduced to percentages. The following breakdown shows what Venezuela received from its oil in the year 1947, the last year of my government, when a total of Bs. 814.5 million was received—an increase of 621.2 percent over 1938 when Bs. 112 million were received. This increase was due to the following:

	Percent
Production increase	130.0
Application of the 1943 oil law	94.1
Price increases	166.9
From nationalistic measures of AD government	230.2
	621.2

Even though our tax income had been considerably increased in 1947, we still had not achieved our objective: that the nation receive at least as much as the net earnings of the companies—in the case of the two largest oil concerns operating in the country. Decree 212 had been strictly applied, but we still fell short of the profits of the Creole Petroleum Corporation (Standard Oil of New Jersey) and the Shell affiliate in Venezuela. This was due to major and unforeseen increases in the price of crude oil (1946: Bs. 24.5 per cubic meter; 1947: Bs. 34.93 per cubic meter).

We were not disposed to permit an element of surprise such as this to thwart the government's intention of never receiving less than the companies from the oil income. We never had a legalistic concept in these matters but believed that national interests should prevail over any fetish of the written word. Since the national will had been clearly manifested and unanimously ratified in the Constituent Assembly, it was logical that we should take other measures to provide what the law had not brought about. When we transmitted this reaction to the companies, they agreed to undertake public works suggested to them by the government up to a value necessary to obtain the principle of 50/50 with the earnings of the companies.

The opposition deputy Jóvito Villalba objected to this measure of the government and asked whether these compensations suggested by Creole and Shell were a tax or a gift. He said that the nation should never receive handouts from the oil companies and complained that the controller general should be involved if the compensations were to be considered as taxes. In forceful reply, production minister Pérez Alfonzo said: "It is not a tax or any kind of obligatory contribution, but simply a payment justified by the intention behind the amendments to the income tax law of 1946."[6]

In other words, a government which was honest and had full public support was able, through the force of its conviction, to obtain from the companies what had been in the mind of the legislators. If the government had limited itself to a legal interpretation of Decree 212, it would not have had sufficient juridical arguments to defend the national interests.

To avoid any similar situations arising in the future, the presidency sent Congress a draft bill which was approved without amendments in 1948. It clearly stated once and for all that if the taxes of the companies did not total an amount at least equal to their net earnings, they would be obligated to make up the difference.

With these changes, it was possible to estimate clearly the national income derived from the oil industry in 1947, including the taxes paid to the government. Unfortunately, this was the last year that such an estimate could be made under AD administration since the government led by President Rómulo Gallegos was overthrown by military coup on November 24, 1947, nine months after taking office.

For the year 1947, the total income of the nation from the oil industry was estimated as Bs. 2119.4 million, divided as follows:

Occasional taxes	Bs.	4.6 million
Regular taxes		814.5
Special 50/50 tax		30.0
Imported machinery and merchandise		476.9
Wages and salaries paid by the industry		743.4
Reserves for worker benefits		50.0
	Bs.	2119.4

All of the above highlights two things: first, the extraordinary impact of the oil industry upon the Venezuelan economy and the vast opportunities for progress opened up by a truly vigilant and concerned government, and second, that Venezuela was well on the road to the recovery of its economic sovereignty and was outgrowing its depressing semicolonial status.

The year 1947 was truly historic—a president of the republic was elected for the first time by free vote of the people; during its 365 days, tremendous advances were made toward national economic liberation. Venezuela was at last beginning to enjoy its own national wealth instead of merely being an economic factory producing wealth for others. The annual report of the Ministry of Production for 1947 showed not only that the oil income had increased 621.2 percent since 1938 but that this had taken place while oil production increased only 130.9 percent. Spokesmen for all the opposition political parties joined at that time in recognizing that the AD government had succeeded in greatly increasing the nation's oil income.

As part of the process, the government insisted on knowing exactly what were the earnings of the oil companies. The time had passed when the financial aspect of the oil industry was considered off limits to us. The state had legal powers to investigate the books of the companies and this power was invoked. Specialized personnel closely followed the variations of market prices and accumulated all the information needed to help the government find its own way through the morass of international prices. We were able to ascertain that the earnings of the oil industry in 1947 averaged around 20 percent of the invested capital, while dividends paid to stockholders averaged 7.5 percent. This meant that earnings in Venezuela were more or less level with those of the oil industry in the United States and with manufacturing industries of that country. We had achieved a relatively favorable position within the prevailing capitalist system and market economy. Now, it would only be necessary to keep a careful eye on the economic cycle and market prices.

It is interesting to note that our total economic benefits were superior to those of Mexico, a country which had nationalized its oil industry as the only way to assure respect for its national sovereignty. However, the AD government was able to take advantage of the bitter experience which the oil companies had in the Mexican nationalization, and the Bolivian expropriation. Tax income was increased from them to such a degree that nationalization was not necessary to obtain maximum economic benefits for the people of the country. Venezuela received an income which was 7 percent more per barrel than that paid by the nationalized industry to the Mexican government, while our production was six times greater. Also, the benefits received in the nation were much greater than those received in Mexico. For example, our oil workers received salaries about the same as those received by oil workers in the United States, appreciably higher than those received by workers in England under the Labor government or by the nationalized oil workers in Mexico.

The income Venezuela was now receiving from its oil was the symbol of profound social change. We were fully recovering our sovereignty. The government was run by men determined to bring about the second independence of the country—economic independence. We stood up to the foreign companies, confident that we were fully supported by the people and invulnerable to the traditional flattery and pressure of which the managers of the companies had made so much use and abuse in our country.

The inevitable question arises: What was the reaction of the companies to our measures? Our relations with the powerful companies were not easy. They called for energy and flexibility, audacity and realism. We would draw a false picture, however, if we presented ourselves as Saint George confronting a dragon spitting fire and smoke. Different opinions have been given to explain why the companies took a respectful attitude and complied with the measures dictated by a government fully determined to exercise its sovereign power. Edwin Lieuwen says that "the oil companies cooperated because of fear."[7] A more generous opinion came from Leonard M. Fanning, a writer reported to have close connections with the oil industry, who wrote: "One of the most important oil company officials in Venezuela described the revolution there as a somewhat violent manifestation of the evolutionary process toward democracy—and urged the industry to adjust itself to the new situation."[8] Whatever the reasons, the truth is that the companies did not take a line of stubborn resistance toward the new official policy.

One final observation should be made, not to aid the historians in their work, but for future reference. It was demonstrated at this time that it was possible for a nationalistic Venezuelan government to maintain normal relations with a powerful oil consortium. This was true because the men who led the government enjoyed public confidence and could not be bribed or intimidated. They were persons who truly governed and did not just use public office for the easy sport of verbal demagoguery.

The Economic Commission for Latin America of the United States (ECLA) in its monograph stated that as the result of the increased income obtained from its oil during the period 1945–49, the usual characteristics attributed to foreign investment in a country were not true with regard to Venezuela. It concluded that "the oil industry in Venezuela could be considered as a national industry, not only in the geographic sense but also because of the economic impact it is having on the country despite the foreign origin of its capital."[9]

Selling Oil Royalties on the Market

There was another simple—but absolutely new—idea with which we sought to demonstrate in our oil policy that Venezuela was the owner of its oil wealth. Under the existing international circumstances, we could not do without the oil companies at this stage of our evolution. But the petroleum belonged to us, it was Venezuelan, and the government was obliged to demonstrate this at every opportunity. That is why we decided to do what no other Venezuelan government had done before—to take royalty payments from the companies in kind and to sell them ourselves on the open market. Venezuelan oil law gave the state the option to receive its royalty either as a cash payment or in oil which it could market for its own account. No government had ever dared to try the latter because of an absurd inferiority complex. The Foreign Minister in the Medina Angarita government, Parra Pérez, had even told newspapermen in 1943 that Venezuela could not sell oil because the oil did not belong to the government.

The AD government decided to break down this taboo and advised the oil managers of its decision to sell royalty oil for its own account. "We had to overcome serious resistance," the minister of production told Congress in 1948. The oil managers did not conceal thier discontent with the surprising official announcement. They argued that the Venezuelan government would upset the market by offering its own oil. However, we had not only the law on our side but also the conviction, repeated again and again to the oil concessionaires, that the oil belonged to Venezuela and that it was for Venezuela to decide what should be done with the royalty payments. The government was motivated first by the question of principle and second by the scarcity of food products from which the nation then suffered. We wanted to make it clear that our oil should not be known simply as "Caribbean zone oil"—as was done in most oil publications—but as "Venezuelan oil" since we accounted for 74.8 percent of all hemispheric production outside the United States.

When we took over the government, the country lacked meat, cereals, fats, and oils. These were the days of the critical postwar food shortages. It was not just a question of having the money to buy foodstuffs. It was necessary to engage in barter, using another product in short supply, such as petroleum, to bid successfully for these foods on the world market. Our royalty oil was therefore offered to buyers with the proviso that preference would be given to deals in which foods we required were offered in exchange. Our oil was bartered for Argentine meat, for Portuguese vegetable oils, and for babasu nuts from Brazil. Other royalty lots were sold for cash. These operations enabled us to ascertain that it was possible in the open market to get a higher price for our crude than that reported by the companies, a fact which would have to be taken into account in their future payments to us.

The rest of the royalty oil was sold back to the oil companies at the higher prices we had obtained on the market. These sales to the companies were put on a short-term basis, on condition that the government could again receive its royalty in kind at any time it wanted to engage in barter deals.

The state obtained many benefits from this policy of selling its royalty in kind on the open market. Needed foodstuffs were obtained for the nation as well as raw materials for industry. Oil income was increased by Bs. 8.4 million in 1947 and Bs. 45 million in 1948. The name of Venezuela was now known on the world oil market as a country where oil could be bought by direct negotiation. The veil of mystery over the marketing of oil—behind which the Anglo-Saxons had maintained a monopoly of rights and secrets—was removed forever.

Some opposition congressmen attacked this sale of royalty oil without sufficiently analyzing its benefits. Jóvito Vallalba, the most eminent of the critics, lamented that we ended up selling the royalty back to the companies for a few more cents per barrel instead of constructing a national refinery. However, government spokesmen set the record straight when they pointed out: (1) that the royalty oil had been sold within the limits fixed by the National Economic Council—25 percent of the total production; (2) that only part of the royalty could be placed on the open market because the oil produced from Lake Maracaibo fields had to be transported in specially designed low-draft tankers possessed only by the companies; (3) that since the government had proved it possible to obtain a higher price for its royalty in the market, this higher price would be demanded from the companies for the royalty oil not taken in kind; (4) that the government remained free to use its royalty oil for barter operations and that there was no obstacle to prevent it from building a national refinery anytime in the future.

Another important factor in loosening the bonds which international capital had placed upon us was the attitude taken by the democratic government regarding the granting of new oil concessions to private companies.

The No-More-Concessions Policy

From the beginning, we had argued that Venezuela should not continue granting oil concessions to private companies but should establish a state oil company to develop national oil reserves either directly or in association with private companies.

It had been Venezuelan tradition for many years that government officials forgot the promises they made when seeking office. Of course, before Acción Democrática, there had never been a political party with doctrines, principles, and a coherent program. However, it was understandable that the concession-hunters would expect us to change our minds and that we would continue the old concessions system. This, at least, is the only way to explain their repeated efforts to obtain concessions despite the reasoned decision of our government not to grant them. Despite the categorical statement I made in my message to Congress at the beginning of its 1948 session and in that by the Ministry of Production in its 1947 report, those hoping to monopolize new portions of our national subsoil did not give up hope.

Various press organs began to publish articles, drafts, and tendentious arguments. These became more and more aggressive in tone and insidious in content. They argued that Venezuela should not keep its oil buried in the ground because there was great pressure for the oil companies to go to the Middle East. They would take their geologists, their oil engineers, and their drilling equipment to that part of the world if they had to wait in Venezuela much longer. Even more venomous attacks were to come. These were the days of the Cold War, the eve of the Berlin blockade by the Russians. A statement by General Eisenhower regarding the importance of Venezuelan oil was used to suggest that we were deliberately holding back on the fuel required for the defense of the West. The author of this campaign, of course, was unidentified. No person or agency claimed responsibility, but certainly all of these articles, figures, and arguments did not reach the editorial rooms of a commercial and venal press by being dropped by witches down the chimney.

The government replied calmly and with conviction to this propaganda of obvious origin, using its own figures and its own arguments to demonstrate the falsity of the argument that the no concessions policy endangered Venezuelan oil production. The figures were easy to understand. Of a total of 91,205,000 hectares making up the national territory, it was estimated that some 25 million had oil-bearing possibilities. Of these, 10,759,567 hectares had already been given out as concessions prior to our government, with some of these concessions due to be returned to the nation by 1950. That meant that 8 million hectares—or 9 percent of all national territory and about one-third of the lands with oil potential—would have remained in foreign hands if we had not adopted a new concessions policy. According to figures published at the time, the companies were only producing in 1.56 percent of the total concessions areas given them through the irresponsible generosity—if one is not to use worse terms—of previous administrations.

Another argument which was used in the press campaign against the government was the threat of the Middle Eastern production. Our response to the veiled threat of the oil companies to look for concessions in Iran if we refused to grant them in Venezuela was to call attention to the tense political situation in the Persian Gulf. The Soviet Union, aided by the Communist Tudeh party in Iran, had tried to obtain oil concessions in a northern part of the country; but the Iranian parliament, on the motion of a then little-known deputy, Mohammed Mossadegh, had passed a law prohibiting the government from negotiating any oil concessions without its prior consent. This thwarted Soviet ambitions for the moment but it was a danger signal for those who, speaking either in the name of socialism or free enterprise, wished to continue considering Iran as open country.

All this had happened before we came to power, but then, in 1946, "the Azerbaijan crisis" revealed the growing breach among the three big powers which had defeated the Axis. Toward the end of 1945, Iranian communists calling themselves democrats, aided by Soviet Russia, overthrew the governor in the northern province of Iran and proclaimed the autonomous republic of Azerbaijan. Iran negotiated directly with the Russians and agreed to include three communists in its cabinet and to form a mixed Soviet-Iranian Oil Company, trying to get the Russians to withdraw their troops from Iranian territory. However, there was violent public protect in Iran against this deal. Some of it was due to true nationalistic sentiment, but there were also subtle intrigues by the Anglo-Iranian Oil Company and English diplomats. The great refinery of the oil company at Abadan was the scene of bloody riots promoted by communists. British troops were dispatched to the nearby port of Basra in Iraq. The Iranians then removed the communists from the cabinet and moved troops into the so-called republic of Azerbaijan, which promptly disappeared. Russian-Iranian tension reached a climax in 1947 when the Iranian parliament unanimously rejected the oil deal with the Russians, who replied with aggressive diplomatic moves accompanied by new street riots by the Tudeh party in Iranian cities.

These events, although they occurred thousands of miles from the Venezuelan oil fields, favored our nationalistic oil policy. We had to be cautiously realistic in the application of new taxes because the production costs in the Middle East were so much lower than those in Venezuela. However, the explosive political conditions prevailing in that part of the world, resulting from the rivalry between East and West and the reaction of local nationalism, encouraged us to maintain our policy even though the oil companies in the country were subtly threatening to transfer their operations to the Persian Gulf.

Toward a State Oil Company

It was not logical to maintain our no concessions policy as a strictly negative matter. We ourselves should take advantage of our rich oil potential. Furthermore, the private operation of the existing concessions might oblige us "to take rapid decisions to prevent concessionaires from damaging or neglecting the oil fields." This last possibility was emphasized in the Ministry of Production's annual report for 1948: "As this situation might present itself in the near future," said the report, "we have studied the problem and believe that its favorable solution would be possible, within our existing legal system, by giving concessions to a state agency." It was explained that a state company might either carry on its own operations, contract these operations out to third parties, or arrange for other kinds of contracts.

On March 11, 1948, the ministry named a commission to study the establishment of a national refinery, either with national capital or as a mixed enterprise, and also to recommend the structure of a state agency to which the oil acreage still in the possession of the nation might be assigned. Its members were Alberto Carnevali, leader of the AD congressional majority, who was later to die in jail as a victim of the Pérez Jiménez dictatorship, the geologist Enrique Jorge Aguerrevere, and Manuel R. Egaña. The nonpartisan character of this commission was one more demonstration of the way we sought to develop a truly national oil policy. However, the policy of AD was not supported by some of the political opponents of the government who saw in oil policy an opportunity for superficial and showy oratory. These adversaries made no serious effort to study the complex aspects of the oil industry with its repercussions in all phases of national life.

The debate in Congress in 1948 on the annual report of the Ministry of Production renders overwhelming testimony to the fact that AD was the only party which had thoroughly studied and reached precise conclusions regarding this fundamental national question. This is not stated with any sectarian satisfaction but with the deep concern of those who wish that all the responsible sectors of Venezuela would exhaustively study the problem to which our national destiny is tied for years to come. The Social Christian party, Copei, represented by Godofredo González, had a mild position compared with that of some of the other parties. However, it echoed the false premise of the frustrated concessions-seekers that an AD no concessions policy might weaken the defense potential of the Western powers. The communist leader, Gustavo Machado, while professing support for the nationalistic oil policy, insinuated that the no concessions policy benefited the oil companies.

Jóvito Villalba, speaking for Unión Republicana Democrática, revealed that he lacked adequate information regarding the problems when he asserted that the no concessions policy actually favored the oil companies because it would impede the investment by independent private capital, including Venezuelan funds, in the oil industry. He also echoed—and I believe he did it in good faith—the shameful argument bandied about by the lawyers of the companies that our policy made it impossible to estimate our petroleum reserves and urged that new concessions be granted.

The government's position was defended by Minister Pérez Alfonzo and the congressional leader, Alberto Carnevali. They insisted that there was no reason to reduce oil production because of inadequate concession holdings since the companies were only producing from a small fraction of the acreage they had already received. They also affirmed that the big companies eagerly wished to obtain new concessions in accordance with their traditional system of monopolizing available acreage. Finally, they argued that the no concessions policy did not mean that future oil activities would decrease but that only those activities conducted for private interest and individual profit would be reduced.

"Production in the future, rather, will be in a very different manner. Instead of turning the rights which belong to the nation over to private parties, we will arrange to participate directly in the production of petroleum," the ministry concluded. It was also demonstrated statistically that it was not true that the no concessions policy had led to a decrease in oil reserves. The country was producing more oil than it was finding. In 1947, proved reserves reached 82.5 million cubic meters compared to production of 69.1 million cubic meters.

Although some of our opponents were not convinced by these arguments, the no concessions policy was overwhelmingly approved by a congressional majority. Thus the representatives of the nation ratified the governmental position: Venezuela definitely resolved that the government itself would determine how the oil reserves shall be developed in the future, but in no case would it be done by the colonial system of concessions to private parties.

The historic projection of this policy will be seen when we analyze what happened to the nation's oil following the coup d'état of November 24, 1948.

Refining Venezuela's Oil at Home

The revolutionary government wanted to get as much Venezuelan oil production as possible refined in the country. Refining our crude at home would mean that the nation would receive a higher income from more valuable products and also that there would be additional employment for Venezuelan workers.

However, in this case, as in others, it was not possible immediately to realize this national ambition. It was stated frankly in the 1947 annual report of the Ministry of Production that "unfortunate circumstances inherited from the past have created a situation which restricts any rapid progress toward our national desire to refine a large part of the petroleum we produce."

Among the "unfortunate circumstances" referred to was the fact that no visible effort had been made by the previous government to impede the enlargement of the refineries located on the Dutch islands of Aruba and Curaçao. It was clear, of course, during the critical days of the war that we could not insist upon moving these plants to Venezuela. But it would have been possible for the government to oppose energetically the construction of new refining capacity on these islands to process larger amounts of our oil. There is no evidence that this was done. Between 1942 and 1945, the Creole and Shell companies were able to build, without any objection, new plants on these islands facing the Venezuelan coast. These included units for the refining of both conventional fuels and 100-octane aviation gasoline.

Meanwhile, the refining capacity of the Middle East oil zone was being greatly enlarged. By 1944 it had been increased by 89 percent over 1938 and had become one of the major refining centers of the world. However, while new refining capacity was proliferating elsewhere to satisfy the tremendous demands of a world at war, only one new plant was going up in Venezuela. This was the Caripito plant in the eastern part of the country, whose 2100-ton daily production was hardly a drop in the bucket. A truly responsible government could have taken advantage of the fact that Venezuelan oil was essential to the Allies and insisted upon more refining in the country. As a matter of fact, official spokesmen of the previous government did insist publicly that this be done, but there was little to show for their alleged concern. The golden opportunity to take action was lost, although Acción Democrática insistently urged the government to take decisive steps and force the oil companies to build refineries in Venezuela, just as they were doing in the Dutch West Indies and the Middle East.

As a result of this official indolence—and that is the mildest term that can be used—Venezuela had three refineries, with a daily capacity of 124,000 barrels, when AD came to power. This was only a little more than 9 percent of our total crude production in 1946 and even less than in 1945 because our production was now increasing rapidly. "It will be understood that this situation is far from satisfactory," said the annual report of the Ministry of Production for 1946.

The government did not resign itself to this state of affairs, even though the new tax measures reduced the advantage of additional refining in the country. As a result of these taxes and of the greater vigilance in auditing company account books, put into effect at the same time, it became less possible for the concessionaires to transfer earnings to their refining affiliates elsewhere. However, there were other benefits to be obtained and we continued, as a matter of principle, to demand more refining of our oil at home.

Our decisive approach to the question became immediately apparent. The agreement between Creole (Standard) and the previous government to build a refinery—larger than any of the existing ones—at the port of Turiamo was set aside because this region was dedicated to agriculture and the refinery would have pulled workers from the fields. The area later selected, the peninsula of Paraguana, was in the state of Falcón, one of the least favored areas in the nation insofar as the distribution of wealth was concerned. The construction of what is today one of the largest refineries in the country was begun there.

When Creole replied to government pressure to hasten the refinery building by pointing out that the United States government was severely limiting steel exports during the postwar period—and this was true—we at once intervened with the Washington authorities on behalf of Creole and other companies for steel supplies. This brought positive results. The Texas Petroleum Company inaugurated a 10,000-barrel per day refinery toward the end of 1947, and Shell and Creole proceeded apace with their plants of 40,000 barrels and 50,000 barrels daily capacity. When these were finished, it was predicted, the refining capacity of the nation would be doubled and would process a quarter of our total crude output. However, the vertiginous growth of crude production during 1947 meant that the disproportion between the amount of our oil refined inside and outside the country increased.

We never harbored the unreasonable idea that all the crude produced in Venezuela should be refined in the country. With such voluminous production, this was impossible—all the more so since many consuming countries insisted upon installing their own refineries and wanted to import only crude. But it was possible to develop special formulas which might further increase refining in the country, in addition to insisting that the companies comply with their obligations under their 1944 and 1945 concession contracts to refine 10 percent of their production in the country. Two such measures were devised. The first was the establishment of one or more refineries by the government, in which our royalty oil—one-sixth of all production—could be refined. The second was the decision to dredge the bar at the mouth of Lake Maracaibo. This would not only transform Maracaibo into a great port for all of western Venezuela and the adjoining area of Colombia, but would also oblige the Creole Petroleum Corporation and Royal Dutch Shell, the two major producers in the lake area, to transfer, ultimately, their big refining operations from the Dutch islands to Venezuela. By opening the lake entrance to a depth of 35 feet, the use by the companies of their fleet of shallow-draft tankers designed especially for crossing the bar would no longer be economically attractive. They would want to convert to using larger ocean going tankers and this would make the stop at the Dutch islands unnecessary.

The annual report to Congress by the Ministry of Public Works for 1947 recounts the background of the bar-dredging operation. It had originally been studied in 1937 under the presidency of López Contreras with the help of U.S. Army engineers, but nothing was done. These studies were now brought up-to-date and it was determined that the work could be done in four years at a cost of Bs. 102.1 million. Late in 1947, the ministry advertised in the local and foreign press, inviting interested parties to file bids for the project. The ministry had explained, in its annual report, that the job would be financed by funds put up by the oil companies under special arrangements then being studied.

These arrangements were ignored as a result of the military coup in 1948, but the promise that I made in my last message to Congress that "we will leave for the succeeding government complete studies for undertaking this major project which will give such vigorous impulse to the western part of the nation and make the capital of Zulia the natural port for vast regions of both Colombia and Venezuela" was carried out. I also made concrete reference to the agreement reached with the oil companies for financing this program. All the plans for dredging and for financing were there for the military junta when it took over. But it was not until four years later that this disorganized regime began to do something about this project of such obvious usefulness to the nation.

Gasoline and Other Fuels at the Lowest Prices in the World

During our long years in opposition, we had faithfully voiced the popular demand that the prices of oil products on the domestic market be drastically reduced. It was incredible that such high charges were made for these products in the country which was the world's leading oil exporter. We made good on our promises as soon as we came to power because we were convinced that our industrial development and the material well-being of our people were closely connected to a policy of cheap energy.

On December 1, 1945, just one month and a day after taking over the government, the prices of gasoline and other oil products were drastically reduced by government decree. We sacrificed our tax from gasoline sales to less than $.01 per liter, a minimum which hardly paid for keeping the statistics. We gave up Bs. 20 million annually in tax income, but we also imposed sacrifices upon the oil companies and the retailers of oil products, who had to give up 1½ céntimos and 5 céntimos per liter, respectively.

The Creole Petroleum Corporation (Standard Oil), Venezuela's largest oil producer, in a press release on December 3, 1945, pointed out that the government had taken an unprecedented step in reducing gasoline prices by 10 céntimos per liter. "There has never been such a large reduction in gasoline prices anywhere before," the company stated, and added that it was also the first time in history that any government, on its own initiative, had given up its gasoline tax income. It concluded that the price in Venezuela for gasoline was now "the lowest in the world."

The reduction of the prices of all oil products had an immediate favorable impact on the national economy. There was a sharp jump in the consumption of liquid fuels—gasoline, kerosene, diesel, and fuel oil. The average Venezuelan at long last began to enjoy the advantages of living in a country with such great oil resources. By 1947 the national consumption of oil products had increased to an index of 470, compared to 100 in 1938. There were some very interesting aspects of this increase. Gasoline use had increased three times but the consumption of kerosene went up twelve times. This means that the oil price reduction policy, together with our concurrent drive to provide more electrical energy at lower prices, had led to a great reduction in the use of charcoal and wood for fuel. Thus we were not only making cheaper fuel available for our people but our policy was protecting our forest reserves in a country with the dubious distinction of being among the most eroded geographical areas in Latin America.

In 1945, 38,154 million kilograms of charcoal had been consumed, but this was reduced to 16,609 million in 1949. Wood use was likewise reduced from 22,681 million kilograms to 8,157 million. At the same time, diesel and kerosene use increased sharply—tripling in just the two years 1946–47.

Oil Conservation and Use of Gas

The idea that nations should jealously conserve their natural resources is relatively new. Humanity now realizes more and more that it cannot make unlimited use of its forests, lands, and waters. They must be conserved for the future and used now in a rational manner. Conservation must be accentuated when it comes to nonrenewable natural resources, such as petroleum.

This precious substance, which has been laboriously deposited by nature over many centuries in a rather capricious manner about the earth, can easily be exhausted by prolonged and intense production. For this reason, many governments—even those with least inclination toward intervention in private business—have carefully supervised the production of oil reserves. For instance, detailed federal and state laws exist to ensure conservation in the United States, where the government does not even possess title to subsoil rights as in our case.

In Venezuela, practically nothing had been done in this regard for thirty years after the oil industry had first been established by private companies. A specialized and efficient personnel existed in the Hydrocarbon Technical Office of the Ministry of Production, but it had no authority and was limited to filing away, each year, the reports presented by the operating companies.

Our democratic administration faced up to this problem, beginning in 1945. It was proposed that the oil fields should be carefully checked to be sure that they were producing only at "the maximum efficient production rate."

The chief engineer of the Texas Railway Commission which controlled production in that state came to Venezuela to advise the government on the subject, while a number of our own engineers were sent to the United States to specialize in conservation. By 1948 the Minister of Production was able to inform the Congress that his office now had the means to determine whether certain oil fields should be worked at different rates to extend their productive life.

Another aspect of the same problem was that of enforcing "unitization"— that is, to coordinate the production of different producing concessions in the same oil zone to achieve a uniform production rate. Wasteful and competitive production of adjoining oil fields had never been much of a problem for us because we had just a few producing companies, but there were areas where the intervention of the state was necessary to ensure that production was in accord with the national interest rather than with the individual desires of the companies.

The new democratic government also concerned itself with better use of gas produced together with oil. The sight of the burning gas flares in the fields always left a negative impression. These flares—or *mechurrios* as they were called—burned day and night, wasting annually millions of cubic meters of natural gas, a precious source of energy. For many years, practically nothing had been done to put an end to this outrageous waste of energy and potential wealth. The companies were using but a minimum part of the gas produced—around 1 million cubic meters per year—as fuel or for reinjection into the wells. A small amount was used for domestic purposes in the city of Maracaibo.

The minister of production took this problem to the Congress for the first time, bluntly expressing our government's viewpoint. He reported that the thermal units of gas burned in 1947 were equivalent to 10 million cubic meters of oil—"more than double the oil production of all Colombia." The government, he revealed, had demanded that the oil companies build conservation repressuring plants to reinject the gas which, up until now, had been wastefully flared. In the debate which followed, in 1948, certain opposition spokesmen engaged in considerable demagoguery. For example, the communist deputy Gustavo Machado objected to the government's promise to obtain " a reasonable solution" to this problem, urging that it was a patriotic matter and that a radical solution was required. He claimed that no gas at all had been flared in the United States for the last hundred years. Minister Pérez Alfonzo refuted this superficial oratory with the facts at his command. Both in the United States and in the Soviet Union, he replied, and in all oil-producing regions, a considerable amount of gas still has to be burned because there is no way to recover it.

Various kinds of projects were now studied by both the government and the companies. There was a plan to bring natural gas from the oil fields by pipeline to urban centers for domestic and industrial use. The use of gas as fuel was also foreseen in the plan for national electrification, which was now being rushed for the states of Anzoátegui and Monagas. The Venezuelan Development Corporation (CVF) was planning a fertilizer plant, using gas. The CVF also was experimenting with hydrogen gas for the reduction of iron ore since we were planning to establish a national steel industry and the major obstacle faced was the lack of coal. Of course, we were not about to make any decisions until we were sure of what we were doing as a result of thorough study. "However," the minister of production reported, "we are determined that within a reasonable length of time, we shall put an end to this action 'against nature'—this destruction of an irreplaceable resource in an epoch when man has become aware of the need to conserve natural resources."

Reinvestment of Some Oil Company Profits in Other Activities

By now the reader will have understood that Venezuela did not have an autonomous economy—that in good part it imported raw materials and manufactured products and that its livelihood depended almost entirely upon petroleum. The destiny of the country depended upon whether we could carry out the goal which our democratic government had set: to win the battle of production.

We utilized different measures to attain this goal. We were not dogmatic in our approach but we pragmatically used any reasonable plan which promised to end our dangerous practice of importing everything from machinery to eggs. Our programs and policies will be examined in detail later. Here we will mention only the assistance which we asked from the oil companies as part of our overall economic planning.

We discussed the economic situation with the oil company managers and pointed out to them that the petroleum industry shared responsibility—even if it were indirect—for the stagnant condition of the rest of the national economy, especially in rural areas. We told them that their help was needed in the government's crusade to promote other permanent economic activities in the country. Some of their profits should be reinvested in the production and distribution of foodstuffs in Venezuela.

It was made very clear to them, at the same time, that this was not going to be another opportunity for them to make money in the country. Neither were they asked to make gifts to the nation or put their money into philanthropic enterprises, without hope of return. The idea was that they invest some of their earnings in nonpetroleum activities, in association with the government, to accomplish unique public interest objectives.

After prolonged discussions, our ideas took shape. The three largest oil concerns in the country subscribed capital for the Basic Economy Corporation, established by Nelson Rockefeller. Creole Petroleum Corporation (Esso) put up $8 million; the Royal Dutch Shell affiliate, $4.2 million; and the Mene Grande Oil Company (Gulf), $3 million. Three companies were set up for cattle raising, fishing, and opening a chain of supermarkets. The Basic Economy Corporation and the CVF each put up half the capital for these companies, but the CVF was given all the preferred stock with interest guaranteed and without risk. It was also given representation on the board and had the right, at any time, to convert its preferred stock into common stock. Both the Basic Economy Corporation, which held the common stock, and the CVF were obliged to put their shares up for sale whenever the companies began to show profit. In any case and under any circumstances, all of the stock should be in Venezuelan hands, public or private, at the end of ten years.

This effort was only a sort of flank action along the broad front of the total offensive we were undertaking to increase production. The public was fully informed regarding all details of the joint enterprise. High government officials, including the president, participated with Rockefeller in a public forum on the subject and there was little reasoned criticism. However, the political opposition raised a hue and cry and a congressional debate was finally held on the subject at the request of the Ministry of Production in February 1948.

The arguments of the opposition during this debate were impressive for their superficiality. Nobody could demonstrate what the risk was in having the oil companies—which already had $2 billion invested in the country in a short-term industry that only left taxes, salaries, and holes in the ground—invest $15 million more in permanent economic activities in association with and under the strict control of the government. The opposition congressmen were so hard pressed for arguments that Gustavo Machado of the Communist party actually stated—with the ineffable nerve of those who argue only from dogmatism—that there would be no objection regarding such investment in heavy industry, but that it should not take place in agriculture. This argument was refuted by the majority leader, Alberto Carnevali, with inexorable logic. He pointed out that the proportion of foreign investment in agriculture would be much less than if it were made in a steel plant. Where then is the danger from imperialism, he asked.[10]

Of course, the opposition did not spring only from political strategy. There was an evident widespread feeling of distrust and suspicion of the oil companies. Many persons of good faith doubted whether they would cooperate without some hidden intention of profiting from the situation. They forgot that the entire idea came not from the companies but from a watchful government which acted without any inferiority complex vis-à-vis the companies. Its only purpose was to produce and distribute the greatest possible amount of basic food articles to meet the urgent need. In any case, the experiment was made as part of the overall effort to obtain as much advantage as possible for Venezuela from its oil wealth.

When the Gallegos government was overthrown, this effort in associating foreign and national capital was in its infancy. The military junta immediately sold the CVF shares to the Venezuelan Basic Economy Corporation of Rockefeller and his associates. Four years later, in 1953, according to an article by Robert H. Hallet in the *Christian Science Monitor*, the enterprise had a net loss of $6 million. None of the three enterprises prospered. Thus the facts demonstrated that risk was really involved in these "Rockefeller deals," as they were called. The government, however, which had obtained preferred stock, would have been able to recoup its investment without loss.

The Oil Workers Make Big Gains in Three Years

The October revolution brought radical changes to the Venezuelans who worked for the oil industry. Prior to October 1945, the life of the unions had been, at best, a languid one. The companies avoided negotiating with them, and only in November 1945 could the workers' unions sign their first collective contract with the oil companies. Company lawyers had always been able to find legal loopholes and maneuver to frustrate the just demands of the workers for improvement in their living standards and working conditions. There were very few inspectors of the Ministry of Labor in the oil fields to oversee the correct application of the labor law, and these frequently tended to favor the companies. The civil authorities acted more often like company employees than like government officials.

There was an immediate change in this depressing situation for the workers. As the great majority of them were militants of Acción Democrática, they did not engage in rebellious violence as when Gómez fell, but followed the party's instructions to maintain public order. However, their intention to achieve justice immediately became clear as they held peaceful meetings and made demands upon the companies. On March 30, 1946, the Second National Congress of Oil Workers was held in Caracas, and unions were now functioning in all the oil zones. The government now did not interfere with this worker organization but sympathized with and actively encouraged their reasonable demands. When I spoke at the final session of the meeting, it was to ratify the government's intention to put an end to the defenseless situation of the workers who produced the black gold from our soil. The workers for their part, "enthusiastically backed the revolutionary government junta for the program being carried out and urged it to continue the economic liberation in the social development of Venezuela." The assembly also decided to negotiate a collective contract with the companies. This was undertaken with the help of Raúl Leoni, Minister of Labor, and for the first time in the history of the oil industry, a collective contract was signed on May 30, 1946. It substantially raised salaries and provided new social benefits and better working conditions, many of which went well beyond the provisions of the labor law.

Daily payroll workers in the industry had their wage increased from Bs. 8 to Bs. 14 per day, including one paid day of rest, which meant a 75 percent increase. Skilled workers had their salaries increased in similar proportion. The contract, for the first time, provided a bonus for night work and sick pay. The labor law had provided one week's vacation, and this was now increased to fifteen days. Company commissaries sold fifteen basic food articles to the workers; by contract this number was raised to seventy-five, including medicine and clothing. The companies traditionally used contractors who hired workers at lower rates of pay and under inferior working conditions. The new contract made the companies responsible for the extension of all the benefits of the new contract to these workers. No pension plan had existed for all workers, but the two largest oil companies now agreed to submit to the government a pension plan within the first year of the contract. Under the labor law, service indemnities were paid to workers only when they were laid off because of a reduction in operations. The new contract provided for obligatory payment of this indemnity after three years of work, even if the worker left his job voluntarily. There were also provisions in the contract for family medical attention, education of children, and worker housing.

According to the *New York Times* of June 1, 1946, the new contract would bring the workers $30 million more during its first year. The newspaper termed the agreement "a resounding victory" for the government headed by Rómulo Betancourt. A strike, it said, would have been disastrous for the Venezuelan economy, and a government arbitration decree would have weakened its prestige among the workers. By acting as mediator, the government achieved an agreement through the normal bargaining process.

After this contract, oil production entered into a time of stability. The workers had obtained many, if not all, of their demands. The companies had accepted the reality of the new conditions existing in Venezuela and the need to adapt to them. The private business community enjoyed the benefits derived from the increased purchasing power of the workers, and public opinion generally was satisfied by the fact that the oil industry was no longer run simply by the imperious dictates of oil company managers.

However, there was not complete unanimity in the way the negotiations had been carried out, and this dissidence was promoted by the small Venezuelan Communist party. It controlled a minority of oil unions, and their leaders took part in the oil workers' congress and participated in the negotiations with the companies. As soon as the contract had been signed, however, they tried to stir up trouble and promote strikes in the oil fields. National and international political motives lay behind this attempt at disruption. The fact that there had not been a single gain for the oil workers at the time when the communists enjoyed bureaucratic power during their alliance with the Medina Angarita government had had a devastating impact upon the prestige of the party. Now, in contrast, under the government of ideological adversaries of the communists, the workers were obtaining great benefits. Furthermore, these were not the days of Yalta and Teheran, with slogans of "no strikes" in the name of "national unity." Rather, from Berlin, the first verbal blasts of the Cold War were being heard. Just as the Soviet leaders, for their own purposes, had wanted the Communist parties in America during 1944 and 1945 to be models of peaceful cooperation to help the Kremlin win concessions in Asia and central Europe from the Allies, now in 1946 and the following years, the "line" was different. The diplomatic tension between Moscow and Washington would show up in the permanent agitation maintained against all companies with dollar investments, especially when they were in American countries. The new version of the Third International organized in September 1947, now called the Cominform, divided the world into two irreconcilable bands, socialists and peace lovers. Not to repeat enthusiastically the chant of the Soviet Archangels was—to the true believers—obvious servility to the Western devils.

Thus it was that the old quarrel between the Venezuelan communists and the majority of Venezuelan workers, who were nationalists and revolutionaries, became particularly intense during those days. The oil workers of Zulia state replied ironically to the appeal for "worker unity" made by the communist union:

> The communists who keep preaching "unity" are those who are engaging continually in irresponsible demagoguery and resorting to all kinds of methods completely contrary to true union democracy. Obviously they are not sincere in their campaign and are only using the "unity" slogan in an effort to bring in members to the Communist party, which is all that they are after.[11]

The communists then tried to instigate strikes in the areas where they had some influence. These were declared illegal by the government since a collective contract was in effect. The government also blocked the attempt by Vicente Lombardo Toledano, encouraged by remote control from "some place in Europe," to hold a congress of Latin American oil workers in Venezuela. All of this had its logical outcome. When the first collective contract expired early in 1948, the communist leaders insisted that new demands be presented to the oil companies with a strike deadline, even before any discussions took place. A strike, they argued, was necessary for the Venezuelan proletariat. The National Federation of Oil Workers accused them publicly of trying

> to transfer the international quarrel between Russia and the United States to our workers. If Russian oil companies were operating in Venezuela, they would not act

this way. The communists are being irresponsible and antipatriotic. They are serving interests which have nothing to do with our worker movement and the national welfare.[12]

The Oil Workers Federation expelled the small group of communist leaders on the grounds that they had tried to involve the Venezuelan oil workers in a strike which would weaken the democratic government, in accord with instructions received from the Cominform. Internationally, the communists have always sought to use the union movement as an instrument of their political game. They had been fervent defenders of union cooperation when allied with the Medina Angarita government, but they sought in every way to instigate conflicts when in opposition to our government. They failed due to their inherent weakness.

The second collective contract in the oil industry was signed in February 1948. Among many other advantages, the workers obtained a 16⅔ percent increase in their wages and a minimum basic wage of Bs. 14 per day.

Although the Acción Democrática government had a favorable attitude toward the oil workers, it did not follow a policy of demogoguery with them. Neither the government nor the party was in agreement with the idea that the oil workers could ask for whatever they wanted from the oil companies on the grounds that the latter could meet their demands. We did not want to create a worker elite while the rest of the workers in the country could not hope for an income at all like the oil workers' income. We also felt that it should be the government which should receive the benefit of the very high oil company earnings because it could redistribute them in an equitable manner among the entire Venezuelan people. Even so, the salaries and benefits of the oil industry during the years 1946–48 reached levels higher than those of any other oil-producing country, except the United States. Joseph E. Pogue, economist of the Chase Bank and therefore closely connected with Creole Corporation, estimated that the cost per worker in the Venezuelan oil industry was Bs. 49.22 or $15.93 per day. Naturally this figure was maliciously used to predict higher risks for the industry due to high labor cost.

The International Labor Office sent a mission to Venezuela in 1949, and its estimates can be considered more accurate than those of Pogue:

	Bs. 1946	Bs. 1948	Increase between 1946 & 1948	
			Bs.	%
Average basic daily wage............	12.90	17.38	4.48	34.7
Other cash payments	3.80	13.02	9.22	242.6
Total daily wage	16.70	30.40	13.70	82.0
Indirect benefits	6.38	12.08	5.72	89.9
Total.............................	23.06	42.48	19.42	84.2

Source: *Liberty of Association and Working Conditions in Venezuela*, ILO, Geneva,

These figures need no comment; they graphically express the change in the status of the Venezuelan oil workers in just three years.

Sowing the Petroleum

The new tax measures meant that the government was receiving a much higher income each year. Reorganization of public administration and the eradication of graft also tended to increase available resources. Although the democratic regime had a revenue without parallel among those of preceeding governments, expenses were increasing at the same time. The nation benefited but did not pay any additional taxes. Oil provided the money for the millions and millions of bolívares now included in the budget to care for the vital needs of the population.

From 1938 to 1945, the annual average public expenditure was Bs. 350 million and the income from oil Bs. 140 million—equivalent to 40 percent of the national expenditures. The remaining 60 percent came from various taxes.

However, the situation changed with the first budget of the Acción Democrática government for the year 1946–47, when public expenditures were tripled (Bs. 1066 million), and quadrupled in 1947–48 (Bs. 1315 million). In this year, the oil income was raised to Bs. 814.5 million—now 63 percent of the public income. The remaining 37 percent was from taxes.

Thus the first difficulty in the great national transformation was overcome. The government now had large economic resources, and our argument while in opposition was justified. We had always said that our problems should not be continued indefinitely without solution, that they should not depend upon routine tax income. We had to devise bold new formulas to bring the state additional income, sufficient to deal with the magnitude of the problems it confronted.

A big question remained, however. Would this enormous income be wasted in a showy and ornamental administration, or would it be used to give vitality to the economy and to upgrade its human resources?

The question was all the more urgent becasue our fiscal prosperity depended entirely upon a nonrenewable natural resource that would be exhausted within two generations.

We chose the second route. In the following pages, it will be shown how public money was invested usefully with the idea of "sowing the petroleum" and giving Venezuela a solid economic-social foundation.

PART FIVE

"Sowing the Petroleum"

6

The Coordinates of a Social Policy: Full Employment, High Salaries, and Adequate Supplies

The Same Reality Seen from Two Angles

Before Acción Democrática came to power, the national scene had been looked upon from two different angles. Like Janus, the mythological god, Venezuela had two faces: the smiling, placid one seen by the government; and that painfully contorted one due to frustration and unhappiness, seen by the rest of the population.

The superficial view from government circles is well summed up in a phrase used by President Medina Angarita with the New York press in 1944: "Happiness reigns in Venezuela." We reflected on the more somber view, diametrically opposed to this rose-colored opinion, in what we said from public platforms, in the press and in Congress.

The foreign trade figures of Venezuela were impressive because the country depended entirely on petroleum. We imported so much only because we produced oil—a product which "cannot be eaten and cannot be drunk," as the famous writer and globe-trotter John Gunther noted when he came to Caracas. The official figures on trade concealed two tragic facts: that Venezuela was a typical semicolonial country in danger of becoming simply an oil reserve for the big powers; and that the great majority of its people were poorly fed, indecently housed, without access to culture, and unprotected from the tropical diseases which continually threatened their health.

Once in power, we did not bear out the saying of Clemenceau that problems are seen much differently from revolutionary barricades than from the government side. We continued to speak with the same blunt frankness in

155

referring to the problems of the nation. We repeated over and over again that Venezuela was becoming a mono-producer nation and that its economic prosperity was illusory because it depended entirely upon oil. In one of my last public statements before leaving the government (message of Janaury 1947), I insisted that there must be a concerted, planned effort to increase national production: "All the different productive factors must be coordinated so Venezuela, once and for all, is freed from the dangerous situation of having its economy depend entirely on the ups and downs—as expressed in dollars and cents—of oil on the world market."

Minister of Production Pérez Alfonzo also revealed the weakness of the national economy in his annual report presented to Congress in 1948:

> Foreign trade makes up the largest part of national income. The true measure of our economy can be understood from the fact that we have Bs. 2000 million of imports for our 4 million inhabitants. Furthermore, it is disconcerting that 95 percent of these imports are paid for with dollars coming from one export product— oil. We are a country of a single product and our economy depends upon foreign sales of this product. This is a dangerous situation which must be rectified.

When we spoke these truths, we demonstrated confidence in our people. We knew that they would join in the noble task of building a different Venezuela if their leaders would show them the way. Events proved that our optimism was well founded. The record of three years of democratic administration—a milestone in our contemporary history and a challenge for the future—was possible only because of public support and encouragement. The objectives of this administration were both to attend to the immediate national needs, and to give a more permanent solution to the fundamental problems of the country.

Immediate Needs

The public mood when we came to power was one of irritation and depression because of unemployment, low salaries, the high cost of living, and the scarcity of basic foodstuffs. The revolution had stirred up the masses, and these social problems rapidly came to the surface. There were no street riots because the people gave the government their peaceful cooperation. However, delegation after delegation, coming from all four points of the compass, brought the same anguished message to us: most people felt overwhelmed by the general poverty and the difficulties of feeding, clothing, curing, and educating themselves. They expected that the government, led by sons of the people, would rapidly solve their pressing problems.

For our part, we had promised to take action. The people had been told in the first radio broadcast from Miraflores Palace, twelve days after the provisional government was installed: "We will make the defense of the human resources of the country our first concern. We will not build skyscrapers but men. Our women and children will have better public services, schools and student dining rooms."

Action could not wait until we had a plan, perfect as Minerva when she sprang from the head of Jupiter. As in the parable of Christ, we had to sharpen our sickle and harvest the wheat at the same time. We had to proceed on two tracks: to give short-term immediate solutions to the most pressing problems, and to undertake the structural changes in our economy necessary for the long-term welfare of the nation.

Elimination of Unemployment and Low Salaries

The annual report of the Central Bank for 1948 described the double process, begun in October 1945: an increase in employment with the objective of full employment; an increase in wages and benefits due to the unprecedented participation in national income by the poorest and largest sectors of the population. For instance, the report noted the substantial increase in oil industry employment which grew from 14,044 employees and 34,880 workers in 1947 to 17,416 and 41,002 in 1948.

Another index cited was the increase in the number of workers enrolled in the obligatory social security system, which at that time functioned only in the Federal District. This grew from 57,333 in 1944 to 77,842 in 1948. Social security statistics also indicated that the income of the workers was rising rapidly. For instance, 10.8 percent of the working population earned a daily wage of only $1.20 in 1944 while 13.1 percent were in the highest salary group. The lowest group had almost disappeared entirely by 1948, with the workers now to be found in the higher wage brackets.

The report made a five-year study of average daily wages:

1944	Bs.	7.09 per day
1945		7.42
1946		10.79
1947		13.39
1948		15.11

Opposition spokesmen kept saying that these wage increases were illusory because the increases in the cost of living nullified them. The fact was that wages increased more than prices. According to the Central Bank, wages increased from an index of 100 in 1944 to 164.74 in 1948, but prices only went up to 129.36. The Economic Commission for Latin America (ECLA) made the same observation and noted that prices actually showed a tendency to fall while salaries continued to go up. Price increases in Venezuela had been much less than in other countries of the continent, including the United States, according to the United Nations. The following are price indexes for September 1947.

1937 equals 100			
Argentina	226	Dominican Republic	296
Chile	313	Peru	352
Costa Rica	228	United States	182
Mexico	253	Venezuela	162

Source: *U.N. Statistical Bulletin*, no. 11, November 1947, p. 58.

Another source of additional income for workers was a government decree of 1938, giving them a measure of profit-sharing in the companies where they worked. This decree had been poorly enforced by the government, but that changed when we came to power. In 1944, only Bs. 17 million had been so distributed. In 1948, the total distribution was nearly Bs. 112 million.

A Real Prosperity

As a result of all these factors, the dispossessed masses of the country now began to have a real share in the national income. Now it could be said that Venezuela was becoming a prosperous nation because well-being was not just a privilege of the highest level of the population.

Prosperity was becoming generalized. Statistics of the Central Bank revealed, for instance, that total worker income in the Federal District increased from Bs. 208 million in 1945 to Bs. 573 million in 1948. Worker income increased more rapidly in the public sector than in private firms (199 percent vs. 163 percent), despite a decree of the revolutionary government which established a maximum salary for top government people, including the president and his ministers, of Bs. 4000. This meant that the salaries of the lower-level workers were increasing more rapidly. Since we were such outspoken defenders of a policy of higher wages for the working class, the government itself had to set a good example.

The first collective contract in Venezuelan history with an official agency was signed in 1946 by the Ministry of Public Works with its 12,000 workers, granting minimum salaries by regions, Sunday pay, fifteen-day paid vacations, and many other benefits. The contract was signed after an interministerial committee had studied different factors such as the cost of living in the various regions and the differences between urban and rural salaries. This was another example of the responsible manner in which we went about increasing workers' earning power. It was not done in an indiscriminate manner, but studied in terms of economic equilibrium.

Another aspect of the wage increases must be examined because it is of continuing interest. How was the new income spent and what were the repercussions on industrial production and business or agricultural income generally? It was often said in Venezuela by business spokesmen that workers wasted this money in superfluous expenditures or on vices and that industrialists were threatened with ruin because higher wages meant less work. Such arguments were not new. They have been used or abused in many parts by that sector of international capitalism which dreams of reviving the archaic times when the employer and the master were one and the same. In Venezuela, this reactionary group still lingered on from the times of Gómez. Opposed to the style and thinking of modern business managers, these people resembled the slave dealers of the colony. When their workers dared to make some timid request, they answered with jail or forced labor on the roads.

Freedom to Organize and Negotiate: The Source of Salary Increases

Our government did not seek to hide its wish to see salaries and wages go up. It increased the wages of government workers and encouraged the same in the private sector. The efficient Labor Minister, Dr. Raúl Leoni, traveled the country explaining to businessmen that it was not only just, but in their own interest to improve conditions for the workers and thus avoid labor unrest. The government did not try to achieve this goal by imposition of decrees, although the governing junta had assumed "the full power of national sovereignty." It did open the door, giving workers freedom to organize themselves and, by their own efforts, obtain better working conditions. At the end of 1945, there were 252 unions legally established in the country; by 1948, there were 1014. It was this organized labor force which won substantial improvements in wages and salaries by normal democratic bargaining, and without strikes or interruption of economic activities. By November 1948, on the eve of the reactionary coup d'état, there were 575 collective contracts stabilizing our production. Entire sections of the economy were able to plan ahead with confidence, knowing that there would not be strikes since they were prohibited by the labor law when work contracts were in effect.

It should be noted that this industrial peace prevailed in Venezuela at a time when class struggle convulsed many other countries. In Italy and France, the communists had abandoned the postwar coalitions and made use of their great power in the worker movement to instigate giant strikes. In the United States, without the ideological problems of Europe, strike after strike affected vital industries in these same years during which Venezuela experienced a violent revolution but was able to settle worker-employer differences by peaceful means.

There were undeniable reasons of social justice for the steps taken to almost double the workers' income in a period of three years. During 1947 and 1948, the cost of living went up sharply (the indices went from 137.1 to 155.6 in 1947 and to 173.5 in 1948). We were "importing inflation" as the Minister of the Treasury, Manuel Pérez Guerrero, fittingly described the situation. No price control or other measures by us would have been effective in view of the fact that the vast majority of the articles of consumption imported in a country with such low production had to be sold at higher prices because they were bought at higher prices from our principal supplier, the United States. The only reasonable formula for a government for which man was the center of its attention was the one we applied: no interference with the spiraling salaries, letting them go up. It was the only way we could avoid having international factors outside our control nullify our social welfare policy.

By the end of 1948, the situation had improved. Many imported articles were now available at lower prices. There had been good harvests for our domestic food production. It was the moment for organized workers to show that they had a sense of national responsibility, and they did. The National Confederation of Workers (CTV) proposed to the Federation of Chambers of Commerce and Industry an overall plan "designed to safeguard social peace and protect the industry and working population of the nation." The basic points of the proposal included protection of national industry, long-term collective contracts, preferential employment for union workers, and establishment of a mixed commission to conciliate labor differences. The employers showed great interest in the proposal, which was being discussed with them when the military takeover of November 24, 1948, dramatically cut short this constructive effort to achieve economic development under their first democratic regime.

The responsible attitude of the CTV had been possible because its leadership was made up of experienced and veteran labor leaders from Acción Democrática. However, it would not serve the truth or help in the future if one were to ignore some negative factors which had appeared in the recently organized labor movement. At the lower levels of the unions, there were many impromptu leaders without theoretical training—some independents, some members of AD. They sought to compete at times with the communists in their verbal excesses. On various occasions, they tried to force weak companies to pay salaries and benefits which they could not afford. Some of the union leaders also showed themselves irresponsible and arrogant in the way in which they abused the freedom given them to organize. Personal antagonisms among certain leaders created unnecessary union rivalries. Excuse for this conduct—one that can only be used for the past because in the future the union movement will surely be more mature—was simply that the earlier obstacles placed in the way of the union movement had not permitted larger groups of trained leaders to be formed or for the mass of workers themselves to develop a responsible attitude. In those years, the sit-down strikes in the United States and the occupation of factories and mines by French workers created a state of mind among the workers in all countries propitious to demagogic slogans. Even in countries where the worker movement had been going on for decades, certain union leaders exhibited a degree of arrogance because of official sympathy for the unions.

Workers Spend Their New Income Usefully

Now we must deal with the question as to how the workers spent their additional income. First of all, it was to feed themselves better. The people began to eat more not because of gluttony but because of what our native irony termed "delayed hunger."

Hunger, like malaria, was traditional in Venezuela. As the Venezuelan author Arturo Uslar Pietri wrote, "Venezuela has never had enough food except in certain areas under Carlos III," and he explained how hunger was one of the factors that drove the people to continued armed struggle during the past century. There were innumerable popular couplets of waggish intent which made reference to this circumstance, such as the following:

When you go out to the Llanos [plains]
And do not carry provisions,
Singing will take away hunger
And whistling will take away cold.

It can be expected that a people of such ironic humor would mock a little at their hunger, but it cannot be understood how Venezuelan governments could have been so indifferent to the problem. Before the government of 1945, there was none which did anything to improve the diet of the people. The following figures are dramatic testimony to the hunger from which the Venezuelan people suffered.

Food Need vs. Actual Consumption

Food	1943 Consumption	Minimum Need[a]
Flour, cornbread, rice, other cereals	265,265 tons	292,560 tons
Cheese, butter, milk......................	248,465	467,760
Meat and fish	81,655	120,720
Eggs	14,400	33,240
Vegetable oils	30,759	37,680
Fats.....................................	9,769	19,920
Citrus fruit and tomatoes	65,265	117,360
Vegetables, potatoes, etc.	76,725	440,640

[a]The minimum is 60 percent of normal, as recommended by the Hot Springs Conference.

Source: *Cuadernos de Infomacion Económica Venezolano*, 1945.

Even though the minimum consumption specified above was 40 percent below that recommended by the Hot Springs Conference as an adequate diet, it will be seen that there was an alarming disparity between what was eaten and what should have been eaten in Venezuela at that time. This explains why workers with more money to spend hastened to satisfy the elementary physiological need of feeding themselves adequately. It is easy to follow what happened with accuracy since so much of our food had to be imported. The figures on imports serve as a very sensitive measure as to how the Venezuelans spent their additional income.

In 1945, food imports were valued at Bs. 63,146 million. In 1948, they totaled Bs. 374,920 million. Food imports were very difficult when our government came to office because of the acute worldwide crisis. Countries which had a surplus asked very high prices and imposed difficult conditions. The Venezuelan government had to intervene and use its fiscal resources to get what was needed. In the two years 1946–47, the government spent more than Bs. 100 million, as compared with Bs. 450,000 during 1944 by the previous government, to acquire foodstuffs abroad. We also resorted to the barter of oil for food, as previously mentioned. Although this was critically described as the "policy of a commercial state," it was the only way possible to avoid aggravating the hunger of the people. Our purchases were in the millions, paid in cash, made on a government-to-government basis and entirely beyond the range of private commerce. However, we used commercial channels to distribute the foods with prices favorable to the consumer and which guaranteed a reasonable margin of profit to the distributor.

The prices of different food articles were fixed lower for consumers than their import cost. Imported lard cost 218 percent more than in 1945, rice 65 percent more, but these and other products were kept at the same price. In the two years 1946–47, the state lost Bs. 20 million. In reality, this money was not lost but invested in the health and welfare of the people. It is interesting to see how food consumption increased. Take sugar as an example. Consumption was 85,000 tons in 1943, equal to total domestic production, and consumption per capita was 20.7 kilograms. In 1944, with the same production, the Ministry of Agriculture declared there was a surplus and allowed 500 tons to be exported at prices lower than those existing in Venezuela. In 1946, national production was 88,550 tons and 35,000 tons were imported, which meant a per capita consumtion of 30.7 kilos. The same trend took place with meat, fish, and milk.

One of our worst deficits was in meat. The country was only consuming half the amount of meat it needed but nevertheless was shipping annually some 30,000 head of cattle to neighboring islands. Once in government, we prohibited this absurd export which was like "placing a candle in the street when there is darkness in the house." Prices were increased for cattle growers. The uneconomic transport of cattle on foot from the far-off plains regions to urban slaughterhouses was replaced by air transport of fresh meat. Frozen meat was imported from Argentina, and arrangements were made with Colombia for cattle imports.

Special emphasis was placed on promoting fish consumption, and the amount of fresh fish eaten jumped from 28,000 kilograms in 1945 to 40,000 in 1947. The increase in imported powdered milk was also notable: from 715,000 kilograms in the first three months of 1945 imports rose to 3,500,000 kilograms in the same period in 1947. In two years, milk consumption was increased 500 percent.

To be sure, these were all temporary measures. We never pretended to have reached the point of satisfying the basic needs of the population. This was admitted over and over again with a frankness unprecedented in a country where pious lies or sweet talk were habitually practiced by the government. What I want to stress here is the incontrovertible fact that most of the salary increase obtained by the working class was spent on food and clothing.

Of course, there was a certain amount of waste. The amount of imported whiskey, brandy, and cigarettes increased. The Spanish and Mexican bullfighters who came to Venezuela charged more than in any other country. Horse racing, which had been the prerogative of just a small monied class now became an attractive form of roulette for a great part of the populace. These problems concerned us and will be dealt with elsewhere. But the essential thing about this significant social experiment was the useful way in which the Venezuelan workers spent their additional income on their basic needs.

Two questions remain: Did this policy of full employment and higher wages help or hurt private business? Did national production increase at this time or did the higher cost of wages act as a brake? The last question will be discussed later when we go into the overall panorama of production under a democratic administration. But let us settle the question once and for all as to whether private enterprise made or lost money as a result of our social economic policy.

Industry and Commerce Increase Their Earnings

Some industrialists and merchants alleged that they were losing money and were on the verge of bankruptcy. Such people were accustomed to sell little and to make much. They were joined by others belonging to those groups which had made huge profits before 1945 as a result of government favor. This rare mix of orphans from official favor and a kind of hybrid of harpy and merchant of Venice proclaimed that both the country and they were at the point of ruin. Persevering observers refuted these prophets of catastrophe by studying the balance sheets of business concerns and industry.

It was evident that the increased purchasing power of the workers, in addition to the government's energetic policy of credits to industry, had not only meant greater social justice but also dynamic general improvement of business. Private firms paid better salaries and obtained at the same time reasonable profits, often better ones, than before 1945.

The 1947 annual report of the Ministry of the Treasury reflected this business improvement when it reported the yearly increase in profit-sharing by workers in various companies and the increase in income taxes paid to the government. The latter rose from Bs. 82 million in 1945 to Bs. 240 million in 1947. The Central Bank reported that the number of business firms in the Federal District increased from 10,919 in 1947 to 12,910 by 1948. The business climate was reflected in foreign investment circles which now understood that while the democratic government of Venezuela no longer accepted colonial treatment, it was led by serious men aware of their responsibilities. *Time* magazine reported from New York that the oil companies planned to invest Bs. 300 million in the next two years, 1948–49.

From Provisional Solutions to Permanent Plans

Until now, our actions had mostly been taken in response to emergencies. The reader is already familiar with the kind of country we found on taking power—overwhelmed by scarcity, high prices, unemployment, and miserable wages. It was our first task to get employment for every man and woman able to work and to see that they got fair wages. Our second task was to cover the deficit of essential products by imports. Our third was to control the high cost of living and to fix prices for rents, electricity, and other public services.

These measures papered over the situation for the moment, but we had to get to the root of the economic and social problems of the nation. We had to transform an economy of limited production of few things to diversified and abundant output. This required farsighted and bold planning by the government. To use the graphic expression of José Martí, it was necessary "to enter the slaughterhouse with sleeves rolled up."

7

From a Semicolonial Oil Country to a Diversified Economy of Our Own

Planning for General Welfare in Freedom

The idea of laissez faire has passed into history. Planning is now the hope of our times. Few today would dispute the fact that democracy means not only public liberties but also economic welfare for the entire population and social security for the workers. It is also generally recognized that the material improvement of a country has much to do with its productivity consumption and the efficiency of its services. Real progress cannot be achieved in underdeveloped regions if the economy is left entirely to private initiative. The faith of Adam Smith and the liberal economists is gone. State intervention to guide the economy toward collective welfare and national achievement is the ABC of modern government policy.

The use and abuse of state interventionism by Nazism-fascism—just defeated when we came to power in 1945—was not a very auspicious precedent for us. Neither was the authoritarian planning imposed by the Soviet police state. The New Deal of Roosevelt and the Welfare State of the Labor government in England came in highly industrialized societies, very different from Venezuela. Puerto Rico was just beginning its admirable effort at planning, but the truth was that we knew very little about this in Venezuela. Nor did India or Yugoslavia (then attached to the Soviet locomotive) have much to teach us in 1946 about how democracy could plan without sacrificing fundamental individual liberties on the altar of progress. Israel, where much has been accomplished in recent years by serious planning, did not yet exist as a sovereign state.

We had to face up to the truth stated by the eminent sociologist Karl Mannheim:

> The democracies have not yet found any formula to determine which aspects of the social process can be controlled by rules; the dictatorships have not yet realized that to control everything is not to plan. Planning will only have a positive value if it is based on creative social forces—that is the say, if it directs social energies and does not repress them.

We knew that the national economy of Venezuela was so deformed that there were chronic defects in the production of basic necessities. We had repeatedly raised our voices against the official inertia that would lead to catastrophe if we did not possess our own permanent source of production once the petroleum was gone. Now that we were in the government, we could not be content with the emergency measures described in the previous pages. The time had come, quoting Karl Mannheim again, "to deal with the defects in the social order, proceeding with full knowledge of the entire social mechanism and the manner in which it functions." So we created two agencies to promote the structural transformation of the country: one to advise and the other to plan. These were the National Economic Council and the Venezuelan Development Corporation (Corporación Venezolana de Fomento, or CVF).

The National Economic Council had been provided for in the 1936 Constitution. It was to be made up of representatives of all sectors of production, who were to advise the government on economic and fiscal matters. However, the post-Gómez governments did not want such a group since they considered public administration as a private monopoly. They were governments of "friends." Only those who had been given the secret signs were allowed to pass beyond the veil. Our government had nothing to hide. On the contrary, we sought to check our official views with those in the street. As I stated at the beginning of our regime:

> To govern does not mean, for us, to shut ourselves up within our ourselves. We do not believe we are self-sufficient nor have we the mistaken idea that we enjoy the papal privilege of infallibility. For us, to govern is to serve; this means to keep in close contact with citizens of whom we are only the representatives.[1]

When in the opposition, we had constantly voiced the demand that a state agency be created to promote national production. This was also the desire of the various private economic groups. The educated people of Venezuela were well aware of the unhappy experience of Spain, Chile, and Peru when the production of their sole economic support—whether silver, nitrate, or guano—began to fail. We wanted to have our own diversified national production ready at the time when petroleum should cease to flow.

In 1946, the CVF was organized, taking into account the experiences of Chile and Colombia with similar agencies, and the Reconstruction Finance Corporation in the United States. However, we were very conscious of the need to use our own judgment in accord with our own Venezuelan characteristics. The CVF was given substantial economic resources—nearly Bs. 400 million to begin with—and it had been planned to raise this to Bs. 1000 million under the Gallegos presidency. Outside directors were included to keep this organization from becoming just another government bureaucracy. A man of unusual social sensitivity and extraordinary dynamism, Alejandro Oropeza Castillo, was named its president.

This state agency had its own unique characteristics for planning and promoting production. We in the Venezuelan government were, and still are, convinced that our country cannot bypass the stage of capitalistic economic development. We require a nationalistic and revolutionary transformation, to be sure, but not one that follows socialist or communist models. Our problem is not going to be solved by taking away wealth but by finding our own way of continuing to produce it. Also we must do this ourselves instead of having the country at the mercy of foreign investors. The government itself, with its vast fiscal resources, must accelerate this transition. It must also orient and condition the process so that it does not produce either anarchy or a new business oligarchy, unwilling to share benefits with workers and consumers.

We knew that we could not carry out this economic revolution in Venezuela on the grounds of historical necessity like the English "landlords" who left such a horrible record of enslaving men to industrial machines, or with Olympian disdain toward the workers as did the Lyon industrialists in France with the triumph of bourgeois capitalism there. In Venezuela this "jump," in the Hegelian sense, from the colonial to the modern in our economy, had to be planned and regulated by a government which responded to the most stable elements of the country—the middle class of professional and technical people: the workers, artisans, and farmers of modern mentality.

Our approach to raising production had three aspects: first, a study of the characteristics of our economy and its promotion in accord with these technical studies; second, the undertaking by the state of those programs, which because of their size or lack of profitability, would not attract private investments; and third, the stimulating through liberal credits and technical assistance to those private businessmen willing to coordinate their efforts with national needs, adjusting their costs to what the consumer could reasonably pay, in agreement with the level of salaries and benefits now being paid to Venezuelan workers.

Economic Panorama: 1946

The analysis of the national economy made by the CVF indicated an excessive development of commerce, the result of the abundance of oil dollars; industrial underdevelopment; and a stagnant agriculture. The statistics of the period show an abnormal growth of commercial establishments dedicated largely to the sale of imported articles, a situation highly unfavorable for the national economy. Our challenge was to produce more merchandise at home and to distribute fewer imported goods.

Because of a variety of circumstances, state action to stimulate and orient the economy was more of a necessity in Venezuela than in most other Latin American countries. The state received most of the oil income, large enough to undertake decisive action. The government could not fold its arms and wait for the private sector to diversify production, because our local capitalists followed the way of least resistance. All too often, they preferred to be shopkeepers rather than farmers or industrialists. Our government had to finance and orient economic activities that would increase and diversify our domestic production. It was also obliged to develop certain activities vital to the national welfare—steel, electrification, radio and telephone communications, and transportation.

Credit Policy of the CVF

The AD government used its credit policy through the CVF and two other previously existing state banks, the Banco Agricola y Pecuario (BAP) and Banco Industrial, to increase agricultural and cattle production and develop industries that would contribute to human welfare.

The need for giving preference to agriculture was obvious. There was a deficit in food products, aggravated by the postwar difficulties in importing food. The amount of land under cultivation—only 4 percent of the potential agricultural lands in the country—was reduced even further during the war by 9.1 percent. Meanwhile our population continued to grow rapidly. Although the need was clear, there were many negative factors which we could not ignore, of both a material and a psychological nature. Much land could not be cultivated because there was so little irrigation. Other land was in the hands of absentee landowners. Erosion had ruined or deteriorated vast areas. Transport difficulties were also discouraging. The mental obstacles consisted of the skepticism which was general throughout the countryside of Venezuela with regard to the agricultural possibilities of the country.

So much was said about agriculture being ruined by the oil industry, and so little had been done by the state to contradict this easy alibi. The rural population was left to stagnate on haciendas or small farms (conucos).

The CVF took the lead in combating this defeatism with its distribution of credits. These were available for twenty years at an annual interest of 4 percent and were issued preferentially for the mechanization of agriculture by those willing to give priority to the production of such deficit items as corn, sugar, rice, vegetable oils, meat, milk, and fish. The credits were closely supervised so that state money would not be used to purchase city mansions, fast cars, and jewels for the ladies of Paris and New York. All contracts contained clauses guaranteeing the payment of wages and the provision of proper living conditions for farm workers. An impressive volume of credits was issued: Bs. 84 million in 1947 and Bs. 109 million in 1948.

Meat, Milk, and Sugar

Geography determined that Venezuela should be a cattle-raising country because of its vast pasture lands, especially in the southeast. A prosperous cattle industry had once existed there but now had so declined that it was threatened with extinction. Alexander Humboldt and other foreign visitors in the early nineteenth century marveled at the animal population on the plains (llanos). The herds of Apure provided horses for the armies during the wars of independence. The cattle herds of Cuba and other Central American countries are descended from cattle imported from Venezuela. At their peak, during the nineteenth century, the Venezuelan cattle herds had some 4 million head, but in 1945 the total was only 2.8 million head. Meanwhile, our population had quadrupled and we needed 7 million head of cattle to supply enough meat.

Cattle raising had prospered as long as there was ample water and natural pasture in the llanos. The irrational destruction of forests at the headwaters of our rivers and the burning of the savanna lands were causing progressive deterioration. Also, the continuous civil wars had greatly reduced the herds so that our writer Tosta Garcia remarked ironically, "Long live the revolution, let the cattle die."

The government could have done something about the cattle industry, but, as we have seen, it took a position of neutrality in matters affecting national economic life. The final blow was given by the dictator Gómez. A cattleman himself, he sought to monopolize the best ranches and cattle as well as the sales of meat. Whatever he did not squeeze from the suffering cattle industry was left for his lieutenants in local government. Shortly before we came to power, the minister of agriculture of Medina Angarita revealed that the country lacked 28,000 head of cattle to fill local market demand. He also admitted that the problem did not arise because of an overconsumption of meat which averaged only 17 kilograms per capita annually, while the normal diet should have been 100 kilograms.

The CVF now assumed the responsibility, which seemed so insoluble according to the prophets of pessimism, of promoting cattle raising and the milk production so closely associated with it. It was not just a matter of handing out credits. The CVF closely coordinated its program with the technical services of the Ministry of Agriculture in cattle raising. A nationwide plan was formulated, concentrating on the areas most suited for cattle raising. Highlights of the plan included technical supervision of credits, the importation of cattle to breed with the native strains, the provision of water for cattle by well-drilling and the construction of reservoirs, and the prevention of cattle diseases. In a single year, 1947–48, more than Bs. 35 million were invested in this program. Credits flowed to the stock breeders. Bulls by the hundreds were unloaded at our ports—Brown Swiss, Zebu, Jersey, and Holstein—to cross-breed with our domestic cattle of which there remained as one rancher said, in the accents of Ecclesiastes, hardly even "good will." In 1947, 100 water wells and 65 reservoirs were completed. Hitherto skeptical cattlemen began to fence their ranches, to resow pasture on eroded lands, and to seek the advice of the veterinarian. Hunger and thirst and disease would no longer continue to decimate our cattle herds year after year.

If this program had been continued for a decade, Venezuela would have recovered its old position as a leading cattle producer. It will be seen, however, how the military dictatorship once again abandoned the cattle industry to an uncertain fate.

As previously noted, national milk production was inadequate and the importation of powdered milk from abroad was constantly increasing. We had to give priority to changing this situation because of our major goal to improve the diet of the people. Some Bs. 16 million were loaned to milk producers in both 1947 and 1948 but since the production and distribution of milk was so important, we felt the state should intervene more directly. A model cooperative was established in Maracay in 1947 with Bs. 5 million in government funds; it selected choice cattle and used the most modern technical methods. It succeeded in producing milk at minimum cost and served as an example for the private producers in other regions. The government also intervened in the pasteurization and distribution of milk and in 1946 acquired various companies engaged in this activity. The idea was to follow the example of Chile, which made fresh milk distribution and sale a public service.

The CVF also planned and promoted the development of the sugar industry. The major sugar mills of the country were controlled by persons with the old-fashioned mentality of the traditional big landholders. Some of them longed for those times when Juan Vicente Gómez had kindly loaned them army troops to silence workers who dared to complain and pursued them like animals through the sugar cane. Their mills had antiquated machinery, and their prevailing philosophy was that of producing very little and selling very dear. It was clear, furthermore, that the multiplication of small mills with obsolete machinery, some of it inherited from days of the colony, would hardly bring about massive production at reasonable cost. The CVF decided that nothing was to be gained by giving credits to those who insisted upon maintaining inefficient and old-fashioned companies. Furthermore, such people seemed convinced of the absurd idea that the workers in their agricultural and industrial plants should get the same wage and living conditions as peons on a coffee plantation.

The CVF therefore established conditions for its credits to sugar growers. They had to show willingness to modernize the industry in both its agricultural and industrial aspects and readiness to improve living conditions of the workers. This was done both to increase the capacity of the sugar industry and to reduce the price of the product.

The leaders of the national sugar industry were not enthused with these conditions. They were caught between the millstones of their traditional routine. I told them frankly when they came together in the presidential office that the government wanted to provide them with abundant credit if they would agree to modernize their industries. However, the state would not hesitate to finance and organize large sugar mills and administer them directly or even advance credits to foreign sugar growers, if the private sugar growers continued with their virtual sabotage of government plans.

That is what we had to do. One of the largest sugar mills, the Central Tacarigua, was among the properties of General Gómez seized by the government. Using the technical recommendations of experts, which were practical and imaginative, this mill soon was producing 10,000 tons of sugar per year with a good profit as well as providing ample social benefits for the workers. After other state projects were undertaken, capitalists appeared willing to operate on the terms set by the government. A Cuban corporation invested Bs. 14 million in 1947 and obtained government loans for Bs. 6 million in 1947. A year later, its first harvest was equal to one-third of our annual sugar deficit.

The blind stubbornness of some of our capitalists of traditional mentality now began to give way. During 1948, various sugar companies were established with the CVF acting as both a participant and principal financier. The results of this policy, evident some years later after we left the government, will be reported in the following pages.

Another Credit Agency, the Agriculture and Cattle Bank (BAP)

The BAP took care of smaller loans—up to Bs. 25,000. Prior to the revolution, this bank had been starved for capital, but new assignments of capital to it as well as to the Industrial Bank enabled both to increase their loans rapidly.

In 1945, the BAP issued credits worth Bs. 57.2 million and loaned money against harvests to 14,146 farmers for a total of Bs. 33.8 million. By 1948, grants were made to 81,093 farmers for Bs. 96.4 million. The BAP also guaranteed minimum prices to the producer through buying surplus crops and storing them in a system of silos that were installed around the country. Some opposition critics complained that these credits amounted to nothing more than donations made by the government to win votes. The foolhardiness of this assertion was demonstrated by the fact that the BAP had collected on 95.5 percent of the loans made the previous year.

The Bonanza for Agriculture

This energetic and well-planned program rapidly brought results. The index of agricultural production in 1948 was 112.8 as compared to 118.2 in 1949. The production of staples in the Venezuelan diet increased significantly, as shown in the following table:

Production in Metric Tons

	1945	1948
Sugar	1,950,000	2,370,000
Peas	8,000	16,000
Beans	8,000	18,017
Potatoes	9,185	16,000

Source: *Cuardenas de Información Económica*, no. 4, 1950.

But was the increase in production really a benefit to farmers? The political opposition in reactionary business circles, including certain commercial establishments that were no longer able to charge the farmers such high rates of interest, insisted that it was not. "Inflation" was an epithet hurled at the government like a dirty word. It was said that the so-called inflationary policy of the democratic government nullified the apparent bonanza for the agricultural sector.

This was completely untrue. Anyone could see, for the first time in many years, economic improvement in the rural areas. This was so patent that even after the fall of the democratic government, the research section of the CVP published figures showing how the farmer was taking in much more with higher prices for his crops than he was having to pay out for goods and services. The farmer now had enough money left over to save. Farm labor became attractive again, and it could even be said that the population began to return to the countryside. The exodus of people from rural areas had been so serious during the years 1938–39 that government circles had even thought of reestablishing the colonial road-control stations, futile though they were. The idea was to try to stop the country population from going to the cities by the use of fines and other arbitrary means. This medieval idea was abandoned and the migration to the city continued until men came to power with clear ideas about the economic-social problems of Venezuela and were ready to put them into action.

Effective encouragement to the farmer began to give immediate and surprising results. The measures taken included credits and technical assistance, guaranteed prices, and the extension of education and health services to the countryside. As production went up and prices improved and as the teacher and doctor appeared in the previously abandoned rural areas, rural inhabitants stayed home. The alleged congenital nomadism of the Venezuelan farm worker, which superficial sociologists attributed to our aboriginal ancestry, proved to be a consequence of a negative social-economic environment.

Large-Scale Technical Farm Production

However, extraordinary importance should not be given to the increase in physical volume of farm production in these years. It really had limited importance because it was achieved without previous transformation of the physical environment, without a true agrarian reform, and without the mechanization of the rural area. The improvement, nevertheless, was sufficient to eliminate the idea, so fixed in the national consciousness, that Venezuelan agricultural development was impossible and that the country was condemned "to enjoy the sun only while it was shining"—to feed itself only as long as it had enough oil to pay for imports of food from abroad.

We wanted to do more than simply do away with this defeatism. We proposed to change radically the inadequate physical conditions, especially with dams and irrigation systems of vast proportions. We also proposed to substitute modern and mechanized agricultural technology for the obsolete methods of cultivation—those of the plough, the hoe, and the machete.

8

Mechanization and Irrigation: Two Major Efforts

"First Place in Mechanization in Latin America"

The observation has been made that when underdeveloped countries learn to operate machines, they enjoy the singular advantage of reaching in one leap the same level of more developed nations. They do not have to go through the same long years of slow development as did the modern industrial nations. This was demonstrated in the way agriculture was mechanized in Venezuela. Machines were needed there as in few other countries to clear land, to sow, and to harvest. The big deficit in farm production required special haste in development. Our rural areas did not have an excess of farm hands, as in so many other countries; and, since Venezuela had financial resources, it was quite logical that our democratic government should have established the mechanization of agriculture as one of its prime goals.

We were pioneers in this field, as in so many others; but there were many difficulties. We had barely 700 or so agricultural machines and there was a notable absence of tractors and mechanics. It was as though we wanted to start the train but discovered that it had neither locomotive nor engineer. We sent hundreds of apprentices to a tractor school at Maracay. Soldiers and demobilized veterans of the armored corps were transferred from driving tanks to farm vehicles. It was not easy to acquire farm machinery because of the postwar scarcities. Mention has already been made of the government's diplomatic efforts to obtain preferential treatment in the United States. These achieved positive results. The number of tractors imported in 1948 was quadruple the number in 1945. Instead of 700 agricultural machines necessary to farm only 39,000 hectares in 1945, there were 2700 machines capable of handling the production of 130,000 hectares by 1948. Our advance was so rapid that the ECLA reported, "Venezuela now occupies first place in the degree of agricultural mechanization in all of Latin America."

Irrigation, a Myth Made Reality

Like a victim of elephantiasis, the Venezuelan economy had one tremendously swollen limb, petroleum, while the others were feeble and deformed. In 1946, this phenomenon had alarming proportions. There was only .21 hectare in cultivation per inhabitant, in contrast to .34 in Mexico and 1.2 hectares in the United States. It should also be remembered that our productivity was much less than in the two other countries.

This negative situation required something more than tractors and credits. We had to modify the physical environment by a water policy of vast proportions. We had to dam streams, catch rainwater, divert rivers, and use irrigation to transform sterile soil. One did not have to be an engineer to know that the great part of Venezuela suffered from lack of water. There were immense areas of eroded land without cultivation or vegetable cover. Looking at the countryside from the air filled one with anguish. There was so little rain in these regions that the land was no longer fertile. In other semihumid zones, the droughts were not so prolonged, but rain was irregular and sometimes came with such violence that the rivers overflowed and flooded large areas.

The lack of water in so much of Venezuela was a result of the destructive action of man. The irrational razing of forests and the systematic use of fire to prepare land for cultivation had been destroying the water sources and changing the climate of the country. Various foreign experts who came to Venezuela left warnings of the somber future awaiting a nation which so depleted its forest reserves. Democratic government tried to put an end to this destruction. A forest ranger service was established. Concessions to private parties for the lumbering of wooded areas were held up. Foreign experts were brought in to advise the minister of agriculture regarding a conservation policy. One of them was William Vogt, author of the book *Road to Survival;* one of its translators was our Minister of Agriculture, Ricardo Montilla. In the prologue to the Spanish edition, Vogt explained how much of the translation had been done in prison and how the conservation program, planned by Montilla, had not been carried out. "This may well be one of the most costly errors in the history of Latin America," concluded Vogt.

Water and Geography

The greatest amount of water power is in the southern part of the country. The Orinoco and its great tributaries flow northward to the sea carrying a fabulous amount of water. They cross areas with little population, still covered by unexplored forests. These rivers will be the highways of a tremendous civilization in the future, but our generation cannot think now about the colonization of this vast hinterland. The immediate task of our own times is to make the northern part of the country habitable and productive—between the great wall of the Andes and the Caribbean shores, where 82 out of every 100 Venezuelans live at present.

This northern area would lend itself to rapid agricultural and industrial development. The major centers of population and consumption are located here. It is crisscrossed by roads and there are airports in all important cities. It has easy access to the sea. It has fresh water, but the problem is to collect it by dams and to distribute it in a proper way. The rivers are torrential, sometimes with little or no water but in the rainy season becoming violent floods. Even during the dry season, according to studies made by the Ministry of Public Works, there is sufficient water, if collected, to irrigate 1 million hectares and to provide enough food, raw materials for a well-developed industry, and electrical energy to satisfy a Venezuela of much greater population in the year 2000—even if not a drop of oil is left in the country.

Irrigation of 1 million hectares should be understood as a goal, not an immediate possibility. At first it would be possible to bring water to 200,000 or 300,000 hectares over a period no greater than five years. This would have assured the doubling of our agricultural production and would have appreciably improved rural living standards.

These are not imaginary figures, but are based on thorough technical studies. In 1946, some 800,000 hectares were under cultivation in Venezuela, of which scarcely 110,000 had permanent irrigation. Studies abroad and in Venezuela itself had demonstrated that properly irrigated soil had five times greater productivity; thus, 200,000 hectares of irrigated land would have produced twice what was being harvested on 800,000 when we began our government.

Other advantages would come from a bold use of our hydraulic resources. Irrigated land could produce two or three harvests each year. This would facilitate large-scale mechanization for agriculture. Agricultural cooperatives with semiindustrial projects in the rural areas could be undertaken with greater financial returns and would lead to the appearance of independent farmers and farm workers, educated and well taken care of, in place of the illiterate peons with their miserable pay and low standards of living. This is not just idle speculation nor based on the experiences of other countries. In one of the first irrigation projects at Swata, east of Lake Valencia, the crops of the first year in only half of the cultivated area were worth double the cost of the project and the earnings of the farmers were the same as urban business.

Another favorable result of irrigation would be to concentrate some of our scattered rural population. Our 5 million inhabitants [1950] are spread out over a vast territory. With irrigation, it would be possible to concentrate 14,000 people on an irrigated zone of 20,000 hectares.

Finally there is another reason, the most important of all. Irrigation would facilitate the settlement of tens of thousands of rural inhabitants on land of their own. Agrarian reform has been the great goal of the popular social movements of our time. Irrigation would make it possible to carry out agrarian reform on a viable economic basis. It would be sheer demagoguery to provide the landless rural inhabitants with farms of their own but continue to leave them at the mercy of the elements, knowing that drought would only drive them to poverty and fill them with resentment. On the other hand, settled on irrigated land and given proper technical advice, the beneficiaries of agrarian reform could rapidly achieve prosperous economic status. This was why an irrigation program was carried out from the start with greatest dedication and energy by the AD government.

Irrigation Policy and the Pilot Project: El Cenizo

When we began our work, we found many obstacles in the way of an effective irrigation program. There were very few engineers who specialized in this kind of installation, or companies which cleared and leveled land. However, we went to work using studies which already existed. At the end of our first year of government, the minister of public works reported that irrigation works were under way for 20,000 hectares—ten times more than that provided for in the budget of the previous government.

These projects were practically completed the following year. One of them, El Cenizo, merits particular attention. This area was carefully selected—the result of a joint study by the CVF and the National Economic Council—as the site for an overall economic development plan. On a very modest scale, we were trying to carry out an experiment similar to the Tennessee Valley Authority in the United States.

This zone was located at the foothills of the Andes between the mountain and the sea in the western state of Trujillo. It had 100,000 hectares of land with excellent soil, alluvial deposits from the mountains washed down for centuries. The area was near the western oil fields, and there were good communications. All branches of government were coordinated to clean up the area and build model towns with all that was required to make life comfortable. Hundreds of rural families were located there to begin work in December 1948, when the first 10,000 hectares were ready for cultivation. It was hoped that this pilot project not only would be economically viable itself, but would also stimulate the imagination and creative faith of the nation. El Cenizo would put to rest, once and for all, the defeatism of those who considered the tropical Latin American man incapable of carrying out an exemplary cooperative project. Many similar projects were under study, and the government had increased its budget for them by 600 percent. In a speech on August 29, 1947, I reported that it would be possible in four years to double the 100,000 hectares of irrigated land the country at present possessed. However, all these hopes were frustrated by the coup d'état of November 1948.

Mechanization, credits, and irrigation were not enough to affect basic transformations in our agriculture. We had to end the traditional system of large landholdings, put undercultivated areas into operation, and give land to the poor country people. We had to carry out agrarian reform. This was another major objective of the revolutionary government.

9

The Agrarian Reform

Historical Nature of the Large Landholdings (*Latifundio*)

As in almost all of Latin America, rural production in Venezuela took place on large landholdings, the *latifundio*. The Venezuelan colonial landowner did not have to overcome resistance like that offered by the Mexican Aztecs of the Quechua-speaking tribes of Peru and Bolivia, both heirs to a great collective agricultural tradition. The Indian tribes in Venezuela were dispersed, backward, and poverty-stricken. They lived and died as indentured servants without the memory of a better life in precolonial times to make them rebellious. The Spanish conquerors and their descendants were able to obtain by royal grant enormous territories, with very poorly defined borders because the property deed of many of them simply stated they extended "as far as can be seen." This occupation—or "primitive expropriation" as Marx put it in one of the best chapters of *Das Kapital*—left the first landholders of Venezuela with dubious land titles.

Monopoly of the land by the very few, and workers virtually bound to the land as slaves—these characterized agriculture during the first three centuries of the colony and explained its nonproductivity and failure to produce wealth.

Gil Fortol, in his excellent *Historia Constitucional de Venezuela*, relates how the Guipuzcoana Company first came to this colony of precarious production with a royal concession to handle all trade. The company was predatory and cruel, but it did introduce new types of cultivation and commercial methods. It even did something more, without intending to. Its ships brought to Ven-

179

ezuela, as contraband, the books of the French Encyclopedists, which became the leavening force of the revolutions to come when the social groups which possessed economic power rebelled against the restrictions imposed by Spain. The monopoly of the mother country over imports and exports of the colonies became an intolerable restraint to their inhabitants. Bolívar, in his famous letter from Jamaica, said that this monopoly and the regulation of all types of cultivation were among the most hated measures imposed by the Spanish Crown.

These economic controls not only hampered production but also stood in the way of local political freedom. The colonial leaders, educated in the Tridentine Seminary of Caracas and often in Spanish universities, felt themselves fully able to run the country and rejected the idea that their public officials should come from far-away Madrid.

These were the economic and social premises for the independence movement; but even so, it never would have come to pass if there had not appeared a group of extraordinary leaders, ready for any sacrifice and capable of all kinds of heroism. This stupendous group was made up of men who, in 1810, had barely reached 30 years of age. The outstanding example was Simón Bolívar.

Our revolutionary war had been likened many times to the French Revolution; however, it differs in that it was not led by members of the bourgeoisie—or the Third Estate—a social class which then did not exist in Spanish Latin America. Rather, it was led by the most liberal members of the landholding class. This accounts for the different forms taken by the two great movements. In France, the people felt that they were well-represented by the iconoclastic bourgeoisie which denounced the dogmas and scorned the aristocracy. In our America, and especially in Venezuela, the people showed considerable skepticism when called on to fight by our revolutionary leaders. They were not easily convinced that these men who were slave-holders, owners of large haciendas, and known for their upper-class prejudices could really speak sincerely of liberty and equality. In fact, as Vincente González has pointed out, it was the Venezuelan lower class, led by the Spanish General Boves, which provided shock troops for the counterrevolution against the First Republic. They felt closer to Boves, himself a man of the people, who played upon their resentment against the arrogant white Creole leaders and promised he would give them the lands of the aristocrats.

After the death of Boves, it was another man of the people who finally succeeded in attracting them to the ranks of the insurgents. The fearless leader of the so-called riders of the plains (llaneros), José Antonio Páez, brought the people into the revolution, offering them political liberties; but he had another inducement that did not appear in the wordy proclamations of the first patriots—land confiscated from the Spaniards. Bolívar, who had already demonstrated that he was determined to give the people a new social status when he decreed the liberation of the slaves in 1816, legalized the offer of land made by José Antonio Páez, and tried to ensure that the promise was kept. In 1816, he issued a decree distributing land to the peasants who had fought in the revolution. The decree was not carried out and the same fate befell a subsequent decree issued in Chuisaca, Bolivia, in 1824. The Congress of Gran Colombia issued agrarian certificates instead of parceling out the land as Bolívar had asked. These bonds were regarded with suspicion by the people, who had well-founded reason to prefer a less complicated and more tangible direct title to the land. Bolívar insisted so much before different sessions of Congress that, at last, a law was passed, supposedly to give land to the soldiers. But it had been so worded by congressmen serving the interests of the big landholders that it really confirmed them in their possessions, except for lands transferred to leading officers and to merchants who had supplied the armies, enriching themselves in the rear guard while the army fought the royalists on the battlefield.

It may be thought that because of my well-known position on social questions, I may be prejudiced. However, the same version of what happened comes from Laureano Vallenilla Lanz, an apologist for military government and no friend of democracy, who wrote:

> Congress listened to the Liberator but did not produce an equitable law. Páez and some of the other leaders backed by speculators bought up the land assignments for the soldiers at very low prices. This meant that the big colonial landholdings were transferred without change to the hands of Páez, Monagas, and the other regional military leaders, who had gone to war as poor men and now became the richest landholders of the new Venezuela. Meanwhile, royalist sympathizers gained control of the courts and annulled the decrees confiscating the lands of the emigrés, demanding them back from the warriors of independence and giving them back to former landholders and their descendants, who now returned to the country.[1]

The swindling of the people took place around 1830 when the revolution was in its twilight hour. The reactionary backlash had driven the Liberator into ostracism despite his efforts during the last years of his life to demonstrate a spirit of compromise with ideas contrary to his own political beliefs. The old economic and administrative establishment of the colony again prevailed. The confiscation of the wealth of the Spanish royalists was annulled on August 5, 1830. Ranches and haciendas were returned to the sworn enemies of the republic. At this time, a so-called Emancipation Law practically reforged the chains of slavery.

The men who had fought the triumphant revolutionary battles and carried the scars of their wounds and honorable mention in the battle communiqués had no land to cultivate because a new agrarian caste had taken possession of it. Their families had disappeared in a vortex of twenty years of constant war. The mass of penniless soldiers and officials survived by rustling cattle.

Highwaymen infested the countryside. The new oligarchy in power was supported by the llaneros of José Antonio Páez. The repression began. In the name of the law, this revolutionary hero shot many of his former companions-in-arms whom poverty and despair had converted into horse thieves.

These facts are basic to the contemporary history of Venezuela, which cannot be understood if it is forgotten how the agrarian revolution was frustrated in its very beginnings. It was a bourgeois and inconclusive movement which did not completely destroy the feudal structures of society, as happened in France. They were left intact, and it was impossible to erect a democratic republic upon them. Instead, there came the violence of civil wars, the dominance of the generals on horseback, and the constant involvement of the rural masses in armed revolts. These facts are all directly connected with the perpetuation of large rural properties. Civil war gave the Venezuelan peasants the chance to break out from the bonds of the debts handed on from father to son that put them at the mercy of the hacienda owners. Instead, they had the prospect of booty and the possibility—always demagogically proposed to them by the instigators of revolts—to win the right to cultivate the land and harvest their own property.

After each of these armed adventures, the people had new reason to feel defrauded and deceived. Resentment and rancor accumulated in the collective subconscious of the people; it finally burst forth with terrifying violence in the days of the Federal War to the cry of: "Let us give the land to the Negroes and Indians."

The landless peasantry erupted over the countryside with the same destructive power as elemental forces of nature. The educated minority in the cities and towns which had been trying to rebuild the culture and economy devastated in the wars of independence now found this an impossible task and they were often physically annihilated themselves. A terrible price was paid for social blindness and failure to perceive the cause of the general instability. Although the leaders had the resources in their hands, they did not give unoccupied, uncultivated land to the landless peasantry.

The federal revolution, when it triumphed, again defrauded the peasantry of the land for which they had fought in dozens of battles. The agrarian problem remained unsolved. One oligarchy replaced another, and the few progressive measures taken lacked effectiveness because they were not based on land ownership. This was true, for example, in a decree emancipating the slaves who wandered about the roads of Venezuela, exhilarated but disconcerted by their new liberty. When not given their own lands upon being declared free, they were left in a tragic dilemma: either to lead a life of nomad wandering without any place to stay or means of making a living, or to return and work under the same master, who at least assured them a roof over their heads and bread to eat. Logically, they opted for the latter.

But there is one unique historical fact that differentiates Venezuela from the rest of Latin America. A kind of social democracy was the residue of those cruel wars. The cataclysm of terrible violence completely undermined the social structures surviving from the colony. Though the peasant did not obtain land or any improvement in his material situation, he did come to feel like someone equal and not inferior to the hacienda owner. Expressions such as "My Lord" and "Your Grace" disappeared from the speech of the Venezuelans. The less reverent familiar form of the verb made its appearance. Semantics and sociology walked hand in hand.

The agrarian problem continued to be as acute during the last half of the nineteenth century as in the colonial period. Again, the best lands were gathered in the hands of a few people.

This process culminated with Juan Vicente Gómez, who had a truly pathological appetite for land. Gómez and his clan monopolized the best lands of the country, using methods such as the forced sale or just plain robbery. Political power coincided with land ownership. This was the classical expression of the barbaric caudillos of Latin America. In Venezuela, this monopoly was not used to develop modern agricultural methods but to leave enormous amounts of territory without cultivation or to use some of the best lands as cattle pasture rather than for crops. After the death of the dictator, the land situation became a matter of public controversy.

The popular democratic movement had made land distribution one of its leading proposals, and it fell to the government which began in October 1945 to take the first steps. All that we found on taking power was a problem as old as the republic itself and the text of a law which no one had paid any attention to after it was printed in the *Gaceta Oficial*.

Large Landholding and Primitive Production

Only one-third of Venezuela's territory is inhabited and is socially useful land. In 1937, 85 percent of this area was given over—a better word would be abandoned—to cattle raising. The other 3 million hectares were the agricultural zone. Only 700,000 hectares were under cultivation, or 1 percent of all of Venezuela. This small amount of land was controlled by a very small number of landowners. There were 50,000 farm owners, of whom 2500 or 5 percent owned more than 2,700,000 hectares (78 percent of the land). There were 500,000 farm workers, of whom only 10 percent had land of their own, the rest being poorly paid itinerant farm workers, farm tenants, or peons who were virtual serfs on the land.

"Large holdings of land meant small areas under production." This sentence characterized the situation in the Venezulean countryside. Most of the landholders were absent. Major domos collected the rents and administered the haciendas. Most of the production came from the so-called *conqueros*—those who farmed a small patch of ground, usually without water, oftentimes on mountain slopes violating not only the best rules of farming, but also the laws of physics. They produced erosion and misery, with an annual income of less than $300.[2]

Plan for Agrarian Reform

We were determined to carry out agrarian reform in a responsible manner. Shortly after the revolutionary junta was installed in Miraflores palace, I told the nation that land must be in the hands of those who work it, but that we were not going to take the position of "the extreme radical left." I recalled that it had been Bolívar himself who had urged the need of agrarian reform. We, however, were not going to undertake the redistribution of land in a demagogical fashion but only "when the government has sufficient plans and technical support to assure the rational and productive development of the land."

There were several fundamental reasons for our caution. As has already been noted, there were many difficulties in the postwar period in obtaining an adequate food supply for the country. Also, we were aware that the changeover in agricultural production for a complete agrarian reform would mean a temporary decline in production, which would have been foolish to undergo at the very time when we were having so much trouble acquiring foodstuffs from abroad.

The other reason was also compelling. We had no experience to guide us, nor were there any plans regarding land redistribution. An Institute of Colonization had been created in 1937, but it had been characterized by bureaucratic ineptitude and waste of public funds. After seven years, by the end of 1945, it had established only seven agricultural colonies, with 2730 hectares under cultivation by 310 farmers. This had cost the government some Bs. 27 million (around $9 million).

The nation owned some 400,000 hectares of agricultural land, not including public lands. These were the properties confiscated from the heirs of the dictator Gómez and other farmlands which had been taken over under foreclosed mortgages by the Agricultural and Cattle Bank. There were no technical studies in the archives for these lands, much less any plans for putting them into production. Furthermore, there was no tradition in our country for the cooperative development of land—a basic factor in modern land reform programs, whether under democratic or socialist political regimes. The *conquero* typified our agriculture with his antieconomic, individualistic work methods. He worked his small patch of ground by himself, living in a hastily erected hut, always prepared to abandon both home and crop if chased off by some landlord. He was like a furtive poacher in the domain of some feudal lord. Sometimes, various *conquero* neighbors did get the work done by some common effort (cayapa), but that was the only group-type farming known in the country.

Another reason which led us to go slowly in turning over land to the poor peasants was the Mexican experience. There, the sociologists and historians had insisted upon a radical redistribution of large landholdings as basic to social evolution. But the economists, with impressive statistical arguments, questioned whether this actually brought improvement in the living standards of the poor farmers.

As a final obstacle, we had no legal statute whereby a democratic state could carry out an overall policy of agrarian reform. Our party believed that it was better to have Congress pass a law which would give a legal basis to its ideas, and this could not be done until the regular session of Congress in 1948 because the National Constituent Assembly took up all its time in debate over the new Constitution.

Nothing has been said regarding active opposition by the landholders. The truth is that very few of them possessed substantial wealth. Whether prosperous or nearly bankrupt, all agreed—willingly or not—that something had to be done about agrarian reform. This had become a sort of moral imperative in the country. The group which reflected the views of industry, commerce and agriculture—the Federation of Chambers and Associations of Commerce and Production—at its Maracaibo convention in 1946, urged the Constituent Assembly to include in the new Constitution "the right of all farmers to own sufficient land for reasonable production, making impossible the continuation of large landholding with idle lands and minimum production."

Also, the reform, as contemplated, would not have punished the large landholders, since they would be paid a reasonable indemnity for expropriated properties. The objective was to eliminate large landholding as antieconomic and antisocial. In other words, agrarian reform in Venezuela was to be simply an administrative procedure without the barbaric orchestration of firing squads, as in other countries. But the communists and others under the influence of their noisy demagoguery wanted to proceed in a different manner. They could not imagine an agrarian reform except in the "Russian manner," with violent occupation of land by peasants brandishing rifles. They had characterized the bureaucratic inefficiency of the Medina government, which they had supported, as an indication of prudence and great wisdom. However, when the AD regime sought to undertake a slow and deliberate program, free of improvisation, this was "making concessions to the reactionaries, and cowardice in confronting the landowner classes."

Agrarian Reform Under Way

It was only the communists and a minuscule group without political support that made these criticisms. Most Venezuelans, including the rural masses, supported what we were doing. This was shown by the massive support AD candidates got in three elections held between 1946 and 1948. The people sensed that those who had the courage to impose a "new deal" in our relations with the powerful multimillionaire oil companies would not hesitate to confront the large landholders, with very little economic and political power.

We began to carry out agrarian reform in all of its many aspects. It would have been easy to treat the reform as a kind of *piñata*, which at a single blow would have poured out land so that each small farmer could grab a piece, much as the children collect candy and toys when the traditional cardboard effigy at a birthday party is broken open.

Just one month after the revolution, November 18, 1945, at the first convention of state presidents and federal territory governors, the following measures were agreed upon to stabilize the small farmer on the land which he was working and thus begin the process of reform:

1. The government would issue a decree protecting the small farmers against arbitrary evacuation.

2. The present situation would be maintained on occupied lands, which landlords were incessantly claiming had been invaded by squatters, until legal title to them could be ascertained. Meanwhile, the courts would refrain from passing sentence in suits brought to expel small farmers from these lands.

3. Efforts would be made to obtain an immediate and equitable adjustment of rent for lands occupied by small farmers.

4. Regional governments would immediately study the possibility of locating small farmers on lands held by the government.

5. The regional governments would ask landholders with surplus and uncultivated lands to rent these on liberal terms to poor farmers.

In December 1945, by Decree 69, the government authorized the Ministry of Agriculture to issue loans for more than Bs. 1 million to the 2044 members of recently created farm cooperatives, for the cultivation of 4021 hectares. The ministry and the Institute of Colonization were authorized to issue another Bs. 9 million credits to farm-worker associations, by which another 25,000 farmers benefited. Decree 183, February 11, 1946, empowered the ministry to divide national landholdings and issue them to small farmers. By the end of 1947, some 73,770 hectares had been given to 6000 farm workers. Also, there were now 9 agricultural colonies where 2000 families were located, each with a minimum parcel of 10 hectares.

A well-planned effort was made to develop farm properties under the CVF. This included the investment of Bs. 37 million to promote model cooperatives, which eventually would farm 70,000 hectares with 7600 farm families, while benefiting from modern machinery, adequate technical advice, sufficient credits, and location in communities with clinics and schools. An experiment in Venezuela, these farm communities were more or less the same as those in many other countries, including the United States under the Farm Security Administration.

It was planned to locate these communities in zones where irrigation projects were improving in the value of the land. From the 10,000 hectares of irrigated land in the first stage of the "El Cenizo" program, 4000 were given to an agrarian community. Hundreds of farm families moved to this region from the slopes of the Andes where they were eroding the mountain soils, deforesting the water sources, and plowing lands that should have produced only the native mountain flower, and never stalks of wheat and corn.

Also, various large farms were purchased from their owners so the land could be issued to small farmers. By the end of 1947, Bs. 3 million had been spent on such purchases. Many small farmers claimed that they were settled on lands which belonged to the nation while landholders insisted that the lands belonged to them. To eliminate this source of controversy, a property census of all unoccupied lands was undertaken. As a result of this inventory, it was possible to prepare plans for 70,000 hectares in four states (Trujillo, Zulia, Falcón, and Yaracuy) in the years 1946–47. The work of determining the real ownership of unoccupied property went forward apace—not just with the idea of giving the poor farmers land, but to increase farm production and better living standards in the countryside.

Reference has already been made to the extensive system of farm credits and minimum prices for crops; the manner in which schools, clinics, and sanitation were extended to the countryside will be detailed hereafter. Another important phase of the work was the attention given to farm roads joining the countryside with the centers of consumption. These were found in a state of complete abandon. By the end of 1947, more than 25,000 kilometers had been restored.

Agrarian reform could not really take place without adequate technical advice and mechanization. To undertake land distribution only to have it farmed by the same primitive colonial methods would have been irresponsible. There were only 70 agronomists in Venezuela in 1947 and only 1244 students of agriculture; the state spent less than Bs. 1 million in teaching farm science. In the first year of AD government, this investment tripled and the number of students went up to 3162; a year later it went to 5173.

There were scarcely any farm unions when we came to power, but by the end of 1947, of the 950 unions registered in the country, 446 were made up of farmers. Furthermore, the farm workers were freed from the political oppression traditional in the countryside, with the large landholders imposing their will through the *jefe civil* or the *comisario* (local police chief). Pernalate, a famous character of the novelist Rómulo Gallegos, was a picturesque example of this type of public official. These were now banished and replaced by officials without arbitrary authority and closely linked to the people. Also, the forcible recruitment of the youths to serve in the armed forces, which had long terrorized the people of the country, how became only a bad memory.

Codification of Agrarian Reform

The 1947 constitution obliged the government to solve the agrarian problem:

> Article 69: The state will carry out a plan and systematic activity to transform the structure of national agriculture to rationalize cattle raising, to organize and distribute credit, to improve the living conditions in rural areas, and to ensure the progressive social emancipation of the farm population. A special law shall be provided to determine the technical conditions which, in accordance with the national interest, will guarantee the rights which the nation recognized for farm associations and for individuals willing and able to undertake agriculture and cattle raising but who lack appropriate land. They shall be provided with land and with the necessary means to put land into production.

This special law was drawn up by Congress in 1948 and signed by President Gallegos on October 18, 1948, just three years after the establishment of democratic government and scarcely five weeks before he was violently over-thrown. The law was not improvised, but was based on three years of continual experiment in the countryside. It regulated "ownership of the land and the use of waters"; declared all of the irrigation works constructed by the government to be public utilities; and created an agency, The National Agrarian Institute (IAN), to administer agrarian reform. To ensure sufficient funds, IAN's intitial endowment was held by the government; its capital was to be increased each year by an appropriation from 2 to 4 percent of the national budget. It was given authority to set up different kinds of farm organizations: it could organize colonies, made up of separate landholdings with individual titles for the colonists but without right of sale; cooperatives, which were associations of producers using common lands, credits, and machinery with land rights held by the association; or individual farms.

With similar elasticity, title to the land could be given through sale; as a rental with an option to buy; in usufruct, with an obligation to cultivate the land and pay a fixed amount; or for temporary use for a trial period. We made it clear that we did not wish to redistribute lands already under reasonable cultivation. Naturally, many of the land-hungry peasants wished to take over this type of farmland, but it would have been absurd on our part to have penalized those who had taken the risks and done the hard work of putting land into production. Therefore, we established an ascending scale of lands which could be expropriated by the IAN: (a) uncultivated lands of greatest area, (b) lands under cultivation by absentee landlords, (c) good farmland which was used as pasture for cattle. Compensation for lands expropriated was to be paid partly in cash and partly in bonds. The bonds were of three types—A, B, and C—paying 3, 4, and 5 percent interest, redeemable in twenty years. The guarantee of the government with no foreign and little domestic debt underwrote these bonds, and they were of obligatory acceptance for the payment of taxes. Finally, expropriation was only to be used as a final recourse when friendly efforts to reach an agreement on the sale price had failed. Another demonstration of our realistic and sincere effort to conciliate agrarian reform with private enterprise was the fact that there would be no expropriation of farms less than 150 hectares when the land was first class (irrigated or with adequate water) or 300 hectares for second-class lands lacking water. Likewise, cattle farms of 5000 hectares, when first class, and up to 25,000 hectares when they were second class, were not to be expropriated. The IAN went even further in its encouragement of private investors when it exempted from expropriation persons or companies who wanted to engage in rational mechanized production of large areas of land.

This drive to redeem the rural populace and to increase production by a carefully planned agrarian reform program was frustrated by the coup d'état of November 24, 1948. The road had nevertheless been opened and the objectives defined. It would be easier, tomorrow, to begin anew the work which had been temporarily stopped because we now had a wealth of experience and a legal basis for reform.

10

Highways and Communications Challenges to Colonialism: The Greater Colombian Merchant Fleet

An Immense Country without Connecting Links

The lack of means of communication between the regions of Venezuela has been a very negative factor in its historical development. Physical geography segments the country into zones, separated by the towering Andes and the coastal range. Within these natural regions, the communities themselves were poorly connected by dirt roads, constructed by the "muleback engineers," as our country people called them.

The separate communities lived a life almost entirely unto themselves, and it could be said that there lived within the same country different Venezuelas, each with its own psychology, production methods, and life styles.

The regionalism of our easterners, plainsmen, and midwesterners, Zulians from the Maracaibo region and Andino mountaineers, did not become as pronounced as in the case of Spain. It was not the result of racial and language differences but rather due to the absence of communication. The integration of our nation was slowed down by this adverse circumstance and in political matters was reflected in the regional aspect of many of our dictatorial governments. José Antonio Páez ruled for many years with people from the central states. The Monagas governed with people "out of the Orinoco forests" to use the phrase of one of our historians. From the end of the last century, the Andeans (Andinos) governed. They had lived in their western mountains in practical isolation for many years, incubating a regional resentment which erupted in 1898 when the troops of Cipriano Castro swept down upon Caracas.

Little was done in the nineteenth century in the way of either roads or railways. President Guzmán Blanco, who sought to copy the construction policies of Napoleon III, began railway construction but under such unfavorable conditions that the whole idea was discredited. The English and German investors were guaranteed against all risk and had no interest in improving their installations. Only two narrow-gauge railways were constructed and these charged such high rates that they made transportation more difficult instead of encouraging it.

Our maritime transport was also neglected. The Orinoco and its tributaries could only be navigated by shallow-draft boats and primitive Indian craft. Venezuela has 1800 miles of coastline, and the Caribbean and Atlantic are a constant inducement to a maritime vocation for our heavy coastal population. However, until the AD government, we only had a scrawny merchant marine and no high-seas fleet whatsoever. General Carlos Soublette, a president in the past century, ironically described the situation when he recommended that the name of the so-called Ministry of War and Marine be changed to the Ministry of War and Schooners.

A "Highway Policy" without Highways

Despotic regimes often coin propaganda slogans to deceive people with regard to what really goes on. Thus, the governments under the control of Gómez masked his prolonged dictatorship with the attractive allegation that it pursued "a policy of highways." Both inside and outside the country, printing presses in the pay of the government wore out their type advertising the building of roads. The falsity of this propaganda appeared as soon as it was possible to speak freely in Venezuela. When the dictator died in 1935, there were scarcely 5000 kilometers of highway in a country which had 900,000 square kilometers of territory. These roads, few in number and badly constructed, were built by the forced labor of political prisoners and common criminals. Most were built under the supervision of self-made colonels who, thanks to their connections with the retinue of the dictator, were assigned these public works to manage as their private property—as a mine. The roads were routed to suit the convenience of the large landowners, who were friends of the government. Even so, these rudimentary roads helped to break down the isolation of important regions of the republic. The trans-Andean highway, narrow and with a thousand unnecessary curves, joined the Colombian frontier with the center of Venezuela.

During the post-Gómez decade, more roads were built but in a spasmodic manner and without an overall plan. Nothing was done about air or maritime transport. In the decade 1936–45, Bs. 208 million were spent on roads, and we inherited 7000 kilometers of highway, as contrasted with the 21,000 kilometers that the republic of Peru had at this time.

An Overall Transportation Plan

As soon as we entered office, we organized a national highway commission under some of the best engineers in the country. They were asked to draw up an overall road plan in accord with good technical standards and the needs of the national economy.

However, while this study was going on, we had to go ahead. In the first year of our government seven times more money was spent than in the previous year on road building. We had to choose between continuing the work of the previous government or starting new highways to satisfy an egoistic desire to originate our own projects. We chose to continue previous work. Our work at first could not be realized with all the haste we would have wished in view of our tremendous lack of communications. This was not due to neglect by the government or to the laziness of road workers, who had just organized a union and were now being treated as human beings. It was rather due to our lack of road-building equipment. It was almost impossible to obtain new machines due to the postwar scarcity. The machinery in use was all more than five years old and could only be expected to work at 50 percent efficiency. We never sought to conceal these problems. Explanation would seem unnecessary now were it not for the tendentious propaganda emanating from government quarters after the overthrow of AD to the effect that our democratic regime was interested only in winning elections and did nothing about the material welfare of the nation.

In 1947, the preliminary national highway plan was put into effect, calling for a highway system of 16,000 kilometers, of which 12,000 kilometers would have to be built or improved. The construction of fifty new airports was also planned, as well as secondary ports for coastal and river traffic. Among the highways recommended was the Caracas-La Guaira superhighway, begun by the AD government after lengthy studies required by the rugged topography it was to traverse. On August 29, 1947, inaugurating the first stretch between Maiquetia and Catia la Mar, I said: "We will leave the study of the highway completely finished. It will place the capital just twenty kilometers and a few minutes from the principal part of the nation."

We also undertook to pave our national highways, but few were paved, with the exception of those built by the oil companies in the eastern and western parts of the country. We had to do this for reasons of efficiency and national pride. "We will end forever this inferiority complex," I said on certain occasions, "which comes from the contrast between the splendid blacktop roads of the North Americans and the dirt roads which we Venezuelans had built."

We sought to give a bold push forward in the development of air transport. Venezuelan Aeropostal Line (LAV), a state company, was badly stunted in its growth. It lacked firm support from the government in the "battle of the giants," as the struggle among the great international trusts for control of the air routes has been called. We proceeded in a different manner. The airlines' flying equipment was increased. The airports—many of them belonging to foreign airlines—were nationalized, and domestic traffic was reserved for national airlines. Transatlantic flights of Aeropostal were begun and it became the first Latin American airline with regular flights to both the United States and Europe.

Also, many new airports were built, including one in Caracas. The coup of November 1948 found the construction of the international airport at Palo Negro in full progress. This was designed to be one of the future key terminals in inter-American air transportation.

We also sought to provide the country with a modern system of trans-Atlantic ports. We built one at La Guaira, our principal port, at a cost greater than any public work built by any government up until then. The port of Cumana was finished and that of Carupano built completely. The ports of Guanta, Maracaibo, and Puerto Cabello were enlarged and modernized.

We were convinced of the need to dredge the Orinoco and its mouths. This enormous waterway was not being used; the window which it opened for the nation to the trans-Atlantic routes was closed. There was no development of the vast Guyana region through which it flowed. This was virgin forest, scarcely touched by the gold seekers and rubber tappers. Our navy, together with civilian experts, drew up studies during the years 1946–48, and it was about to begin work when President Gallegos was overthrown.

We were eager to get ahead with the unfinished work of settling the interior of the country. We wanted the Venezuelan to have useful control over his national territory—to really possess it; for this, it was essential that our riverways and seas be used.

The Automonous State Railways Institute was created with a capital of Bs. 7 million; and an interministerial commission went to work, aided by foreign experts, to determine what should finally be done with our railways—whether to abandon them or improve their condition. Four different gauges were used in the country, so it was impossible to have a single rail network or even connecting lines.

An extraordinary push was also given to postal, telephonic, telegraphic, and radio communications. In the nine years preceding our government, only twenty-two telegraphic offices had been opened in our country. In the first two years of our government, thirty-five were opened. More than Bs. 42 million were spent in extending and modernizing telephone and telegraphic services and in improving postal services. A contract was signed with the Swedish Ericsson Company to construct the first regional telephone network and a vast national and international communications system.

A Merchant Marine Under The Venezuelan Flag

Our coastline, with many harbors, bays, and gulfs, looks out on the Caribbean and the Atlantic, yet our waterways were little used for commercial traffic, and the nation spent millions annually to import and export merchandise. Nothing had been done to create our own merchant marine.

Different economic sectors in Venezuela chafed under the extortionist policy of the shipping cartel which controlled maritime traffic. In 1939, the Venezuelan Foreign Office lodged protests with the U.S. State Department and the Inter-American Maritime Commission regarding the conduct of the shipping cartel in raising rates whenever it pleased. But there was timidity in deciding upon the only true solution, the organization of a merchant marine of our own.

When we got to govern, we reorganized the old inefficient Venezuelan Navigation Company (CVN) and provided it with adequate capital. In 1945, this company had only sixteen ships, totaling 8000 tons; two years later, it had twenty-four units of 20,000 tons.

Latin American governments have been blind to the signs of the times and until recently have failed to pay attention to the development of a merchant marine. Immediately after the war, the United States made the decision to subsidize private companies in building merchant ships, but there was no parallel concern by our government. In addition, there were the twin complexes of inferiority and timidity. Only more advanced people, it was felt, could sail the seas and successfully organize merchant fleets. Also, there was the fear of confronting the powerful shipping trusts which adopted such high-sounding and misleading titles as "Conference of the Caribbean" and "Conference of the Pacific." Their capital totaled millions of dollars and they had powerful influence in the Foreign Office and the State Department.

A high price was paid for this lack of vision during the Second World War. The Latin American people will long remember the difficulties of supply which prevailed in 1941 and the war years following. The international shipping consortium took advantage of these circumstances to increase their freight rates scandalously. This experience convinced us of the need to have our own merchant fleets, which the Inter-American Conference of Chapultepec in Mexico in 1945 recommended as essential for the growth of our economies. But this formal statement remained a dead letter for most of the American governments. We took it seriously. I promised the nation in my New Year's message of 1946 that "not many months will pass before the glorious tricolored flag with the seven tropical stars will be seen waving from the highest masts of Venezuelan ships at trans-Atlantic docks."

In working at this project, the possibility was seen of giving it a regional dimension. The Foreign Offices of Venezuela and Colombia had discussed this matter in previous years in a rather metaphysical manner.

It was logical to unite the efforts of the three nations which had once formed the single state of Greater Colombia in Bolívar's day—Venezuela, Colombia, and Ecuador. All three states had long coastlines (7500 kilometers on the Atlantic and the Pacific). Together they had 18 million inhabitants in 1945, and their foreign trade (not including Venezuela's oil) amounted to 2 million metric tons per year. They were joined by history, language, customs, and common economic needs, which guaranteed harmony in the proposed enterprise.

Despite the good sense which this project made, it was not until men of modern mentality came to power that the vague idea was put into effect. After conversations with Colombia, it was agreed to invite Ecuador to participate. Ecuador was enthusiastic but lacked capital. With the ease which our small countries had for reaching agreements when they are not struggling in political or commercial rivalry, the matter was arranged. Venezuela and Colombia loaned Ecuador money on very liberal terms.

The Regional Merchant Fleet Is Launched

There were no lengthy bureaucratic delays in organizing the Greater Colombian Merchant Fleet. On April 24, 1946, I presided over the inaugural session of the conference in which the three nations organized the company. Less than two months later, June 8, in the presence of Alberto Lieras, then president of Colombia, the organizing documents were signed in the historic Quinta Bolívar of Bogotá.

The company began to function with a capital of $20 million, divided as follows: Colombia and Venezuela, 45 percent each; Ecuador 10 percent. Venezuela committed itself to immediately establish a naval school where youths of all three countries could be trained in high-seas navigation.

Not many months afterward the first ships put to sea. On July 6, 1947, the first two units of the eight ships with which the fleet began its activity put into dock at La Guaira.

The extraordinary success achieved by the Greater Colombian Merchant Fleet is a great encouragement to our sense of national pride. It shows that we can plan and organize when opportunity comes. In the five years, 1947–51, the fleet's gross income was $200 million and its net earnings were $25 million; it had paid-in capital of $31 million, assets of $56 million, and some thirty ships displacing a quarter-million tons.

What was absolutely new in Latin American history was the demonstration of the advantage of subregional economic agreements. The success of the fleet was due especially to joining up an importing country, Venezuela, with Colombia and Ecuador, which were big exporters of agricultural products. Furthermore, by breaking out of the cartel operating under the name of "Caribbean Conference," the fleet made it possible to save 25 percent on freight charges. But again, it should be emphasized that the major stimulus our peoples received from this success was the destruction of the colonial complex fostered by well-known "sociologists." We Latin Americans are capable of undertaking big projects, extending our influence beyond our frontiers and of succeeding.

Foreshadowing the Latin American Merchant Fleet

Of course, organizing the shipping line was not free of risks and pitfalls. It was inconceivable that, given the implacable logic of their monopolistic capitalism, the shipping trusts would peacefully accept our challenge to compete fairly in the open marketplace. They reacted immediately and sought to hamper their unexpected rival with all kinds of maneuvers, ranging from the threat of reprisal against merchants who used the fleet, to subtle diplomatic pressures.

They failed at first in their efforts. They were bluntly informed that the governments financing the fleet would not tolerate monopolistic practices. Nor did diplomatic efforts succeed. When the U.S. State Department reminded Colombia that a certain treaty obliged it to give North American ships the special advantages enjoyed by the Grand Colombian fleet, public opinion was aroused. University students stoned the Bogotá offices of the United States shipping line, and the press bitterly recalled that in the same treaty, the United States had promised to guarantee Colombian sovereignty over the Isthmus of Panama.

This faux pas of the State Department coincided with the arrival of the new Colombian ambassador in Caracas. When he presented his credentials, I took advantage of the protocolar speech to make some very categoric affirmations:

> This shipping company is not just another commercial enterprise. It is a landmark on the road to our economic independence. It was organized with the express intention of competing with a monopoly that had been exercising an irritating control over the maritime commerce between the United States and the nations of the Caribbean. . . .
>
> There have recently been various judicial efforts in the United States in the field of antitrust against domestic monopolies. It would certainly be a contribution to good inter-American relations if the State Department would also begin a similar investigation of the actions contrary to the independence of our economy by the shipping monopoly which has baptized itself with the fancy title of The Caribbean Conference.

Although the shipping trusts failed to abort our fleet, it must be admitted that they achieved success in later years. But this will not last since they are dealing with a dictatorial clique hostile to the true interests of the country. The military government yielded to the pressures of the cartel and agreed to join the Venezuelan section of the fleet with the Caribbean Conference, abandoning its useful association with Colombia and Ecuador. Those two countries bought the Venezuelan share of the company.

The negative aspects of this myopic isolationist conduct will not be analyzed here. There is no reason for excessive alarm because the adverse circumstances of which we speak are transitory. When Venezuela again is governed by people with a true sense of national pride and American responsibility, it will surely rejoin the regional fleet, the best means for our economic liberation. The extraordinary significance of this earlier experiment for Latin America and countries of the Caribbean should be stressed. Just imagine the possibilities such a company could have were it to be transformed into the Latin American Merchant Fleet, engaged in transoceanic traffic and coastwise trade, promoting commerce in a vast area of common language, interests, and historical objectives. Such a Latin American Merchant Fleet, organized along parallel lines with a supranational airline, would give these countries control of their sea and air routes and would be the decisive factor in coordinating the creative efforts of a disunited archipelago of twenty republics.

11

Industrialization – Carefully Planned

Venezuela, like other underdeveloped countries, feels it necessary to industrialize. No country anywhere today wants to have only a secondary role as a source of raw materials for manufacturing nations while at the same time importing products it could produce itself. No contemporary nation accepts that arbitrary division; even the most backward countries legitimately aspire to end their dependence on foreign production.

More than economic interest is at stake. There is also the need to assert the individuality of each nation. No nation can be truly sovereign while accepting the role of exporter of raw materials and importer of manufactured goods. This is not to propose economic self-sufficiency as our goal. The economic interdependence of nations in our time is fully understood by us.

We also wanted to industrialize our country but it had always been a vague national wish without solid foundation. Our national industrial tradition was very weak. Credit instruments did not exist and the government attitude was not such as to transform the wish into reality. The slow development of our industry from the days of the colony and the affirmative response which finally came from the government when we took over in 1945 will now be analyzed.

A Poor Tradition

Venezuela was one of the least brilliant jewels in the imperial crown of the Bourbons. Its poor economy had a scant export trade of tropical fruit, coffee, cacao, and indigo—sold to Spain. Manufactured goods came from the motherland, but Spain's production was reduced because the Industrial Revolution stopped at the Pyrenees. A nation which did not use machines to process raw materials could not export them. Spain continued using the artisan systems of the Middle Ages. Believers in the mercantile theory, the leaders of Spain and its colonies, were only interested in gold and other precious metals from overseas possessions to purchase products manufactured in other countries. If a colony was not rich in these metals, it was abandoned to its fate.

This was the fate of Venezuela. There was only the most rudimentary industry. Nothing more than the weaving of heavy wool cloaks for the cold mountain moors, twisting tobacco, the distillation of rum, and the fabrication of primitive construction materials existed in the country before the War of Independence. This destructive hurricane eliminated life and the squalid wealth of the country. Later came the continuous civil wars, the ruthless autocrats, and a few short parentheses of civilized government—nothing propitious for the development of manufactures.

The turbulent process continued throughout the nineteenth century and finally led to the Gómez dictatorship. A few industries appeared then, the most important controlled by the despot or his family—textiles and cement. Others—shoes, clothing, bottled drinks, furniture—slowly developed and supplied only part of the population's consumption or, better said, underconsumption. In 1926, only 15 percent of the population used shoes; the rest wore native sandals or went barefoot. Petroleum was flowing in a swollen stream of black gold while most of the people dressed in tatters. In 1925, oil worth Bs. 173 million had been exported.

In 1930, the figure had reached a spectacular Bs. 858 million, but these exports did not bring any appreciable increase in industry. During the early 1940s, the new negative factor of war made it difficult to import industrial machines, which led to very low investments of capital. According to the Central Bank, the highest capital investment in the war years was in 1940— no less than Bs. 52 million—but in 1943, only Bs. 11 million were invested, the largest proportion in construction. At the end of the war, our industry was in very poor shape. Its old-fashioned equipment could hardly compete with the products that now commenced to flow from North American factories. A definite, positive stand was required by the government to confront these difficulties. We took such a stand.

Acción Democrática Supports Industrialization

Our party had consistently proposed and defended the thesis of industrializing Venezuela. This had been done with special emphasis because among influential sectors of the country there existed openly, or shamefully, a contrary attitude. Perhaps because they were irresponsible or because their thinking had been deformed in a colonial way, these enemies of Venezuelan industrialization claimed that it would be artificial. Their reasoning ran more or less as follows: in a country which has an abundance of foreign exchange and solid money, why bother to undertake the difficult manufacture of goods, often of poor quality, when these can be bought easily in the great markets of the United States and Europe. In accordance with this criterion, the country should fatalistically accept the fact that it can only be an oil producer and should spend the oil income to buy most of its needs abroad.

Our reasoning was diametrically opposed to this. Venezuela should try to produce the greatest amount possible of what it consumed—above all, because of the oil boom. Our situation was the same as that of entire continents such as Africa, much of Asia, and Latin America. We paid tribute to foreign industry and saw our own money disappear. The maturing of the country was thus made impossible.

We had the advantage of our oil income, which should have enabled us to accelerate a process of industrial growth more than in other underdeveloped countries; however, this could also become a disadvantage because the possibility of diversifying our economy would last only as long as the oil. We would have to hurry. The exhaustion of the oil wells was not just a possibility—it was a predetermined fact. When that moment arrived, our country not only should be able to supply itself sufficiently for civilized life, but should also have opened up new sources of foreign trade. To compete in the export of typical tropical products, such as coffee and cacao, with European colonies on various continents did not offer much hope. On the other hand, there were great prospects for the manufacture of goods which could be sold in the vast Latin American market. Thus it was necessary to push— by plan and firm will—the industrial development of the nation.

Definite factors favored such a policy. With the increases in wages and in the national budget following 1946, the country had much greater purchasing power. There was abundant fuel at low prices after the measures our government had taken. Unlike many other Latin American countries, where industrial workers had to be drawn from the countryside, Venezuela already had a large urban population. There were many sources of raw materials; those that we did not have could be imported.

The negative factors could not be ignored, however. The near parity of the bolívar with the American dollar and the volume of our dollar reserves were a permanent stimulus to imports. Our population had acquired the habit of buying products from abroad. We lacked an efficient labor force because there were few technical schools to train workers and because their working conditions had conspired against a high level of productivity. There was lack of official encouragement for the manufacturing industry in a country where the government had such a decisive role in the economy. Electricity-generating capacity was small and demand was high—so high that it could not be supplied in Caracas and other cities. Finally, high tariff barriers, erected more to collect custom duties than to protect national production, meant that our industry reinvested little of its earnings to modernize equipment, produced goods of doubtful quality, and did not apply the rigorous methods of organization and cost control which characterized contemporary industry elsewhere.

In view of these factors, both favorable and unfavorable, how did the government go about industrializing Venezuela? Our first effort was to promote agriculture and cattle raising. Liquidation of the pronounced deficit in foodstuffs was our obvious first priority but "sowing the petroleum"—that felicitous phrase inoperative for so long—meant that we also had to use credit policy and other state incentives to promote urban manufacturing. This had to be done under definite guidelines. It was not reasonable or in accord with national interest to supply the oxygen of credit to parasitical industries kept alive behind a protective tariff wall.

We did not intend to favor privileged groups at the expense of the consumer or at the sacrifice of public funds. This philosophy was expressed to industrialists with the sincerity characteristic of our government. Loans were to be made on liberal credit terms to those companies ready to modernize their production methods and accept the supervision of the Venezuelan Development Corporation (CVF). Well-managed industries would also get help from the state, ranging from exemption from raw material import duties to the establishment of import controls on some products to protect nationally manufactured goods.

The initial program of the CVF gained support from most of the Venezuelan industrialists, and we undertook to place men from the private sector in directive posts of many of the state agencies. This was not simply a superficial tactic of trying to neutralize such individuals; rather, it reflected our concept that the present economic, political, and social transformation of the country required the collaboration of all sectors, including what might be called the national bourgeoisie. Our interests did not really conflict. The only problem was distinguishing between those with sufficient mental clarity and lack of prejudice to support a truly popular government, and those who would not support one if it did not grant privileges to any special group or individual.

Accomplishments

The CVF undertook its program of industrialization in four stages. We did not want to imitate what was being done at that time by Perón's government in Argentina—to force an artificial industrialization for reasons of prestige or even less defensible motives.

The first stage was to promote basic industries: electricity, which was necessary for any industrial growth, and those related to human welfare—food, clothing, fuel, and housing. It was also planned to encourage mining and industrial chemistry. The second stage was to include industries complementary to the first. The third stage was semiheavy industry, and the fourth was to be machine manufacture and heavy industry. This was not to be a rigid schedule; it was to be administered with flexibility. As will be seen, it became necessary to establish a steel industry almost immediately instead of waiting for the fourth stage.

The programs of sugar and milk production have already been described earlier, but a description of what was undertaken with regard to oils, edible fats, and the fishing industry might be added. The Food and Agricultural Organization of the U.N. (FAO), in a survey of our country, had determined that the consumption of fats and oils was only four kilograms per year, in contrast to the eight kilograms which dietary experts had established as minimum need. This was true although oil-bearing plants were easily grown in the country. Also, raw materials could be easily imported for lard and vegetable oils, while the growth of milk production made butter manufacture possible on a large scale. Taking these facts into consideration, it was possible to raise the consumption of oils and vegetable fats from 13,000 tons annually in 1945 to 25,000 in 1948, cutting deficit to 10,000 tons with respect to a minimum diet.

In another area, the country was taking only partial advantage of its prodigious seafood resources. Fish consumption in 1946 was 29 million kilos, but experts said that it should be around 66 million kilos. The problem was attacked on all fronts. Fishing equipment was imported in massive amounts and sold at cost on liberal credit terms. The CVF helped motorize the fishing fleet; docks were installed at the principal fishing ports. Loans were made to canning factories, and a fishing company was set up with the Basic Economy Corporation. By 1948, the physical volume of fish preserved was the highest in history — 9 million metric tons, with a value of Bs. 26 million. According to the ECLA, the fish catch increased by 400 percent between 1939 and 1948, and there were 400 motorized fishing vessels, compared to 72 in 1946.

The textile industry was the object of special attention. While production increased, there had been no reorganization of this industry, nor was its old equipment replaced. A credit fund of some Bs. 20 million was made available for those industrialists who were willing to improve installations and methods and to produce merchandise of a better quality and lower price. A study was also undertaken of the shoe industry, which revealed that it, too, required a complete overhaul; of 138 existing factories, only 6 had shoe-making machines. The rest depended upon handwork.

More tangible achievements came in the construction industry; cement production was of first importance for the new public works and increased activity by the private sector. Our industry manufactured about 136,000 tons in 1946 but we needed 400,000 tons. Despite the sure market, the CVF encountered considerable resistance when it offered to finance expansion programs. The situation resembled that in the sugar industry — the Malthusian economic tendency of producing little and charging much. It was necessary to emphasize that if government financing was not accepted, the state itself would enter the cement business. Resistance gradually gave way, and the

CVF was able to loan Bs. 9 million in 1948 and Bs. 16.5 million by 1950. This vigorous impulse given by the AD government to a slowly developing industry made cement among the most important products of the country.

Also, in this first stage, the government sought to increase mining under the supervision of the Ministry of Production. Work in the Guyana gold mines was put on a more technical basis and reorganized so as to function as a single economic unit; diamond mining reorganized and a joint enterprise was created with a private firm which had been lagging in its production. Coal production was also of great interest to the government. The coal mines at Naricual had to be closed down following a bad accident in 1947, but a cooperative was organized to develop the coal reserves in the western state of Táchira. By 1949, this company was producing 75 percent of national coal production—30,000 metric tons.

The Ambitious Electrification Program

It is common knowledge that civilization today cannot exist without electricity. Industrial development presupposes the availability of abundant low-cost energy. The cost per kilowatt-hour of energy for a community largely determines what its living standard will be.

Venezuela is a country with optimum conditions for generating electricity. It has many waterfalls. It also has unlimited amounts of fuel oil at low prices plus enormous reserves of natural gas to use as fuel for thermoelectric plants which, in some respects, are more advantageous than hydroelectric installations. However, it was not until our time in government that a serious program for electrification was undertaken. Until then, the energy generated was always less than needed; tariffs were extremely high and there was no state supervision of the private companies, which offered a deficient and costly service.

As soon as the revolutionary junta was installed in Miraflores, a decree was issued lowering electricity rates by 15 percent. The same companies which had persuaded the government to annul the timid decrease of 5 percent two years earlier now had to contribute Bs. 5 million to the consumer in the first year of this decree.

In this, as elsewhere, our democratic government tried to conciliate the emergency needs of the present with plans for the future. In two years (1946–47), the number of electrical plants doubled and the number of towns using electricity rose from 319 to 660. Half a million Venezuelans stopped using candles and kerosene lamps. An overall plan for the nation was meanwhile being drawn up by the Ministry of Production and the CVF with assistance from well-known New York consultants. Under this plan, the map of Venezuela was divided into seven geographical zones and in the last two years of the government, much was done to electrify various areas despite the difficulty of obtaining equipment during the postwar period.

The most spectacular development plan was in the southeast, in the so-called Bolívar-Caroni area, a region of extraordinary possibilities for future economic development. Here was located what would eventually become the generating center of a complete hydroelectric system installed at the falls of the Caroni River. Its potential is capable of satisfying all of the electrical needs of the country and becoming one of the world's most important hydroelectric programs. The Caroni flows into the Orinoco from its source 400 kilometers to the south. There are numerous waterfalls along its route, the highest known as the Caroni falls, some 30 meters in height, where the river has a flow of 5000 cubic meters per second.

The first studies of this area had been carried out in 1939, commissioned by Standard Oil. A more complete investigation made in 1947 predicted that hundreds of thousands of kilowatts could be generated at the site. The initial steps were taken for building a plant with an estimated capacity of 200,000 kilowatts, and the dream which many Venezuelan patriots had held now began to take shape. With this energy, it would be possible to develop a fabulously rich area which possessed all of the elements needed to create a great industrial center. Here were abundant reserves of iron and other minerals, including great deposits of bauxite for making aluminum. Nearby were immense reserves of natural gas and oil. And the Atlantic is easily reached via the Orinoco River. If cheap electricity could be made available here, it would become a natural center for enormous economic development.

We did not have sufficient Venezuelan personnel to carry out an electrification program of the size contemplated, so training in electrical engineering was begun at the Central University. Also, a law was prepared making it possible to control and coordinate the entire electrical industry throughout the state. Ours was perhaps the only modern country where such a public service industry functioned entirely without government regulation. This legislation was prepared using United States laws as a model; but it was never discussed in the 1948 Congress.

The results of the program were impressive. According to the Ministry of Production, electrical energy generation increased from 317 million kilowatt-hours in 1945 to 453 million in 1948. The increase in the last year was 21.4 percent, the highest registered in any country in Latin America for many years.

The Discovery of Iron

Another gift of nature found in Venezuela was iron ore. The history of its development began in 1938 when the Iron Mines Company of Venezuela, an affiliate of Bethlehem Steel Corporation, found an iron deposit of around 60 percent purity not far from the port of San Felix on the Orinoco River. This was estimated to have a reserve of 100 million tons.

There was great discussion under the government of Medina Angarita as to how this ore should be transported, once mined. The Iron Mines Company could not justify dredging the Orinoco at its own expense, nor was the government at that time ready to undertake it. The company wanted to transport the ore in shallow-draft carriers and transfer it to oceangoing vessels at Trinidad, the nearby English island. Acción Democrática had vigorously opposed this idea, believing the transfer port should be located in Venezuela. We insisted upon this when we took power in 1945; Puerto de Hierro was therefore constructed by the company on the Venezuelan coast.

At the time of the López Contreras government, the Oliver Company, an affiliate of United States Steel, was interested in a concession in the Guyana highlands to mine iron ore. The Ministry of Production named a commission of geologists to study the area, and their report stated that iron existed only on the right bank of the Caroní River, not the left. On the basis of this report, the right bank was declared a national reserve and the left bank was made a free zone. United States Steel continued its exploration there and in 1947 found a huge reserve of high-quality iron at Cerro Bolívar. The discovery was on the left bank of the Caroní in the free zone and a claim was filed with the ministry. Fearing there might be other finds, our government declared the rest of the left-bank zone a national reserve so any new concession would have to contain special conditions.

These concessions were given under an old and inadequate mining law which had been on the books since 1928. We were not able to change this law during our three years of government because not even one full session of Congress was held. The lack of a law, however, did not prevent us from carrying out a policy in defense of the national interest; we had not forgotten our experience with petroleum.

Iron ore differs considerably from oil. Petroleum exists in limited amounts in just a few countries capriciously scattered on the five continents. With iron, it is quite different. The world's proven reserves are more than 50 billion tons, and in Latin America alone there is a total of 10 billion. Our realization of this fact conditioned the policy adopted by our government after thorough investigation and on the basis of reputable technical advice. Our policy had three principles: first, to promote the establishment in the country of companies already at work there when we came to power and to orient their investments in accordance with our general needs; second, to keep careful track of the earnings of these companies and to obtain an adequate share for the nation; third, to proceed without delay to create a national steel industry managed directly by the government so the long history of oil shipped only as crude would not be repeated.

With regard to the first aspect of this policy, we had to be realists. To apply restrictive regulations to the companies already working in the country would simply have caused them to depart. They had found very valuable deposits in Labrador, Liberia, and other places. Their advantages in our country included easy access to United States ports, the excellent quality of the mineral, and the fact that extraction was under the open sky without costly investment for underground mining. It was up to us to take advantage of these favorable aspects. The fact that iron ore was exported under the existing concessions at a relatively low tax lacked importance because of the new deal in income taxes we had promulgated for all mining industries after 1945. Under this juridical tax system the mining companies had to pay not only the production taxes called for under the concession agreement, but also income tax at the new rate of 50/50.

The system had to be carefully supervised to avoid the transfer of profits to other affiliates or to the holding company. Company accounting ought to be based upon a fair price for the iron ore, which turned out to be no more difficult to establish than in the case of petroleum. Both Canada and Sweden, other iron-ore producers, published price quotations which could be used as a guide. Furthermore, we were categoric in our administrative thesis that concessions so vital to the public interest could only be granted as an "expectation." The government would not agree to maintain indefinitely or for any fixed period of years any established tax rates or other conditions which unduly favored the concessionaire. The government reserved its sovereign right to modify the terms of the contract when in the national interest.

This criterion was explained clearly to United States Steel and the Bethlehem Steel Corporation. It was also made public in a document of singular importance in the history of Venezuela and perhaps of Latin America because it stated, as a government norm, a doctrine which has been put forward by advanced thinkers in the field of public law.

Without delay, special advantages for the country were sought from the iron companies. Conversations were well advanced with Orinoco Mines, the affiliate of United States Steel which had begun iron-ore production, to secure the construction of a broad-gauge railway from the river 300 kilometers northward to Puerto La Cruz at a cost of more than $100 million. The railway would have increased the value of the lands through which it passed and would have enabled Puerto La Cruz to become a great industrial center. A big thermoelectric plant was already programmed for this city, which would have made possible a "low temperature" steel industry. Also, a bauxite-refining plant was to be constructed there. The railroad projects did not exclude the dredging of the Orinoco, for which our experts also had plans.

Finally, we were determined to immediately create a national steel industry. All of the iron ore would not be exported at low prices to be returned later, after manufacture in the United States in the form of steel bars or plates at high prices. We would make enough steel in our own country to take care of domestic needs and to export some abroad. We had favorable conditions: large reserves of iron ore and a domestic market sufficient to justify a steel plant of a certain size. The unfavorable factor we faced was the lack of coke in the country.

Existing iron ore reserves in 1947, before those of Cerro Bolívar had been fully evaluated, were 216 million metric tons of 60 percent iron and 490 million of 51 percent. These U.N. estimates changed substantially when Orinoco Mines announced in 1950 that its Cerro Bolívar property had 1 billion tons of high-quality iron. In addition to the internal market for steel —

more than 200,000 tons annually—there was a vast potential market in Latin America, where the amount of steel used per person was very low in 1948, hardly 24 kilograms, in comparison with 545 kilograms in the United States and 130 kilograms in western Europe. We were very happy to think that steel made of Venezuelan iron could be exported in the near future to our brother countries on reasonable economic terms, giving commercial unity to countries which today are so much prey to foreign domination. Integrated in a regional economic pact, they will cease to be exploited and demeaned.

Venezuela lacks the coal reserves for a steel industry of the classical type with blast furnaces. To refine the metal and eliminate impurities, iron ore is smelted, eight- or nine-tenths ton of coke being required for each ton of smelted iron. But this difficulty could have been overcome. At the time we were in government, the reserves of Cerro Bolívar had not been defined and production plans were relatively modest. The possibility of exporting great amounts of iron ore with the carriers returning loaded with coal could not have been foreseen. According to the possibilities then understood, electricity or natural gas, instead of traditional blast furnaces, could have been used for the smelting process.

The concessionaire companies were not scheduled to begin production until 1950, but the democratic government was already actively at work, hoping to gain time so the initial output would not only be exported but would also supply Venezuelan steel plants where the iron would be smelted and rolled to provide steel in many different forms. Our first exploratory effort was to bring to Venezuela the knowledge accumulated in the United States, Canada, and Sweden, whereby iron is reduced using natural gas.

The CVF carefully studied this matter and, at first, was going to try the Brassert method and had appropriated money to build a pilot plant in New Jersey. However, after tests had been carried out in Sweden with our iron ore, it was decided to use the Wiburg method, and plans were proceeding when the 1948 revolution occurred.

The CVF continued its work under the de facto government which followed. Thanks to the law of inertia, the momentum of our program carried on for some time. In any case, in 1948, we were at the point of rapidly establishing a domestic steel industry. We had abundant iron ore, a great electrification program under way, the petroleum and gas which are necessary for whichever smelting system is used, and financial resources. Above all, the country was governed by creative men without colonialist inferiority complexes, who were determined to serve Venezuela and not to appease foreign interests.

The situation changed when the military dictatorship took over. Even when more favorable developments in iron ore mining occurred after the ominous events of 1948, nothing was really done to establish a national steel industry. Iron ore, like oil, left the country as a raw material.

The plans of the companies to export the mineral were just as ambitious as those of the oil companies in their time. The idea was to mine and ship the greatest possible amount of iron before a responsible Venezuelan government would take note of their earnings and put an end to this absurd system—not only of underpricing the product but also of continuing to buy iron from Cerro Bolívar which was made into steel at Pittsburgh or Sparrow Point. It is poor business to exchange cheap iron ore for high-priced steel. To permit foreign capital, technology, and labor to fabricate the iron—something which could have been done in our own country—was merely to deform further the conscience of a people which had been so exposed to colonial influence.

From the Material to the Human

The foregoing chapters, I admit, may have been tedious or even somewhat deadly for the reader because of the many figures used. But it seemed worth sacrificing style for the moment because this report should be useful not only to Venezuela but to other countries as well. The democratic system of government is so often questioned because of its alleged inefficiencies in material accomplishment that it was important to recount the facts of what was planned and what was done by our free government during only three years in office.

No claim is made that the record is exceptional. It was carried out in a limited period of time, with a human margin of error, and with all the shortcomings inherent in any undertaking to try so many new things by men who do not insist upon pretending that they are always right. However, the record was constructive. It was planned coherently and carried out with great enthusiasm. Finally, it tended to make our land more habitable for the men and women who live there and our economy less vulnerable to the ups and downs of the international oil market.

Our intention of serving the men and women who lived within our territory was shown in an even more direct manner: to educate them better and raise their cultural level; to protect them from disease and heal them when they suffered; and to give them decent housing—these were the central concerns of the AD government, as detailed in the following chapters.

12

School and Pantry: Keys to Educational Reform

From the Pharonic to the Human

Like other Latin American nations that had suffered from continued tyrannies, Venezuela has often heard it said that there should be "less politics and more administration." To administer was to build; to govern was to mix cement. Massive public works, whether needed or not, were the only mark that these providential men-on-horseback left behind.

The satraps of Babylon and the pharaohs of Egypt had shown the way. Those who ruled in the turbulent tropics took short lessons in their primitive and inhuman methods.

When we changed administrative direction in Venezuela, we did not seek to blaze any glorious new trails: we simply wanted to lay the foundations for a modern country—electrically equipped, traversed by means of communications, and ready to take advantage of its own natural resources. But this was not all. The state had to take greater concern for its people, bringing them better education, a better diet, decent homes, land which they could work, and preventive and curative medicine for their chronic diseases. In other words, we had to hurry, making up lost time if we could, to implement a social policy similar to that of nations where the gendarme and tax-collector state had been replaced years ago.

Our determination was to carry out a truly national policy—not just an urban and metropolitan one confined to the capital city of Caracas. We wanted to change the center of gravity, away from things and toward people. Ten days after arriving in Maraflores palace, I told our people that "we will not construct showy skyscrapers; but Venezuelan men, women, and children will eat more, dress better, and pay less rent, have better public services, and there will be more schools. . . . We will decentralize the state and turn our attention to the forgotten countryside."

We were consistent in this policy. In my last message to the National Congress in February 1948, reciting what had been done to improve the lot of our people, I expressed thoughts that challenged the past and pointed to directions for the future:

> We think that monumental engineering works and material wealth mean little to a nation if its people are poor, few in number and badly fed, with their physical health undermined by devastating diseases and spiritually depressed for lack of culture. That is why populating our semideserted land with immigrants and undertaking to feed, cure, and educate the Venezuelan people have been the principal objectives of the government I have led.

The same was true of the government which Rómulo Gallegos headed for just nine months. Both our administrations had a common ideology set forth in the program of AD.

"The Ignorance of the People is the Instrument of Their Own Destruction"

The phrase is Bolívar's. But it was forgotten by almost all of the republican governments of Venezuela, even though they always called themselves "Bolívarian."

If any American country stood in need of an aggressive educational policy, it was Venezuela. It had been the least favored of all the Spanish colonies, for it was poor in precious metals and sent little tribute to the royal coffers. The printing press did not arrive in Caracas until two years before the first independence effort in 1810. The university was not established there until a century and a half after those of Mexico and Peru. A few primary schools scattered over the vast territory were the only educational efforts during three centuries of Spanish rule.

After independence was proclaimed, Bolívar placed special emphasis on bringing education to the people, as expressed in his message to the Congress of Angostura in 1819: "Popular education should be first in the love of Congress. Morality and culture are the pillars of the republic. Morality and culture are our first needs."

But these were the years to make war, not to go to school. The Venezuelans, adolescents included, rode on horseback behind their captains, fighting the troops of Ferdinand VII throughout South America. When the Second Republic was founded in 1830, power fell into the hands of a conservative oligarchy bent on forming a government elite. Without saying as much, they echoed Carlos IV when he said, some fifty years earlier, "It is not a good idea to educate the Americans."

As a result of the Federal War and the triumph of liberalism, the Constitution of 1864 guaranteed free and obligatory education and proclaimed freedom of teaching. It was not until six years later, however, when General Antonio Guzmán Blanco seized the presidency that free and obligatory education was decreed. His administration had many shortcomings but his work in education was truly commendable. The number of schoolchildren reached 100,000. But this momentum was lost during the rest of the nineteenth century and for much of the twentieth. When Luis B. Prieto became minister of education in 1945, only one-third of the 800,000 children of school age were getting any education and more than 1 million of the adult population were illiterate.

"If the People Are the Sovereign, the Sovereign Must Be Educated"

If we were ever virulent and aggressive during the years in the opposition, it was when we fought against the bureaucratic parsimony in facing up to the backward education of the country. As soon as we were in government, we showed that we were faithful interpreters of the Bolívar message. We undertook a crusade, using as our motto Sarmiento's phrase, "If the people are the sovereign, the sovereign must be educated."

The budget is a government tool, and the manner in which the state uses its money reflects its true policy, especially in a country such as ours where the state, thanks to its great tax income, has a predominant influence on community activity. Thus we tripled the budget of the Ministry of Education from Bs. 38 million in 1945 to Bs. 119 million in 1948. This was not all, since the state governments spent Bs. 60 million on primary education, the Ministry of Public Works invested Bs. 53 million in new school buildings, and other ministries contributed Bs. 12 million. The true educational budget was thus more than Bs. 250 million—around $80 million.

It was not just money spent on education but money well spent. Venezuelan and foreign experts drew up a National Education Plan, designed to coordinate education from kindergarten to university and make it relevant to the life of the country instead of bookish and abstract, and also to make up for the deficiency of teachers and of schoolrooms. The plan was submitted to the National Congress in 1948, just a month before the coup d'état. However, the plan was preceded by a tremendous effort to improve the school system immediately.

More Schools and Teachers—and Better Ones

Instead of 131,000 children in primary school, there were now 500,000. The number of teachers had increased from 8520 to 13,500, including 1200 teachers in private schools.

Secondary schooling underwent the same growth. The number of high schools increased from 29 to 47; the number of students from 11,500 to 22,000. In 1945, half of the high school students were in private schools; by 1948, only 22 percent were—which may help explain why some individuals and religious organizations opposed our educational policy, asserting that there was official hostility toward private schools. It should be admitted that there was some truth to this argument for a while when the junta promulgated Decree 321. This decree, later withdrawn by the junta itself, was the result of disloyal machinations by a group in the Ministry.

The schools urgently required furniture and student materials in incredible amounts. We found that in all educational institutions there were only 55,000 school desks, which meant that 60 percent of the students either stood in class or sat on boxes or the floor. After the three years, not a single pupil remained without a desk, not a single high school without a laboratory. This in itself amounted to a revolution in the Venezuelan schools.

Encouragement to Vocational Education

Whatever previous regimes had done for education, practically nothing was done to prepare skilled workers. The criticism of Miguel José Sanz, who taught the Liberator that the schools of the colony disdained teaching applied arts "because decent people did not work on the land and orderly people avoid mechanical occupations" was still true. There were only two industrial technical schools, with poor equipment and 300 pupils.

Venezuela urgently needed skilled workers for its factories. The low productivity was due, among other reasons, to the lack of training, for our workers had native intelligence but no knowledge. This problem acquired new aspects when immigrant workers began to compete favorably with local people. Therefore, we decreed the establishment of various schools of technology and applied arts throughout the republic, to train our people not only how to learn what was written in books but also how to do useful things with their hands.

Frontal Attack on Illiteracy

In 1817, General Pablo Morillo, chief of the largest expedition which the Spaniards sent to reconquer South America, wrote to one of his aides in Venezuela: "Do what I have done in New Granada—cut off the heads of all who know how to read and write. This way America will be pacified."

The despotic governments of Venezuela did not apply the bloody formula of the Spanish "pacifier," but did systematically deprive their people of culture. Collective ignorance and passivity before political oppression go hand-in-hand. One of the most negative problems we faced was the high percentage of the adult population that could not read or write. The figures are horrifying. According to the 1941 census, Venezuela had more than 2 million people between 14 and 59 years of age. The illiteracy rate among this active population was 56 percent. In some of the agricultural states, the figure went as high as 77 percent. An agency had been set up a year before we took over, but it worked on a tiny budget and had only taught 600 Venezuelans to read and write.

We took the bull by the horns and trained hundreds of teachers in a crash course. We also established the National Agency for Illiteracy and gave it large resources. The results were immediately seen. In 1946, 15,000 adults were taught to read and write; the next year 45,000; and 37,000 more in the first half of 1948. If we had been able to maintain this pace, not a single illiterate would have remained in the country at the end of ten years.

The Teaching Profession Given a New Dignity

Miguel de Unamuno once said that in Spain the ninth sons of prolific families either went into the clergy or the army, which he termed a kind of "Malthusian recruitment" for the two professions. In Venezuela, this seems to have been the way teachers were found.

The schoolteacher was looked upon with considerable disdain, a frustrated person who could not make good in other fields. Teachers made up a kind of bureaucratic proletariat. Obviously, unless our teachers could be given a sense of professionalism and freed from their inferiority complex, they would not be able to carry out the national cultural regeneration with much success.

At the outset, we found that seven of every ten teachers lacked professional certificates. In 1942, using the pretext of the war, their salaries had been cut by 10 percent and the base salary of a graduate teacher was only Bs. 340 a month. Those without certificates received Bs. 230. We immediately increased salaries by 75 percent and provided various social benefits, but this was not enough. We had to dignify the profession and make teachers more respected in our national life. Their eunuchlike political status was ended, and they were encouraged to become active in all political parties, including those of the opposition.

Success was achieved in attracting young people. Public expenditure on teacher training quadrupled in three years. In 1945, there were only five normal schools with 1200 students; we left twelve schools with 4500 students enrolled, one-third of them on official scholarships. Another 1000 students studied in private normal schools.

The Autonomous University

We were resolved to end the deficiencies of our universities. In 1946, the revolutionary junta decreed administrative and teaching autonomy for our institutions of higher learning.

One of the major problems had always been the lack of economic resources. We increased these from Bs. 5 million in 1945 to Bs. 14 million in 1948. The education law of 1947 sought to ensure continuity between teaching at lower levels and at the university. The experience of other Latin American countries had taught us that universities with absolute autonomy in educational policy often became strongholds for extremist political groups.

The university accelerated the process of democratization. The ethnic mosaic of the country—black, white, and mestizo—was fully represented in its classrooms, and the son of the worker and the son of a millionaire walked side by side in university halls. Higher education was no longer the privilege of the rich. The number of students increased by 65 percent during our first two years and had reached 6000 by the end of our regime.

More rapid growth was not possible because of limitations previously mentioned in primary school education, but it could be foreseen that enough students would be coming to the universities during the following five years to make up our deficit in the professions. We guaranteed sufficient financial resources for the universities by decreeing and later incorporating in the 1947 Constitution the clause that the annual appropriation for universities should be from 1 to 2 percent of the national budget. We also sought to make the universities something more than "a factory which produces doctors." Even though we could do little within so short a period of time, we encouraged the university to place itself more at the service of modernizing the country.

New Importance for Venezuelan Culture and Folklore

Artistic activities were stimulated and the national soul was encouraged to express itself in dance, music, and painting. Our National Symphony Orchestra, with government help, was able to become one of the best in the Caribbean area within a few years. When I gave Maestro Vicente Emilio Sojo, its conductor, the news that the government had assigned it an annual subsidy of Bs. 1 million, he embraced me with emotion and said from the complicated maze of his enormous Dali-like mustache, "It is symbolic. Under your government, the orchestra to which I have given such effort will achieve a great reputation." We both are from Guatire, as was the colonial priest, Padre Sojo, who began the study of music in Venezuela.

The Ministry of Education published thirty books by Venezuelan authors during our three years and printed for the first time the complete works of Bolívar. A Department of Folklore Investigation was set up in the Ministry of Education under the fine poet, Juan Liscano. We wanted to preserve our prodigious heritage of popular artistic traditions which testified to our unique national personality. It was all the more urgent to preserve this legacy because of the deforming effect upon our national culture which the avalanche of foreign immigrants would bring. We wanted to assimilate that which was useful from abroad but absorb it within a way of life and a culture which are and should continue to be Venezuelan.

For this reason, we especially wanted to have our folklore popularized and its excellent quality made known to all, both Venezuelans and foreigners. The excellent presentation of national dances at the time of the inauguration of President Gallegos brought warm praise from the intellectuals who came from all over the Americas for this event. The Negroid frenzy of the Barloventa dances, the mountain rituals of the Andes, the violent prancing of the plains Joropo, the dionysiac sea dances of the coast people from Nuevo Esparta and Sucre, and the melancholic Indian movements of Maracaibo and the territories—all this vast register of music, rhythm, and different customs expressed the strong creative power and proud national traditions of the people.

"The School and the Pantry"

The formula of Joachim Costa, the tormented Spanish thinker, has universal application. Hungry people cannot develop a culture. The need to coordinate education and diet was something that could not be postponed in Venezuela. Along with the golden privilege of being the world's leading oil exporter, we exhibited the national shame of being among the typically underfed countries of Latin America.

In preceding pages, there have been figures supporting this affirmation. Let it just be recalled here that one month before we came to government, 65 percent of the 15,000 children checked in the capital of the republic were threatened with tuberculosis because of inadequate diet.

This widespread problem of undernourishment was attacked with the same energy that our government devoted to other problems of community welfare. We created an Institute of Popular Diet and a Patronate of Student Dining Rooms, coordinated by the Ministries of Health and Education. The number of students who received a balanced diet rose from 1000 in 1945 to 38,000 in 1948. This service was assigned Bs. 9 million and was providing 4 million meals annually. Various industrial firms also made arrangements with the Institute to provide low-cost healthy diets for their workers, who paid 30 céntimos for each meal. We also gave resolute support to the state agency responsible for poor children, the Venezuelan Children's Council, which had a ridiculous budget of Bs. 180,000 annually. We told the president of this institution that the only limit he need accept upon the activities of his agency should be those of a technical nature because the government would assign him all the financial resources he needed; Bs. 8.5 million were budgeted.

Education with a Goal and Doctrine

Long-range goals for Venezuelan education were presented in 1948 to Congress in a four-year plan. Priority was assigned to primary education, so at the end of President Gallegos' term in 1953, Venezuela would have 80 percent of its student population going to public schools. This plan, drawn up by educational experts with full awareness of the social realities of the country, had more than just figures and estimates. The idea was not just to teach humanities and technology. The educational process must fit within an overall philosophical concept in tune with our political situation.

The AD governments did not hesitate in this regard. We agreed with the sociologist Karl Mannheim that "society can be formed either as a hierarchy or as a democracy" and that "the ancient ideal of liberty can only be achieved by planning for liberty." Our schools were oriented from top to bottom in accord with the concept of active, aggressive, and militant democracy. Reactionaries of the extreme right and communist militants criticized our view because a neutral education, impotent and without a position on the ideological conflict, is fertile ground for the confusion they wish to sow.

Luis Prieto expressed our philosophy when he wrote, "If the school educates for liberty then it must teach the children to be free and to practice democracy." I expressed similar concepts when I spoke at the National Teachers Convention in 1947:

> The school teacher cannot be neutral in this battle fought in Venezuela between new times and the remains of the past, between democracy on the march and those who yet dream of the lost autocracy. The government does not ask the teacher to join any single political faction for this battle, under one or another of the parties. What the government does ask is that teachers be passionate defenders of the ideas that sovereignty resides with the people, and not with selfish oligarchic minorities which have tried to usurp power since the earliest days of our nation.

This was the way in which work was carried out and doctrine was converted into fact during the democratic interlude of the years 1945–48. New routes were opened up and others already opened were followed with more confidence and clearer objectives.

13

Human Capital

Venezuela: A Purgatory Because of Health Conditions

Emile Ludwig wrote in a bad book about a privileged land that the earthly paradise was to be found in Cuba. If he had written about Venezuela, knowing of its health conditions, perhaps he would have called it purgatory.

The depressing health picture was the result of the criminal lack of concern by the government during three decades of the Gómez dictatorship and the inadequate attention given by the following governments to public health. In 1945 we found a Ministry of Health with a considerable degree of technical resources but with a budget of scarcely Bs. 28 million (6 percent of the national budget) and a deficit of specialized personnel which would be difficult to overcome. Edmundo Fernández, a distinguished physician without party affiliation, was placed at the head of the ministry. Adequate physical resources were provided, and the budget was increased to Bs. 110 million by 1948. In addition, approximately 20 percent of the expenditures of the states were applied to health and social services.

The situation in the countryside was pathetic. Rural inhabitants were abandoned to their fate without medical or hospital attention and were defenseless before implacable disease. They died by the hundreds while the survivors worked little because of their chronic diseases. A minimum of 4000 doctors was required, but there were not more than 1000 in all the rural areas where 61.5 percent of the population lived. It was necessary to provide medical services, rural water supplies, and sanitation to a population dispersed in thousands of small settlements over an immense geographical territory. The

216

magnitude of the task did not overwhelm the government, motivated by a fervent patriotism and a desire to make history.

The Battle Against Tropical Diseases

The first obstacle was the lack of medical services. Of the 124 rural medical stations, only 64 were occupied. In just a few months 175 doctors were sent to the countryside to fight against disease. Although it scandalized the dehumanized professionals of the oligarchy, it was decreed that students in the last year of medical studies, after an intensive eight-week course, would receive their degree without final examinations or presentation of a doctoral thesis. Instead, these new professionals agreed, after one year of service in public medical centers, to write a report describing their experiences as doctors in the area to which they were assigned.

When the constitutional government was overthrown, three times as many doctors were in the rural medical stations as when we began. In a single year, 1947, some fifty buildings had been erected for rural medical service. Half of the Venezuelans living in the countryside—in a nation where migration to the city was an alarming phenomenon—now were receiving adequate medical attention. All of the national territory would have been covered by medical assistance services at the rate things were being done by the time the Gallegos government should have finished its term in 1953.

Sanitary engineering is basic for hygiene, but in previous government budgets there had been assigned only the incredibly small amount of Bs. 500,000 annually. This budget was increased ten times in the first year of the revolutionary government and progressively thereafter.

Diseases transmitted by water were widespread because most of our people drank from wells or rivers. There were few water mains or sewers in the cities, for they were invisible underground and therefore of no interest to those regimes which wanted to have buildings to show off. During the 115 years of republican life, sewers and waterworks valued at Bs. 55 million had been constructed in 47 towns where there were 98,000 homes with a total of 600,000 inhabitants. In only three years the AD governments invested Bs. 150 million in this type of installation—three times as much as in the course of a century.

Only one rural water supply system had been built before 1945. We tackled this problem head on and did not hesitate when the experts of the Ministry and the Inter-American Public Health Service estimated that an investment of Bs. 60 million was needed to provide pure water to the country villages throughout the nation. Despite our inexperience in this kind of work, twelve rural aqueducts were finished in 1947. Twenty more were well under way and seventy were planned for 1948, but this was not enough to win the fight against intestinal parasites, which ravaged the bodies of a majority of Venezuelans and reduced their work capacity.

It was also necessary to bring shoes to the countryside because feet that were bare or poorly shod with the Venezuelan sandal (the *alparagata*) made it easy for various parasites to enter the body. I had written many articles in the press during the years in opposition and now in the government tried to convert this preaching into putting shoes on people's feet.

A Policy of More Hospitals, Better Equipped

We found hospital services in lamentable shape. Their financial resources were so scanty that many had only Bs. 2 daily per hospital patient, far less than the Bs. 10 needed daily. The situation was so urgent that it was necessary to act immediately without waiting for next year's budget. By decree, the 1945 budget of Bs. 7 million was doubled to Bs. 14 million while the regional governments also doubled their expenditures.

A plan was drawn up to build hospitals and health centers needed to make up the deficit in beds. In 1947, hospitals with 660 beds were finished and those for an additional 1600 beds were begun. The building of University City in Caracas, whose foundations had not yet been laid, was accelerated with the injection of more than Bs. 100 million. It was finished in good part when we lost power, and its hospital with 1000 bed capacity was half built.

Many doctors were sent overseas to specialize in public health services. Nursing and laboratory schools were enlarged. Public opinion came to believe that disease actually could be eliminated. These were the most important tasks for the Venezuela of our time. We understood the protection of public health to be a responsibility of the government. Without theorizing about the nationalization or socialization of medicine, a very controversial subject, we pressed ahead toward our objective, to guarantee to all the population preventive and curative medical services.

If this policy were continued for some years, the results were foreseeable. We took but the first steps. Medicine as a private and lucrative practice would have receded and finally would have been eliminated before the progressive development of public health services. The private hospitals and clinics available only to minority sectors would have been confronted by the overwhelming competition of state hospitals, provided with the best equipment and organized in a completely different manner from the obsolete institution of charity. The remnants of the Spanish Catholic tradition of charitable care would have given way before the modern idea of public health protection as one of the primary responsibilities of the state.

Malaria—A Plague Put to Rout

It was in the fight against malaria where the first great battle was won for the physical redemption of the Venezuelans. Malaria had been a terrible scourge. It was said that there were a million new persons infected each year and that the loss to the economy was some Bs. 200 million annually. The human cost was much greater, even though it could not be expressed in monetary terms.

The antimalaria services in Venezuela were in expert hands—those of Arnoldo Gabaldón. A recognized expert, he had been a high official of the World Health Organization and had advised the government of India on its sanitary campaigns against malaria. In the school which he headed, attached to the department of malariology of the Ministry of Health, officials from all over America, including the United States and Canada, came for specialized training. We gave him carte blanche to carry out his plans for eradicating the disease and he asked for Bs. 10 million, two and half times his previous budget. This was immediately granted. Thus, for the first time in any American country, the division of malariology was able to make massive use of DDT, the insecticide used to clean up the Pacific Islands during World War II.

The results obtained after two years were so extraordinary that Dr. Paul E. Russel, a noted United States specialist, declared in 1947, "Venezuela is the first tropical country that is doing away with malaria." By 1948, a third part of the malaria zone had been completely cleaned up. It was foreseen that in two more years the disease would have been totally eliminated. The dedicated group of technical people working on this redeeming enterprise were supported by a government more interested in saving human life than in constructing avenues and cementing public plazas.

To govern is a harsh and depressing task, especially when one is motivated by intense patriotism and the will to serve. But there are moments of emotion during the exercise of power which are so intense that they alone make up for all the frustrations. I owe a wonderful memory to this war to the death against malaria, which turned to victory under my government.

In August 1947, I was touring the eastern part of the republic on an official visit. The progress of our auto caravan was slow because the villages through which we passed were congested with country people who came down from the hills with their women and children to give testimony of their support for the revolution. We arrived one midnight at the town of Caguaramal in the state of Monagas, known as "the capital of malaria." There had not been a single case of malaria in that town for the past year. My throat choked to see tears pouring down the bronzed country faces and through the wrinkles of ancient visages. One old lady, coming up to where we stood upon the planks of an improvised speakers' stand, cried out to me: "We cry, my son, because we no longer must worry each year about which grandson will be carried off by the fever."

Obligatory Social Security

Obligatory social security had been in effect for a year when we took over in 1945. A law had been promulgated in 1940, but only four years later was it put into effect. Its services only covered maternity cases, labor accidents, and work-related diseases. Even so, it was already discredited with the workers because its services were so deficient.

The reason was plain: it lacked financial support. The employer contributed 5 percent, the worker 2 percent, but the state only 9/100 of 1 percent. We immediately appropriated Bs. 4 million to cover the deficit and raised the state contribution to 4 percent. Additional contributions brought the annual appropriation to Bs. 12 million for 1947, and the first social security hospital was constructed.

However, it was not an easy matter to overcome the deficiencies of this institution which is so important in modern society. We lacked statistical experts capable of reorganizing the service. We brought some from England and Chile since we did not hesitate to import experts when we needed them. Social security protected only about 20 percent of the total urban population while the rural workers, the most numerous in the country, were not covered. The labor law provisions regarding dismissal, indemnification, and death were no substitutes for what we understood to be the modern norms of security—total protection against all risks from cradle to grave.

The experts worked very hard accumulating statistics and records; their efforts would give a more solid basis for social security in the country. Personally, I feel we should have done more, much more than we did despite the fact that we governed for so few years. The experts always want to have perfection; they want to have their models function like clockwork. But those of us who govern, especially when we are dealing with peoples whose historical evolution has been long delayed, must apply that maxim of Sarmiento's: "Take action, even when everything does not come out well."

A Housing Policy with a Goal: A Decent House for Everyone

Our government of necessity had to adopt an aggressive housing policy, for here there was a most dramatic expression of the paradox of a country that was wealthy and a people that were poor. The capital city of Caracas included beautiful districts for the delight of privileged minorities. In contrast to the luxurious mansions of a few dozen rich families, the rest of the population lived in modest homes and *ranchos* (hovels). The 1941 census revealed the primitive conditions in which the majority of the Venezuelans had to live. Only 36 percent of the houses were made of brick and mortar. Only in the capital city and in three of the most advanced states did they make up half of the housing. *Ranchos* predominated in the remaining states and two territories, and in some of them they reached 90 percent or more of the total.

The typical *rancho* found throug. out the rural areas is of primitive construction, little different from the Indian dwelling which the Spanish conquerors found in the fifteenth century. There is one difference, favorable to the Indians, because at that time most of the diseases now widespread in the tropics did not exist. Of the 660,752 dwellings in the census, 406,460 were *ranchos*. Of these, half had earthen floors and thatched roofs, while 72 percent lacked sanitary facilities of any kind. Some 63 percent of these houses—if they could be called such because they were really just hog-pens—had but a single room, with all of the crowding and promiscuity that resulted from having an average of 5.5 persons in each. Even worse, the unsanitary *ranchos* harbored, especially in their thatched roofs, insects carrying various tropical diseases.

We understood the problems and faced up to them even though we had little experience. We were not prepared to undertake mass housing programs simultaneously in various cities. We did not have the necessary architects and city planners. We lacked not only the imported construction materials; we did not have modest lime or brick factories, and we had to provide these. Public sanitary services (water and sewers) were lacking in many of the urban areas where housing was in short supply. Once again, we had to employ that simile from the railroad: everyone—conductor and passengers—had to get off the train while new rails were laid so the trip could continue. The fundamental thing was for the government to admit that behind the golden facade of its showy and maldistributed wealth, Venezuela has been hiding the fact that the greater part of its people lived in as dirty and poorly furnished conditions as the inhabitants of darkest Africa, or the peons on the sugar plantations of the European colonies in the Caribbean. It was high time to undertake a feasible method of housing in Venezuela.

The first step immediately taken was to give the Workers' Bank (Banco Obrero), the state agency for financing public housing, the kind of money it needed. Its capital in 1946 was only Bs. 20 million. In the first year of democratic government it was given Bs. 60 million more and Bs. 90 million were added in 1947–48, so that in the three years of AD government, its financial resources to carry out a housing program were unprecedented in Latin America. The rents of those living in apartments were reduced from 5 to 15 percent, but since there were so many ways of getting around rent controls, the important thing was to rapidly build housing within the reach of workers and the middle class.

The Workers' Bank had been in existence sixteen years before we came to power, but had constructed few housing developments. The best was El Silencio in Caracas, built under President Medina Angarita, which showed it was possible for the government to develop large-scale housing projects. However, this was but a single effort, and in Caracas.

We faced the problem in its full dimension. The housing program must be extended over the entire country. Venezuela was not a city-state like ancient Athens, but a modern nation with a vast and depressed provincial hinterland. The construction of new housing was accelerated; the results were soon seen on a national scale. In the first two years of AD government 5000 housing units were built—equivalent to six and a half times the capacity of El Silencio, and ours were distributed throughout the republic. At the same time, the Workers' Bank made loans of more than Bs. 10 million to private individuals to construct their own homes, and the Mortgage Bank was organized with an initial capital of Bs. 20 million, provided by the government.

At the same time, a program of rural housing was started. The idea was to rebuild a typical country dwelling and provide it with sanitary facilities, roof, and floor. The first experience, using the cooperative labor of the community and construction materials provided by the government, successfully transformed existing hovels into decent habitations. Plans were made to extend this program to the rest of the rural areas.

A national commission for city planning was also organized in connection with this program. Its need was evident. Our cities, Caracas among them, had proliferated in a rather perverse manner. The problems which disorganized urban growth had created were particularly acute in the areas adjoining the oil camps. To introduce order in this chaos and to plan the future rational development of our cities were the tasks assigned to this official city-planning body.

Massive Immigration

Our policy of upgrading and improving our human resources was held back by the thin density of our population, one of the lowest in South America. The problem of populating the country had concerned many Venezuelans since Bolívar. In 1824, he had called for "the immigration of people from Europe and North America to come here and bring with them their arts and letters." Little was done to follow his directive throughout the rest of the century. During the despotic regimes of Castro and Gómez, covering a dark period of thirty-five years of our history, the foreigner who arrived enjoyed a status similar to that of the ambassadors in ancient cities. There came but a few dozen North Americans, English and Dutch, with their checkbooks for the banks in New York and London, to benefit from the venal distribution of the nation's oil reserves.

In the post-Gómez decade, the need for an open-door policy for hard-working foreigners was continually talked about, but once again it was proved that autocratic governments always fear programs which signify change in the existing situation. For instance, the government of López Contreras rejected the opportunity for bringing Basques from Spain after the Franco victory, as Mexico did to the great benefit of its industrial development. López distrusted the men who had had the courage to confront the totalitarian hordes of the caudillo. So it was left to the government of Acción Democrática to begin a bold immigration policy. In my last message as chief of state to the Congress on February 12, 1948, I reported on what had been achieved:

> From 1939 to 1944, only 3500 immigrants entered the country. From 1945 to 1947, 16,000 have arrived as a result of official efforts, and 25,000 more have come

as a result of their own efforts, some bringing with them their own industrial machinery, and most of them determined to make Venezuela their homeland.

In 1948, the last year of democratic government, 20,000 immigrants entered the country as the government of President Gallegos continued the policy initiated earlier.

To Bring the People Needed by the Country

This flow of immigrants was not gradually deposited like river alluvium. Times were quite different from Sarmiento's day when, presiding over the Argentine government, he announced, "To govern is to populate," Venezuela sought to adjust the immigration to national requirements. Most of the newcomers came from Italy, Spain, and Portugal. Some were refugees from Central Europe fleeing from political intolerance. An agreement was signed with the Internal Committee on Refugees (IRO) to bring in 15,000 immigrants per year. However, these were to be selected by Venezuelan missions which were instructed to exclude all those who were physically, morally, or politically undesirable. We did not want those who were chronically ill or affected by war psychosis. This was not a philanthropic crusade but a realistic demographic policy. Also, we did not want people of totalitarian thought, whether of the left or the right. We had enough at home and it would have been stupidity to augment their number through importation.

We decided that immigrants of the same nationality should not form separate communities. I remembered the negative experience during the war in southern Chile, where there was a German minority which sympathized with Hitler. Also, we reacted against the idea—hurtful to our national pride—of treating the immigrant as a special person who should be given benefits denied to our own people. We wanted them to enter into integrated communities, mixing those of our country with those who came from abroad.

Our immigration policy followed a definite sociological concept. We wanted the immigrant to increase our production and to fill the country. We did not consider the white man as such or the European as superior to the Venezuelan of mixed blood. We were not interested in a transfer of civilization as one might bring some Swiss pine saplings to give style to a tropical garden, filled with our mango and tamarind trees. On the contrary, we wanted to nationalize the immigrants, adapting them to our soil and to our way of life. The best way to achieve this was to have them live in communities where they would mix their blood with that of our native people, with their own racial characteristics of which they were justly proud.

We do not idealize our typical man of mixed race, nor do we believe that there is any "cosmic race" chosen by the gods as the basis for a new humanity. We do believe that our people, formed from various races with all their virtues and defects, are just as capable of creative thought and activity and just as able to live a civilized life as any other. They are people who live in their own land, in a nation descended from the forefathers whose values should be exalted and preserved. An immigration policy which gave privileged status to people coming from outside, just because they had a skin without Negro or Indian pigmentation or because they came from countries with some centuries more of history than Latin America, would not contribute to this goal.

Emphasis was placed on the selection of farmers, but there were others who were urgently needed, such as doctors, laboratory technicians, skilled workers, and craftsmen. Contrary to the short-sighted idea that only farmers were needed, a less exclusive criterion was applied. The beneficial results were soon seen. The Economic Commission for Latin America of the United Nations (ECLA) estimated that 35 percent of the nearly 39,000 migrants entering the country from 1945–49 were industrial workers.

Population Growth Greater than Brazil's

Three years after this government action in the protection of our human resources and their increase by an open-door immigration policy, very positive results were reported by the Central Bank of Venezuela in its 1948 annual report:

> There was a growth of the population by 130,000 persons due to the total of 190,000 births in contrast to 60,000 deaths. If the immigration of 20,000 persons is added, the total increase is 150,000, which means that the population growth during the year is more than 3 percent. The importance of this figure is seen when it is compared with the 2.5 percent annual growth which occurred from 1936–47. In Brazil, during this period, the population grew by little more than 2 percent per year.

Thus Venezuela began to cleanse and populate its territory and to free its people from the diseases which had had all the destructive effect of the biblical plagues. The challenge of the wilderness was faced, as was the threat of becoming an enormous unpopulated region with a ravaged countryside perforated only by the steel towers of petroleum rigs through which "a man suffering from malaria stumbled upon a bony horse."

14

Administrative, Monetary, and Bank Reform

Obsolete and Inefficient Government Organization

The reforming urge of our three years of democratic government had a most serious obstacle—the lack of effective means to carry it out. The Venezuelan government was among those which conserved the greatest resemblance to its long-gone predecessor—the administrative organization Spain brought to its colonies. In 1808, the observant Frenchman Depont, in his book *Viaje a la Costa Oriental de Tierra Firma,* had noted ironically how the royal government functioned in Venezuela. Many of the same characteristics survived in the twentieth century: paper shuffling and bureaucratic lethargy; multiple and complicated accounting systems; duplication of functions among different state agencies; absence of a civil service career; and the deep-rooted idea that the public official is not there to serve the community, even though his salary is paid by the taxpayer, but somehow is above the common citizen who has business with government offices.

In a country such as ours, where power had so often been seized by armed uprisings, government positions were considered as war booty. The triumphant caudillo would distribute jobs among his retinue like spoils taken from the country. Under the long period of mechanical peace imposed by Gómez, there was no improvement in the dignity, stability, or efficiency of the public employee. The confusion between what was a sinecure and what was public trust was, on the contrary, accentuated. Furthermore, government employees were recruited from among those legions of flatterers who frequently signed public tributes describing the despot as "irreplaceable for the present and future of the homeland."

During the post-Gómez decade, little change was made in this situation. There were a greater number of technically competent people in administrative positions, without whom some of the new services established after 1936 could not have functioned. However, nothing was said or done to reform the administrative organization of the government or to establish civil service careers.

With the coming of Acción Democrática to power in 1945, there was an acceleration, often a violent one, of government activities. There was a substantial increase in bureaucratic payrolls and salaries were increased. But even with all our emergency measures, government machinery continued rusty and creaking, and administrative services were deficient and costly. Our careful plans were often put into effect with painful delay or were not acted upon at all. The unhappy tradition of inertia was a deadweight throughout the government. Many employees lacked ability to do their work or even the desire to do it.

We were not embarrassed to admit this publicly or to discuss the weakness of our national organization and our customs frankly. This was characteristic of the new government. In my last message to Congress, I evaluated the situation with absolute candor:

> At the start we imagined that executive decrees would be sufficient to establish or improve a public service or that we could make it more efficient by assigning adequate funds. Now we know differently. The desire to render public service on the part of the individuals heading up government agencies and adequate funding are important factors, but not the only ones to guarantee efficient administration.
>
> We will never get the kind of efficiency that we want until we reorganize the administrative machinery of the state and train specialists in the modern machinery of government. We need these specialists and the machinery urgently. Venezuela, like other underdeveloped countries now hurrying to attain civilized standards, must face all of the problems of modern states without adequate organization or trained personnel.

This statement was an indirect reply to criticism made of democratic government, even by many who sympathized with it, including members of our own party. Administrative failures, it was claimed, were due to "sabotage" by a hostile fifth column hidden in the bureaucracy. The basic fault was something else—lack of adequate organization and trained personnel. It is true that there were enemies of the government in public positions, but this is a phenomenon characteristic of any popular revolution.

Parties based on the masses, in Venezuela as elsewhere, usually do not include many technical experts or even many good stenographers. In his *History of the Russian Revolution*, Trotsky tells how the police, soon after the overthrow of czarism, surrounded the quarter where most of the bureaucrats from the old regime lived—not to arrest them but to force them to return to their jobs.

Our government was not content just to complain about the situation. We tried to do something about it through administrative reform. The principal figure in this effort was one of the most capable men in the government, Manuel Pérez Guerrero, Minister of Treasury.

A Basis for Administrative Reform

The decision of the democratic government to undertake administrative reform was set forth in the November 27, 1947, decree of the revolutionary junta. Responsibility was assigned to the ministry of treasury, and the commission of administrative and financial studies was established there to prepare the necessary legislation. Various foreign experts were brought in as advisers, but the fact was that there was not much experience from abroad we could apply.

We took some initial steps, nonetheless, to demonstrate that we were serious. The first was to make a census of public employers and to study the government agencies, one by one, to determine whether they were properly staffed. After the census and a job performance survey of four ministries, recommendations were made for greater efficiency.

Various legislative bills were presented to the 1948 Congress, but most of them never got to a vote. Among these, the public employees law is worth mentioning because it defined the rights and duties of government workers and proposed to encourage better performance through an adequate system of job stability, promotion, benefits, and pensions.

The studies of administrative reorganization sought, in the first place, a better distribution of services to avoid duplication of effort. Beginning in 1936, various autonomous institutes had been created. Some were credit institutions and others had specific administrative duties. Often their duties were not well defined and overlapped with those of the ministries to which they were attached. The reform also sought the creation of a central government purchasing service to end dispersion of the function among twelve different government offices, a situation which presented obvious difficulties in reducing costs and eliminating corruption.

Also, it was sought to speed up administrative procedures and to reduce paperwork in public offices that put the patience of the public to such daily trial. Under the reorganization carried out by the law of public treasury in 1948, one of the first approved, the minister no longer had to personally sign 75,000 orders of payment each year. He was thus able to use his time for more important tasks, and the creditors of the government could hope for more rapid payments of their accounts. Similarly, government accounting systems were simplified and unified, putting an end to the great variety used previously. Because of the positive results achieved, in the 1948–49 budget the recently created General Department of the Budget was able, for the first time in our history, to discriminate between capital investment and general expense. Such an effort, perhaps routine in other countries, had singular interest in Venezuela because of the overwhelming impact of the budget on the economic life of the nation. Work was done on a new tariff law to bring our practice into line with universal norms approved years earlier by the extinct League of Nations. Our customs law resembled a mysterious code, decipherable by only a few persons.

Finally, legislation was drawn up to regulate and simplify appeals procedures. The complex and difficult method of obtaining justice in disputes with the government was another evil legacy from colonial times. It was so difficult that many persons preferred to accept rulings which they considered unjust rather than appeal governmental decisions to the tribunal.

Clearly, it was not enough just to issue new laws if the performance of government personnel did not improve. The reforms would be a dead letter if the men who were to carry them out lacked a minimum of efficiency in their work. Various schools were set up for specialized training in fiscal and administrative studies, post and telegraph operations, forestry, and so on.

Finally, an agency for national planning was created to coordinate government activities and set goals for official action within definite time periods. Actually, since 1946, a group had been functioning in the presidential palace without waiting for legal authority. It met weekly under the chairmanship of the chief of state to make decisions of an economic and fiscal nature and to oversee development plans. The CVF had been asked to draw up legislation for a Planning Council and this was ready by March 1947. Its fundamental purpose was to coordinate all public and private activity in a long-range plan, giving priority to matters of national interest and social welfare. This was to be accomplished largely through private initiative and enlarged economic democracy, and should provide Venezuela with a healthy, solid, and stable economy.

A New Monetary and Banking Policy

In 1948 the economic and financial situation of the country seemed very favorable. The national production was increasing, the large budget was financed without excessive taxation, and the huge foreign exchange reserves accumulated by the central bank gave strong backing to our currency. Venezuela, like many other countries of Latin America, had accumulated a large surplus of gold and exchange, but unlike other nations, it did not exhaust these reserves during the first years of the postwar period. On the contrary, they increased. The new investments of the oil companies and our energetic tax policy to obtain a higher share of oil income made this possible. Our exchange balance grew despite larger imports to meet deferred demand as the purchasing power of the public increased. In 1947 our foreign exchange reserves had reached Bs. 662 millions, seven times as much as those of 1940.

But behind this favorable panorama lay a reality which could not be ignored—our excessive dependence upon the growing oil production of the postwar period, truly the fuel and lubricant of the Venezuelan economy. Politicians of the old school would have preferred to silence the truth and portray the existing bonanza as a great achievement of the government. However, we wanted to awaken the nation to its dependence upon a single product. We continued to insist that our national economy would be unstable as long as it lacked support other than the transitory oil industry. It was not enough just to proclaim this fact. It had to be modified. In the monetary and banking field, for instance, we tried to provide the country with defensive reserves against possible decline in oil production or a fall in prices.

Our monetary unit, the bolívar, enjoyed universal prestige because of its solidity. I have heard persons of various nationalities, in the most diverse walks of life, speaking in different languages, express the same idea in more or less the following terms: "The bolívar is the only money as strong as the American dollar." Their tone of respect for such solid currency reflected the idea that Venezuela was a happy Eden.

The strength of the bolívar masked a grave vulnerability. We had known this, we had said this, and we proposed, now that we were in the government, to change the situation. In 1947 Venezuela obtained Bs. 465 million in foreign exchange—34.5 percent more than in 1946 and 83.3 percent greater than in 1940. However, 97 percent of this income came from oil, and only 3 percent from such permanent products as coffee and cacao.

The vulnerability of the bolívar had a close connection with the national economy. To defend both the economy and its monetary symbol, various legislative proposals were presented to Congress in 1948, but it was not possible to conclude their discussion that year because of the accumulation of legislation being debated. These reforms included amendments to the central bank law to give this institution greater power in the regulation of money supply and national finance; amendments to the currency law to give greater protection and stability to the bolívar; creation of an anticyclical fund for use in any crisis resulting from unfavorable oil prices; creation of a fund to stabilize securities which, together with the stock exchange, would channel saving into productive activities; and reform of the bank law with special emphasis on the regulation of mortgages and capital operations.

State supervision of private banking operations came relatively late in Venezuela and still were very deficient. The central bank had been created only in 1939 to supplement the bank law from the times of Gómez. When the dictator died, Venezuela enjoyed the dubious privilege of being the only country in the world where there were various banks issuing currency. This multiplicity made it impossible to follow a monetary policy in the national interest. The volume of circulation was not determined by the government, in accord with national needs, but by private bank directors in accord with their own needs. Furthermore, the power to issue currency of obligatory circulation provided the banks with an easy business of scandalous profit— about 24 percent since the bills they issued were backed by a reserve of only one-third their nominal value. There were many other privileges that the

private banks enjoyed, thanks to the lack of official vigilance over their activities. Our backward industrial and agricultural production was due in part
to the way the Venezuelan banks behaved, more as medieval pawnshops than
as modern credit institutions.

The bankers reacted in a choleric manner in 1938 when the Congress had
discussed changes in the banking law and prepared the statute of the central
bank. They used all imaginable resources to torpedo the reform and were
successful in part. The powers of the Central Bank were reduced to a
minimum and private banks continued to circle in their own orbit outside the
area of state regulation.

The reform prepared in 1948 gave the central bank much more extensive
powers and would have integrated the private banks into the development
plan of the country. There was no thought of nationalizing them. This was
not necessary in Venezuela because the institutions most directly connected
with regulating the credit mechanism for productive activities were official
agencies — the Venezuelan Development Corporation (CVF), the Agriculture
and Cattle Bank (BAP), and the Workers' Bank (Banco Obrero). The private
banks operated almost exclusively in the commercial field.

The reforms of 1948 gave special emphasis to bank capitalization. It was
hoped to stimulate individual saving which the spendthrift Venezuelan of our
times had been so little interested in. There was need to create a useful substitute for gambling. The government was greatly concerned because people,
in the wake of the oil boom, immediately spent most of the money which
came to their hands. In saving not at all, or saving very little, Venezuelan
behavior was typical of mining communities, as in the California gold rush
days. There was a national urge to spend until one's pockets were empty.

In 1938, according to the statistical annual of the League of Nations, savings in Venezuela were among the lowest of the continent, $6.75 million,
while those in Argentina were $680 million. Even savings in countries of
lower per capita income, Chile and Peru, were higher—$45 million and $15
million, respectively. Although the situation began to improve and savings
visibly increased, they did not bear a satisfactory relation to the per capita
income. In 1949, Venezuela held third place in Latin America with $315
million, following Argentina and Uruguay.

This reluctance to save was due, in the case of the average Venezuelan, to
the failure of schools to develop habits of thrift. State agencies did not stimulate savings, even though it was urgently needed. The ease of buying abroad
encouraged waste. The sectors most favored by the petroleum lottery wasted
their winnings with the carefree exuberance so characteristic of the miner.
The contagion spread throughout the population, especially among the middle class. In Miami and Puerto Rico, in Havana and New York, not to speak
of the European countries with their devalued currencies, the Venezuelan
became synonomous with the big spender. The principal object of the banking reform we prepared was to channel part of this wastefully spent money
into savings and capital investment.

Landmark and Signpost

So finishes the recital of the government activities under two Acción Democrática administrations, those headed by Rómulo Gallegos and myself. They constitute a permanent landmark left as a challenge to contemporary Venezuela. They were made possible by a multiplicity of effort, by unflagging dedication, and by the confidence of the people that democracy would modernize and transform the country.

They also constitute a signpost for the tasks of tomorrow, no matter who may be the men to carry them out. If there is historical continuity, their government action will be characterized by economic nationalism, agrarian democracy, political liberty, administrative honesty, and encouragement for all creative welfare and cultural activities. Those who follow with their own programs will have ample precedents due to the work we finished or planned.

PART SIX

Neo-Fascism in the Government

15

The Background of
the Military Coup
November 24, 1948

"The military spirit is incompatible with civilian government." (Bolívar)

"It is always dangerous to have soldiers, sailors or Air Force men intervening in politics. It is a world of very different values from that to which they are accustomed." (Winston Churchill)

A Government that Lived Dangerously

The Nietzschean formula—adopted by Benito Mussolini—of living dangerously might well have been applied to the democratic regime which followed the revolution of 1945. It lived dangerously, facing reactionary conspiracies, aborting some before they broke out and overcoming others which got underway. This continued until the coup d'état of November 24, 1948 overthrew the political regime in which the Venezuelan people had placed their hope.

The eternal second-guessers can theorize—and they often do—regarding formulas that might have given the political situation a stability resembling passage over a quiet lake. They forget—or they pretend to forget—that the price paid to achieve this tranquillity would have restricted the government to administering the status quo. If we had made only a simple change of the men at the wheel, leaving the course of administration the same as that of the previous regime, a new autocracy would have presided over the stratified injustice and profound disorder of a government which only had the appearance of order. It is ingenuous to believe that changes as profound as those

235

which occurred in the direction of political democracy and economic reform could have been possible without the desperate resistance from those reactionary groups ousted from their arbitrary abuse of power.

There were other factors in Venezuela which made the whole process of the rescue of popular sovereignty and serious economic-political reform more difficult. For the previous fifty years, no civilian had occupied the presidency of the republic. Also, since 1899, no one born outside the Andes region had held that office. Castro, Gómez, López Contreras, and Medina Angarita, all were Andinos from the state of Táchira. Regional resentment, an important factor in what happened in our case, was added to the force of those who traditionally opposed democratic government in Latin America. Feudal landholders, many among the military, the clergy and business circles, both national and foreign, were hostile to the unionization of labor, to modern taxation, and to government supervision of the production of resources which belonged to the nation. Ex-president López Contreras was the prime exponent of this regional feeling as revealed in documents which left no doubt of his intentions.

On April 13, 1947, the revolutionary junta published the text of a confidential memorandum which López Contreras sent from New York to Colonel Delgado Chalbaud, the minister of defense. In this document, he urged Delgado to use army pressure on the national constituent assembly to get himself elected president of the republic, using as his principal argument the need for what he called Andino hegemony. He claimed that Delgado had the right combination of qualities for the presidency because he was the son of an Andino father and his mother was from Caracas. He claimed that there was a separatist movement in the Andean states and others of western Venezuela—something which existed only in the fantasy of this fanatic regionalist—and added: "All of this is due to the imprudent attitude of Rómulo Betancourt, who is unnecessarily persecuting these people."

Finally, he counseled Delgado that, if he could not get himself elected, "it would be necessary to resort to force."

There was nobody in Venezuela, not even the most bitter adversaries of the AD government, who would dare to assert publicly the existence of official hostility toward the Andes. Our government's program was national in scope, without preference for any region. We thought and acted like Venezuelans. Our patriotism was not a pretense. However, what López said shows the kind of whispering that was going on and the way conspiracies were being hatched in dark corners.

This disgraceful campaign appealed to the most provincial feelings and was contrary to the national outlook with which the most thoughtful and authentic representatives of the Andes looked upon the country. It caused irreparable harm, especially among the officers of the army. While people from all regions were found throughout the government, the military officers largely continued to come from the Andes. But the idea of Andean superiority was receding generally in public life. In politics, for instance, the Christian Socialist (Copei) party, which was a national party led by a native of Caracas, Rafael Caldera, won all of the elections between 1945 and 1948 in the two Andean states while AD always was second. It was also significant that many Andino officers loyally supported the democratic regime and were among the most decided adversaries of the military government. Various Andinos, civilian and military, had died fighting against it.

The Caribbean Dictatorships, Arsenal of the Counterrevolution

Certain American dictators joined in the conspiracy against our government. The AD governments, in their stand on international politics, were faithful to their doctrine. We broke relations with the totalitarian Spanish government months before the United Nations voted for the collective withdrawal of diplomatic missions from Madrid. We withdrew our diplomatic representatives from Santo Domingo and Nicaragua and our relations with the government of Perón in Argentina were cool and even hostile on occasion. I made many public statements during an official tour of the Caribbean in 1946, denouncing the tropical dictators for undermining representative governments and for violating human rights. At this time, I urged that a "prophylactic cordon" be established around antidemocratic governments of the continent. As long as there was a single government in America which did not guarantee freedom to all the political parties, to the press and to all ideological currents; as long as there was a single government which did not guarantee the four freedoms of Roosevelt, the liberty of all the others was menaced.

The Democratic Government Helps the Military

I want to stress that our democratic government harbored no hostility toward the military. The members of Acción Democrática have always believed that it was necessary to have a well-equipped and organized army. We supported the armed forces in bringing technical training and better living conditions to both officers and rank and file. Testimony of this was given in the public letter with which Lieutenant Colonel Delgado Chalbaud and Lieutenant Colonel Vargas replied July 3, 1946, to a letter from former president López Contreras: "In only eight months, the revolution has done much more for the army than your government ever did."

I told the national constituent assembly on January 20, 1947, how much had been done for the military. Official salaries had been increased 37 percent and those of the soldiery by 57 percent. Bs. 4 millions were contributed to the military pension fund to which only Bs. 1 million had been previously given.

While we wanted to better the professional and technical status of the military, we insisted that the army be clearly under civilian executive control and not intervene in the political and administrative activity—faithful to the most orthodox, Bolívarian tradition. It was the Liberator who coined the phrase which should be our permanent doctrine: "Unfortunate the people when the man of arms takes over."

This is not to downgrade the armed forces. On the contrary, it has been the prolonged military autocracies which have opened breaches between the man in uniform and the man in shirtsleeves. Never has there been such close understanding between the army and the people as in our years of democratic life. Fervent multitudes applauded the military parade that took place at the first anniversary of the revolution. The people expressed their sincere and spontaneous identification with the army for the first time in many years— perhaps for the first time since the liberating troops entered Caracas in 1813—because they considered the soldiers to be the guardians of the revolution that was underway.

One Conspiracy after Another

Those who wanted to return to the past were sure that the people would defeat them if given a chance to vote. That is why seditious plots always coincided with electoral events. The first plot took place in Maracay, the site of an important military garrison, at the same time that a commission was drawing up the electoral statute and a draft of a constitution. Several civilians, brothers by the name of Bello, were seized in Caracas with a small quantity of arms. This led AD to mobilize its members in the streets to support the new government. We really did not know what the situation was except that our support was very precarious in the army—the second military garrison of the country at Maracay was frankly out of control.

The recently organized opposition parties knew of our weakness. They knew that the true danger did not come from the Bello brothers but from the barracks in Maracay. If they had been truly conscious of their own survival, the other political parties would have supported the government at this critical moment. They did just the contrary. They belittled the danger that the revolutionary junta was of being overthrown. Only the rapidity with which we moved to arrest a group of military and civilians enabled us to survive this grave situation.

When I confronted Major Alborñoz, commander of the Maracay garrison and demanded that he explain what had happened, he said, significantly: "It was impossible to maintain discipline. The rebellious officials are angry that your government is not led by an Andino, as has always been the case before."

In the middle of this same year, 1946, when the electoral process was well underway, there was another barracks conspiracy directed from the United States by General López Contreras. In North America, the police uncovered a vast plot involving exiles, adventurers in search of oil concessions and arms merchants in the diplomatic service of Rafael Leonidas Trujillo, the dictator of Santo Domingo. A United Press dispatch from Augusta, Georgia, on December 2, 1947, reported that a federal judge had declared two persons guilty of a plot to steal surplus arms from the United States army to supply a revolution against the Venezuelan government. According to the testimony of one of the guilty men, Dominican consular officials were involved in the plot. Spokesman for the State Department, Michael J. MacDermott revealed that the State Department had been following the matter actively and had passed along to the Venezuelan government all of the information it had obtained.

The New York *Herald Tribune* of May 11, 1947, reported that North American police had learned of the conspiracy when agents of the enemies of the Venezuelan government had promised a United States businessman lucrative returns if he supported the movement and purchased an oil concession after the triumph of the counterrevolution. General López Contreras was cited repeatedly as being the key man in the conspiracy. However, when our Washington ambassador was asked by the United States government if we wished investigations to be pursued against the ex-president, our reply was a resounding no. Our government had a sense of decency in relations with other states which did not permit us to use foreign police to persecute the enemies of our regime.

After the national constituent assembly had been elected, another more serious revolt broke out, in an effort to prevent the assembling of the newly elected body. This was on December 11, 1946. The rebels took two cities less than 200 kilometers from Caracas—La Victoria and Valencia. They also captured most of the military installations in Maracay, and there were outbreaks in various other spots in the interior. We were again able to dominate the outbreak, but it was a very difficult situation. We believed, although we did not have evidence, that various other garrisons were almost ready to revolt. We knew the military chief of Caracas, Rincón Calcaño, had connections with the insurgents.

The situation was more serious because at that critical moment, Lieutenant Colonel Mario Vargas, who had helped put down the other revolts, was out of the country and I had to take personal responsibility for the situation. I explained to my military aides that I was going to the Ministry of Defense and that they should be alert for whatever might happen, as I was fully aware of the possibility that I might be taken prisoner. Delgado Chalbaud and Marcos Pérez Jiménez were in the minister's office, the first pacing up and down with his habitual nervousness and the other sprawled on a chair because he knew that his brother, Lt. Col. Juan Pérez Jiménez, chief of the garrison at Valencia, was among the rebels. To avoid alarm, they had not yet explained the situation to the barracks commanders in Caracas. I saw to it that things were changed immediately. The barracks were placed in a state of alert and their officers were told that the government intended to fight and not surrender. I personally gave these orders in many cases. In the presence of the military chiefs, I called the AD party headquarters ordering our people to get ready to go for arms to the barracks where there were officers friendly to the government.

Late that night, news came that two planes had taken off from Maracay to bomb Miraflores and the Ministry of Defense, then located side by side. Delgado urged me to go to the cellar of the Workers' Bank which could serve as an anti-air refuge, arguing that the chief of state should not run risks. I am not going to express any judgment now as to whether this suggestion was made in good faith or not. In any case, I replied with asperity, since I was very suspicious, more or less as follows: "We are in Venezuela, Delgado, and here whoever shuts his eyes, loses. I will leave this office only when we defeat these people or when they carry me out."

The planes arrived and flew over our buildings. The guard commander ordered that the planes be fired upon setting an example for the troops by firing his submachine gun. Even the police fired their revolvers. The bombers flew off without dropping their explosive cargo. The following day the counterrevolution was over.

After Rómulo Gallegos had been elected and just before his inauguration there was another conspiracy which sought to use massive terrorism. Pirate planes were reported preparing to bomb Caracas from bases in Nicaragua and Santo Domingo. I telegraphed the puppet president of Nicaragua, Roman y Reyes, the docile cousin of Anastasio Somoza, and sent copies of my wire to the Pan-American Union and all the foreign offices of America denouncing the fact that two planes had left the United States after giving false flight information to the authorities there, to pick up bombs in Nicaragua for a pirate air raid on Caracas. In his reply, the unfortunate cousin had to admit that the planes had arrived in Nicaragua. He protested that his country would never allow machinations against the fatherland of Bolívar. Our Ministry of Foreign Affairs reported to Congress on February 11, that twenty-seven Venezuelans and a number of foreign mercenaries had arrived in Nicaragua with arms and bombs in an airplane which had taken off from an identified Dominican airport. Our information was so precise that it could not be denied by the dictatorial governments of Trujillo and Somoza. Later, one of the Venezuelans involved confirmed that the expedition was bringing bombs of 1000 kilos to finish off the regime in Caracas, but that its members had unexpectedly been arrested in Nicaragua.

These plots, with the exception of that of December 11, 1946, had not involved many of the military. However, they were all strongly encouraged by the rancorous and persistent propaganda campaigns the opposition parties carried on against the government. There were also specific incitements to the army to rise against the democratic government. Four months before the coup of which he declared himself the leader, Defense Minister Delgado Chalbaud denounced the encouragement given to military insubordination by civilian groups. He said with deceptive dignity:

People who try to influence the military are very mistaken. The men of our armed forces are not puppets. They are men who think for themselves and who repudiate attempts to encourage them to disregard their obligations. All ranks know what their obligations are under the constitution and know that the national interest demands strict regard for this obligation. Speaking on behalf of the armed forces, I can say that they are pledged to follow the orders of the supreme command exercised by the president of the republic, with the decided collaboration of all of those who have been named by the president.

This message read on the "Day of the Army" was generally interpreted as the reply to the inveterate conspirators, including those who were to be found among the opposition political parties. The press also served as a mouthpiece for the underground conspiracy against constitutional government and helped open the road for the coup d'état.

There were also people of good faith, but small courage, including some Acción Democrática people, who questioned the big changes taking place. Perhaps unaware of the many difficulties being faced, they helped weaken democratic government with their contagious defeatism. It became almost a sport to criticize the failings of a government which had inherited so many problems. One cannot but recall that expression of Jan Huss, the Czech reformer, when he noted the saintly simplicity of the old lady who walked for miles to throw a faggot on the fire which was consuming that apostle of religious decency.

But the people—the man on the street and the workers—had a different attitude. They believed and trusted their government. They instinctively sensed the dangers surrounding the regime elected by their votes. That explains why the great public meeting in Caracas, commemorating the third anniversary of the revolution which took place on October 18, 1948, just four weeks before the coup, drew the greatest throng that had ever gathered up to that time in Venezuela. By their massive turnout, the people offered fervent support to the government they considered their own.

The Manifest Destiny of the Military

The conspiracy meanwhile continued, along with the encouragement which Juan Domingo Perón gave to the military throughout the continent. A well-known circular from the Argentine colonels in April 1943, with its profession of barracks faith, became a sort of Bible for the crusaders of military neofascism: "Civilians can never understand the greatness of our ideal. They must be eliminated from government and given the only mission which corresponds to them—work and obedience."

The religion of the sword found its prophet in the megalomaniac from the River Plate. The man who was going to be, within a few months, the most active chief of the armed assault against Venezuela's democracy, now went to Argentina, the Mecca of the American military crusaders, to get instruction and learn the slogans. Lt. Col. Marcos Pérez Jiménez, Venezuelan chief of staff, conferred with Perón early in 1948. He listened to Perón's advice and, on the return trip, stopped off in Lima. There, he certainly must have agreed on common tactics with his old professor at the Peruvian Superior War College, General Manuel Odría, who at the time was preparing to overthrow the Peruvian civilian government.

On return, Peréz Jiménez inaugurated an active campaign to demoralize military officials in active service. All sorts of calumnies were circulated to discredit those of us in power and the party giving loyal support to the government. Along with this corrosive propaganda, a theory of messianic content was circulated assigning the army a manifest destiny, a providential mission as the savior of the country. The Argentina of Perón was cited as the paradigm of stability and progress.

The victorious insubordination of General Odría in Lima accelerated the plans of these disturbers of order, as Bolívar would have called them who were centered in the Ministry of Defense in Caracas. The military chiefs entrenched in the general staff sought to impose a political policy upon President Gallegos. When he categorically refused, they decided to stage a coup. In the days immediately preceding Venezuela's so-called military "bloodless" revolution, the Washington government recognized the de facto regime of Odría in Peru, the result of a military coup. As the Washington press was later to point out, the Caracas conspirators took this attitude of the United States as a "green light for an uprising."*

The uprising took place with impunity because the thief was also the policeman. The insurgents ran no danger at all because they treasonably used Ministry of Defense communications to order the deposition of the legitimate authorities.

People Helpless before Armed Uprising

Acción Democrática had no way to arm the people against the subversive military commanders of a large well-organized army, but an effort was made

---

*Did the government of President Truman only commit a mistake when it recognized the Odría government at a time when the military in Caracas was visibly stirring or was it trying to encourage the Venezuelan uprising? I do not believe it was the latter. Whoever has read these pages will appreciate the fact that expediency—a defect or a virtue, whichever way you want to look at it in the conduct of public men—is not a characteristic of mine. If I believed that the North American government had any participation in the events of November 4, I would say so. The first to give a calm appraisal of the dramatic downfall of our democratic government was Rómulo Gallegos in a communication of extraordinary dignity and statesmanship, addressed to President Truman from Havana, the first stop of his exile. He said: "I have accepted the statement in reply to my query made by the State Department denying any proven participation by United States officials or of North American interests in the military coup which has criminally seized power in Venezuela."

In his reply, dated February 3, 1949, despite the fact that Washington had already recognized the military government in Venezuela, President Truman said: "I am so happy that you have accepted the sincere declaration by our State Department regarding the non-participation of American citizens or of members of this government in the coup d'état and I want to reiterate them personally to you at this time. It was very kind of you to make public your acceptance of our disavowal."

to block their disregard of the constitution. In accord with President Gallegos and the AD leadership, Valmore Rodríguez, president of the Senate, who was next-in-line for the presidency, went to Maracay where Lieutenant Colonel Jesús Manuel Gámez, a loyal government supporter, commanded a large garrison. Valmore Rodriguez organized a new government after Gallegos was arrested, but the Maracay troops chose to obey orders coming from the Ministry of Defense. Lieutenant Colonel Gámez, on the other hand, preferred to resign his command rather than obey them.

In a book later written from jail, *Bayonetas sobre Venezuela*, Rodriguez quoted Stefan Zweig to explain why honorable military men of democratic belief will obey superior instructions in circumstances such as this even against their most intimate convictions. "Those who have been educated under the iron rule of the military," wrote Zweig, "succumb to the psychosis of an order as if it were an irresistible force."

Andrés Eloy Blanco wrote later from Havana on the role of the army, refuting the allegation that AD had an armed militia force: "The military junta tries to make out that the civilians of AD had arms in their homes and even in the schools. The facts demonstrate the falsity of this charge." He went on to point out that the army itself was not responsible for the overthrow of constitutional government since only a small group of high officers had conspired to take over the government, annulling the progress made in creating a profsional military institution.

The insurgents did not carry the day without opposition. Students mutinied, oil workers went on strike on the outskirts of Caracas, and a few men of the party who had guns skirmished with army patrols until they ran out of ammunition.

At other places throughout the republic, there were outbursts of public protest but the army war machine was used with Prussian brutality to crush all manifestations. Barricades in the street, used in civil wars of past centuries, are not possible in this era of armored tanks and bombers.

The general staff had deposed the constitutional government. It focused on three problems: the makeup of a new military junta, the arrest of the AD leadership throughout the country, and the formulation of a theory that would justify its crude disregard of the will of the people. When the new junta was established, Pérez Jiménez was not at its head. He was a complex, hesitant man, consumed internally by self-doubt. He had encouraged subversion in the military commands but instead of collecting for his dirty work, he gave way in the military triumvirate to the minister of defense, Delgado Chalbaud. The third man was Llovera Páez, who had been chief of the general staff.

Lieutenant Colonel Mario Vargas, in the midst of a crisis of his lung disease and a virtual prisoner of his companions in arms, watched the scene from a cot in the office of the minister of defense. He later recalled the exchange between Pérez Jiménez and Delgado Chalbaud:

Pérez Jiménez: "There should be a military junta of three persons. Llovera Páez and I will be two of them. You should be the third."

Lt. Col. Delgado Chalbaud: "I cannot accept because I was minister of defense in the constitutional government."

Pérez Jiménez: "But you were the one who gave the order for the army to take charge of the situation."

Delgado Chalbaud: "That is true, I will take part in the junta and I must preside over it because I have the highest rank."

Once again Delgado Chalbaud, the introvert, the man of timid temperament, stepped to the front at the critical moment as he had done on December 18 and Pérez Jiménez again took a secondary post. This would prove to be but the first act of a drama which would have its epilogue in blood and violence two years later.

Once the new government was installed, its first effort was to fill the jails of the country with political prisoners. Accompanying President Gallegos and his cabinet to prison were all of the congressmen and party leaders of AD. At least 10,000 Venezuelans filled the jails to overflowing from one end of the country to the other. A few were able to escape and go underground. I was one of these until the police had me virtually surrounded; then I sought asylum in the Colombian embassy.

After many delays by the military junta, I was able to obtain safe conduct out of the country because of the insistence of the government of Chile. This led to a break in diplomatic relations between Venezuela and Chile. The Chilean foreign office issued a note describing the stalling tactics of the junta in issuing my safe conduct and expressing Chile's satisfaction in helping obtain freedom for the democratic former president of a sister nation, persecuted for political reasons. The note ended ironically: "Perhaps the members of the Venezuelan military junta will themselves some day have reason to be thankful to Chile for the defense of the sacred right of political asylum."

The Attempt to Justify the Coup

Desperate efforts were made to justify and explain the military takeover. Civilian advisers prostituted themselves to devise theories and lies to defend what had happened. On November 24, the document of justification was ready. Entitled "A Statement of the Armed Forces to the Nation," it was a parade of falsehoods and specious arguments. It admitted that a majority of the people would have voted for the party which had been in power when it said, "Venezuelan people voted for those whom they believed were the best interpreters in the spirit of the revolution but Acción Democrática took advantage of the results to give the country a constitution which suffered from fundamental defects." It accused the party of having "fomented permanent agitation," and having promoted "the complete breakdown of the republic." In a maze of contradictions clearly revealing that many alleged experts had taken part in its editing, it went on to say: "Today when the armed forces expected that the installation of a new government would restore normality, they were surprised by the decision of an Acción Democrática union (one controlled by AD) to declare a general strike."

Apart from the fact that this was untrue and that no strike had been called after or before the coup, it should be noted that the alleged "breakdown" never existed. Otherwise, how could the usurpers claim that something so routine as a simple change of cabinet would make possible the "restoration of order."

Their feeble arguments were quickly replaced by other statements given to the press and spread abroad by diplomats and confidential agents. These can be quickly summarized and refuted. On November 25, it was said that extremists controlled the party and also were trying to take over the armed forces. Venezuelans know this was false. Acción Democrática's moderate leadership never tolerated divisions and always controlled the party. AD was also accused of possessing an armed militia. The fact that the party could do nothing in the streets to defend a legitimate government is eloquent proof that it lacked arms. It should also be added that just a month before he made the charge, Delgado Chalbaud had hotly rejected the accusation made by Rafael Caldera in a congressional debate that AD was organizing an armed militia.

After having admitted the legitimate origin of the AD government, the president of the military junta, without embarrassment, said a few days later: "It is evident to the Venezuelans that undue advantage was taken from positions of power to favor the party in the elections." What was evident for the Venezuelans was that for the first time in the history of the country there had been free elections. Another reply to this false assertion was the testimony of the instigators of the subversion themselves. In a document signed by all the officers on duty, represented by Delgado Chalbaud, Pérez Jiménez, Llovera Páez and the rest of the high command at the time, and addressed to the national constituent assembly, it was stated that this body was "representative of the popular will, elected on October 27, 1946, in free elections that were under their supervision. They therefore certified that elections were carried out with the greatest honesty."

The agent of the triumvirate in Washington was José Rafael Pocaterra, who had catapulted to this position from his post under the constitutional government as ambassador to Brazil. He had also been a member of the Venezuelan delegation to the ninth Inter-American Conference in Bogotá. I had headed this delegation and named Pocaterra a member of the commission that drew up Resolution Twenty-three, which condemned the activities of agents at the service of international communism or any other kind of totalitarianism. This same personality, of such versatile and indecorous political conduct, now tried in Washington to impute communist sympathies to the overthrown government. This gross opportunism was an effort to take advantage of the anti-communist hysteria then characteristic of important United States political circles.

It is easy to refute this charge. Within and without Venezuela, it is well known that AD and its leaders maintained an ideological position which cannot be confused with the theory and practice of the Communist party. Furthermore, that branch of this international organization in Venezuela was always hostile to the governments headed by Gallegos and myself. Other arguments could be made: Delgado Chalbaud had been minister of defense in both governments, but he had never shown any sign of alarm at alleged communist sympathies of the government; the activities of AD were well-known before October 8, 1945, and when the young military approached us before carrying out their uprising, they were "perfectly aware of the political tendencies of the men who had formed part of the government," according to a public statement issued on April 6, 1947, by Lt. Col. Carlos Delgado Chalbaud, Lt. Col. Marcos Pérez Jiménez, and Lt. Col. Mario Vargas. After the November 24 coup, AD was dissolved by decree and its publications suppressed. But the various agencies of the Communist party continued to enjoy freedom. They published their press organs and named members to interparty commissions formed to investigate the conduct of the overthrown administration. When a newsman questioned Delgado Chalbaud as to whether the Communist party would be declared illegal as Acción Democrática had been, he replied, "the other parties have nothing to fear if they obey the laws of the republic."

The spokesmen of the triumvirate contradicted one another. Delgado Chalbaud in Caracas denied to newspapermen that the general staff had tried to impose political conditions on President Gallegos; "There were no negotiations with Gallegos. The armed forces merely let him know that the party was arming against the nation." Pocaterra in Washington completely contradicted this statement: "For five months before the coup," he told the press, "the military leaders repeatedly urged President Gallegos to form a new non-partisan cabinet that would include the army and representatives of various political parties, including the conservatives."

Finally, an effort was made to smear the deposed government leaders by accusations of dishonesty. The press hostile to AD charged that our leaders had made huge bank deposits in Canada. Those who were about to plunder the public treasury had the impudence to claim that the only Venezuelan government of the twentieth century—and even for most of the nineteenth—which had used water and soap when it handled public money, had enriched itself illegally.

The accused were not long in replying. Those who had been ministers and occupied other high administrative posts sent a letter from jail to the comptroller general of the nation on May 11, 1949. They demanded that any accusations be presented in court and affirmed the idea that public officials should be obliged to give public accounting of their actions. The signatories offered to cooperate in the fullest possible manner with any investigation.

The bitter enemies of Acción Democrática searched the archives of the ministries, inquired of stock brokers and real estate salesmen, and investigated bank records—all in a desperate search for one single case of fraud during the three years of democracy. All was in vain. Not a single AD leader of significance could be accused then or later of lying or appropriating public funds.

Erroneous Perspectives of the Opposition Parties

At first, other political parties acted as though only AD's fate was at stake, ignoring the fact that constitutional order had been abruptly ended. One after another, the leaders of the democratic Republican Union (URD), the Social Christian (Copei) party, and the two wings of the Communist party climbed the stairs of the ministry of defense to interview the military triumvirate. Possibly they were promised that their parties could continue to act freely. Some of their members accepted a state governorship or other lower posts here and there. They did not protest the violent removal of the constitutional president or the dismissal of the elected congress in which their representatives had seats.

When they made public statements they took care not to condemn the coup d'état. Instead, they preferred to criticize the political party which had so decisively contributed to the democratic climate in which these parties had been able to organize and function freely. Out of respect for historical truth, this error should not be overlooked. Later, it will be noted that these parties joined with patriotic zeal in a common front to fight the dictatorial regime.

The inevitable now came to pass from a government without respect for human rights. Union headquarters throughout the nation were assaulted and sacked by soldiers and police. Various newspapers and weeklies were closed. In jails, political prisoners were given inhuman treatment.

That which happened to Valmore Rodríguez, who was invested with the presidency at the time he was imprisoned, has special significance. There was special ire against him because of his frustrated attempt to rally support for the government at Maracay. He suffered two successive heart attacks in jail, but the attempts of his family to get him transferred to a hospital were obstinately refused by the self-appointed government. "He will be cured with baths of cold water in the early morning," replied Pérez Jiménez to one of the doctors trying to save the life of this illustrious Venezuelan. Finally he was sent from his jail cell to a clinic, which was actually aboard a ship taking him to exile. Although practically a corpse, he managed to live six more years because of his dogged determination not to die and to continue from exile the eternal fight to dignify Venezuela.

The exile of Valmore Rodriguez from jail and others was not the result of generosity by the triumvirate. They had proposed initially—at least that is what Pérez Jiménez and Llovera Páez told many people—to keep prisoners in jail indefinitely. However, international pressure made itself felt. Rómulo Gallegos, Andrés Eloy Blanco, and I presented the case of the political prisoners held without trial in Venezuela to the United Nations. We contacted the heads of numerous delegations, and the ambassadors of Uruguay and Guatemala promised action. When the Uruguayan delegation sent a note to the secretary general of the United Nations, Trygve Lie, asking for all available information regarding the recent violations of human rights in Venezuela, Carlos Eduardo Stolk, who had represented the constitutional government of Venezuela but now joined the dictatorship, denied that the world body had authority to investigate. He invoked the same paragraph 7, article 2 of the United Nations charter, which Russia and its satellites had so often used to reject investigations of human rights violations within the Soviet area. On May 9, 1949, the Uruguayan delegation advised that the matter would not go to the General Assembly but had been turned over to the United Nations Commission on Human Rights. We were informed that various delegations, including that of the United States, did not want the case to come up in the general assembly but offered to use their good offices to influence the Caracas government. We do not know what methods were used, but for a time at least, Venezuelan jails were relatively empty of political prisoners.

Active Voice of the Resistance

After the coup, the principal leaders of AD were either in jail, exile, or in asylum in foreign embassies. The party, nevertheless, spoke from underground catacombs. Its first manifesto to the nation was dated December 8, 1948, a day that will live in history because on it began one of the most heroic eras of Venezuelan life—the resistance. The day before, the military junta had published a decree outlawing Acción Democrática. This decree displayed the blatant ignorance characteristic of political adventurers who believed it was a decree sufficient to eradicate a people's party which had a program, discipline, revolutionary faith, and real leaders. Events would convince them of their mistake. This first underground communiqué of the people did not seek to deceive its vast membership or the public in general. It foresaw that there would be blood and sacrifices in the fight now beginning. It called for courage and decision, a capacity to accept defeat, with faith in the final triumph. Our dissolved AD spoke in this manner to the nation in its manifesto of December 8:

> Our party declares to the nation that it begins its political underground work on this date. We seek to organize the vanguard of opposition of the people and to recover public liberties which are usurped today. The party enters a stage of sacrifices and of organized resistance—an undertaking for which our movement has unlimited sources of dedication and capacity. We know that the battle will be cruel and brutal because our adversaries will resort to violence in seeking to silence the people and to stifle opinion so as to survive as a police regime. This will not stop us, and nothing will make us desist from the sacred commitment which we have to Venezuela. It is a time for harsh persistent work, for selfless labor, for permanent

sacrifice. We do not hide the magnitude of what must be undertaken or the promise of terrible combat that awaits us. With full responsibility for what this undertaking signifies, with a clear concept of our duty and with sure faith in the final triumph, AD begins today its underground resistance which will continue until Venezuela has a government of liberty, political dignity, administrative honesty and public decency.

The following pages will reveal the prophetic lucidity of the analysis made then by the National Executive Committee of AD.

16

Contempt for Human Rights

No one can be deprived of his liberty except under existing laws. . . . Every person who has been deprived of his liberty has the right to immediate judicial review of the legality of his detention. He should be tried without unreasonable delay or be set free.prisoners have a right to humane treatment while detained.[1]

At Geneva, on August 31, 1955, the first United Nations Conference on Crime Prevention and the Treatment of Prisoners approved a charter of the prisoner, forbidding inhumane treatment and degrading punishment, condemning corporal punishment and the use of chains, irons, straitjackets, dark cells, and solitary confinement.

After several revolts instigated by the illegal AD party, the strong man decided to eliminate its underground leadership. He selected Pedro Estrada, a police veteran, voluble and without anything to lose, to do this job. As chief of national security, he had built up an efficient spy apparatus with eyes and ears in every restaurant, hotel, office, and oil camp. His officials jailed thousands of people, and often forced captives to reveal secrets either by seating them naked on blocks of ice, or through other torture, or by the time-honored method of beating. Whenever an AD official or an activist member of the party planted bombs, he was imprisoned or shot in the street.[2]

Jails were not sufficient to terrorize a people determined to recover their liberties. More brutal methods were used. Men of the resistance were sent to concentration camps. The police used the worst kinds of torture, physical violence, and even assassination against captured members of the opposition.

Political Prisoners Treated as Common Criminals

On October 8, 1949, the progovernment newspaper *Ultimas Noticias* featured the news that twenty-three political prisoners had been sent to mobile penal colonies in the southern jungle where the worst criminals were usually confined. The press was not as heavily censored then as later; editorials were printed protesting this harsh measure. The public was angry. An important group of prominent personalities issued a statement protesting the confinement of political prisoners in jails designed for common criminals.

This protest movement spread beyond our national frontier. Exiles of AD throughout the hemisphere supported a widespread publicity campaign against this outrage in Caracas. Teachers' associations, intellectuals and workers, unions in the United States and Latin America, as well as newspapers of various political tendencies, joined in the protest. Headlines from one end of the western hemisphere to the other denounced the establishment of concentration camps in Venezuela.

The dictatorship's response to this international uproar was typically insolent. An official advertisement published in the Caracas press October 12, 1949, stated that prisoners were not being punished for their political activities but "they had been caught in the acts of sabotaging highways by spreading tacks, painting slogans on the walls of public and private buildings, and repeated acts of subversion." The notice concluded with the arrogant threat that the authorities would continue to punish all those arrested in the future for illegal activities such as these.

This desperate measure of treating political prisoners as though they were common thieves had no effective results. The democratic resistance was not intimidated, and the vast opposition front which had been formed now grew even more. Repudiation of the de facto regime became greater day by day.

The Nest of Vipers

Trouble in the streets coincided with progressive deterioration of the relationship between the two members of the triumvirate who had most of the power. Delgado Chalbaud and Pérez Jiménez each wanted the pluralistic government to evolve toward a single-person presidency. It was obvious that one of the two must disappear from the scene if the other were to monopolize the stage. Delgado Chalbaud had no very demanding ethical standards, as his conduct on November 24 had shown. But he was clever and intelligent. He was spinning his web and sought to immobilize his rival. However, his defeat was almost guaranteed in advance. He could not get close to people because of his reserve, and he nourished a rancor because of the scarcely disguised popular dislike for him. He was a typical aristocrat, associating only with the upper class of Caracas and not interested in invading the territory of his rival, the defense minister, in the barracks or in competing with him there for power.

In two ways Delgado Chalbaud and Pérez Jiménez were similar: neither possessed moral political scruples and neither had any respect for public opinion. This is why they could work together in the dictatorial adventure which began November 24. But the outcome could be predicted. As has always happened in political partnerships where there is no common ideology; their relationship would degenerate into a personal feud.

In the struggle for power, Delgado sought allies in the city among office-seekers, flatterers, has-beens, and by foolish alliances formed with big names. Pérez Jiménez made friends among the army officials and formed a sort of praetorian guard. He was also advised by the so-called Uribante group, a sort of political lodge whose members came from the Andean state of Táchira and who fancied that they were born in the Prussia of Venezuela. The truly worthwhile people of Táchira had nothing to do with this group of ambitious office-seekers: lawyers without any cases, doctors without any patients, and poets without any readers. This group was nourished by a kind of small-town provincial regionalism. Its members had an intense desire to leave anonymity behind, to become public figures, and to obtain economic benefits from a government without administrative ethics. The circle which surrounded the minister of defense constantly whispered in his ear the witches' litany from the Shakespearean tragedy: "In the future you will be king."

Delgado Chalbaud, meanwhile, began to talk openly about the need for elections. He offered benevolent neutrality, were elections to be held, to the leaders of the URD and COPEI parties, who had not yet broken with the military government. Was Delgado thinking of an audacious political move of the sort that he may have recalled from his years in France? And did he perhaps aspire—by some strange combination of electoral forces—to gain the presidency by means of a popular vote?

The Assassination of Delgado Chalbaud

Whatever his private plans may have been, he carried them with him to the grave. He was assassinated on November 13, 1950, under strange circumstances. It was the first murder of a chief of state—even one of questionable authority—ever to have been committed in Venezuela.

Rafael Simón Urbina (a wealthy landholder from western Venezuela), leading a gang of drunken thugs, was the executor of this crime which was carried out in a manner unique among the political assassinations of our times. The president of the military junta was seized at midday on the streets of Caracas by a group of armed men. These had been able to meet, organize, and then to act without being seen by any of the hundred eyes of Argus belonging to the vast political police network, nor by the no less inquisitorial military intelligence. The police were under the control of Llovera Páez and the military intelligence was controlled by Pérez Jiménez. It seemed as though the police knew what was going to happen. On the eve of the assassination, political prisoners in jail and their families outside were notified that reprisals would be taken if there were any attempt made against the life of any government leader.

Sufficient facts are not available to establish all the details of the palace conspiracy that led to the murder of Delgado Chalbaud; however, objective evaluation of the facts as well as such evidence as was brought forth in the cursory investigation made by fearful judges throws considerable light upon what took place. It is really not necessary in this case to wait for the delayed judgment of history. Contemporaries have already reached a verdict that indicates the direct beneficiaries of the crime.

Persons who have studied the circumstances of the crime believe the original idea was to kidnap Delgado and force him to resign, and that his assassination was contemplated only in case he resisted. However, unforeseen factors frustrated these plans and guns had both the first and the last word. Rafael Simón Urbina, who could have cleared up the mystery, was never able to talk before a judge. He was already badly wounded when he left the asylum of the Nicaraguan embassy to surrender to the police. Once in prison, as if to confirm the widespread suspicion regarding the instigators of this bloody deed, he was murdered in his locked cell. However before he died, Urbina left testimony in his own handwriting and other evidence by which it has been possible to reconstruct, with sufficient credibility, the political crime which had so many repercussions both outside and inside Venezuela.

The links between Pérez Jiménez and Urbina before the crime were overwhelmingly established in 665 pages of testimony in the official report.[3]

Urbina's widow was among the persons questioned. She had driven the automobile carrying Urbina from his home to the place where Delgado was seized. She told the judge how, the day before the crime, Urbina had instructed her to take word of the capture to someone who would pass it along to Lt. Col. Marcos Pérez Jiménez. She also told how her husband had a permit to carry a gun as well as a pistol, given to him by Pérez Jiménez. Other important testimony was given by Domingo Urbina, a relative and aide of the leader of the plot. He declared that Rafael Simón Urbina had said the kidnapping was carried out in accord with a plan made with Pérez Jiménez, who had promised him control of three western states if it succeeded. It was explained to him, furthermore, that to avoid problems of recognition by foreign governments, Pérez Jiménez did not want to engage in another military coup. The widow of Delgado Chalbaud, in declarations to the press, indicated that her husband had feared being kidnapped and forced into exile.

Domingo Urbina further testified that the conspirators had been ordered to avoid killing Delgado Chalbaud. He was taken by car to an unoccupied house and during this trip, his military aide, Navy Lieutenant Carlos Bacalao

Lara, also taken prisoner, had heard Urbina tell Chalbaud that he would no longer be president and that Pérez Jiménez was aware of everything that was taking place. The plans were abruptly modified, however, when one of Urbina's gunmen misfired his pistol and wounded Urbina so badly that he fainted. His men, drunken and confused, and not aware of the nuances of the plot, took Delgado to the house and murdered him. Urbina then sought refuge in the Nicaraguan embassy and from there sent the following letter:

> Commander Pérez Jiménez, my dear friend: I now have the people of Venezuela mobilized. As I told you when I arrived in the country, I do not want any president other than you. Delgado has been badly wounded, although I did not want them to kill him as the policeman who was with him can testify. I hope that you will support me in the Nicaraguan embassy where I am to be found badly wounded.

Urbina's widow testified that her husband had given the note to the policeman, telling him to take it personally to Pérez Jiménez. This policeman had served as Delgado Chalbaud's motorcycle police escort at the time of the kidnapping. Urbina's widow testified further, "when I asked my husband who the policeman was, he told me that he was from Urbina's home town and that he worked for Pérez Jiménez."

Our underground obtained a copy of this mysterious document and saw that it was widely circulated. Nevertheless, it was not until a month and a half after the event that the person in charge of National Security sent the note to the investigating judge, saying that it had been immediately turned over by him to Pérez Jiménez.

Urbina was in critical condition when he reached the Nicaraguan embassy and could not reply clearly to questions put to him, according to a communiqué later issued by the Managua foreign office. He agreed, upon receiving a safety pledge from the police, to leave the embassy and go to a clinic. However, he was taken to the notorious El Obispo prison and there he was killed, with significant haste, before he could testify before a judge. The official version was that this man, who was bloody, helpless, and dying, tried to attack those who were guarding him.

It seems that there was no regret—but only boasting—at the elimination of Urbina. He was the only person who might have defended the instigator of this political assassination—if any defense were possible.

Antonio Arnaguren, another one of the plotters, testified that when he had been questioned by Pérez Jiménez, Llovera Páez and others had asked to call a lawyer. Pérez Jiménez replied that this was not a matter for lawyers, but of life and death. "Is Urbina not sending you the message that you are in danger of following him?" he was asked.

Despite the fact that his name appears dozens of times in the thick court report, Pérez Jiménez was never called to testify. When Delgado Chalbaud's widow pressed for a more exhaustive investigation of the murder, she was first put under house arrest and later expelled from the country. She wrote Pérez Jiménez a public letter from London accusing him of blocking full investigation:

In summary, you fear the suspicions which surround you and that is why you are impeding justice. The suspicions are not gratuitous. They are based on the fact, in the first place, that you are the great beneficiary of the crime. They are based on statements of some of the killers. They are based on the benevolent protection which your government has given those who killed Rafael Simón Urbina in his defenseless condition—these agents who hurriedly did away with the key figure of the investigation before it was ever begun. They are also based on the existence of the strange message the assassin sent to you after the crime which was impossible to suppress was finally published. Finally, they are based on the fact that you had at your side at the time of the crime, as private secretary, a lawyer named Victor José Cedillo, also known to be one of the closest friends of the assassin Urbina. It would be ingenuous to think that he had not established close relations between the two of you and that he was not aware of the plans under way.

The crime remained unpunished, and only secondary personages of the drama went to jail. The tribunal of public opinion, both in Venezuela and abroad, however, has brought those truly responsible to court and has given its verdict.

The Zero Between Two Aces of Spades

It was expected that Pérez Jiménez would succeed Delgado Chalbaud as president of a new military junta or as dictator. But once again, doubt and hesitancy, so predominant in his complex personality, prevailed over the urgings of his supporters. Macbeth does not always immediately sit upon the bloodied throne of Duncan. Public opinion, moreover, was so insistent in pointing out who the true beneficiary of the murder was that the temporary result was, unexpectedly, a military junta presided over by a civilian. Pérez Jiménez and Llovera Páez, with the real power, installed a weak and docile figure as president in Miraflores palace, who carried out the graceless role of armor-bearer for the two military commanders.

First to be selected was Arnoldo Gabaldón, a sanitary engineer with an honest reputation. He had accepted the job and had even issued a presidential statement to the news agencies but, at the last minute was dropped for unknown reasons. Could it have been that Odría, from faraway Peru, counseled his devoted disciple to select some other puppet, or "political doll" (*muñeco político*) as we say in Venezuela? The next choice was the lawyer Germán Suárez Flamerich, who, at the moment of his promotion or, better said, his fall, was ambassador to Peru. If there was any change due to this political arrangement, it was for the worse. The jails continued to be full of political prisoners, press censorship was complete, and the police state was absolute. The administration was venal, inept, and disorganized.

National repudiation of the government became more violent. No one took too seriously the official announcements regarding elections because the country was in submission to permanent martial law. *The New York Times* in an editorial regarding a possible political eruption in Venezuela, stated that nobody could blame democratic elements for not taking the vague promises of elections seriously.

Official Announcements and Assassination Attempts

On April 19, 1951, an electoral law was published along with a decree regulating individual liberties. These decrees were only a maneuver to divert the opposition; there was no intention of having elections or restoring liberties. It was not by chance that just the day before, on April 18, gangsters (according to all the evidence, hired by the Caracas government) made an attempt on my life in Havana where I was then engaged in the struggle against the dictatorship in my country.

The crime had been planned in Caracas months before it was attempted. On January 2, 1951, the underground command of AD circulated a document within Venezuela revealing that the military government was planning an assassination attempt against me. Much has been published about this affair. Since it was against my person, I will avoid personal narration and simply repeat here what was written in Cuban newspapers, as well as the testimony collected by the police there. As I was opening the door of my automobile, parked in front of the home of a medical friend in the center of Havana, the following events occurred, as narrated by the magazine *Bohemia* of April 29, 1951:

> The sound of steps coming closer to him were heard from behind and he turned around, surprised. A tall man of mixed blood, with a strange object in his hand, rushed up to him. He scarcely had time to push away his assailant, when the strange object nicked the arm of the former Venezuelan president and fell to the ground. Betancourt felt almost nothing for the moment. Stupefied, he saw the object fall to the ground while his assailant fled. He instinctively took out his revolver and pointed it at the fugitive but did not fire because a woman and a child were passing precisely at that moment. He began then to feel a pain in his shoulder and looked around for the mysterious object which he found in the grass.
>
> With it in his hands he returned immediately to the clinic he had just left and told the doctor he believed he had been scratched by a poisonous needle. He showed him the syringe. Fortunately the assailant had not had time to inject the needle. The substance contained was not known to the doctor, but he decided to cauterize the scratch after applying a local anaesthetic. The patient did not appear poisoned but was kept under observation while the liquid was sent to a laboratory. It was tested immediately on a rabbit which died within ten minutes. Later tests revealed that the syringe contained a deadly poison.

The official report of November 15, 1951, by the Cuban police to President Carlos Socarrás of Cuba, was based on the confession of a person involved in the crime. It revealed that it had been carried out by a group of gangsters from Tampa, Florida, who had been paid $150,000 by the Dominican consulate in Miami. The money, the confession said, had been provided by the Venezuelan government.

Three members of the gang had arrived in Havana to carry out the operation. They were identified. One man had escaped to Venezuela, another had been imprisoned by Florida authorities for a thirty-year prison term, and a third was later murdered in Tampa. The poison used in the assassination attempt was cobra venom.

On the night of September 23, 1951, the political police ambushed the car carrying Leonardo Ruiz Pineda, the underground general secretary of AD. This time he was able to escape the sentence of death.

The next act of political gangsterism started some days before the violent events known as the Columbus Day Mutiny. Students of the three state universities were on strike, backed by most of the faculty. The air was tense with anticipation. Numerous military officials were conspiring almost openly against the dictatorship. On September 22, Pérez Jiménez called together more than 200 officers to active duty at the Ministry of Defense and warned them that the high command had exact information regarding a rebellion planned by certain military units. He added that the government intelligence service had proof that the insurrection was instigated by AD and that the plotters were planning to kill the families of all army officials.

The Events of October

In that tense atmosphere, on October 11, a homemade bomb exploded in the Mariperez zone of Caracas. Two men were injured and taken to the hospital. Pedro Estrada, the national security chief, and other men, pistols in hand, threatened to shoot the two men unless they revealed the names of their fellow resistance members. The next day the Caracas press published, without commentary, an official communiqué claiming that the bomb was part of a widespread terrorist plot directed at high government officials. It pointed out that the house where the explosion occurred was only 300 meters from Plaza Colón where ceremonies were to be held the following day with top officials of the government. It held AD responsible for the bombing plot and—for the benefit of external consumption amid the cold war between Soviet Russia and the United States—claimed that the party was allied with the communists.

According to *Time* magazine, there was a bomb planted in one of the floral pieces at the ceremonies but it did not go off. In any case, Llovera Páez claimed in a radio speech that the junta had smashed an insurrection and that there had been fighting in sixteen cities.

Whether or not there was such a bomb, it was used by the dictatorship as a pretext for unleashing a kind of Saint Bartholomew's Day purge to liquidate AD. Six thousand Venezuelans, from all parts of the country and from all social levels, were imprisoned without trial. Police raided and ransacked homes day and night. No distinction was made between AD members and those who were not.

Many people without any political affiliation whatsoever were seized. At various points in the eastern part of the country, in anticipation of arrest, members of AD seized various police posts using machetes, hunting rifles, and rusty revolvers. At Río Caribe, Tuna Puy, Tunapuicito, and Puerto La Cruz, site of a large oil refinery, many of our people desperately confronted regular army forces with their own guns. The Associated Press reported that there were nine killed, at least one hundred wounded, and hundreds arrested in the mutinies.

The reaction of the controlled press in Perón's Argentina revealed the close ties between the neofascist dictatorships in the Caribbean and their Argentine sponsor. The papers there claimed that the events in Venezuela were "low blows from Wall Street" and the result of the efforts by foreign imperialists to dominate the oil wealth of the country. The newspaper *La Epoca* even claimed on October 15, 1951, that the rebellion had been organized by Nelson Rockefeller and myself. Similar language and accusations were made by the Venezuelan communists exiled in Mexico. This was not a sporadic coincidence. It is continually true in Latin American politics that the totalitarians of extreme right and extreme left use the same slogans and the same tactics.

Torture in the Prisons

The repression took on an unprecedented ferocity, even for a country that had been governed by Gómez. The government brought out the most primitive and barbaric instincts in the Venezuelan subconsciousness; and its orders were carried out by sadistic men who undoubtedly were mentally ill. The most brutal physical violence was applied to hundreds of political prisoners in torture chambers.

They were hung by the feet and by their sexual organs. They were beaten by machete blades (the so-called *peinilas* or "combings," an ominous legacy from the times of Gómez), whacked against the back, the face, the chest and stomach. Electrical charges were applied to the heads of the prisoners, using the technique developed in the prisons of Perón called the *goad*. There was also the famous *penguinazo* or penguin-squat, forcing the victim to sit naked for lengthy periods upon a block of ice. There were deaths, such as the case of the businessman José Vicente Gutiérrez in Cumana, at the hands of the torturers. So many Venezuelans were subjected to torture that to record them all would take many pages of this book.

However, that which passed all previous limits in Venezuela and probably in all Latin America for savagery was the imprisonment, indignity, and torture inflicted upon numerous women. Josephina Guerrero do Troconis, an honorable lady of 70 years, and her daughter-in-law, the teacher Alicia de Troconis—mother and wife, respectively, of the AD leader Luis Troconis Guerrero—were locked up with prostitutes and common thieves, together with dozens of other mothers, professionals, schoolteachers, and students.

This was a new horror introduced by the worst despotism in Venezuelan history. It had been a national tradition, inherited in part from the courtly Spaniards, to always respect the female sex. In the terrible nineteenth century, with its cruel wars and authoritarian governments, jail and exile were reserved for men. Even Juan Vicente Gómez respected the female sex. The Pérez Jiménez regime, so closely akin to fascism, violated the limits which had been set by the most barbarous autocracies of the past. Great numbers of women passed through the jails, often tortured and kept for years behind bars. Ligia de Vargas, widow of the deceased army officer Mario Vargas, was expelled from the country in 1951 with five children, all under ten years of age, after the police had broken into her home and destroyed all that they could lay hands on. The list of other victims is interminable.

While this torturing was going on, the anger of the people rose to fever pitch. Something must be done—something desperate—was the spontaneous slogan whispered through the underground. What followed was another example of fearless heroism, revealing that courage never had been lacking among those who fought despotism but also showing clearly that it was not possible for isolated groups to undertake successful insurrection. At midnight on October 21, some fifty poorly armed members of AD tried to assault the cadet school of the national guard, located in Caracas.

The assault was poorly synchronized with the uprising that was supposed to occur inside the barracks and the attackers were cut down in a suicidal attack. Even so, they kept up their fire until their ammunition was exhausted. Many fell, and the rest who were taken prisoners were tortured together with fourteen cadets and officers from the barracks.

America Has Its Dachau: It is Called Guasina

At this time, *The New York Times* commented that the military junta in Caracas was uncomfortably seated on a powder keg. Instead of trying to conciliate and pacify the country, the regime promoted new insurgencies, as demonstrated by the treatment given to political prisoners. Now, instead of sending them to jails with common criminals, a concentration camp was opened especially for them: Guasina, a name that would be inscribed in the annals of infamy.

Dachau, the German concentration camp, symbolized Hitlerian barbarism with its torture chambers and lethal gases and mobilized the free peoples over the world against Nazism. In America, "the continent of liberty" as it is called by the diplomats, a tropical jungle version of Dachau functioned for some time. It was located in a country where the Tenth Inter-American Conference was held in April 1953, when hypocritical delegates held up the western hemisphere as the paradise of human happiness and liberty in contrast to Russian totalitarianism.

Guasina was located on the banks of the Orinoco River in a part of the country where Venezuela ceased to be a nation and was just simply land undisturbed by man. *Time* magazine, on August 18, 1952, described the place as a muddy key, four miles long, seventy miles above the principal mouth of the Orinoco. It was covered by mangrove swamps and its temperature was usually well over 100 degrees Fahrenheit. The magazine could have obtained additional details about this inhospitable region from the archives of the Ministry of Health, where a report by a special commission headed by Arnoldo Gabaldón in 1943, condemned Guasina as unfit for human habitation. Investigation was made after the Congress had received criticism because a prison had been created there. It found malaria mosquitos, amoebic dysentery, and endemic typhus, as well as terrible flies whse bite brought great swelling on the body. It was also the refuge of poisonous snakes and the lice known as *chipo*, transmitting agent of the then incurable Chagas disease. As a result of this investigation, the camp for murderers and other criminals was closed in 1943.

Now it was reopened in 1952 for political prisoners. More than nine hundred men were sent to this death camp that year—almost all of them leaders or members of AD. Four of them were buried there, and the survivors will forever keep the memory on their bodies of the barbaric treatment and the diseases suffered there.

Men whose only crime was to seek liberty and decent government for their country were subjected to terrible punishment. However, the United Nations Commission on Human Rights never tried to investigate this tropical Siberia. The government responsible for this genocide lined up regularly and voted with the West in the struggle between the two blocs in the United Nations. Furthermore, it was so cooperative with private enterprise that it won the enthusiastic eulogy of one of the leaders of the Republican party in the United States, Secretary of Treasury George M. Humphrey, who said in November 1954:

> Venezuela is an example of what can be done when private enterprise is promoted by a climate of economic freedom. I think the philosophy of President Pérez Jiménez is profoundly nationalistic. The security and liberty under which the economy of Venezuela is operating is especially noteworthy. This is something which is in the air, in the activity of the people.

The commission in the United Nations which was supposed to protect human rights gave all of its attention to other parts of the world, especially to what was going on behind the iron curtain. Vishinsky and Malik, the Russian diplomats who were so clever in debate, did not reply to western accusations against Russian concentration camps by bringing up Guasina because there were few communist prisoners in Venezuela. They had all the liberty they wanted to collect signatures on peace petitions in the country. The only worker federation, so repressed as to hardly exist, was led by communists and their newspaper in Caracas published a front-page picture of one of their leaders, Rodolfo Quintero, in animated conversation with Giuseppe de Victorio, leader of the World Labor Federation. This explains why both blocs in the United Nations, east and west, concealed what was going on in Guasina, just as the sons of Noah covered their drunken father when they found him naked in his sleep.

Time magazine described the insufficient diet and the hard labor given the Guasina prisoners. It reported how dysentery, typhoid, malaria, beri-beri, and pneumonia ravaged the prisoners who drank the muddy river water and who had to sleep without protection from mosquitoes. It was possible for some to escape from Devil's Island, the infamous French penal colony farther east, but flight from Guasina was impossible, said *Time*. It was surrounded by an electrified fence, illuminated at night. Furthermore, the waters surrounding the island were full of crocodiles and voracious caribe fish, which would convert any person or animal into a skeleton in a matter of minutes. Press versions such as this were amply confirmed by the pathetic accounts given by the victims of these Hitlerian experiences suffered a decade after Hitler had committed suicide. All this took place in a country in what is conventionally called the free world.

The Protest in Venezuela and Abroad

There was an outrage and valiant protest in the country because of Guasina. University students denounced it in a public document; the families of the prisoners also denounced the situation to the presidents of the Venezuelan Medical Federation and the Venezuelan Red Cross in a document printed by the underground press. Pérez Jiménez, now a colonel and minster of defense, told one of the mothers who managed to speak with him personally: "Do not complain. Your son is in Guasina, along with the others, enjoying his love of liberty."

The international protest aroused by this violation of human rights was heard from all corners of America, but the colonels of Caracas maintained disdainful silence and officially ignored the existence of Guasina. The leadership of the Social Christian (Copei) party, on June 20, 1952, published a forthright letter to the junta, denouncing conditions in Guasina. As a result, party leaders, including Rafael Caldera, were taken to the national security offices and questioned for forty-eight hours without interruption. This may not seem like much when it is remembered that others spent years behind bars, but another Copei leader, Edecio la Riva, was picked up again after being released and beaten with iron construction bars and steel cables into unconsciousness. Rafael Caldera and Pedro del Coral then went to court to accuse the government of trying to assassinate a leader of the opposition. This outrage was also denounced by the leaders of the URD Party as a fascist attack. The junta replied to the latter by stating that an investigation was under way and asking, with ineffable effrontery, what basis there was for terming the event fascist.

All this protest had its effect, or perhaps it was the fact that the rising

Orinoco river threatened to flood the island. In any case, the inmates of Guasina were transferred to another jungle concentration camp, somewhat less rigorous, at Sacupana del Cerro. Their life was less difficult, but the daily humiliations continued.

Later, the prisoners were again transferred to the jail at Ciudad Bolívar. There was one change: Instead of being surrounded by electrified wire, they were confined behind the high cement walls of the half-finished jail. There were no medicines, no doctors, no nurses. They received the same diet of fried beans and fish as on the banks of the Orinoco. And they continued to receive machete beatings and all kinds of other humiliations.

They were beaten for writing only the "subversive" word liberty on the outside of a notebook or for singing the party hymn written by Andrés Eloy Blanco. The situation of the prisoners there was identical with that of thousands of other Venezuelans in the Carcel Modelo and El Obispo prisons in Caracas and the San Juan de los Morros penitentiary, as well as in other jails of the state capitals.

Neither Judges to Judge nor Courts to Sentence

All these men and women, deprived of their liberty and victims of brutal treatment for months and years, never got to be heard by a judge nor sentenced by a court. Very few cases of political imprisonment reached the courts, and the results were such that it was preferable for the government arbitrarily to lock people up without any judicial proceedings. This, of course, was in open violation of the laws of our country and of principles proclaimed by the international charters of San Francisco and Bogotá.

On June 2, 1953, I was formally received at a special session by the Chamber of Deputies of Uruguay. In my speech there, I told how human rights were being systematically violated in my country. After citing Article 25 of the Declaration of Bogotá, quoted at the beginning of this chapter, I said:

> This norm is being violated consistently, deliberately, systematically by the present government of Venezuela. Numerous congressmen have been in jail for three years. Thousands of political prisoners are being held. The Central University has been closed by the police and more than 7000 students and inumerable professors have been scattered throughout the Americas. . . . I denounced before this high-ranking audience the refined methods of cruelty against political prisoners used by the Nazis which are also being used in my country.

With certain resentment, I compared the interest at that time of the United States and two European governments in rescuing a North American citizen, an Associated Press correspondent, from Czechoslovakian jails to the widespread official indifference found in both Americas to the prolonged and illegal confinement of hundreds of Venezuelans.

"We have read, with great satisfaction," I said, "that Mr. William Otis, the former AP correspondent in Czechoslovakia, has been pardoned after being condemned to ten years of prison. Presently he is home in Boston or Maryland with his wife and children. It is said that he regained his liberty thanks to an emotional letter sent by his wife to the head of the Czech government but it is understood there were other measures, perhaps more effective—trade between the United States and Czechoslovakia had been shut off and this would have meant a loss of $20 million annually to the latter country. The governments of the United States, England, and France undertook a joint action to slow down the granting of passports and visas for travel between their countries and Czechoslovakia. One may ask why if so much was done to obtain the liberty of the just one newspaperman among all of the American journalists. Cannot there be a joint action in America to rescue from prison and death the intellectual and political elite of one of the American states?"

The fact of the matter is that of more than thirty thousand Venezuelans thrown into prison during this time, scarcely one hundred sentences were handed down by the courts. The arbitrary repression against individuals was accompanied, as always, by similar action against institutions and organizations without political affiliation which sought to defend the good name and dignity of the country. In the pages that follow, it will be seen what happened to the press, the universities, the labor unions, and the teachers.

17

The Abolition of Press Freedom

> No newspaperman is told what to write, but he is forbidden to write anything that in our opinion, may be bad for the morale or progress of the country. In a word, the press is censored. Very mildly indeed, but censored.[1]

The climate of respect for press liberty that existed during the three years of democratic government changed radically after November 24, 1948. Thereafter, the country did not know a free press. Freedom of thought was asphyxiated by a typically totalitarian censorship. Some newspapers were suppressed outright. Those that were able to survive were subjected to rigorous control.

The first victim was the newspaper *El País*, the official organ of the AD party. It was closed by decree, and army troops occupied its premises. Its editors had been implacably persecuted. Its first editor, that exceptional Venezuelan Valmore Rodríguez, was expelled from the country after suffering several heart attacks in jail and died in exile in July 1955. Luis Troconis Guerrero, who edited the paper at the time of the military coup, went underground and after three years of heroic labor suffered a serious heart attack. He also was exiled and died in San José, Costa Rica, in December 1951. Antonio Piña Salinas, who had been the financial editor of the paper, was seized in 1953 and assassinated by the police. Ana Luisa Llovera, who had been news editor and a congresswoman, was exiled.

Press censorship also indicated what should be published and how it should be handled. As a result, the Venezuelan press took on a uniform tone of deadly gray as it followed the one rule that was laid down—all news printed should be in praise of Pérez Jiménez. Even foreign press agencies were affected by the censorship. The United Press customarily warned its newspaper clients about any questionable news reports: "Take care, editors. Remember the censorship!" Any news from abroad which referred to difficulties encountered by democratic governments anywhere had the green light. On the other hand, foreign news which might reflect upon the regime was forbidden. A typical case was a news dispatch on a speech made by General Douglas MacArthur in Lansing, Michigan, May 15, 1952. The orator was not precisely a model democrat, but in this particular speech he expressed an opinion adverse to military governments. It was deleted by the Venezuelan censor.

First Repression, Then Bribes and Intimidation

Repression of the press did not end with the closing of the AD party organs. The newspaper *El Gráfico* of the Social Christian (Copei) party was systematically persecuted; its news editor, Luis Herrera Campins, was imprisoned and later exiled. The newspaper ceased to publish. The same thing happened with the weekly URD, organ of the Unión Republicana Democrática party, and its chief editor, Santiago Herrera Suárez; and with the magazine *Signo* and its editor, the lawyer Alfredo Tarre Murzi.

Other newspapers of democratic commitment that were not suppressed outright had to be sold by their owners as a result of government pressure. This happened to the newspapers *Panorama* of Maracaibo and *Ultimas Noticias* of Caracas. Other newspapers such as *Fronteras* of San Cristóbal, *El Día* of Valencia and *Onda* of Coro, as well as the weeklies *Atalaya* of Mérida and *Acción* of Valera were closed.

Censorship

Censorship began with the coup in 1948, but in 1951 it was given a more agreeable name, Committee to Examine the Press. Its mission was always the same—to gag, to inform, to imprison, to deport newsmen who showed the slightest kind of disagreement with the regime. Two persons of very doubtful reputation presided over this commission: Vitelio Reyes, who had been an official under Gómez; and Edwin Burguera, a communist youth leader who pledged allegiance to the dictatorship.

The Press Examination Committee worked closely with the national security police. When the censors found in 1952 that many articles on nationalistic themes were written by members of a recently formed literary group named after the national tree of Venezuela, Araguaney, the authors were called in and threatened by Pedro Estrada, chief of national security. Notable writers such as Mariano Picón Salas, Eduardo Arcilia Farías, Mario Briceño Iragorry, Eduardo Arroyo Lameda, and others were told that if they kept on writing press articles deploring the colonial tendencies in the country, they would be jailed or exiled. The Araguaney group ceased to exist.

Strictly literary magazines such as *El Perfil* and *La Noche*, edited by the poets Vicente Gerbasi and Juan Sánchez Peláez, and *Cantaclaro*, edited by Guillermo Sucre Figarella, were likewise affected. In 1949, the big newspaper *El Nacional* of Caracas was shut down for some days because a linotypist with a sense of humor had interpolated in the text of a news report a reference to "the three little pigs," the term with which people were referring in those days to the members of the military junta. The same fate befell this newspaper when it published, without comment, a picture of Hitler and Franco embracing on the same day that the dictatorial Venezuelan government established diplomatic relations with the dictator of Spain.

One day, after *El Nacional* was closed and its personnel arrested, there was a meeting of the Venezuelan Press Association in Caracas to protest the measure, and the forty newsmen present—all of different ideologies—unanimously approved a protest. However, this was never published because the police invaded the meeting hall and arrested all those present, including the notable writer, Lucila Palacios. Before *El Nacional* was allowed to circulate again, it was forced to drop a number of columnists, as specified by national security. Among them were: Juan Liscano, Lucila Velásquez, J. M. Martínez Siso, and Luis Esteban Rey. All four were exiled.

The conservative newspaper *El Universal* of Caracas, which during its long life had never opposed any government except ours, was fined because a reference to the "three little pigs" also found its way into one of its columns. Various editors were arrested and a printer was sent to the Guasina concentration camp. The *Diario de Occidente*, published by a group of Maracaibo businessmen, was fined various times because it published innocuous news which managed to irritate the sensitive skin of the regime. The church newspaper the *Diario Católico* of San Cristóbal was obliged to change editors.

In 1951, when President Gallo Plaza of Ecuador visited Venezuela, the newspapermen who came with him were given a dinner by their Caracas colleagues, and the youthful newspaperman, Simón Alberto Consalvi, in a welcoming speech, uttered these courageous words:

> Since 1948, we have been gagged by the most absurd and stupid press censorship. More than a hundred periodicals have been closed and not even the least offensive provincial sheets have been allowed to circulate again. But do not think that we are pessimistic. We are determined to regain our liberty. Having enjoyed it once, we have learned that we cannot live without it.

Consalvi was promptly jailed and spent years behind bars. He was expelled from the country at the end of 1955.

A beating by gangs of thugs—actually the political police—was another way to teach the newspapermen how to behave. This happened in 1953 to José González González, and in 1954 to Julio Ramos, both columnists for *El Universal*. One after another they incurred the wrath of the dictatorial clique for something they had written. Each was abducted by mysterious persons, taken by car to the outskirts of Caracas, and thoroughly beaten. The police, of course, never caught up with the attackers, for only in metaphors do snakes ever bite their own tails.

On occasion, the wrath of the police was provoked by something published abroad, as happened in the terrorist attack upon Rafael Caldera and his family. The Social Christian leader, who was also a university professor, had written an emotional eulogy at the time of the tragic death of Andrés Eloy Blanco. His article did not allude in any way to the domestic political situation, but only praised the conduct of a man who had been his opponent in ideological debates. When the article was published by the newspaper *Excelsior* of Mexico, an editor's note explained that it had not been published in Venezuela due to the rigid censorship there. Some days after this, in the early morning of August 4, 1955, two automobiles of the national security stopped in front of Caldera's home in Caracas. Their occupants threw hand grenades at the windows, shattering them and setting fire to the curtains. Caldera's newborn son was in danger of suffocating when the smoke of the explosion filled his bedroom. The police termed the case "without solution."

Various newspapermen were confined in Guasina. Others were badly beaten. At least two of them died as a result. Many more paid with bodily suffering and exile for their dedication to freedom of thought.

The Censorship Affected Foreign Journalists

The restriction of liberty also affected foreign correspondents and international news agencies. In 1949, the Caracas correspondent of *Agénce France Presse*, Alberto Brun, was imprisoned and later expelled because he had sent a dispatch reporting a strike in the oil camps. Later, the same year, the police ransacked the offices of the United Press and arrested two of its employees.

In 1950, the chief of the Associated Press office was expelled, and so were two editors of *Time* magazine. It seems that after these experiences the international news agencies were instructed by their home offices to send as little as possible from Venezuela, or, in any case, not to offend the government. This situation led me to write an open letter to the managers of these agencies on April 22, 1952, in which I vehemently protested because the wire services had sent dispatches based on a communiqué from National Security describing two AD underground leaders as "fugitive terrorists." I also wrote in this letter:

> These two Venezuelans, who are my political comrades, together with others of similar talents, tomorrow may be able to help in the reconstruction of the civilization of our country if they succeed in avoiding the sentence of death presently threatening their lives. This is no figment of my imagination. Political crimes have official approval in Venezuela. This fact plus the careless manner in which the international press agencies have circulated the slanderous imputations against Ruiz Pineda and Carnevali is a way of cooperating—I am sure without meaning to do so—in the sinister plans of the dictatorship.

This grim forecast came to pass. On October 21, 1952, just a few months after the above letter was published, Ruiz Pineda fell before a hail of bullets on a Caracas street. On May 21, 1953, Carnevali was left to die without adequate medical assistance in a penitentiary cell.

The Underground Press

Obviously if the national press was not allowed to publish any criticism of the ominous conditions in the country, unfavorable criticism from abroad would not be allowed to circulate either. Various Spanish-language publications were completely prohibited from circulation; the *New York Times* and *Time* magazine were frequently picked up by the police. The Inter-American Press Association regularly protested the absence of press freedom in Venezuela at its annual meetings. As its president, the United States editor James G. Stahlman, said in a speech in Hamilton, Bermuda, April 8, 1956:

> We must see through the black cloud of censorship that today covers Venezuela with the idea of hiding the atrocious vengeance of President Pérez Jiménez in suppressing the so-called riots by students. Venezuela may have a lot of wealth, but it is in total bankruptcy when it comes to freedom of thought.

But the truth of the well-known phrase that Sarmiento coined was demonstrated in Venezuela: "Barbarians cannot cut the throats of ideas." Along with the regimented, corrupt, and cowardly press, there circulated in clandestine form the newspaper *Resistencia*, the organ of the underground AD party, as well as other publications of the opposition. These were reproduced on multigraph or written by typewriter, but they circulated widely and brought to the oppressed people a message of faith in the future. They analyzed the problems of the day and brought instructions for the fight—everything that was completely absent from the press crushed under the iron heel of the censorship. All the dramatic developments of national life during the time when the country suffered this brutal repression are recorded in the underground press for posterity.

18

Offensive Against the Universities

What the Press Did Not Say

On February 8, 1952, newspapers throughout the hemisphere published a brief United Press dispatch from Caracas—brief because the press agencies for the most part accepted censorship:

> Official reports state that a group of university students has occupied a building, formerly the site of educational activities, now used for public offices. The administrative personnel there have been detained. All the doors have been locked, and public order has been disturbed by the constant ringing of bells.

Uninformed newspaper readers might have concluded that a few rowdy students were playing typically juvenile pranks and that a group of paternal professors and understanding police had tried to persuade them that this was not a civilized way to behave. The facts were quite different.

A violent skirmish took place the day before in Caracas between university youth and armed police accompanied by some university professors in the service of the government. The scene of the encounter was not a public office but the two-century-old main building of the Central University. The ringing bells were the same ones that sounded on a clear Caracas morning in 1814 when this building housed the Tridentine Seminary, from which students emerged under the command of José Felix Ribas to combat the Spanish troops of Ferdinand VII. The brief censored United Press dispatch, seemingly a picturesque anecdote amid the daily monotony, in reality reported the climax of a bitter battle fought between the university and the despots, between civilized intelligence and retrogressive ignorance, between culture demanding its rights and barbarism reverting to the worst of the past.

The battle began as soon as the constitutional government was overthrown. The universities became the center of active democratic resistance. There were many encounters there between the forces of repression and students armed only with their courage and their wonderful youthful devotion to Venezuela. Faithful to the tradition which goes back to the beginning of our republic, students claimed a front line position in the fight to regain liberty. The innumerable skirmishes always left a number of students wounded, beaten, imprisoned, and exiled, not only in Caracas but also in Mérida and Maracaibo. In mid-1950 there was an especially grave encounter between students and the university authorities, who used the same tactics to subordinate intelligence to force that the tyrannical government was using throughout the nation. This was demonstrated when they asked the National Guard to occupy the university. One student was shot and badly wounded, others were imprisoned, and the university was closed for months. The rector who had called in the troops was Eloy Davila Celas.

The student rebellion was vehement but disorganized. In an attempt to coordinate their efforts, two important documents had been drawn up and sent to the puppet president of the junta, Germán Suárez Flamerich. These documents demanded an end to all repressive measures, condemned the way the junta was exercising arbitrary power, and stressed that an election held under these conditions could never be considered legitimate.

The anger of the government reached the boiling point at this display of civic courage which, it should be noted, was supported by numerous professors. Official response quickly followed. The university authorities of Caracas were all dismissed. A man who had demonstrated his talent for the hard line, Eloy Dávila Celis, was named rector. The university accepted the challenge. The students went on a general strike, and the nation watched with pride while its educated youth once more took the initiative against the usurpers of power.

Their courageous stand proved to be contagious and concentrated national resistance to the government. It had to be suppressed and this was one of the main reasons why the plot of October 12, 1951, was "discovered." More than 6000 Venezuelans were thrown into jail and the road was open to the elimination of a free university.

University autonomy—administrative and academic—ceased on October 18, 1951, when Decree 321 was issued. Five docile persons, completely subject to the repressive will of the government, were given complete authority as the University Reform Council.

Students and Professors Defend the University

The day after this arbitrary decree was published, hundreds of professors from all faculties raised their voices in courageous protest. A document signed by two former university rectors, Julio de Armas and Rafael Pizani, stated that university autonomy, which AD had put into effect while I was president, had been "the result of many years of struggle and of dedication to the cause of higher education and the raising of the standard of culture in our country." It asked for reconsideration of the decree and warned that if this were denied, the signatories would resign their university posts. The Federation of University Student Centers issued an even more violent protest. The government's answer came from the pen of that obedient scribe in Miraflores palace, Suárez Flamerich, and—more convincingly—from guns. Suárez Flamerich's letter replying in threatening tones to his old fellow professors at the School of Law coincided with soldiers firing on a student parade in Mérida, where the father of one student died and various people were wounded. Now the connection between the University Reform Council and the National Security Office became evident. Many university professors were either imprisoned or expelled from the country.

Repression of the students was even more ferocious. Many were jailed or sent to Guasina, and some were subjected to physical torture. The universities were closed provisionally and it was announced January 30, 1952, that they would be reopened February 7. Nine students had been expelled for three years and 128 for one year. The president of the reform council said that if there was any further student violence, the universities would be closed permanently. Such threats only added fuel to the fire, and further resistance could easily be foreseen. On February 7, the students expressed their solidarity with their companions who had been imprisoned or exiled, as well as with their professors. The "incident" to which the United Press gave such a brief report was actually the complete occupation of the university by the students. Police and army troops battered down the doors of the old building and arrested all those within.

Closure of the Central University

On February 22, fifteen days later, the reform council closed Central University indefinitely. There was but one single precedent for this action, the closure of the university by Juan Vicente Gómez. But the circumstances were very different in those days. Scarcely four hundred students went to the university, and they lived in a climate of defeatism and passivity following long years of dictatorship. South America was a group of national islands, all isolated from each other. Now times were different, both in Venezuela and abroad. In 1952, there were more than 6000 students. They did not come just from the small group of the well-to-do in Caracas. The economic growth of the nation and of the middle class had brought increased university enrollment. Now students from all social strata had access to the source of culture. Thus, arbitrary action against the university affected not just the rich, who could continue their studies at Harvard and the Sorbonne, but also thousands of poor students who were unable to continue their professional studies abroad. The damage to the country caused by ths action was incalculable. The lack of professional personnel being trained for responsible positions would soon be felt throughout the country.

Other facets of this conflict between the university and the despotic government should be noted. It had long been the tradition in Latin America for students to take the lead in the fight against arbitrary government. Their activism has often been criticized by foreigners unfamiliar with our reality. University faculties have rarely given much support to the students. This was true during the Venezuelan student uprisings of 1928; however, things were very different in 1952. The decree closing the university blamed "a group of students, encouraged by some irresponsible professors, of having made it impossible for the majority of students to go to classes." Apart from the fact that it would have been impossible for a group of students to do this, the phrase referring to "some professors" was misleading. The overwhelming majority of all the faculties supported the students. More than 80 percent of the professors signed the protest against Decree 321 which ended university autonomy, and carried out their threat to resign when the decree was not repealed. This demonstration of civic responsibility and resistance among the most educated circles of the country was most encouraging.

The government reacted with great rancor to the stand of the professors, and in the decree said "that the payment of salaries of professors and other expenses related to the university could no longer be justified." In other words, the money spent on guns and police was more worthwhile than the Bs. 18 million budgeted for the universities.

There were many protests from abroad. The Latin American Union of Universities cabled protests signed by the rectors of the universities of Mexico, Guatemala, and Panama. Other faculty protests came from Cuba, Costa Rica, and Puerto Rico; student associations from around the continent added their word of solidarity. Once again, American democratic opinion, much more vital and sincere than that of such ossified agencies as the Organization of American States, made it clear that no one on the continent was deceived regarding the totalitarian character of the government in Venezuela.

University Against Dictatorship

Two years passed before the university was reopened. Tension between the government and students, as well as police intervention in the classrooms continued.

On the eve of the Tenth Inter-American Conference, held in Caracas in February 1953, the persecution against the universities became especially intense. The national security police took drastic repressive measures against democratic groups to ensure the peace for the continental assembly. The University City area, where the sessions were held, was declared a military zone and occupied by the National Guard and hundreds of security police.

Barbed wire surrounded the buildings. Nevertheless, when February 17 dawned, the walls of the building housing the law faculty were covered with slogans painted there by student activists. Three days later, this building was invaded by troops and seventy students were arrested and sent to join the AD student leader, José de Jesús Alvarez, arrested forty-eight hours earlier after a shoot-out in downtown Caracas. At this time, the police began to use the hostage system—arresting members of families of persons sought by the police. A student, Pablo Penaloza, could not be found so his father Francisco, who was the New York representative of the Grand Colombian Merchant Fleet, was arrested in his stead.

Again in 1956, from February 15 – 22, there was a continuous battle between student and the forces of repression. It began when the high school students of the Liceo Fermín Toro staged a peaceful demonstration to protest arbitrary changes in the examination system. The police charged the students and there were dead and wounded. The *New York Times* of March 1 recorded that the students raised the bloody dress of a seriously wounded girl on the university flagpole. An army officer shot and killed the policeman who was beating his daughter with a sword. Some seventy students were taken to the national security prison and tortured. Students in other high schools throughout the nation took to the streets; there were new victims resulting from these encounters with the police. The press was forbidden to publish funeral notices of the dead students, and the police seized news photographs taken of these dramatic events. Student strikes spread to other institutions. Police entered the Industrial Technical School of Caracas. Its faculty and students were arrested, and the only technical school of importance in the country was closed. The cynical response of the government to this wave of collective protest was a joint communiqué by the ministers of interior and education blaming the trouble on "communist youth," a small group in a small party that was completely incapable of promoting this vast spontaneous protest. As always in Venezuela and other countries of the continent, the university was the trigger activating the permanent conflict between the nation and those who governed it against its will.

19

Repression of the Labor Movement and Teacher Organizations

Persecution of the democratic union movement began as soon as the constitutional government was overthrown. The unions were a bulwark of resistance to arbitrary government. Organized labor of Venezuela was not backward in its thinking, not concerned merely with its own welfare, but was a strong defender of public liberty, recognizing that a strong labor movement could only exist under a democratic system. The military junta sought to reward the most reactionary national and foreign businessmen for their support by destroying the unions, the only real instrument the workers had to defend their interests.

Dissolution of the Workers' Confederation

I have already described how union headquarters were occupied, sacked, and closed throughout the republic after the November revolution. Police hunted down labor leaders and the jails became crowded. Many industrialists and hacienda owners fired workers without paying them legal indemnities, lowered salaries, and declared collective contracts null and void. The result was a series of strikes in different sectors of the economy. Finally, on February 25, 1949, the powerful Confederation of Venezuelan Workers (CTV) was dissolved. More than half a million workers—80 percent of all organized labor in the country—were adrift without any centralized labor command. The arbitrary decree did not eliminate the unions but put them under what amounted to police control. A resolution of the Ministry of Labor on March

9, 1949, decreed that the officers of the unions—all of whom had been elected democratically—were to be dismissed. The unions were given one month to elect other leaders. The assemblies where these elections were to be held had to be authorized and supervised by the Ministry of Labor.

The ILO Mission

The youth conference of the western hemisphere members of the International Labor Office was held in Montevideo at this time. From exile, Augusto Malavé Villalba, secretary general of the CTV, had protested to the ILO in Geneva the suppression of unions in Venezuela, a protest supported by the veteran French unionist and Nobel Prize winner, León Jouhaux. Now, in Uruguay, the matter was energetically pushed by a strong defender of the Venezuelan labor movement, Serafino Romualdi, of the American Federation of Labor. It was agreed to ask the ILO to investigate the labor situation in Venezuela. It was very significant that at this same time Vicente Lombardo Toledano, speaking before the United Nations on behalf of the communist-affiliated World Labor Federation, attacked the Cuban government of Carlos Prío Socarrás and the Chilean government of Videla, but had not one word to say regarding the situation in Venezuela. The reason was that only AD labor unions were being persecuted while the communist labor leaders in Venezuela were at that time getting along with the military junta.

The triumvirate government responded to the Montevideo demand for investigation by a maneuver that must have seemed very clever to Rubén Corredor, formerly juridicial advisor to the Ministry of Defense and now the minister of labor. In a note to David Morse, director general of the ILO, on April 7, 1949, the Venezuelan government asked that "one of the ILO officials visit the country to obtain complete, impartial information regarding social problems, general working conditions, the extent of benefits and protection which the present laws gave the workers and their organizations."

The ILO turned the tables on the government. They did not send just one official—someone whom Caracas thought might be manipulated—but a commission of three high functionaries from Geneva led by Jeff Rens, undersecretary general and close associate of David Morse. By the time the commission arrived in Venezuela in June, there was a new minister of labor, J. T. Rojas Contreras, president of a nonexistent socialist party.

A summary of the Rens commission's conclusions was published by the ILO. It is an extraordinarily significant document because it was perhaps the first time that an affiliated organization of the United Nations spoke out frankly on violations of human rights.

The mission had wished to interview labor union leaders imprisoned without trial, but the minister of labor advised Rens that only a courtesy visit could be arranged. The imprisoned leaders could not be interviewed or questioned because that would offend national sovereignty. Rens replied with cold courtesy that since conversation with labor union leaders was impossible, the entire purpose of the visit was lost but that he would not insist upon it. Nevertheless, the mission was able to talk with labor leaders who were still free, and accumulated much firsthand testimony regarding what was going on. It summarized its findings with these words: "The mission did not find anyone among public officials or in industrial circles who denied the extensive repression to which labor union leaders are submitted."

Nor did the presence of the ILO mission moderate the repressive mania of the authorities. Labor leaders who were still free had taken a calculated risk in speaking frankly to Rens and his associates; many of them, as the Rens report related, were later arrested. Before leaving Caracas, the mission was supposed to interview the military junta, but this interview was cancelled. When the junta saw that the mission members could not be bought with tax dollars or flattered by decorations, it decided to let them leave the country without talking with them.

The mission's report noted that labor freedom is necessary not only to ensure social justice but also to obtain stable production. But labor unions in Venezuela did not enjoy freedom to act and to organize and added, "The labor movement in Venezuela is an indispensable factor in the normal functioning of professional relations. Its disappearance or weakening means that the regulating element so needed for the social life of the country has disappeared or been weakened."

The mission urged Venezuela to comply with the fundamental guarantees of human rights proclaimed by the United Nations General Assembly. It especially stressed the two that were least observed in Caracas: the right of every person to trial by jury, and the right which says that no one can be arbitrarily arrested, imprisoned, or exiled.

When the ILO report was published, there was angry protest. The dictatorial government circles had been submissive in their foreign policy before the big powers; they had been docile before the demands of the international petroleum cartel. Now they took refuge in a hypocritical flaunting of "national sovereignty." They tried to say that the ILO officials who had come to Venezuela at their invitation had offended national sovereignty by telling what they saw and heard and not what the triumvirate wa ed them to say. In effect, the Caracas reply to the ILO admitted many of the accusations. For instance, the Ministry of Labor stated that there were 1053 unions in 1948, but by 1950 there were only 397. In other words 656 unions had disappeared, liquidated by the combined action of the national security police and the inspectors of the Ministry of Labor.

In 1950, there was an outburst of strikes and great popular agitation. A vast strike occurred in the oil fields, which paralyzed production, refining, and tanker shipments. An audacious group of men, most of them rural workers, attacked and captured the important military air base at Bocca del Rio. The base was retaken and the survivors placed in solitary confinement. No demonstrated connection with the oil workers' strike was found, but it was used as a pretext for repressive action that will be related when the oil policy of the dictatorship is examined.

The Dictatorship Exposed by the Democratic Labor Movement

In 1950, the international labor unions inflicted the first defeat upon the Caracas despotism. The American Federation of Labor (AFL) and the Congress of Industrial Organizations (CIO), together with democratic worker organizations in Latin America, ceaselessly denounced the arbitrary measures of the Venezuelan government. Once more, I want to state that it is unfair and even stupid to confuse the organized labor movement in the United States with those North American investors who pursue profits so avidly that they do not concern themselves with human rights in the countries where they operate. The United States labor movement has concerned itself with human rights throughout the continent, and also supported our efforts to obtain fair participation in the production of our natural resources. In other words, imperialism is a distortion of North American society, representing the attitude of plutocratic minorities there.

This needs to be said in a responsible way even though it may disconcert some political and labor leaders in Latin America. These include not only communists but others who have accepted as dogma the charge that the United States labor movement is just another tentacle of powerful American corporations. Many individuals and groups chorus this opinion either because they do not have sufficient information or for reasons of simple demagoguery. To counter this claim, they should remember the support United States labor gave to the Bolivian revolution. It might be noted that American capital investment was not large in Bolivia's nationalized tin mines but how about Venezuela? United States oil companies were fervent apologists for the Pérez Jiménez dictatorship and cooperated in every way possible to maintain a situation so convenient for them. But the AFL and the CIO maintained a constantly belligerent position against the dictatorial regime.

Largely because of the influence of the United States labor movement, the ninety-five delegations at the twenty-third international labor conference, held in Geneva in June 1950, refused to admit the Venezuelan labor delegation on the grounds that it was nonrepresentative. The credentials committee unanimously recommended that the supposed worker delegates be turned away because they were really political police. George P. Delaney, an AFL official, led the attack; his most immediate proof was the news that forty-six oil worker unions had just been dissolved by the Caracas junta.

Faced with this kind of international pressure, the dictatorship felt obliged to allow the traditional worker parade on May 1, 1951, in Caracas. Thousands of workers marched in the streets demanding freedom of organization, the liberation of prisoners, the return of exiles, and the right to strike. Their representatives wanted to speak at the Pantheon Plaza where Simón

Bolívar is buried, but the police and National Guard dispersed the parade. There were many injuries and arrests.

Controlled Labor Unions

Defeats on international fronts, as in Geneva, and the worker discontent clearly evident on May 1 led the government to create a regimented labor movement. The experiences of the Argentine and Spanish dictatorships in regimenting the labor movement showed the way. The effort made in 1952 was a terrible failure because from the start Venezuelan workers refused to support a regime which they detested and wished destroyed.

In a coded circular to state governors on March 27, 1952, the Minister of Interior, Col. Llovera Páez, ordered labor delegates to be recruited by the official labor inspectors and sent to Caracas for the first so-called National Convention of Independent Labor Unions. All costs were to be paid by the government. Members of the resistance procured copies of this circular and decoded it, and officers of the dissolved CTV circulated the document widely. The convention took place on April 5 under the greatest secrecy. Only official photographers of the government and public officials were allowed to attend the meeting, which lasted only twenty-four hours. This squalid official union movement freely elected the supposed worker delegates who were to be sent to ILO meetings.

The Dictatorship Challenges the United Nations

Protests continued to be presented before various United Nations agencies regarding violations of labor rights in Venezuela, and it might have been thought that the junta would have been more careful. But the head of government was so taken with his own inept oratory and so anxious to show off his uniforms covered with tawdry decorations that continued efforts were made to attract international conferences to Caracas. No doubt this effort was encouraged by the success enjoyed in reunions of obsequious diplomats and professional political neutrals, who lacked all human feeling. In any case, the annual meeting of the industrial oil committee board was held there in April 1955. This was a tripartite group of governments, workers, and employers, an adjunct of the ILO, and it turned out to be harder to handle than a saucy serving wench. To take on the workers turned out to be the height of folly. They really knew what it meant to be free and were more capable than intellectual circles of creating a crisis. The International Federation of Free Labor, including the vast majority of workers outside the Soviet orbit, succeeded in getting ILO officers to urge rejection of the invitation to Caracas, although the governing board, with its majority of governments and employers, insisted on accepting it. However, the labor agency did persuade the regional labor organizations in the western hemisphere to boycott the meeting. George Meany and Walter Reuther, presidents of the AFL and CIO in the United States, issued a joint statement announcing that neither organization would be represented at Caracas because the military government had suppressed the free labor movement. The labor federations of Mexico, Canada, and Colombia followed suit, as did the International Federation of Oil Workers.

The meeting began on April 25, with 120 delegates meeting in the Aula Magna of the University City in Caracas. The "Little Colonel" was there seated on a chair covered with gold and velvet trappings. On his coat, covered with decorations, he displayed the Order of Merit, grade commander-in-chief, given to him a few months earlier by the United States government. All seemed to be going well when suddenly the storm broke. Adrianus Vermeulen, a Dutch labor leader who was the worker delegate sent by the Industrial Oil Committee, had been welcomed by the Caracas government as a discreet and conciliatory individual, but when his turn to speak came, he failed to use the language diplomatic protocol called for. Instead, he acted like an elephant in a china shop—his words crashed through the monotony of the gathering like hard, burning rocks. "During the last six years," he said, "the ILO has continually received protests regarding violations of labor rights in Venezuela," and went on to list the names of labor leaders held in jail. He referred to the many messages received by the regional labor organization from Venezuelan unions affirming that they operated freely in the country. Yet, since these messages were all more or less identical, it was obvious that they had the same inspiration and could only be attributed to "a well-prepared spontaneous movement." He concluded with the demand that the Venezuelan government free all unionists not accused of criminal acts and allow them to leave the country, if they wished; that trials be held as soon as possible for unionists accused of crimes; and that a truly free labor movement be allowed to function in accord with ILO standards.

The dictator was furious. Those who saw him there thought he might suffer a stroke. A few minutes after the session was over, the head of the political police was ordered to seize Vermeulen, take him to the international airport at Maiquetia, and put him on a plane for the nearby Dutch West Indies. A few hours after exercising his right to free speech at an international conference, Vermeulen was in Curaçao.

The despot thought he could get away with this kind of conduct because he had paid the price of allowing uncontrolled production of oil and iron in the country. But, on this occasion, he was dealing with a United Nations agency, not so subject to regional pressures. Vermeulen cabled David Morse, head of the ILO, protesting his expulsion, and Morse cabled Pérez Jiménez, demanding that Vermeulen be allowed to return and take his place at the conference. Vermeulen refused to modify his language in any way as the price of his return, and the 119 other delegates in Caracas decided to put an abrupt end to their meeting without even considering the agenda.

The little despot and his sycophants responded by taking Venezuela out of the ILO on May 3, 1955, and a graceless bureaucrat named Otañez, who used to hold a very low position in the foreign office but now was foreign minister, accused the ILO of "political maneuvering and becoming a demagogical forum."

In the light of these facts, George Meany of the AFL stated that the military dictatorship of Venezuela had exhibited its brutal ways to the whole world. Nevertheless, the military usurper did not learn his lesson and continued to seek international conferences for Caracas. When UNESCO announced that it would hold a meeting there on immigration in December 1955, the international free labor union movement again protested. At first, UNESCO refused to change its plans, but the wave of protest was so great that the meeting was transferred to Mexico.

The Persecution of Teachers

Similar suppression was suffered by the teaching profession, for the majority of Venezuelan teachers were staunchly democratic. The Venezuelan Federation of Teachers was a professional body which had functioned since the days of Gómez—at first underground—but now it had two decades of useful public existence.

The history of the persecution of the Teachers' Federation is a tale of offenses against teachers of both sexes. It cut deep into our national sensibility, as the teachers of a nation are the very roots of its culture. After the November revolution, dozens of teachers were jailed, including our most representative teacher and former Minister of Education, Luis B. Prieto. Many others were sent into exile or deprived of their positions—this in a country which suffered a serious lack of teaching personnel.

The Teachers' Federation, trying to put an end to this situation, obtained an interview on January 3, 1949, with the minister of education, Augusto Mijares, a writer who once had given superficial support to democracy. In their memorandum, the federation asked that the 1948 education law, which equated education with democracy, be continued in effect, that imprisoned teachers be released, and that educators be assured of job stability. The minister replied by replacing the law with a so-called provisional education statute, under which teachers continued to be dismissed, imprisoned, and deported. When the educators were unable to obtain an interview with the military junta, they sent them a memorandum, which pointed out that as the teachers had been prohibited from meeting by the suspension of constitutional guarantees, it had been impossible for them to formulate policies that would keep schools free from political influences.

Attempts to Divide the Teachers

No reply was made to this reasoned document, but the government now tried to divide the teachers. The minister of education and his acolytes, convinced that the traditional teachers' organization would never serve as an escort for the victorious praetorian guard, sought to form an independent teachers group, with much the same expectation of being able to control it that had prompted the organization of government labor unions. The split reached its climax at the fourteenth national convention of the federation in Trujillo in August 1950, when Minister Mijares made a speech critical of those teachers who did not support the government. In reply, Luis José Bellorin valiantly spoke for the majority of teachers on behalf of democracy. The few so-called independents were voted down by a great majority and left the assembly to form their own peripheral group.

Now the repression of the teachers took on a progressively more violent form. Security police seized and occupied the federation's headquarters. Members of the federation were systematically persecuted in an effort to intimidate them. There was a brief time of hope when Mijares was replaced by a professor, Simón Becerra, an intimate of Pérez Jiménez and a member of the Uribante group. He declared an amnesty for the teachers and called for a political truce.

The Teachers' Federation became active again and was able to secure the signatures of 5000 teachers backing its positions. This vigorous recovery led the government to abandon its promise of pacification, and repression became even more serious. In mid-1951, the president of the federation was jailed and later expelled from the country. When the organization tried to hold its national convention in August, the security police arrested officials who were giving a press conference as well as the newspapermen who attended it. On August 19, when 216 delegates met in the name of 6000 teachers, police arrested them all and Caracas contemplated the shameful spectacle of army trucks carrying the best teachers of the nation off to jail.

Jail Cells and Torture

The wave of barbarism did not stop here, as various cases picked at random will demonstrate. Professor José Antonio González, member of the federation's board, was thrown into El Obispo jail in October, 1951. He was beaten with machetes, tortured, and put into solitary confinement; as a result, he contracted tuberculosis. When released from jail he was dying but was still required to appear daily at the police offices and submit to interminable interrogations. He died June 8, 1952, with the serenity of a stoic, and confident in the final triumph of democracy.

Professor José Angel Agreda, another federation official and vice-president of the Teachers' Professional College, was jailed in the Carcel Modelo of Caracas. Later, he was sent to the Guasina concentration camp where he contracted typhoid and nearly died before being released. When he had recovered, he was again thrown into jail.

Professor Manuel Vicente Magallanes, another leader, was jailed and savagely beaten. Later, the "sweetheart," a pointed iron instrument which cut through to the bones, nearly breaking them, was applied to his wrists. A similar fate befell many other well-known educators. One of them, René Dominguez, one-time president of the federation, related his experience as a political prisoner:

> I was imprisoned December 26, 1951, and placed in a cell in the National Security Building, measuring two by one meters. The floor was of gravel. As no mattresses were permitted, one either had to sleep on the floor or on some newspapers if they could be obtained. Some cells had eight prisoners in them; those that were a little larger had fifteen. Some people had to stand while others were seated with their legs extended through the bars. They would alternate positions from time to time in order to rest. It was very difficult to sleep since agents kept coming down to the cells to take prisoners upstairs. Since this meant that they were going to be tortured, the rest of us were left to worry lest the torturing would break their nerves and they would reveal some of the secrets of the party. . . .
>
> I was taken twice before Ulises Ortega, head of the political brigade, for questioning, but was returned to my cell when I refused to make any statement. The final questioning followed a three-day period of torture. After taking off my clothes, they applied what was called "Number Eleven." This consisted of making me stand about a half a meter from the wall, bending forward to support myself on the wall with my outstretched index fingers. My face was near the wall but could not touch it nor could I use any other part of my body for support. Several agents, armed with machetes, watched me constantly, questioning and threatening me. I do not know how long I was able to resist but I remember that first of all my fingers became numb, then my hands, finally my arms. Afterward, the muscles of my face and abdomen, then the muscles of my whole body and my legs began to knot. I fell to the ground without power to make a single move to defend myself against the blows because my muscles would not obey. The guards, believing me to be pretending, hoisted me up against the wall smashing my face against it but I fell bleeding to the ground again. They left me there to recover and when I could stand again, the questioning and the threats continued, now mixed with the promise of better treatment if I would talk about the party organization. As I continued silent, they left me under guard, not allowing me to sleep, to eat, or go to the toilet.
>
> To this torture was added the maddening noise of two clocks that sounded the quarter hour at different times and whose "tick-tock" became unbearable, especially at night. I suffered from asthma and a strong attack seized me. They finally allowed me to put on some clothes. However, I had to continue standing for seventy-two hours. My sight became cloudy and I began to see spots on the wall that moved and took the form of animals or rare beings. The questioning did not stop and began anew with each changing of the guard. I do not remember when I fell to the ground because I could no longer stand. The guards kept lifting me up and letting me fall. At last I became unconscious. Before they finally stopped, one

of them struck my legs various times, breaking open the flesh. When I recovered consciousness they dragged me before a stenographer who took my statement. I repeated what I had said before, that I knew nothing about the internal organization of the party.

It was in this climate of violence—with the torture chambers in the overflowing jails operating day and night and with tight censorship of the press—that the country was called to elections.

20

The 1952 Elections and the Coup d'État of December 2

The Prospect of Elections with the Majority Party Excluded

On April 19, 1951, three decrees were issued calling the country to elections at an unspecified date. The first, Decree 118, was an electoral statute and the next two decrees regulated constitutional guarantees as well as freedom of association.

The electoral statute was quite like the one in force during the democratic period. The leaders of the two legal, independent parties—Rafael Caldera of the Social Christian (Copei) party and Jóvito Villalba of the Unión Republicana Democrática—had collaborated in its preparation. But the voting age had been raised from 18 to 21, over their opposition, and the provision for having all political parties represented in the organization which supervised the elections was eliminated. Voting was made obligatory, with fines and other penalties for those who failed to go to the polls.

One hardly needs to stress the point that there was a complete absence of human rights in Venezuela at this time and that the manner of governing the country was wholly incompatible with a free electoral process. Perhaps for this reason, the military junta issued another decree which liberalized the absolute lack of liberty to the extent of permitting "meetings in closed areas without weapons and without disturbing public order, as well as freedom of association, both to be conditioned by restrictions separately established." These additional restrictions empowered the government to dissolve any meetings "in case of an insulting or degrading reference to a political, judicial, or administrative official or the organizations which they represent."

Obviously real elections could not be held without the participation of political parties. Decree 119 authorized them to function but specified that local or national officers of dissolved political parties could not take part—a measure aimed directly at excluding Acción Democrática from the election. The significance of the prohibition will be understood if it is recalled that AD had obtained 75 percent of the vote in three successive elections between 1946 and 1948. Also remember that the military had publicly testified as to the honesty of these elections.

Two Confidential Circulars Typical of the Government

Even so, the decrees offered some promise of liberty. The real intentions of the dictatorship did not appear in the text of the decrees but in the secret orders sent out by the Ministry of Interior and the national security police. Clandestine resistance forces succeeded in obtaining, deciphering, and publishing two of them. The first, January 4, 1951, by Lt. Col. Llovera Páez, a junta member and minister of interior, and sent to state governors, referred to the "restitution" of constitutional guarantees. The regime's true purpose is seen in a paragraph on the process of legalizing a political party:

> In order to get legalization, we must receive copies of the documents relating to the statutes and programs of the parties as well as lists of their founding members. At the same time, you should send a report recommending whether or not it is convenient to legalize this organization, taking into account the past history and other data regarding its members.

The second confidential document was sent by the head of national security at that time, Jorge Maldonado Parilli, on January 18, 1951, to security officers in various states. They were ordered to exercise a "systematic vigilance over all of those people who had prominent political activity and especially those who had been members of AD and therefore can be considered enemies of the government." The order contained the following literary pearl of fascist police activity: "The purpose of this order is to identify those who conspire against the government, those who should also be watched, and those who have abandoned political activity and are devoted only to the exercise of their professions or habitual activities."

Following the publication of the decrees (and the secret orders), nothing more was heard for some time about the proposed elections. The matter came up again in 1952. Those who had previously opposed a vote now favored it. Why? One version worthy of credit was that the government wished to acquire a legal aspect so that it might serve as host for the Tenth Inter-American Conference early in 1954; Caracas had been designated as the site, and the United States State Department had been bringing pressure on member states to attend the meeting.

Another reason cited for the elections was that some among those avidly seeking new petroleum concessions insisted that the sale of the subsoil rights be authorized by the Congress—no matter how elected—to give legal basis to the doubtful deals. Two recent events were precedents—the elections of Laureano Gómez in Colombia and Manuel Odría in Peru—who both had pulled the fancy trick of being elected constitutional president without having either rivals at the ballot-box or liberty in the streets.

The dictatorship needed a political instrument of its own for the elections, having failed in its efforts to utilize either of the two legally functioning parties for its own ends. Copei and URD had ended their period of hopeful waiting and now took a definite opposition line. Suárez Flamerich was told to recruit a civilian group to serve as an electoral front for the dictatorship; it was baptized with the colorless name of Independent Electoral Front (FEI). An electoral stage manager showed up in Miraflores palace, with offices there for his use—Rafael Heredia, who before 1945 had been leader of the communist group in the municipal council of Caracas.

AD, URD and Copei Take Positions

The elections for a constituent assembly were called for November 30, but it was not until the middle of September that the two legal opposition parties decided to participate in the voting, showing how little faith they had in elections held under such questionable auspices.

AD decided to abstain from the elections. Our reasons were stated in a lengthy document signed by me as president of the party in exile, and by Leonardo Ruiz Pineda, secretary general of the underground party. This document was circulated on September 13, the twelfth anniversary of our party's founding. It published more than one hundred secret telegrams of the Interior Ministry, revealing how government funds and offices were being used to distribute electoral propaganda and bring pressure on individuals and groups. Despite formal abstention, the party nevertheless authorized its members to vote for non-party candidates "if it would effectively support the evolution leading to recover popular sovereignty."

AD leaders had another reason to boycott the election, a very important one. Information received from groups in the military indicated that the accumulated discontent in the barracks against Pérez Jiménez and his clique would break out in violent form before the elections.

URD and Copei, however, both decided to take part in the elections. They announced their decision with penetrating and courageous analyses of the national political situation, making it clear that they would not recognize the results if the elections were carried out in a fraudulent manner. These statements made it clear that the organized political forces of the nation were now acting in a kind of tacit common front against the dictatorship. As the opposition now included all social sectors and ideological viewpoints, the dictatorial regime had only one source of support left, the army. The precarious nature of its support was demonstrated by subsequent events.

Boca del Rio and Maturin—Two Signs of Crises in the Army

On September 29, Pérez Jiménez again called together a large group of officers on active duty; he said a new conspiracy had been discovered among the military and he threatened repressive measures. Luis Emilio Gómez Ruiz, ironically nicknamed "the pocket foreign minister" because of his anatomy and other characteristics, also briefed the officers on the recent commercial treaty signed between the United States government and the dictatorship. There had been bitter public criticism of the treaty; even some in the barracks. When an agreement is made with counterfeit governments which do not allow any free discussion of public issues, the agreement is sure to be considered a betrayal of the country by suppressed public opinion.

Repressive measures began on the morning of September 30, when various officers under the command of Captain Wilfredo Omaña rebelled at the Boca del Rio air base, the largest in the country. The uprising was put down but had immediate repercussions elsewhere. Civilian groups armed with machetes assaulted the National Guard posts at Villa Bruzual and Turen in the state of Portugesa. They were bloodily repressed, and bomber planes, acquired from England and the United States to contribute to "continental defense," strafed the insurgents. No prisoners were taken. All captives were shot.

Meanwhile, at Maturin, capital of the eastern oil state of Monagas, the garrison rebelled and the city was in the hands of the champions of liberty for several hours. Only an unfortunate fatal accident prevented this uprising from spreading throughout the country. A chance patrol killed Captain Juan Bautista Rojas and gravely wounded Jorge Yibirín, the AD leader, the two in command of the rebels.

The dictatorship responded in savage fashion. All the leaders of both URD and Copei were arrested. Hundreds of AD members and many military officers were thrown into jail without trial and denounced by the political police.

The government now lost its head completely and resorted to naked terror and political murder. Previously, various freedom fighters had died in jail or in Guasina, but now the government not only began to kill, but also to boast of what it was doing.

There was the case of Castor Nieves Rios, a man of the people and the mayor of a small provincial town at the time of the 1948 coup. With a few old guns he and fellow party members had continued fighting until their ammunition was exhausted. He escaped from Venezuela but returned later to participate in the underground resistance. Captured, he managed to escape when being transferred from one prison to another. His courage became something of a legend, and a source of demoralization for the government. Again captured on October 4, 1952, he was tortured and finally shot in cold blood. The official communiqué in the Caracas press said that an incident had occurred when Nieves Ríos had tried to wrest away the gun of an agent and security officers had fired in self-defense. But Pedro Estrada, head of this tropical Gestapo, boasted of having personally fired the shot.

The Murder of Leonardo Ruiz Pineda

On October 21, Leonardo Ruiz Pineda was shot down in an ambush deliberately staged by the police in a busy Caracas street. This terrible crime which ended the life of a man who had organized the vast underground resistance of AD to become a national hero and the symbol of civilian resistance, exhilarated the government. The police sent dramatic pictures of the body to the newspapers.

Leonardo Ruiz Peneda was a man of singular gifts. A magnificent orator, he possessed a keen intelligence and a native vocation for heroism. An Andino, born in the state of Táchira in 1917, he fought with a truly Venezuelan vision against the regional doctrine of "Andinism" and became the AD political leader in Táchira, where he founded the newspaper *Fronteras*. When AD came to power, he was successively secretary of the revolutionary junta, governor of his native state, and minister of communications, demonstrating remarkable administrative ability in each post. For four years, he was the main force behind the underground movement. His assassination confirmed what the AD leaders in exile had been saying, that Pérez Jiménez had ordered him apprehended—not alive, but dead.

The owner of the car in which Ruiz Pineda was riding when shot was Germán González, a lawyer. He was not a political activist but a personal friend of the victim. On his own initiative he went to the police to explain that he had no connection with the underground. His body was found riddled with twenty machine-gun slugs. Auraelena Ruiz Pineda was imprisoned when she went to beg for the body of her husband to bury him.

The display of official terrorism produced national and international commotion unforeseen by the government. All Venezuelans now understood that the regime was incompatible with our national dignity and survival as a civilized community. In both Americas, congresses, newspapers, and many different institutions raised their voices in protest. Panic grew among the supporters of the dictatorship. The children of the ministers and other officials had to leave school because their fellow students were so hostile to them.

Caracas society repeated the indiscreet news from certain druggists that the high officials of the dictatorship were consuming sleeping pills and tranquilizers to an extraordinary degree.

The demoralization of the government also fed the secret personal rivalry between the two military men in power. Mistrusting Llovera Páez because of his control over the electoral machinery—the Independent Electoral Front, Pérez Jiménez created his own political arm, and the country learned on October 26 that an agency had been created to promote "massive support for the army and for Colonel Pérez Jiménez." The adjective massive was ironically received because it turned out that the head of the movement was the disreputable P. A. Gutiérrez Alfaro, a gynecologist who had gained entry to palace circles by delivering the numerous illegitimate offspring of the prolific dictator Gómez.

Pérez Jiménez had himself nominated for the provisional presidency by his improvised organization, but Llovera Páez did not hide his disgust at the haste of his partner. On August 23, he sent a circular telegram to all the state governments which the AD underground obtained and promptly published:

> It is possible that some persons may come to you claiming to organize on behalf of the candidacy of Col. Marcos Pérez Jiménez and trying to obtain signatures. You should be advised that these people do not have the authorization of Col. Pérez Jiménez for this campaign, and act accordingly.

The Irrevocable Popular Decision—Defeat the Dictator at the Polls

Now a double phenomenon occurred: angry crowds thronged the political rallies of the opposition parties as never before, openly voicing their defiance of despotism; and the frightened authorities tolerated the bitter criticism of opposition orators. Villalba and Caldera, in rapid and hard-hitting campaigns, traveled throughout the country, criticizing the political and economic situation before excited crowds. At an extraordinary popular URD rally in Caracas, just a few days before the election, the people groaned with sorrow and anger when a minute of silent tribute in memory of Leonardo Luis Pineda was proposed; then thousands of white handkerchiefs—the color that AD traditionally used—fluttered in the tropical night like banners of defiance.

By election day, November 30, it was clear that the populace intended to convert the vote into a plebiscite against Pérez Jiménez and his clique. The cold chill of defeat penetrated the bones of even the few sincere adherents of totalitarian government and frightened the unscrupulous businessmen favored by the government. At the same time, the growing difference between the two colonels at the top of the government could not be bridged. The civilian presiding over this farce, Suárez Flamerich, was like a hapless rag doll jerked to and fro, the object of universal scorn and ridicule.

The succeeding events can be described through the reports of international news agencies and well-known publications. As described by the *Economist* of London in its issue of December 11, 1952:

> The elections on November 30 were impressive in their orderliness. Secrecy of the ballot was observed and more than 80 percent of the electorate voted. The two principal opposition parties allowed to function legally, the left-of-center URD and the Catholic Copei, had no criticism of the voting. As the first results came in, URD was getting 54 percent of the votes, Copei 15 percent and the FEI, the government party, only 25 percent.[1]

How did this news of the overwhelming defeat of a government which maintained such iron censorship over communications get abroad? The vote against the government was so overwhelming that it simply could not be hidden. Radio stations throughout the republic had been transmitting election bulletins revealing the tremendous defeat being administered to the dictatorship before they realized what was happening. The entire world was aware by the next day that the opposition had won the elections in twenty-two out of the twenty-three electoral regions of the republic.

The international news services reported from Caracas on December 1 that the only two states where URD was losing were the same ones AD had lost in 1946. This indicated, the news agency said, that 1,500,000 AD voters had cast their votes for URD.

The truth was that AD had reversed its original decision to abstain from the elections and encouraged its supporters to vote for the other opposition parties. It was not necessary to make a formal pact with them. We trusted the promise of their leaders that there would be immediate democratic change if they won. The massive vote for the opposition parties was a plebiscite against the dictator, which explains why AD acted the way it did. The victory of URD came from the votes of AD.

The Military Elect a President

On December 1, the transmission of news from Venezuela to the outside world was suddenly interrupted by censorship. Local radio stations were occupied by police and transmitted only music and commercial announcements. On the night of December 2 there was a no less sudden and surprising announcement: Colonel Pérez Jiménez had dissolved the triumvirate and had proclaimed himself provisional president with the support of six chiefs of the armed forces.

Let us read what *The New York Times* said about Venezuelan events in its editorial, December 4, 1952:

> What happened in Venezuela these last few days comes as a shock to all who cherish the growth of democracy in Latin America. The shock is no less great because the leader of the military junta, Col. Pérez Jiménez, appears to have done just what everybody expected. He took several years to arrange an election for a

constituent assembly, thought he had it sewed up, and then, when—according to the only credible figures—he saw that he was losing, he reacted in the old-fashioned way and is retaining power by force.

This is not the way that he and his supporters explain what happened. According to them, the electoral tide, which was running at two and a half to one against them for at least one-third of the votes, took a sudden turn and gave the Government group (the FEI) a numerical superiority. Thereupon—although even the total claimed by the military clique represented less than 30 percent of the electorate—Pérez Jiménez, "by decision of the armed forces," proclaimed himself provisional president. Yet, according to the electoral law which the junta itself drew up, the constituent assembly was to choose the provisional president on Jan. 10.[2]

Upon proclaiming himself provisional president with only the backing of a praetorian guard, Pérez Jiménez had actually not only defied the popular will expressed by the balloting but had violated the decree he himself had signed. With typical shamelessness, the usurper also chose to forget what he had said just two weeks earlier in La Guaira, as published by the Caracas newspaper *El Nacional* on November 16: "The provisional presidency falls under the constituent assembly. This sovereign body is the only one with the power to choose whomever it sees fit to select."

These events apparently did not upset foreign offices throughout America or the Organization of American States. A little game of chess took place whereby the credentials of César González as ambassador to Washington, signed by Suárez Flamerich, were replaced by others signed by Pérez Jiménez. The White House, hastening to accept them, implicitly affirmed that "normal relations were continuing between the two governments," as the stereotyped language of diplomacy would phrase it. The same attitude was adopted by almost all of the other hemispheric governments. Only the free press of the continent voiced the indignation felt throughout America at the way the good faith of a people had been put to ridicule.

The unseemly haste with which the Department of State received the credentials of the ambassador of Pérez Jiménez, as if there had not been a new coup d'état, rightfully evoked bitter criticism. Even years later, this attitude, which had no justification in the light of moral principle or the precedents of inter-American relations, continues to receive the adverse judgment of true democrats throughout both Americas. The editorial of the *New York Times* on Columbus Day, October 12, 1955, is especially significant:

> Nonintervention is a precious and necessary principle of hemispheric affairs, but it can never be forgotten that the United States is so powerful economically and politically that whatever we do or do not do greatly affects the individual Latin American countries, and in that sense is a form of intervention, whether we intend it or not. It is an open secret that if the United States had expressed its displeasure at the stealing of the Venezuelan election by partisans of Colonel Pérez Jiménez in November, 1952, he would have drawn back, or at least compromised with his opposition. By keeping strictly out of the conflict and recognizing the Pérez Jiménez regime quickly, we, in a sense, intervened.[3]

Vacation Tours, A Message of Gibberish, and a Stupid Telegram

Meanwhile in Caracas, the tragedy continued. After his second armed assault on the popular will, Pérez Jiménez proceeded to announce that Llovera Páez and Suárez Flamerich would make "vacation trips" to Honolulu and Switzerland.

He named Laureano Vallenilla Lanz, son and namesake of the theoretician of American despotism under Gómez, minister of interior. Like his father, Lanz was a person without ethical scruples but lacked his father's talent. Pérez Jiménez named a cabinet selected from the ranks of old Gómez supporters. Finally he blurted out a radio message to the country and sent a telegram to the leaders of URD.

In his message, he proclaimed the sibylline formula of "the national welfare," by which he and his clique sought to superimpose themselves upon constitutional law. In his illogical reasoning, "If it is true that the fundamental factor in a republic is the normal development of constitutional order, it is also true that even above this is the obligation to achieve the national welfare which will bring to Venezuela the prestige which it merits." This was followed with his habitual diatribes against AD. As reported by the United Press: "He added that he would invite political leaders from every sector to collaborate with his government but made it clear that he would exclude AD, which he described as 'an offense to national dignity' and which he accused of 'efforts to undermine the military forces'."

His telegram to Ignacio Luis Arcaya and Jóvito Villalba, leaders of URD, was of singular stupidity. It was sent at 3 a.m. on December 2, after it was known that the vote totals had been falsified to give the government candidates the majority. Notwithstanding this, Pérez Jiménez admitted that the electoral triumph belonged to the opposition. Here is part of the text of this curious and cynical telegram:

> Your categorical denial of the grave fact which the underground and anti-national parties attribute to you is not enough to prove the good faith which you profess. The ideas put forward by URD speakers at different meetings and the votes cast by the AD and the communists for your ticket has corroborated the fact. The armed forces you have mocked will not permit treacherous agreements to damage the national prestige—so adversely affected by the electoral triumph of AD and the Communist party that URD has organized.

Brutal repression became the order of the day. Strikes called in protest of the election results were smothered by shots, beatings, and jailings. Curfew was established in the petroleum camps. Students were beaten without mercy when they took to the streets. The majority of the members of the electoral council, which included men placed in their positions by the government, were persecuted by the police when they refused to sign the falsified results of the elections. Those who did not succeed in hiding themselves were thrown into jail. Jóvito Villalba and Luis Hernández Solis, together with other URD leaders, were arrested when they went to interview Vallenilla Lanz, despite the fact that he had "guaranteed their safety on his word of honor." They were later deported when the URD leadership announced that its deputies would not take their seats in the constituent assembly; otherwise it would be vulgar mockery of the opposition's triumph. The Copei party conditioned its attendance on the reestablishment of constitutional guarantees and freedom for political prisoners. The dictator's reply was to jail hundreds of additional people from all political camps and others who the police simply believed were unfriendly to the government.

The Spurious Constituent Assembly

This was the situation when the spurious constituent assembly was installed on January 9, 1953. Army tanks and troops, Tommy guns in hand, patrolled the legislative palace, closed for four years, as if they expected an attack. There were 104 delegates who should have attended, but only 71 appeared, with those of URD and Copei absent. Out of the seventy-one, only fifty were delegates, the other twenty-one being substitutes. By an act of magic, worthy of Houdini himself, the dictatorial clique had changed an overwhelming defeat into a pyrrhic victory, assigning to its own party fifty-nine seats. The fact that only fifty delegates attended indicated that at least nine who had been rounded up had jumped the fence of the corral and were either in hiding or in jail. It was this caricature of the sovereign body, this farce of clowns, that ratified and received his oath in a rapid ceremony "which scarcely lasted five minutes," according to the Associated Press.

At this dramatic moment, a document of the "Party of the People" reached the hands of all Venezuelans: "AD calls for civil rebellion" was its title, and it was signed by Alberto Carnevali, the successor to Ruiz Pineda as secretary general of the underground party. This document will remain one of the great political pronouncements in Venezuelan history because of its vigorous democratic faith in the country's destiny. It recounted how the opposition had triumphed at the ballot box and the way the usurpers had ignored the popular decision. It added firsthand information on the mechanics to make the takeover appear a "decision of the armed forces." Just as in November 1948, a minority of military chieftains substituted their decision for that of hundreds of officers and thousands of soldiers.

Carnevali accused Pérez Jiménez of having sent emissaries to the barracks to announce that the government had lost the election but that the political parties were planning to dissolve the army and assassinate the families of officers. This was the pretext, he said, for Pérez Jiménez "sacrificing himself." And he added:

> In general, the officers were not consulted but simply "notified" of this second crime against popular sovereignty as if the army were a docile herd of armed indi-

viduals whose opinions and feelings did not have to be taken into account. In the few barracks where there was any discussion, the true response of most of the officers was not passed along "to the higher level."

Visible discontent in the army paralleled the agitation in the streets. Many officers opposed the falsification of the electoral results. In the months of December and January, there were at least two military conspiracies and many officers were jailed, retired, or exiled.

Alberto Carnevali Dies in Jail

The underground resistance continued its activity without interruption and with great perseverance. Alberto Carnevali, now its leader, was one of the most able men of AD. A 36-year-old lawyer, kindly in demeanor, he possessed an analytical mind and had exceptional leadership qualities. The police searched for him tirelessly, ransacking homes and apartments throughout Caracas, and finally found him in the heart of town. Early on January 18, 1953, dozens of security agents surrounded the block where he was hidden and began an assault with all kinds of arms, including machine guns and hand grenades, as the order had been given to kill Carnevali. He was meeting with a group of party members; they courageously defended themselves. A number fell wounded, including Ramón Alirio Garcia, who died a month later from his wounds; the labor leader José Vargas; the university student Germán Pacheco, and another party member, Pedro Barrios Astudillo. As all the shooting attracted many people to the area, the presence of these witnesses prevented the elimination of Carnevali then and there, and he was taken prisoner.

Carnevali was isolated in solitary confinement. He fell ill and presented symptoms for which he underwent an exploratory operation by military doctors; their diagnosis revealed a widespread malignancy in the intestinal track. All efforts to get him transferred to a private clinic were in vain. Carnevali was one of my best friends, and I personally requested various foreign offices to act on his behalf. All these efforts, however, failed because of the sordid cruelty of a regime under men of primitive instincts, incapable of overcoming their hate. Carnevali died in jail because of the inflexible refusal by the dictatorship to have him sent to a cancer hospital. I received news of his death in Chile a few hours before I was to make a speech; I did not mention it because had I done so, I would not have been able to contain tears of pain and rage. Crying by men in public is a display of emotion which old-fashioned prejudice has prohibited.

Those in power now concentrated on three principal goals: to kill off the men of the resistance; to prepare a scenario for the Tenth Inter-American Conference; and to organize the facade of a constitutional state.

A police ambush on February 24 cut down another fugitive from the summary justice of the regime, Captain Wilfrido Omaña who had gone underground in 1952 after the unsuccessful uprising at the Maracay air base. Sante Gómez, an AD member who acted as chauffeur for the army officer, was subjected to terrible physical torture.

On June 10, Leparvanche Parpaicen, who was the representative of the dictatorship to the Organization of American States and also president of its general council, advised the secretary of the OAS that all was ready in Venezuela for the solemn inter-American conference. On the evening of the same day, Antonio Pinto Salinas was arrested in the small town of Pariaguan in the eastern oil zone. He was another leader of the AD underground, 34 years old, an economist and writer. He was lean of body, with fine features and a faraway look in his eyes—like a frustrated poet. The next night he was sent to Caracas, handcuffed and bleeding from various injuries. He never arrived. Early in the morning, he was forced out of the car as it crossed the plains in Guarico state. Two shots at close range finished him off, and eight more slugs were poured into his body by the butchers.

The False Predictions of the State Department

At that time, a monograph prepared by the United States State Department was put into circulation. Entitled *Venezuela: Oil Transforms a Nation* (Office of Public Affairs, Department of State, February, 1953), it contained this revealing paragraph:

> Although the first return from the elections showed the government party FEI running behind URD, the final figures published by the junta claimed victory for FEI, with 788,031 votes (59 seats). URD got 638,366 votes (29 seats). Copei obtained 300,359 votes (14 seats) and there were 60,483 votes (2 seats) for other parties. Immediately after the elections, the government announced that the junta had resigned and Col. Pérez Jiménez selected by the armed forces as provisional president. This action, later ratified by the constituent assembly, left Pérez Jiménez—formerly minister of defense and member of the old junta—as the only executive authority until presidential elections can be held. At this time, the constituent assembly is preparing a new constitution. When this is ready, the road will be open for presidential, municipal, and congressional elections.[4]

The road that was to have been opened by popular election for constitutional government remained closed. The usurpers tried to achieve constitutional status by and for themselves in April 1953 in one of the most cynical parodies of constitutional government that can be recalled. In a single day, the constituent assembly designated twelve thousand essential officials of the legislative, judicial, and executive branches of government. It named the members of Congress and the state legislatures, municipal councils, the Supreme Court of Justice, the attorney general, and the comptroller general of the nation, and Pérez Jiménez as constitutional president.

The Constitution Which Annulled Human Rights

The rubber-stamp constitution approved by the constituent assembly had one great innovation—it abolished individual rights. This was really quite a novelty in the history of Latin American despotism, which had always, at least formally, respected them. It was traditional for dictators to proclaim the essential principles of democracy in their constitutions, even if only in letter. The constitution written by the docile lackeys of the usurper in Venezuela did not even observe this formal scruple.

Title III of the constitution enumerates the individual rights guaranteed by it, but at the end of the document there are reservations which suspended all individual guarantees and left the government unbound by any limits other than those fixed arbitrarily by the persons in power. The special laws to protect human rights vaguely promised by the new constitution were never promulgated. Thus, the guarantees of life and safety have no legal force today in Venezuela, as the facts demonstrate. The rights of property, labor, and contract are suspended. In other words, the government declares itself to be above any law.

This loosely-defined constitutionality, even though the negation of any kind of public law, was taken as giving a moral and juridical basis for the regime to play host to the Tenth Inter-American Conference. Brigades of construction workers, upholsterers, and carpenters worked around the clock in order to prepare a sumptuous spectacle for the delegations. Other details were not forgotten, such as continuing to jail or kill opponents capable of stirring up popular protest in the streets against political oppression while the delegates of the American governments were in Caracas.

On April 24, the police took another prisoner, Eligio Anzola, who had become the head of the underground resistance and secretary general of AD. The car in which he rode in the residential zone of El Paraiso of Caracas was machine-gunned and Anzola, a former minister of interior, a jurist and a man of outstanding civic virtue, was handed over to the torture chambers. His teeth were kicked out and the base of his spine crushed. His wife was also jailed. At this time, other AD leaders were seized and tortured, including Rigoberto Henríquez Vera and José Angel Ciliberto, young lawyers among the best of our younger leaders; also Ramon Quijada, president of the Rural Workers Federation; and the labor leaders, Tomas Alberti and David Nieves. Three members of the party perished in jail, victims of torture: Victor Alvarado, Ruben Perdomo, and Jésus López. None of them were leaders but simply members of that innumerable legion of anonymous combatants. Their martyrdom symbolized the best of what it meant to be a Venezuelan.

The Tenth Inter-American Conference and the Historic Action of Costa Rica

Now the scenario was cleared of obstacles for the tenth conference. Bullets, jail cells, and torture chambers had eliminated the foremost leaders of the democratic underground. There was no risk that the metaphysical speeches on behalf of an abstract liberty would be interrupted by explosive popular demonstrations demanding real freedom for the Venezuelans. The ritual could be carried out in a country terrorized by the totalitarian machine of the dictatorship. Col. Pérez Jiménez, in golden epaulets and shining decorations, could give the opening speech. The newsmen present could note the curious coincidence in the enthusiastic response from two personalities otherwise in antagonistic positions: John Foster Dulles, the United States secretary of state, and Guillermo Toriello, the Guatemalan foreign minister in the leftist Arven government.

This was not the only time in which the United States and Guatemalan attitudes coincided during the Caracas meeting. Both delegations abstained from voting—which, under the circumstances, constituted a negative vote—when the Uruguayan delegation proposed that all American governments decree an amnesty for political prisoners and exiles. José Mora Otero, head of the Uruguayan delegation, courageously brought up the subject, knowing full well that not far from where the heavily protected conference was meeting there were jail cells and concentration camps full of political prisoners. It might have been expected that the foreign minister of the United States would argue that his government, under a Republican party administration, was interested in protecting free enterprise and concerting military alliances against communism, rather than in obtaining respect for human rights in Latin America. However, what justification could be given for the conduct of the Guatemalan minister who spoke for the highly vocal and aggressive revolutionary regime of his country?

The inter-American meeting at Caracas was held despite vast opposition. Rarely has there been seen in America such a wave of protest as occurred because of the Caracas meeting. The protest movement urged that the member states attend only if the host country put an end to the permanent state-of-siege under which it governed, free its prisoners, allow the return of exiles, and restore basic freedoms. There were two basic arguments for this thesis, one juridical, the other moral. First, it should have been obligatory for the member states of the regional system to comply with the Charter of Bogotá and the Declaration on Human Rights. Obviously the nation where the conference was being held did not even pretend to do this. Second, the moral authority of an organization which sought to affirm democratic principles as America's response to the threat of Soviet totalitarianism would be badly tarnished by holding the meeting in a country ruled by police methods similar to those of Stalin and Beria.

These arguments were energetically put forward by both houses of the Chilean Congress, by numerous congressmen of Uruguay and other countries, by the labor movement of the United States and Latin America, by students, by some of the most prestigious intellectuals of both Americas, and by the free press of the continent. Only two foreign offices expressed their view publicly: Costa Rica was against attending; the United States favored making the trip to Canossa.

The attitude of the United States was set forth by the man who was then assistant secretary of state for Latin America, Moors Cabot. Speaking to newsmen in Bolivia, he said: "I want to insist that the United States does not intervene in the internal affairs of another country. In my judgment, to refuse to go to Caracas would be to interfere in its political affairs." Then, turning to another subject, he affirmed that "the United States is determined to defend the free world."

After the Caracas meeting, it seemed as though the regime felt free of any remnants of scruple. The presence of almost all of the hemisphere's governments in Caracas was interpreted as a sort of license to do whatever it pleased, despite the widespread opposition to attendance at Caracas. From now on, it would not limit its challenges to civilized behavior to the territory of Venezuela itself.

Costa Rica and its democratic government were the first objects of its fury. The government of this small but dignified nation was the only one absent from the Caracas meeting. Under the inspired leadership of José Figueres, it refused to attend the tenth conference. In language worthy of the American founding fathers, it explained why its seat was left empty:

> The government council, after prolonged study, feels that Costa Rica should not attend the conference. Our absence should be seen as a reflection of American feeling adverse to the holding of the meeting in Caracas as long as present conditions exist there with regard to human rights.
>
> This opinion would be silenced if all member states attended the meeting. This opinion holds that two simultaneous battles are being waged in America: one, the global front against foreign aggression; the other, the internal conflict between democracy and dictatorship.
>
> Costa Rica believes that while the other American States, present in Caracas, consider the general needs of Pan-Americanism and hemispheric defense, at least one country, by its absence, should emphasize the agony of people being sacrificed in the fight against our own totalitarianism in America.
>
> In this way, we will contribute, at the same time, to both battles—the worldwide one and the internal one.

Aggressions Against Costa Rica

This attitude of the Costa Rican government, even though discretely expressed, infuriated the Caracas despot, already angered because of the generous asylum offered in San José to various exiles, including me. He now engaged in actions which were an open challenge to inter-American treaties and to the most basic norms of behavior in international relations.

The Venezuelan dictator had close ties with his Siamese twin in Nicaragua. Somoza was a most honored guest of Pérez Jiménez, and the schemes of the two dictators soon became evident. One day in June 1954, Venezuelan military planes flew over the unprotected capital city of Costa Rica. There was not a single anti-aircraft gun in the entire country, and the demilitarized government of Figueres did not possess even a single light plane. The Venezuelan aircraft boldly violated the airspace of Costa Rica to carry out an ignominious mission: tons of pornographic pamphlets with obscene drawings were dumped upon the city.

After the paper bombardment came another assault with machine guns. An invasion planned by the dictatorships was launched from Nicaragua into Costa Rica. Pérez Jiménez and his clique were active in all of this, and the collaboration of the Venezuelan dictatorship in this disgraceful invasion was well-known throughout America. In the diplomatic maneuvering which followed, the names of Pérez Jiménez and Somoza were never linked, but the two will go down in history as the co-authors of this unprovoked attack. Calderón Guardia, the former Costa Rican president and a leader of the invasion, had come to Caracas four times in the preceding six months, according to the Social Christian leader of Uruguay, Venancio Flores. The aerial incursion over San José immediately followed his first visit. Also, just before the invasion, Venezuelan Air Force planes brought arms to Managua. The Costa Rican government charged that Venezuelan combat planes machine-gunned camps and cities during the invasion, while the United Press reported from Washington that the Defense Department confirmed sighting Venezuelan warplanes flying north over Panama toward Costa Rica.

The Week of the Fatherland: Trumped-Up Nationalism

Militarization of the country became more pronounced. July 5, the national holiday when the signing of our first Declaration of Independence of 1811 is celebrated, was now declared Army Day. Another celebration was added, the so-called Week of the Fatherland. This was given a theological-military tone by Monsignor Ramon Inocente Lizardi, who said the inaugural mass dressed in the uniform of an army major. Blackouts were held in the cities during mock air attacks, and all the members of the Inter-American Defense Board in Washington made a special trip to Caracas to witness these martial fireworks. Tanks, cannon, and military battalions paraded before the dictator, and schoolchildren were also called out to march to military tunes. Public employees obliged to dress in the traditional high-collared suit of the Venezuelan plainsmen—the *liquiliqui,* now declared the national costume— were also compelled to appear in these fascist parades. These were climaxed by flamboyant oratory, seeking an impossible objective—to convince the Venezuelans that the army personified the fatherland and alone possessed the highest civic virtue and creative capacity.

This half-baked nationalism, served up in military sauce, was also shown in provocative attitudes taken toward Ecuador, Chile, Costa Rica, and other Latin American countries, all orchestrated with brass by the official press and speeches made in the caricature Congress. This posturing chauvinism against brother peoples was very contrary to the true feeling of the Venezuelan people. It contrasted with the obsequious position taken before more

powerful states, whether large or only half-sized. The beggarly posture before the oil companies was paralleled by the indiscriminate support given to
the big powers in the United Nations. It is with great shame as a Venezuelan
that I recall the coarse oratory heard in the pseudo-Congress of my country
against other peoples and governments of Latin America. Persons without
ethical or intellectual authority voiced the scorn of this arrogant government
for sister nations and its submission before the big powers. On May 1, 1953,
the Associated Press reported the speech of deputy Luis Garcia referring to
the alleged traitorous blow of Ecuador and Columbia in connection with the
Grand Colombian Merchant Fleet. He was applauded when he declared "every Venezuelan is ready to go to the trenches to defend the dignity of Venezuela." Another deputy claimed that Venezuela had always been victimized
by Colombia. Other deputies stormed against Chile, which was termed a
country "without social, political, or economic standing." On another occasion it was claimed that the Chilean Congress had been bought out by money
furnished by Rómulo Betancourt.

In order to ingratiate itself with the European nations still having colonies
in America, the dictatorship left the chair of Venezuela empty when the
Commission on Territorial Dependence, convoked by the OAS, met in
Havana in 1949, despite the fact that Venezuela had been one of the most
outspoken critics of colonialism at the Bogotá conference. Venezuela's absence meant that this inter-American agency had a short life instead of being
used, as it should have been, to pressure England and the Netherlands to
modify the status of their island colonies close to the Venezuelan coast. In
1952, Venezuela was one of the few countries that did not vote for Resolution
33 sponsored by Uruguay in the United Nations, supporting the right of
nations to control their raw material resources. This occurred after the
nationalization of Bolivian tin mines; it was opposed by a minority led by
the United States and England. Even Santo Domingo did not vote with
the minority, but Venezuela did.

The "National Ideal"

Public morale was now degraded by the reappearance of the worst kind of
adulation and flattery of government officials, like the personality cult of
Stalin and the officialized servility in Santo Domingo under Trujillo. The
country was nauseated as the front pages of the regimented press were
monopolized by eulogies of Pérez Jiménez. Sculptors by the dozen made
busts of the dictator. Docile municipal councils and state legislatures declared
him to be their adopted son. Imaginative courtiers daily dreamed up new
medals or decorations to pin on the breast of this trinket-collector. He placed
them on uniforms covered with so much gold braid that they resembled the
dress of a bullfighter, trying to conceal his own mediocrity.

Bishops, chambers of commerce, and professionals from all over the country lined up in 1954 to sign petitions to the so-called Congress, asking that this strategist who had never planned a battle be promoted to general. Then Pérez Jiménez suddenly discovered with moving modesty that he did not yet merit that rank. Scarcely a year after this farce, his political and military partner ruling in Lima made him a Peruvian general. With this recognition, he returned to Caracas and coyly accepted the rank of general.

His despotism was described by his sycophants as the government of the "National Ideal" (thus completing a ridiculous and tragic triad with the "National Restoration" of Castro and the "National Rehabilitation" of Gómez). This was a sort of Perón-like *Justicialismo*, supposedly providing a doctrinaire basis to an administrative record completely lacking in ideological content.

The authorized summary of the regime's "doctrine," given its source, came from Pérez Jiménez himself in a speech July 5, 1954. In prodigious synthesis he said: "The 'National Ideal' gives rise to a doctrine: the 'National Welfare!' The doctrine gives rise to plans that lead to the realization of objectives. The plans give rise to works based on the definition of the doctrine."

The Police State

The logical sequel of this retrogression in public affairs was the predominance of the police. The government was controlled by the police much more than by the military. The national security police and their leader, Pedro Estrada, controlled almost all the levers of power. The army itself had become a virtual prisoner of the vast apparatus of espionage, informers, torture, and assassination run by the political police. In due course, Estrada was named minister of security. A large building was erected to house his tropical Gestapo, and the dictator in person swore in the new officers of this agency. The sinister personality who directed it had acquired such power as the executor of top level orders that he named and removed ministers and other high administrative officials. Venezuela suffered under a regime acting in the name of the armed forces, but the country was actually governed with the almost sole support of a Himmler-like police, which ransacked homes, jailed, and killed, opened private correspondence, violated the privacy of family life, and terrorized the country with constant fear. Citizens of all social classes were persecuted, as was the military.

A few examples will back up these statements. On September 14, 1954, a certain Francisco Espejo, a member of AD without political rank, was arrested in La Guaira. A month later, the National Security police issued a communiqué in which it was announced that on October 18—the anniversary of the revolution which had brought AD to power—a band of terrorists was discovered trying to dynamite one of the bridges on the superhighway from La Guaira to Caracas. In the fighting which ensued, it was claimed that Francisco Espejo and another person were killed.

On other occasions, the order to kill was carried out beyond the borders of the country. Lieutenant León Dros Blanco had been arrested for conspiracy but had managed to flee prison and leave the country. He was considered one of the best shots of the army and had won international medals. The dictator was warned that with such an expert sharpshooter at large, his life would be in danger. On June 10, 1954, Dros Blanco was shot from behind at close range in Baranquilla, Colombia. As the victim lay dying, he accused Pérez Jiménez of having ordered the assassination. The killer was caught and found to possess credentials from the National Security police, as well as an airline ticket from Venezuela paid for by the ministry of interior. The Venezuelan consul visited him repeatedly in jail at Baranquilla and arranged for a lawyer. In view of the incriminating turn the investigation was taking, the murderer was allowed to escape from jail, and later reappeared in Venezuela as an assistant of Pedro Estrada. When the parents of Dros Blanco went to Colombia to seek an indictment of the murderer, they were abruptly ordered out of the country.

On December 9, 1954, the turn came for Mario Briceno Iragorry. This distinguished Catholic writer was aged and ill. He had been elected to the constituent assembly in 1952 but had gone into exile and had published various accusations against the government. When he entered a Madrid church to hear mass, he was attacked from behind. He fell unconscious to the ground but recalled that his assailant had whispered to him before striking: "This is to pay part of what you owe." The accent was Venezuelan.

On January 2, 1955, the president of Panama was assassinated. The chief of the national security announced in Caracas that a clean-up was needed in case anyone should think of doing something similar in Venezuela. On January 6, Jesús Alberto Blanco, an AD member, was taken from jail at Ciudad Bolivar where he had been held for three years. The next day, the Caracas press published a national security announcement that he had been shot while trying to escape. Handcuffed and defenseless, taken from jail under heavy guard, he had been subjected to the "fugitive law" or, to put it plainly, assassinated.

On June 16, 1955, I was visited by a high official of the Mexican police. He warned me that a plot had been discovered to assassinate me that night at the airport when the body of the deceased poet, Andrés Eloy Blanco, was to be returned to Venezuela. From that time on, I was always guarded by various detectives.

International Impunity

There was one more demonstration of this lawlessness. The expulsion of Adrianus Vermeulen and the challenge to the ILO and the United Nations in April 1955, recounted in preceding pages, demonstrated that the dictatorial government was ready to defy all international rules. The despots completely lost their sense of balance due to the deference paid them by the foreign offices of Washington and London. These governments were so pleased by the colonial oil policy tolerated in Venezuela, that they took no notice of the outrageous conduct of the government in other respects. As long as unrestrained exploitation by the oil cartel was permitted to continue, there was little possibility of any criticism from international organizations. For the contemporary governments of powerful western nations, crude oil weighed more on the scales than offenses against international political morality.

A summary has been presented of the political conduct of the Venezuelan dictatorship. Restraining my anger as a patriot, I have tried to narrate the facts as they occurred without the use of tendentious adjectives. This was but one phase of the conduct of the dictatorship—so contrary in every respect to the true national interest. Two other aspects are described in the following pages: its administrative practices, and its colonial behavior in the petroleum question.

21

Disorganized Economic Social Policies and Immoral Administration

Political repressions were accomplished by governmental disorganization and administrative dishonesty. The simple primitive mentality of dictatorship is incapable of serious planning and the establishment of long-range goals in accord with national needs. Dictators construct impressive and spectacular projects—Hitler building the first superhighways in Germany or Mussolini erecting a railway station for Rome bigger than that of New York. These costly public works make it easy to pick up "commissions," the quick way to illegal wealth. Also, they are good propaganda material for well-paid publicity agents in the United States and other countries who try to picture Venezuela as progressing in seven-league boots.

This may seem like a hasty judgment but it is as easy to prove as to state. Let us look at the economic and social development of the country under the dictatorship.

Human Underconsumption and the Deification of Cement

According to statistics put out by the Development Corporation in 1954, the underconsumption of meat in the country was even more serious than before. Although a little meat was produced, it was hard to sell. Despite rigid press censorship, surprising facts come to light which show that the alleged Venezuelan prosperity was fictitious. The newspaper *El Nacional* of Caracas on May 28, 1954, announced that the amount of meat available in Maracaibo had been reduced by 5000 kilos daily due to speculation and the economic situation—this in opulent Maracaibo, the oil capital of the new Canaan.

There was no planned development of cattle-raising with state assistance. All the projects which the AD government had begun were abruptly cancelled. Francisco Morrillo Romero, a cattle grower and president of the Federation of Chambers of Commerce, complained in 1954 that, without far more state assistance, it would be impossible to supply the meat shortage in the country. A year later, nothing had been done to aid cattle production, the second most important sector of the Venezuelan economy.

The ruin of the cattle-raising program was admitted even by government officials. In May 1955, Pedro Segnini, director of cattle-raising planning in the Ministry of Agriculture, revealed that there was a deficit of 16,000 head of cattle annually and only 7.6 percent of existing herds could be used for meat annually in contrast to 25 percent in other countries. The average weight of cattle had gone down considerably, by more than fifteen kilos per head, so more cattle had to be slaughtered to obtain the same amount of meat. He recommended various technical improvements but did not dare refer to the fact that cattle-growers had been starved for credit. This would have admitted one of the worst injuries inflicted upon the economy by the "National Ideal." The commercial distribution of meat at prohibitive prices became once again, as under the Gómez dictatorship, a monopoly of certain privileged colonels. The readiness of this clique to use their power to get rich was also responsible to a great extent for the outbreak of hoof-and-mouth disease which decimated the already scanty herds.

The monopoly of the sale of meat was a typical manifestation of despotism in a country that should be swarming with cattle feeding on rich pasture lands. The statistics of international agencies corroborate the fact that Venezuela ranked with the lowest consumers of meat in Latin America (only 24.4 kilos per capita annually) and had the same low level of meat production as Honduras and Nicaragua. The same was true regarding milk. Headlines in Caracas papers on September 22, 1955, read: "Only one liter of milk is drunk per day for every five Venezuelans."

The same sad story can be told about other primary articles of consumption. The country was being covered with cement and steel construction: aerial tramways up Avila mountain, spectacular boulevards, and a replica of New York's Rockefeller Center (but three times as costly) on the central avenue of Caracas. Yet with all this ostentatious display, the country continued to get most of its food, even eggs, from abroad. In 1952, Venezuela paid $5.7 million for eggs imported from the United States. Of the total United States powdered milk exports in 1951, 67 percent went to Venezuela. In 1952, according to the chamber of commerce of La Guaira, Bs. 360 million in food was imported. From 61,000 tons of food imports in 1943, the total had more than quadrupled to 274,000 tons in 1950.

Figures like these, demonstrating the lack of national production, show that the country was not sowing the petroleum adequately or developing its own diversified economy. Each day it was becoming more and more dependent on a single diminishing resource.

It was not that consumption was growing so rapidly in the country that it was overtaking production. On the contrary, Venezuela was consuming less and less in the way of primary foodstuffs. The simplest index of a nation's prosperity is its capacity to consume its purchasing power. Official statistics of the volume of sales in the federal district in the years 1948–53 reveal that sales dropped off sharply after 1948, the last year of democratic government, despite the fact that the Caracas population grew rapidly in those five years. During this same period, the government's budget increased from Bs. 1600 million to Bs. 2500 million, yet the growing population in an area where, theoretically, more money should have been circulating, was spending less. In 1948, the Caracas public had purchased Bs. 109 million worth of clothing and Bs. 26 million worth of shoes; in 1953, these figures had dropped to Bs. 84 million and Bs. 20 million, respectively. Meat consumption was the same as seven years previously. On the other hand, jewelers sold Bs. 13 million worth of merchandise in 1948 and Bs. 19 million in 1953. In short, the basic consumption of the working population, whose wages had gone down in real value, was less, but the luxury buying of privileged minorities had shot up.

These figures for the federal district indicate what was happening elsewhere in the country, although the dictatorship concentrated most of its showy construction projects and spent at least half of its public works budget in the capital. The working population in the interior received little economic help, and its income was far below that of the workers in the capital.

Lower Income for the Worker

Without freedom to organize for the collective defense of their economic interests, the workers and the peasants had increasingly lower living standards. The real income of the Venezuelan workers had gone up sharply during the three years of democratic government (1946–48). For instance, the average daily wage in the federal district, which was Bs. 7.15 during the first three months of 1945 (practically the same level at which it had been for years) doubled to Bs. 15.11 by 1948. But the real value of this increase must be adjusted to purchasing power, as determined by the cost-of-living index. Official figures of the Central Bank of Venezuela show the following picture:

Workers' Wages

Year	Average Daily Wage	Percentage Increase	Cost-of-Living Index	Real Wage	Percentage Increase
1945	7.15	—	100	7.15	—
1948	15.11	111.32	126	11.9	67.7
1953	17.33	14.69	148	11.71	−2.3

These figures reveal the economic loss suffered by Venezuelan workers during the years under a dictatorship. During the three years of democratic government, the worker broke through traditional wage barriers and increased his purchasing power by 67.7 percent. During five years of despotism (1949–53), his actual wages were held down and he lost ground in purchasing power, by 2.3 percent. In other words, he worked more, he produced more, but he received less.

Abuse of worker productivity was another aspect of how the so-called National Welfare regime oppressed the people. An analysis of oil industry conditions is very eloquent. In 1948, there were 48,418 workers in the industry; their number was reduced to 43,884 by the end of 1953. During the same period, production grew from 79.9 million cubic meters to 102.4 million. Whether the worker was forced to work harder (which is really what happened) or whether "labor was used more efficiently" (as some oil company managers like to say, praising the absence of unions), the production increase represented a 58 percent increase in worker productivity, according to a Central Bank study. It does not explain why this increase in productivity coincides with a decrease in real wages and purchasing power. The exploitation of the working class led inevitably to economic and cultural stagnation and an abrupt interruption of the steady yearly growth of national income.

The figures show very clearly the substantial impulse the economy received during the three years of AD government and its deterioration under the military dictatorship. According to Central Bank estimates, the national income in 1936 was around Bs. 1500 million, and was more or less maintained at this incredibly low level until 1945. By 1947, however, two years after we began to govern, the national income had more than tripled to Bs. 5000 million. At the beginning of the dictatorship in 1949, national income had risen to Bs. 7000 million. But in 1953 (according to United Nations figures) national income was only Bs. 7195 million, a minimal increase of Bs. 115 million in four years. The absence of growth was due, of course, to the limited gains of the working population, which accounts for about three-fourths of total national income.

These negative figures were juggled by government propaganda both inside and outside the country. Using costly publicity, it sought to portray Venezuela as the best of all possible worlds. Certain personalities of international capitalism, which had such a solid grip on our oil wealth, acted as volunteer spokesmen for the regime. One such was George M. Humphrey, the Republican secretary of the treasury in the United States, who enthusiastically eulogized Venezuelan prosperity. During a visit to Caracas in 1954, he said "here two and two make twenty-two instead of only four."[1] It should be added that this arithmetical correction favored the oil industry and a small number of local potentates, not the impoverished majority of the population.

International agencies and reputable foreign economists were not deceived by the false claim of widespread Venezuelan prosperity. They revealed the dramatic truth. The nation was not receiving true benefit from its prodigious natural resources. According to studies of the United Nations Economic Commission for Latin America (ECLA), gross income per capita was $373 in

1945 and reached $519 by 1948. Total per capita investment rose from $182 in 1945 to $918 in 1948 but fell to $498 in 1950. In a monograph on the economic problems of development in Latin America (published by the *Encyclopaedia Britannica* in 1955), the section on Venezuela was written by Professor Raymond E. Crist of the University of Florida. He did not join the enthusiastic chorus of the oil coupon-clippers in New York and London, or cite Venezuela as an example for other Latin American countries. On the contrary, he urged them to avoid Venezuela's precarious situation. He stressed especially the low purchasing power of the Venezuelan masses, noted that it was getting lower, and concluded that "the apparent stability of Venezuela is illusory since there is an underground democratic ferment which may break out at some future time."

This evaluation must have been read with astonishment as so much publicity had been given to the fact that Venezuela had the highest per capita income in Latin America—around $800 per year. But serious economists were not deceived and sought the real reality—the redundancy is deliberate—behind this figure. For instance, a study by the Rural Welfare Council on the economy of the Venezuelan Andes reported the per capita income there as only $250 per person in 1951, less than half the national average. Even so, the study warned, living standards throughout Venezuela were not that much higher than the Andes. There was an incredibly unjust distribution of wealth—a tremendous income gap between a few hundred multimillionaires and the vast majority of the population.

Decline of Production

The previously cited figures on heavy food imports do not mean that the national production fell or remained stationary under the dictatorship. In absolute terms, it went up. The vigorous impulse given to the national economy after 1945 made possible further progress in agriculture, cattle growing, and industry. However, for lack of continued government stimulation, the increase was unnecessarily slow. In food production, the increase, based on an index of 100 in 1948, was 169 for 1953. With the exception of rice, the only items which were substantially increased in production were those for which we had provided an ample amount of credit during the democratic period: oils, vegetable fats, and sugar. The abrupt reduction of credits for the cattle-raising and fishing industries meant that these increased more slowly (the index rose from 100 to 109.7 five years later).

The textile industry actually went into decline after 1948, falling from an index of 100 in 1948 to 84 in 1950, reaching such a state of crisis by 1954 that imports had to be increased. Although the leather industry expanded, the production of shoes declined. It is noteworthy that the output of alcoholic and nonalcoholic drinks rose substantially; the country supplied itself with beer, rum and, of course, Coca-Cola. The chemical industry also made little advance. The ambitious plans of the Development Corporation to use natural gas and phosphates were put aside.

This retarded development of the Venezuelan economy was closely connected with the history of the Economic Development Corporation, the agency we had created to increase non-oil production. At the same time that other credit institutions of the government specializing in agriculture, cattle-raising, and industry were virtually abandoned to their fate, the dictatorship also changed the statutes of the Development Corporation, removing the obligation to assign it from 2 to 10 percent of the annual budget. It also ended the requirement to have business representation on the board, and the agency became a center for fraudulent deals to enrich government officials. The actual amounts assigned to the Development Corporation for long-term credits were greatly reduced, with adverse repercussions on economic activities.

Similarly with the operations of the Agricultural and Cattle Bank. In 1948, the last year of democratic government, 81,000 loans totaling Bs. 116 million had been made by the Agricultural and Cattle Bank, but only 21,000 loans for Bs. 83 million were granted in 1952. Short-term loans against crops, the seasonal credits required by poor farmers, were drastically curtailed. The bank's operations in the Andean region had gone down by a third, and its reduction of credit in the rest of the country was even greater, having diminished by 73 percent during a five year period.

On the other hand, more than Bs. 400 million were being spent annually on defense and the police. The prestige of the military had plummeted because the armed forces were regarded by the citizenry as a sort of occupation army, although more than two hundred officers of all branches were in jail or exiled and many others lived under constant surveillance. The praetorian guard of Pérez Jiménez enjoyed outrageous privileges and utilized the army commissaries to engage in blatant contraband. Another scandal was caused in building the Military Circle, a luxurious club in Caracas. Sidney Gruson of *The New York Times*, in an article published December 14, 1953, described the strange contrast of this marble palace in a country where thousands were unemployed, half a million children had no schooling, and two-thirds of the population was illiterate. *Time* magazine estimated that the true cost of this luxurious club was double the official figure of $7,600,000—6.5 times greater than what the government spent on social security and two times more than what it invested on irrigation annually.

A full-page advertisement in the Caracas press on December 5, 1954 listed the military buildings constructed during the year at a cost of more than Bs. 100 million. Improvements in the target range in Caracas—"the best in the world"—cost Bs. 8.5 million. Another Bs. 1.5 million was spent to construct the reviewing stand on the "Avenue of the Heroes" in Caracas for the little colonel and his clique.

These excessive military expenditures led, of course, to a corresponding decrease in expenditures for education, health, public services, and agriculture. For example, the budget of the armed forces for schooling—there were seven military institutes with 1500 cadets—reached nearly Bs. 11 million, approximately the same amount spent on secondary education throughout the country, with its 45 high schools and 16,000 students. As the regime sought to militarize the country, the purchases of war equipment reached record levels. In a two-year period, they amounted to more than Bs. 557 million, in addition to the Bs. 400 million spent annually on regular expenses by the Ministry of Defense. Fifty-five percent of the budget presented by Pérez Jiménez to his caricature Congress for the fiscal year 1955–56 was devoted to the ministries of what was termed "high policy," dealing primarily with the suppression of the democratic feelings of the people. Let us examine the repercussions of this irresponsible spending on education, irrigation and electrification.

Educational Bankruptcy

The catastrophic situation of primary education—the basis for the entire cultural process in any country—was revealed in a 1954 study by Vicente Costezano and E. Rivas Casado, published by the Caracas newspaper *La Esfera*, which could never be accused of hostility to the dictatorship. Of one million children aged seven to fourteen years, only 570,288 were registered for schooling. And of these, only 440,747 attended—in other words, less than half the children eligible for primary school. The remaining 600,000 swelled the ranks of the enormous legion of illiterates. Repetition of this situation year after year left the country mired in ignorance and hopelessness. In his message to Congress on April 23, 1955, Pérez Jiménez reported an increase in enrollment of 30,514 children for school during the year, less than half the annual child population increase of more than 75,000. The AD governments, in vigorously promoting primary education, had planned to have 800,000 children in school by 1952, about 80 percent of those eligible. The military regime was hostile to the people and hated intelligence. It was incapable of following through on such plans. Data published by the Ministry of Education in 1953 revealed Venezuela was going through an educational crisis as bad as that under Gómez.

In the school year 1948–49, the last budgeted for by democratic government, there were 13,500 primary school teachers. Three years later, the figure was only 15,146, and private schools largely accounted for the difference since they had 1370 more. Private schools also doubled their enrollment from 36,053 in 1948 to 72,398 in 1952. The ministry tried to ascribe this big increase in private education, where fees must be paid, to the greater freedom given to private schools. This is a false and specious argument. Private schools grow to the degree that the state fails in its duty to provide sound, free education to all the population. When this happens parents place their children in private schools, especially in the cities, the only place these institutions are found.

The only conclusion to be drawn is that the government deliberately turned its back on educating the Venezuelan people and was not interested in solving the problem of illiteracy. This is borne out by other official figures. The Ministry of Education reported in 1953 that the campaign against illiteracy was no longer limited to the big towns but had been extended throughout the country, adding that "this logiically means that after 1948, there was a decrease in the number of training centers, the number of which is now 1744." In reality, 2094 of these centers had been shut down, but the ministry cynically tried to justify the decline of the literacy campaign by claiming that it was being extended.

A logical corollary of the neglect of primary education and literacy was the lack of interest in the training of teachers. As previously mentioned, the AD governments had begun a program which, within six years, would have provided certificates for all of the nation's teaching personnel. Twelve normal schools had been set up, but the dictatorship immediately reduced this number to nine. In 1949, 3178 students were training to be teachers; three years later their number had been reduced by more than half.

As for secondary schools, the AD government had planned to increase high school attendance to 40,000 in public schools and 20,000 in other institutions, which would have doubled the enrollment of 1948–49. However, the dictatorship put an end to this: total registry in 1949 was only 22,747, and 2000 more students were turned away when the system of alternate turns in classes was eliminated. More and more students had to go to private schools, which increased from fifty-two in 1949 to eighty-one in 1952.

The educational crisis reached its climax in the universities. The university system had been revolutionized by the AD government; educational and administrative autonomy was put into effect, and liberal economic resources were provided. Many youths from the middle and working classes now were able to attend, and university enrollment tripled during the three years that we were in power.

Along with the military reaction against democratic institutions, a peculiar oligarchic mentality now prevailed in Venezuela—that of the stingy aristocrat trying to bring back the ways of the colony. This reactionary mentality characterized the dictator's minister of education, Augusto Mijares. He announced a reform of the mass education policy of AD that was nothing less than a return to the obsolete educational theories of the colony. In his Provisional Statute of Education, the government renounced control over private education. The Organic University Statute was replaced by a university law which required the payment of tuition fees, thereby reserving higher education for the monied class. This law broke the tradition of free universal education in the country that went back to the time of Guzmán Blanco in 1870, a tradition which even Gómez had respected.

The Central University, after being shut down for two years, had reopened in September 1952. Now the students were required to pay Bs. 115 to register—tuition ranging up to Bs. 1050—and an examination fee of Bs.

24. This backward step had a twofold purpose: first, to impede the entrance of lower-class youth to professional education, with the idea of eliminating the more revolutionary elements of the population from the university. Second, it was sought to create future professional elites who were not interested in reform but were imbued with the view so popular among the capitalist sectors of Venezuela that "order"—even if imposed by whiplash—better assured the peaceful enjoyment of material wealth than did democracy, which gave free play to the different social forces.

The results of the deterioration of higher education, due to police persecution and the discriminatory entrance policy of the universities, were alarming. There was an exodus of university students from the country. Some 7000 went to study in the universities of Europe, the United States, and Latin America. Some went because they were deported, others because the financial burden of studying in Venezuela was so great. This exile in the formative years of youth had unfavorable results for a whole generation of students. Postgraduate studies abroad may be useful, but basic professional education should be on one's native soil, in the environment where one is to work and live. This is not a chauvinistic idea but is generally considered valid by those who look to education for the solution of the problems of modern society.

In consequence of all this, the enrollment in national universities totaled only 6533 students. The monumental University City in Caracas had only 4000 students because Pedro Estrada and his police had driven many of those wishing higher education to universities in the interior where they would cause less trouble. The total university enrollment in 1955 was scarcely equal to that of 1948, even though the increase in population and the completion of the University City construction made possible a considerable increase in the student population.

The training of technical personnel so badly needed by the country was crippled by the brutal dictatorship. At this time, Cuba, which had a population more or less equal to ours, had 14,000 students in the University of Havana, and 4000 more in other universities—three times the number of Venezuelans studying in our universities. Furthermore, no attempt was being made in Venezuela to encourage studies in areas where professionals were badly needed, as shown by the situation in engineering. The president of the College of Engineers in Caracas, Pascual Chalbaud Cardona, reported in 1955 that Venezuela had only twenty-six petroleum engineers, thirty-six electrical engineers, and nine mechanical-electrical engineers, apparently because the courses begun in 1947 at the Central University and sponsored by the minister of production were not continued. There were only nine industrial engineers and twelve chemical engineers. Most of the total of 1847 Venezuelan graduate engineers worked at building pretentious public buildings in the cities and mansions of dubious architectural taste for members of the military-petroleum caste.

It might be said that even if the dictatorship failed in the area of education, it at least accomplished something in the less complex material field. This at least is what certain benevolent apologists say about strong governments— seeking to excuse the assaults against liberty by an alleged administrative efficiency. The Venezuelan dictatorship showed the same incompetence in other government activities as in education. Let us take the example of what happened in the program of irrigation. An irrigation program of ambitious proportions was required to upgrade the Venezuelan physical environment. This had been one of the major concerns of our democratic government but this program failed dramatically under the dictatorship, which devoted only minor sums to the program. In 1949, little more than Bs. 26 million were invested and in 1953, the sum was Bs. 25 million. At the tenth Convention of the Federation of Chambers of Commerce and Industry held at Maracaibo in 1954, an ironic resolution was passed urging the government, whose annual budget was now Bs. 2500 million, to seek loans in order to develop irrigation projects more rapidly.

The well-planned El Cenizo project, whose first stage was ready in 1948, with the irrigation of 10,000 hectares, was paralyzed and a vast fertile plain of 100,000 hectares remained without irrigation. The projects under way were stopped. New ones were not begun. Even the censored press of Caracas managed to publish some criticism of the tragic situation in a country whose soils were being destroyed by erosion and fire but where less than one percent of the total budget was devoted to soil conservation. It was not until 1953, five years after the beginning of the dictatorship, that the first irrigation project of any importance was begun in the state of Guarico. Five years had been completely lost in an area of government action which should have had top priority.

The military government also let the ambitious electrification programs begun by the AD regime run down. Inadequate resources were devoted by the state to this problem. Much of the investment consisted of loans to private companies.

When we took over in 1946, we channeled Bs. 5 million into an emergency program for a national network of small generators. In 1947, these expenditures increased to Bs. 8 million and in 1948, with a national electrification plan now fully developed, Bs. 16 million. According to the plans, these investments should have kept going up. Instead, the military government began to reduce its investments in this area and a good part of the funds assigned to electrification were loans to private companies.

In the last year of our government, electrical energy generation increased by 25 percent—this was the highest rate of increase in Latin America. However, by 1952–53, a study of the Economic Commission for Latin America of the United Nations (ECLA) showed that Venezuela—the country with the opulent treasury and the astronomical state budgets—was far behind in its per capita generation of electricity. While Argentina and Chile generated more than 300 kw-hours per capita and Uruguay, Cuba, and Costa Rica more than 200, Venezuela was one of those states which produced 100–200 kw.

According to the study made for the Federation of Chambers of Commerce in 1953, it was 123.5 kw. Finally, in 1955, the government began the much delayed electrification of the Caroní river.

Planning for this program was divided among various state agencies including the Office of Special Studies, the inefficient and pretentious superagency set up under the inept leadership of Col. Llovera Páez, one of those who enriched himself most from the November 24 movement. This office functioned in Miraflores Palace and sought to orient national productive activity according to the basic principle of Pérez Jiménez' doctrine: "prepare the country for war." The unthinking followers of this viewpoint simplified the slogan in the barracks: "The colonel is going to enlarge our map for us." These unrecognized military geniuses never said, of course, against whom they were going to fight a war or whose territory they were going to take over. They had never fired a shot except against their own defenseless people.

Crisis in Social Security and Winding Down of the War Against Malaria

There was continual tension between the government and the medical profession under the dictatorship because of the Venezuelan Institute of Social Security. The government tried to get the doctors to praise the services of this agency and, at the same time, blame them for its bankrupt and discredited status.

In 1954, a study presented to the medical college of the Federal District by M. Acosta Silva, pointed out that the government's contribution to the institute was only one-fourth of what it was supposed to be (Bs. 7 million out of nearly Bs. 27 million). Furthermore, the dictatorship had failed to provide adequate physical facilities for the social security services. In 1954, Bs. 10 million were spent on such constructions—a little more than what was spent to enlarge the shooting range (Bs. 8.5 million)—and in 1954, a special commission of the medical college urgently called for the provision of such facilities. This might have seemed strange to movie-goers of the period, accustomed to seeing propaganda films showing Pérez Jiménez inaugurating public works, especially the "biggest and best hospital in Latin America," the University City hospital of Caracas, on December 2, 1954. This event was also written up in *Time* magazine, but neither the movies nor the magazine pointed out that this hospital had been planned by the Medina administration and had been built in good part by the AD government, despite which six more years were needed before it could be inaugurated and two more years before it could operate. Medical and nursing personnel were lacking, not only here but elsewhere in the country. The country at that time, according to studies by the Red Cross, needed 10,000 nurses but there were only 1285 nursing graduates in the nation, of whom 25 percent did not practice their profession.

In any case, the entire social security operation was falling far short of what the democratic government had planned: an overall system of welfare similar to the Bererid Plan in England. The only coverage offered was for labor accidents and maternity cases. Old-age pensions, family bonuses, unemployment benefits, and other welfare payments could not be offered in a country where tax money was thrown away like confetti. Instead of a functioning social security system, there was simply a petty cash distribution in each government office.

There was not much that could be learned by those who came to Caracas in March 1955 for the fifth inter-American conference on social security convened by the OAS. Like all the other international meetings held with exceptional frequency in the Venezuelan capital as part of a propaganda strategy, the meetings also satisfied the exhibitionist craving of the colonel who always inaugurated them with a babbling speech and the customary display of decorations on his uniform. After the initial session, the working sessions would be alternated with sumptuous social affairs at which champagne and whiskey flowed like water. It was hoped to gain the gratitude and blur the judgment of those who attended these conferences with these inelegant displays of "nouveau-riche" hospitality.

The lack of true concern for the health of the country can be seen in the incredible stinginess with which this spendthrift regime treated the fight against malaria. Arnoldo Gabaldón, former director and founder of the department of Mariology of the Ministry of Health, took the risk of speaking out clearly about the problem on April 8, 1954, when he described what had been accomplished under democratic government. Some 65 percent of the Venezuelan territory had been infested by malaria, he revealed, and Venezuela had suffered more from the disease than any other Latin American state except Haiti. Some 20 percent of national territory had been completely freed of malaria, he added, so that half the national population now lived in malaria free zones; however, despite the obvious need for continuity in this work of sanitation, the government had not increased the budget for four years. Gabaldón then said as much as anyone could say without being sent to jail: "The budget of the department is less than that assigned for the collection of garbage in Caracas."

This was the government which merrily spent public funds on trivial activities, on propaganda displays, on entire editions of the *Herald Tribune* of New York, on so many unimportant magazines and newspapers either lacking in funds or ethics or both.

No More Agrarian Reform and Immigration of Undesirables

The unpopular dictatorship truly had an allergy to any kind of planned administration and always showed its preference for the privileged classes. Nothing showed this more than the way it abandoned the agrarian reform program and distorted the immigration policy.

The provisions of a 1948 law by which the state would appropriate Bs. 100 million for land reform and authorize the issue of bonds to pay for expropriation were never carried out. The agrarian communities founded by the Fomento Corporation were abruptly liquidated. It was claimed they had produced losses during their first year, as if any type of enterprise is supposed to show an immediate profit.

The credits of the Agricultural Bank no longer went to poor farmers without favoritism but now were assigned to those who had family connections or political influence. In some states, the old land-holding caste recovered control of local government and took revenge upon the poor farmers. Those who had been given land were evicted and a workday from sun-up to sun-down for the peons again became common. The big landholders insolently coined a phrase with which to reply to the complaints of the peons: "Go tell AD." Without wishing to do so, they were helping to make sure that two-thirds of the rural population would identify its fate with those of this political party.

Hundreds of families had been settled on the 10,000 hectares under irrigation by the end of 1948 in El Cenizo, but this land was now given to not more than fifty friends of the government. In 1951, the National Economic Council timidly criticized what had been done and the manner in which the cultivation was now being carried out without regard to erosion and the misuse of the irrigated lands.

The dictatorship installed a costly and unscientific farm colony at Turen. Foreign visitors were flown over this site without landing so that they would not see the desolate sight of fallow lands held by the big landowners and peons cooped up in miserable huts. The leaders of this colony were not agricultural technicians but flunkies of the dictatorship who ran the place with military discipline. It cost a tremendous amount—nobody knows how much—to install a few hundred families at this site, most of them immigrants. However, the fundamental objection is not that money was spent to promote agricultural development, because enough money will never be spent in the country for this purpose, but that there was nothing more done. The best lands of the country continued in the hands of 10 percent of the landholding aristocracy which now opened its ranks to include some of the leading figures of the regime. Many government-owned properties were transferred to these new land-holders who interpreted the doctrine of national welfare to mean the accumulation of national assets for their private use.

The paralysis of the agrarian reform program led to a decline of farm production and aggravated the social problems of the Venezuelan countryside. According to a study published in August 1956 by Alonso Calatrava, Jr., secretary of the Venezuelan Milk Council, only potatoes, sesame, and sugar cane were increasing in production out of the twenty-five products studied. Such basic dietary items as corn, rice, black beans, yuccas, copra, and cotton as well as sisal showed sharp reductions. While agriculture was in this critical condition, the dictatorship continued with its ornamental and militaristic policy. Pérez Jiménez made one of his habitual vainglorious presentations in Miraflores palace on August 31, 1956. With maps and models, he explained how the regime of national welfare was about to inaugurate a tunnel underneath Lake Maracaibo which would cost Bs. 250 million. The purpose: "The tunnel will offer military advantages."

Hatred of foreigners became common and the number of families allowed to immigrate into the country was sharply reduced. Our plans to bring Puerto Rican farm families to the country were cancelled. The dictatorship exploited the economic difficulties of the newcomers, using them for public services in Caracas instead of settling them on the land. This guaranteed a cheap source of labor and eliminated the risk of strikes. Portuguese drove buses. Italians were encouraged to form construction companies—often simply fronts whereby officials could assign public work contracts to themselves. Traffic in passports and visas became such a scandalous affair in many consulates that there were complaints from foreign governments. Prostitutes and adventurers of all nationalities descended upon Caracas, which now became a city on a permanent spree, with the government officials as the primary clientele. This was a shameful hour for Venezuela. Any kind of austerity in government disappeared. The official orgies characteristic of the time of Cipriano Castro returned. The country's government resembled a pig sty, a brothel, an outhouse.

Submerged as they were in this licentious morass, those responsible for public administration had little time to reflect upon the true problems of the country. Together with the habitual aristocratic stupidity of autocratic governments, this helps to explain the lack of planning for those activities not paralyzed altogether after having been begun by the democratic government. Such was the case with housing. Housing continued to be built under the dictatorship but on a retarded timetable which did not correspond with the magnitude of the problem. The dictatorship has widely publicized its construction of buildings and individual houses, making this subject especially interesting to examine.

It has already been explained how the AD governments had to start from scratch in housing policy—planning, selecting, and obtaining land; organizing constructions services; and even improvising the supply of materials. These difficulties were overcome in the first two years. In 1948, 2000 units were considered to be constructed in an effort to reach the goal of 4000 annually then thought necessary. This program was in full swing when the military took over. However, in 1949, the junta limited itself to finishing the construction begun in 1948.

Even though new construction was begun thereafter, by 1952 the government was still 10 percent under the amount of housing construction by AD in 1948. By now, however, the increase in population of a quarter million each year required the construction of 40,000 new houses per year as well as the improvement of the deplorable conditions under which most Venezuelans were living.

Apartments and Super Apartments—Without Plans

It is generally admitted that the problem of housing cannot be solved in any country without relating it to the other problems of the country. In the case of underdeveloped peoples, it is closely connected with agrarian reform and industrialization. The rural dweller must be given land if his exodus toward urban areas, accompanied by a shortage of housing, is to be avoided. Industrial development of any given zone must coincide with massive construction of new housing. The dictatorship however, did not have any criterion of this sort. It simply constructed houses and apartments in the capital without trying to corollate its construction with economic development or extending construction to the rest of the republic.

In a country such as Venezuela, government action on housing should have three aspects: financial assistance to construct housing, encouragement to house owners to improve their own dwellings, and protection against speculation by landlords for those who rent.

The dictatorship appointed people of little integrity to head the regulatory commission and, certainly as a result of bribes by landlords, they raised rents. This discredited the rent control office to such a degree that it was finally abolished. The population remained without any kind of protection. In 1949 and following years, prices at last began to go down somewhat, but this saving was not reflected in the cost of living because of the increase in rents. Professor Francis Violich, in a United Nations publication (*Housing and Town and Country Planning*, New York, 1954, page 94), pointed out that although Venezuela had the highest per capita income in Latin America, even those with the highest income often had to pay at least one-third of their income in rent.

Not only was the policy of rent control abandoned; programs to improve housing through community cooperation were also terminated. Plans to construct new housing in cities of the provinces were ignored. All efforts were concentrated in Caracas in order to make it a tourist showplace—a kind of mirror where those who governed could admire and congratulate themselves for the way they were amassing quick fortunes and providing work for propaganda film-makers.

At least half of all public expenditures were made in Caracas. Taken together with the end of agrarian reform, this meant a continual migration from the countryside to the city. By 1955, 15 percent of all Venezuelans lived in the narrow valley where the capital was located. The population of Caracas grew out of all proportion to the rate of increase in the country. The torrential accumulation of people in the federal district did not coincide with industrial development there. Sao Paulo in Brazil had a similar population increase but it came along with a growth of new industry providing jobs. In the Venezuelan capital, on the contrary, employment grew in commerce and construction due to the distribution of foreign merchandise and the transitory spurt of building avenues and edifices, but industrial activity declined.

Between 1936-41, Venezuela increased its population by 14 percent while the capital area increased 34 percent. Between 1941–50, the republic increased 29.47 percent while the capital increased 92.6 percent.

Professor Violich, in the United Nations study cited above, used the Venezuelan case to warn that urban construction should not be carried on without relating it to the other problems of the nation. He declared the growth of Caracas was producing an "unbalanced and backward" situation with a need for low-cost housing to be used by a population which itself was working mostly in construction. "Caracas can never be an industrial center of the country," he warned. "Once the wave of construction falls off, there will not be the employment which exists today. Meanwhile the construction of more housing will only serve to attract more people to the city." He urged overall national development as the logical solution for the problem of excess population in Caracas.

The dictatorship indignantly replied to these warnings. The pro-government newspaper *El Heraldo* on October 27, 1954, said the Venezuelans could solve their own housing problem without advice from United Nations experts. It attacked Professor Violich as a political refugee figure from Europe. Perhaps the editorialist was unaware that this man was an urban planning professor for the University of California. Marco Antonio Casanova, head of the Workers' Bank, also accused Professor Violich of "bad faith" and boasted of the "Cerro Piloto" project then in construction at a cost of Bs. 250 million, the first stage of a Bs. 600 million project to eliminate the huts from the poverty-stricken hillsides which so marred the monumental Caracas.

Pérez Jiménez inaugurated this project on December 2, 1954, the second anniversary of his takeover. The official propaganda told of forty super apartments which could house 30,000 people. *Time* magazine of November 1, 1954 described the manner in which the dictatorship went about these projects as a military occupation with armed police guarding cleared land and preventing families evicted from huts to squat on the land again. "With this combination of energy and firmness," the magazine wrote, "Pérez Jiménez proposes to eliminate all the ghettos in the capital in the next five years."

However, the magazine did not mention how Cerro Piloto turned out to be another mess as the result of the improvisation. Just the buildings' facades were inaugurated on December 2. Apparently there was not enough money to finish the interiors. Also, nobody had figured out how to get water up to the hillsides in a city which was only half-supplied already.

The above should make it clear that even if Venezuela is constructing houses and apartments with public funds at a rate now superior to other Latin American countries, no lasting solution has been devised for the housing problem. On the contrary, it is sowing the seeds for great future difficulties. There is much yet left to write concerning other areas of public administration, which will reveal how this arbitrary government had an almost vicious tendency to make mistakes. I will continue to describe these errors, although with bitter reluctance because of my love for my country which prevails over my political instincts.

22

Venezuela: Oil Factory

Beginning a Surrender Policy

On May 9, 1949, several United States newspapers published an interview in Caracas with Pedro Ignacio Aguerrevere, the first minister of production of the military government. It was the first public expression of what the new government's oil policy would be. It was apparent that there would be a return to the old colonialist surrender policy of Juan Vicente Gómez. Reversing the policy of national liberation begun by the AD governments, he said: "The new Caracas government may lighten the tax burden of the United States oil companies." After explaining that he had been "educated in North America," at Stanford and in the Colorado School of Mines, he went on to recall his long years of service with the oil companies.

Aguerrevere announced disapproval that the previous government had taken half of the profits of the foreign companies. He spoke just like an oil company lawyer when he said: "Venezuela is fundamentally an exporter; the cost of production is basic. We cannot play around lightly with taxes."

He recalled that no concessions had been awarded for three years, but mentioned that the AD minister of production, Juan Pérez Alfonzo, who stood for the no concessions policy, was in jail and that "the new government would change this policy." With simple mercantile logic, he deliberately ignored the solid doctrinal base for AD's policy when he said: "It is not logical to shut the door on the national treasury and throw away the key." He concluded by repeating the propaganda of the avid new concessions hunters to the effect that synthetic fuels or other energy sources would soon replace petroleum.

320

At the time these words were spoken, the Paley report prepared for the president of the United States had been published. Its main conclusion was that world demand for petroleum would continue to increase for the next twenty-five years.

It should be no surprise that the representative in Venezuela of the Inter-American Council of Commerce and Production, Tom Lumpkin, confessed the sympathy of the exclusive millionaire syndicate for the new regime.

The oil companies surveyed the Venezuelan panorama after the November 1948 coup and found it very much to their liking. They had their reasons, as Lumpkin confessed with candor. Instead of having to deal with a democratic government, strong in moral authority because of winning power by a majority vote, they now faced a military group with inferiority complexes due to the spurious nature of their mandate. The democratic government's coherent ideological program had been executed by men with high personal and political ethics. The adventurers who seized power, however, had no clear idea of a desirable relationship between Venezuelan state and foreign investors. They completely lacked moral scruples and had an almost sensual appetite for power as well as an urge to command, so typical of people with a Spanish heritage. This government clique, just like totalitarian groups installed in other nations, engages in all kinds of fraudulent practices, influence peddling, and administrative corruption—a sewer in which companies organized during the Gómez regime would operate with great familiarity.

Finally, the usurping government hated the working classes because they openly repudiated the politicians. They were consequently predisposed to liquidate the union movement and leave the workers completely defenseless. The worker movement was persecuted after the coup, and the National Confederation of Workers was dissolved by executive decree on February 25, 1949. The oil companies prepared to take maximum advantage of favorable circumstances arising from the facts that a responsible popular government had been replaced by one imposed by force, whose leaders did not worry about the future of the country. They had an easy time in their relations with officials of the new government. But it was different with the public. The ordinary Venezuelan citizen now had a fair idea of what the petroleum problem was all about. In this situation, companies had to go beyond their lobbying in ministerial offices and so mounted a clever campaign of confusion in the press. Their purpose was to convince the public that it was necessary to reverse the AD oil policy, arguing that it had been leading the country to economic and fiscal disaster.

The *Scientific American* spokesman for this crusade of confusion was an economist who worked for the Chase Manhattan Bank and Standard Oil—Joseph Pogue, author of many works on oil economics, but well-known for his preference for big companies. Pogue visited Venezuela early in 1949 and gave a highly publicized talk at the College of Engineers in Caracas, profusely illustrated with statistical charts and graphs. These were published in the press and edited later in a booklet, thousands of copies of which were distributed free of charge in all the schools of the country. Pogue's basic idea was that the great national slogan, "The oil must be sown," must be complemented with another, "Let us not lose our customers." In order not to lose them, he said frankly, Venezuela must tax the oil companies less, turn over its national oil reserves for production to the foreigners and go back to the colonial system of the days of Gómez.

Pogue sought to instill fear among the Venezuelans regarding a nationalistic oil policy. To do this, he used concepts familiar in commercial circles where keeping the customer happy is a very important matter. However, he silenced the fact that the customer had a very secondary role in the oil business, especially in Venezuela. Petroleum is not merchandise produced according to one's desires. On the contrary, it is a natural resource found only at certain places in the world, in limited quantities. While oil cannot be manufactured by man, there are more and more new uses for which it is employed. Thus, anyone halfway familiar with the industry knows that demand is not the determining factor in the oil business; rather, it is the oil reserves available and those which can be found.

The founder of Royal Dutch Shell, Henry Deterding, reportedly said on the eve of the First World War: "Petroleum is the most unusual product in world trade—its sale is only limited by what can be produced. There is no other article in the world of which it can be said that its consumption is assured from the moment that it is produced."

However, in his effort to prove that markets, not production, are the "key to the oil industry," Pogue stressed that the domestic consumption of oil in Venezuela was small in comparison to that produced. Since so much of Venezuela's oil was sold abroad, he tried to emphasize the importance of cost differentials in the alleged fight for markets. Trying to portray a bitter contest among the producers, he even made false statements. Pogue showed himself bitterly unscrupulous in his use of facts and manipulation of figures. He was obviously trying to demonstrate that the taxes levied by the AD government made oil production unprofitable. In describing the oil law of 1943, he claimed that the government had given information to Congress showing that the sum of the oil royalty payments plus other taxes would give the nation an income equal to the net earnings of the industry. Anyone in Venezuela who has followed the oil question knows that this was not the case. The officials of the Medina Angarita government had always claimed that with a royalty of 16.66 percent of gross production, the nation and the companies would benefit equally from industry profits. Pogue's further claim that the evolution of the 50/50 formula involved a tax on capital—and was therefore hidden confiscation—was also untrue.

These arguments of the Chase Manhattan Bank economist and the Creole Petroleum Corporation regarding the difficulties Venezuelan oil would have in the world market in competing with other producing areas because of high production cost found their way into the Venezuelan press, along with columns, editorials, and manipulated statistics. Those able and willing to combat this poison were in jail or in exile; their writings banned from the Venezuelan newspapers.

An unexpected move by the companies was synchronized with this psychological offensive in the press. The big three—Creole, Shell, and Mene Grande—reduced their production by some 200,000 barrels daily. This was about 15 percent of the 1948 output, averaging 1,350,000 barrels daily. The restrictions had a crippling effect. New plants were delayed as investments and production went down. According to *U.S. News and World Report*, between 15–18,000 workers were laid off by oil companies or the contractors working for them. Pogue insisted that the drop in production was due to "increased competition and less demand throughout the world." However, he did not mention that as production decreased in Venezuela, it increased by more than a half a million barrels a day in the Middle East. Also, there was another contradiction: if production was falling due to a decline in world demand, then how could he attribute the decline in output to the fact that Venezuela was not assigning new oil concessions.

Plot by the Cartel to Gain Control of New Concessions

The publicity campaign of the companies in 1949 and the reduction of production the same year were obviously intended to encourage public support for new concessions promised by the military government. It was also hoped that future departures from AD's policy giving the country a higher percentage of the oil income could be justified.

There were various reasons why the oil concessions were not immediately forthcoming. The most important was the need for the companies to maintain reduced production for a year to reinforce their argument for new concessions. By 1950 the production was backed up not only over 1949 but also more than 1948, which had been a record year in the history of the national oil industry. In 1950, production was 546 million barrels—12 percent more than in 1948. This increase was achieved by intensifying production from already active wells, and by drilling new wells. This confirmed our two viewpoints: the existing concessions were fifty times larger than the oil fields in production, and the decrease of exploratory activity in 1949 was due to the companies' deliberate policy of limiting production in order to pressure the government for new oil concessions and thus control all oil reserves in the country.

At the beginning of 1952, John Laudon, director of the Shell group in Venezuela, told the press that "to increase Venezuelan production, it is necessary for the companies to have new concessions where they can carry out widespread exploration. Representations are being made to the government in this regard." With a lack of embarrassment which would have been amazing if it had not been so habitual among the oil managers, this spokesman for the English oil interests propagated a great falsehood—to increase oil production, which topped 600 million barrels in 1951, it was not necessary to obtain new concessions. The companies already had enough to increase production from operating wells and to drill hundreds of new wells in the vast area handed over to them as concessions by government before AD.

More precise information about those "representations to the government" to which Loudon referred were published in the foreign press. The *Oil and Gas Journal* of January 21, 1952, said that the military junta was going to issue new concessions. Offers of more than 100 million dollars had already been received, the magazine reported. Among the new companies interested were Cities Service (with which the former minister of production, Pedro Ignacio Aguerrevere was connected), the Coronado Petroleum Corporation, and Superior Oil. The magazine also mentioned that there was some opinion against new concessions. It was something more than an opinion. It was a resolution of the legitimate Congress of 1948, after free and open debate, by which all new concessions had been suspended. From the underground, the AD party invoked this resolution on September 13, 1952, by issuing a manifesto denouncing the secret negotiations taking place and stating:

> These negotiations carried out behind the backs of the Venezuelans and without their consent do not legally commit the nation in case they are finalized. The oil companies and the governments of the countries from which they come are fully aware that the government representative of the people's free choice has been overthrown and that a small military clique without popular support has temporarily usurped power.

Italy and France had invoked similar resolutions, providing precedents for nonrecognition of concessions made by the present government. After the fall of Mussolini and Petain, the governments which followed annulled or changed their administrative actions in accord with the public interest. In France, the process was regulated by the ordinance issued in Algiers by General de Gaulle on August 9, 1944, referring to the "reestablishment of republican legality in continental territory." This instrument proclaimed that the republic had never ceased to exist in law and nullified all actions of the government which had been imposed upon France.

Two Fallacious Arguments: The Need for New Concessions and the Need to Diversify the Industry

It is well known that the oil industry must retain a satisfactory margin of proved reserves if it is to maintain a normal production rate. Since 1948, there had been much speculation—sometimes the result of ignorance, sometimes to serve the interests of the oil trusts—that the no concessions policy made it impossible to discover new oil fields and thus to guarantee production at a certain level. The industry needed ample land in order to maintain this favorable ratio between proved reserves and production. New fields must be discovered or existing ones enlarged so new reserves could more than make up for oil produced during the year.

Although the future of petroleum seemed very bright, no one could contend under prevailing economic conditions in Venezuela that it would be a good idea to postpone the discovery of new reserves, thus reducing the future ratio between reserves and production. The oil cartel possessed a great number of concessions on which there had been no drilling or even exploration, so it would have been quite possible to increase or maintain the reserves in Venezuela.

By the end of 1947, the oil industry had explored 168,485 hectares and had discovered 1160 million cubic meters of oil reserves. In the six years following, it produced 546 million cubic meters, leaving 462 million cubic meters of the 1947 reserves. By this time, however, the total reserves were actually 1.550 million cubic meters, despite the oil taken from the wells during the six previous years. A total of 926 million cubic meters of new reserves had been added as a result of additional exploratory drilling on this acreage, as well as by new exploratory wells on 55,695 other hectares of existing concessions. The additional 55,965 hectares explored were scarcely one percent of the total concessions held by the industry. The amount of new acreage drilled averaged 9282 hectares annually. If drilling were to be continued at this rate it would take 635 years for the companies to explore all of their remaining concessions.

This state of affairs should convince us that at no time in the immediate future will there be a need for new concessions to maintain the present high production level. The amount of non-explored concessions is so great that it would be possible to increase our oil output even if that were necessary.

During the six years after 1948, production rose from 1,338,800 barrels daily to 1,900,000 in 1954. The 1948 production was 2.5 times that of the war years average, but the 1954 level was 43 percent more than 1948. This was accomplished by drilling new exploratory wells on only 9282 hectares annually.

An even more decisive argument against new concessions was the fact that the companies did not want to release any of their existing concession acreage. They continued to pay taxes on acreage not being explored since they were sure that millions of barrels could be produced there when they decided to drill them. The oil business in Venezuela is no longer a matter of high risk. The possibilities of finding oil on the non-explored territory, according to published work, can be measured with considerable accuracy by studying the results of wildcat wells drilled in previous years.

In 1948 and 1949, one well out of a little more than three was productive. For these same years in the United States, only two wildcats out of every fifteen drilled was commercially productive. In other words, it was 2.7 times easier to discover new oil wells in Venezuela than in the United States.

The trend during the following three years was even more significant. The percentage of success in Venezuela went up; that of the United States went down. The Venezuelan success factor was 47.37 percent, or almost one out of every two wells. The United States had success in only 11.06 percent of the wells drilled. In other words, it was 4.2 times easier to find new oil in Venezuela during these years than in the United States. This ratio of success was due more to the higher percentage of successful wells found by Venezuelan drilling each year than to the decline of American wildcat results.

For 1952, the risk differential between Venezuela and the United States—1.11 versus 8.05, was 4.2 times in favor of Venezuela, which meant that while it took 9.05 wildcats in the United States for one producer, this number of exploratory wells would have established 4.2 producing wells in our country. It is claimed that a ratio of sixteen hectares for every barrel of oil produced is required in the United States to maintain production. However, if the productivity differential is applied to Venezuela, a ratio of only 2,232 square meters—or slightly less than one-fourth of a hectare—would be required per barrel of oil. Thus, production of 1,800,000 barrels daily would require 420,000 hectares to be under production. However, the actual facts are that production in 1947 was 1,338,000 barrels daily on just 168,485 hectares; by 1952, production had gone up to 1,900,000 barrels just by putting 55,695 additional hectares to use.

The amount of potential oil-bearing national reserve lands remaining is not as great as believed. The petroleum office of the Ministry of Mines and Petroleum in 1952 increased—without explanation—the estimated amount of such land to 35 million hectares—40 percent more than estimated in 1947. Existing concessions make up 19.9 percent of this total as compared to 25 percent in 1947.

It should be remembered, however, that much of this acreage—a total of 5,241,946 hectares—was formerly held by the oil companies but, under the law, was returned to the nation after having been evaluated. Other lands were also returned to the nation as concessions expired. The companies, first of all, selected those lands which seemed most promising to them, keeping them for production. The land returned by the companies was considered second grade at the time. If they had another chance to evaluate it now by new geophysical methods, they would be able to take the best of what is still in the hands of the nation.

The above facts demonatrate, first, that a minimum percentage of the enormous concessions presently held by the companies has actually been explored. Second, by increasing the production on relatively small acreage, the companies were able to greatly increase their production during 1948–53. Third, reserves have been greatly increased without adding to concession acreage. Fourth, the U.S. estimates of acreage required to establish reserves do not apply to Venezuela because of our greater productivity per well. Fifth, much of the present national reserves have already been previously held by the companies, evaluated, and returned to the nation. Sixth, a new round of concessions to the companies would give the oil cartel practically total control of all the nation's remaining oil lands.

Since all of these arguments were irrefutable, another propaganda line was brought up—that the new concessions would be put in the hands of "small investigators." Robert Brinsmade, one of the most active of those that were flocking to the Ministry of Mines and Petroleum and Miraflores palace in pursuit of new oil concessions, claimed to represent a group of independent investors from Texas. He suggested that monopolistic control by the Big Three of the oil industry would be loosened if competitors from among the so-called independents disputed matters with the giants already there. This would bring about a healthy degree of diversification in the industry. The small companies which operated or wanted to operate in Venezuela, and which ingeniously sought to win concessions on the basis of confronting the big companies already there, were actually affiliates of the powerful trusts. They did not have acreage in our country because they arrived late to the concessions carnival, but in the United States they were included among the most powerful companies. Four of these small companies ready to confront Standard Oil were the Texas Company, the Cities Service Corporation, the Phillips Petroleum Company, and the Atlantic Refining Company. All were among the twenty largest oil companies of the United States.

"With an understanding of the international nature of the oil industry, it can be affirmed that this alleged 'diversification' is impossible in practice and is merely a verbal expression," Pérez Alfonzo commented. In one form or another, the Big Seven control most production, refining, transport, and marketing in the non-Soviet world. It will be pointed out later in this book that they are not interested in encouraging market competition with Venezuelan oil but would prefer an agreement for international regulation.

Likewise, it is of interest to Venezuela to choose the best method of developing its oil reserves without resorting to concessions. In any case, the concession system cannot be continued because we know all about our natural wealth and are determined to defend it. We are through turning over our wealth for extended periods of time for exploitation by foreign companies under contracts written in colonial terms.

These foreign companies know that the Venezuelan people support this viewpoint. They know that it will finally prevail and that their present concessions expire after forty years in accord with the 1943 law. That is why they have resorted to all kinds of maneuvers and pressures upon an irresponsible government to obtain renewal of their concessions and to continue their positions of privilege.

The dictatorship balked. It knew that public opinion, including sectors of the armed forces, was hostile to going back to the old Gómez method of handing out concessions as if they were the private possession of government officials. Symptomatic of the hesitation was the report of the Ministry of Mines and Petroleum—the first in three years of government—presented in 1953 to the national constituent assembly. It not only failed to mention plans to award new concessions; it even included statistics and arguments that seemed contrary to the idea. For instance, it pointed out that the oil fields had increased between 1948 and 1952 from 168,488 hectares to 270,720 hectares. With this small increase in acreage—scarcely 100,000 hectares—production had increased from 1,300,000 to 1,700,000 barrels daily. The area under production covered all but 4.31 percent of the vast land under concessions— 6,281,279 hectares. The proved reserves had been increased by 24 percent, the report concluded, so the increased production "has not had the significance of checks issued against a bank account into which no new funds have been deposited."

Just a year later, however, the theme of new concessions was again big news in the oil publications in the United States, although inside Venezuela nothing was said. Officials of the Venezuelan embassy in Washington wrote an article with a Cold War title of *Venezuelan Oil: Fundamental Pillar of the Free World* for *Oil Forum* in New York in November, 1954, in which he said that the Venezuelan government would definitely issue new concessions under the traditional system of free enterprise and respect for private investment—a system which has proved superior in all practical situations as well as by scientific analysis.

Another year passed without much talk about the subject but in November 1955, the president of the chamber of commerce in Caracas, Feliciano Pacanins, in a sudden and unexpected move announced support of his organization for new concessions. This was taken as evidence that the negotiations between companies and the government, carried out in secret, were very advanced. A few months later the regime decided to take the plunge. No doubt Pérez Jiménez and his partners were worried, given the memory of the violent events which led to the overthrow of Juan Domingo Perón after it was announced that oil concessions would be given to Standard Oil of California. However, there were other factors which led the Caracas government to open the spigot: the pressure of the Big Seven of the international oil cartel who saw their only opportunity to get what they wanted in Venezuela; plus the bankruptcy of public finances due to the disorganized, wasteful, and corrupt administration. There was also, of course, the irrepressible hunger of the influence-peddlers to increase their already huge wealth. They were sure to obtain commissions of at least six digits in what would be the business deal of the century.

On February 11, 1956, just four days before the student repressions in Caracas, a spectacular was staged in Miraflores palace with Pérez Jiménez—uniformed and super-decorated; his docile ministers; a pompous and ineffective National Council of Production; industrialists and businessmen, fawning upon those in power; newspapermen, photographers, and television cameras. The dictator himself, acting as a ventriloquist's dummy, tamely repeated the two arguments constantly voiced by the cartel in favor of new concessions: "We must prevent oil investment capital from going to other countries. Our oil reserves must be maintained or increased."

Nothing was said, of course, about production and refining of petroleum by ourselves or for the exclusive benefit of the country as was done elsewhere in Latin America: in Mexico, Brazil, Chile, Uruguay, and even in impoverished Bolivia. A government that acted in multimillionaire fashion and wasted huge amounts on propaganda and political espionage did not have any money left to invest in the development of oil reserves itself. The humble vassal did not dare to enter into the prohibited lands of his lord and master. *La Espera* in Caracas of February 12, 1956, wrote, "General Pérez Jiménez stated that the government could not at this time get involved in oil production since it was interested, or rather, committed to the development of other economic activities."

He did not list those activities, but he probably meant the aerial tramway up the Avila Mountain, the luxury hotel that the government built on the highest peak, or the city boulevards where the Cadillacs of the dictator and his body guards could race at 100 kilometers per hour.

The arguments which were made to justify the unjustifiable can be easily refuted. How could Venezuela, in 1956, when it had full knowledge of what the oil business was all about, repeat the same wasteful policy Juan Vicente Gómez had applied thirty years ago? "Oil investment capital must be prevented from going to other countries," said Pérez Jiménez. Was it not enough to have Bs. 8,635,000 of foreign capital invested in this single industry at the end of 1954? The threat that the oil cartel might be tempted to leave the country was the kind of fairy tale with which Venezuelan grandmothers in times past used to frighten their grandchildren. Anerica is the most attractive zone for oil investment, as demonstrated in June, 1956, when Texas Oil (Texaco) acquired the assets of Trinidad Oil Company in Trinidad for $170 million, double the value of the capital of an oil company which produced barely one million metric tons per year.

Outside of the western hemisphere, where would the oil money go if it left Venezuela? The only other large producing zone is the Middle East and there the cartel members have already staked out positions. Economically, it is an occupied zone. Furthermore, it is an area bristling with problems and insoluble conflicts and very much within reach of Soviet maneuvers. At the present time, there is no zone in the world more subject to risks for western investment, because of political upsets, than the Middle East where Jews and Arabs—the latter armed by the Russians—live in a permanent state of undeclared war, and where there is a constant underground diplomatic struggle between the Russians and the Anglo-American bloc. There is even a harsh fight there between London and Washington because of oil. The English accuse Saudi Arabia of using dollars provided by the Arabian American Oil Company (Texaco) to finance anti-British campaigns throughout the Arab world.

These and other problems arising from disputes over spheres of influence in the Middle East, were among the most important issues discussed in the 1955 meeting of Prime Minister Eden with President Eisenhower. It should therefore be discounted that the oil companies will pack up and leave the Venezuelan oil fields, or move their equipment and capital to those desert lands over which the shadow of the prophet still passes and where his call to holy wars still resounds.

"The oil reserves must be maintained or increased," added the dictator. In terms of being reelected, Pérez Jiménez had one thing in common with certain American politicians: "The oil companies would not be against him," according to a phrase attributed to the former United States Ambassador to Venezuela, Fletcher Warren, in an interview published by the *Washington Post* and the *Times Herald* in January 1956. The government, through a company of its own, by direct exploration or by contacts with third parties, could have and should have carried out the work of exploration, located new pools of oil, and thus increased the total volume of reserves.

These considerations were not taken into account by the arbitrary government which acted without any congressional control or public criticism. The immoral influence-peddling in Venezuela was known both inside and outside of the country. A communiqué of the Ministry of Mines and Petroleum on February 11, 1956, which accompanied the statements of Pérez Jiménez, ended with this hymn to administrative morality: "It must be emphatically stated that payments to obtain concessions must be made only and exclusively to the national treasury. The government does not have and does not need intermediaries inside or outside of the country's territory."

It may have been hoped that these statements would be amplified when the dictator presented his annual message to his pseudo-Congress, but not the least reference was made to the new concessions. When he spoke on April 21, 1956, clear demonstration of the incredible absurdity of the situation and his subconscious disdain for Congress had already been shown by the manner in which he picked his docile menagerie trained for a congressional circus. Now he even forgot to carry out the charade. According to the oil law, it should have been this Congress, which he did not even bother to inform, that should have given the stamp of apparent legality to the new concessions.

The first lot of concessions was awarded in June, 1956. Venezuelans who read the *New York Times* were able to learn about it on June 3. The press in Venezuela was not allowed to publish the news transmitted by the press agencies. The first concessions went to the members of the international oil cartel already in the country or, to paraphrase a Venezuelan saying: "The same foreigners smoking the same pipe." The concessions were in Lake Maracaibo, the most fabulous oil pool in the world, where petroleum spurts out almost as soon as the drills scratch the lake bottom. The companies favored in the first fraudulent giveaway were all North American or British. They got eight blocks covering 80,000 hectares.

The foreign press also informed the Venezuelans of the details of later concessions—grants which were not allowed to be publicized in Venezuela. Up to the time when this was written, the new concessions covered 400,000 hectares, many of them including national reserve acreage that, as *Time* magazine stated, could be considered money in the bank.

The Minister of Mines and Petroleum, Luongo Cabello, made it clear that this was just a beginning, as the official plans contemplated awarding 7,400,000 acres more, which together with the 6,000,000 hectares already under control of the companies, would have meant the virtual occupation of the nation by foreign concerns. The so-called Big Three—Creole (Jersey Standard), Shell, and Mene Grande (Gulf)—which already controlled 90 percent of the production, were favored in this extraordinary operation resembling horse trading at a gypsy fair. Most of the other companies receiving acreage were conspicuous members of the oil cartel, but there were several newcomers. According to the *New York Times*, one of these was "the subject of many commentaries." It was the Venezuelan leasehold, whose president, Enrique J. Brandt, was an intimate friend of Pérez Jiménez. It received various concessions, including one of 800 hectares in the best part of Lake Maracaibo. Since none of the directors were oil men, according to the newspaper report, it sold its concessions to the San Jacinto Oil Company of Texas. This kind of agreement was reminiscent of deals by the so-called Venezuelan Petroleum Company, understood to be the "Company of General Gómez" during the early days of the industry in Venezuela.

Various comments might be made about Venezuelan Leaseholds. There was no valid reason why the state itself could not have operated the concessions directly or through drilling contracts similar to what the concessionaire arranged with the company from Texas. The same argument could have been applied to all of the concessions but the case of Venezuelan Leaseholds is particularly significant; the beneficiary was not an operating company but simply a suspicious intermediary.

Venezuelan Leaseholds was a mysterious company incorporated in Liberia under the presidency of Leon Ross, while Brandt was the head of the Venezuelan affiliate. Its directors included such personages as Reinaldo Herrera Uslar, who gained fame in New York for the parties that he gave at the Waldorf Astoria; and Nikita Harwich, brother-in-law of Laureano Vallenilla, Minister of Interior in the Pérez Jiménez government and one of the most influential members of the palace set. With this kind of sponsorship, the plans of this particular company rolled on well-oiled tracks and Venezuelan Leaseholds received $3 million from San Jacinto, plus a permanent royalty on any production for the original owners of the concession: Brandt, Herrera Uslar, Harwich, and Ross. But were they alone?

There were more mysterious companies mixed up in the concessions scandal. Another one which received a big slice of national reserves was the Superior Oil Company, whose president, Howard Beck, was being investigated at that very time by a federal grand jury in the United States for having used company money to finance the so-called gas lobby, a criminal offense. These were the new people with whom Venezuela was making contracts to "diversify its oil industry."

It could not be alleged that the new ground for oil concessions was needed by the United States and the west in general because of the Suez crisis. The Egyptian nationalization of the canal and the aggressive attitude of the Arabs came after the events in Venezuela. Also, Venezuela was producing 2.5 million barrels of oil daily by that time, more than anyone had forecast.

The new concessions were for forty years, the same amount of time allowed by Gómez at the beginning of the century and to d'Arcy by the Persian monarch, in contracts inherited by the Anglo-Persian Oil Company. At this time, no one anywhere was handing out concessions for such a long period of time. The basic clause in these contracts signed in Caracas between midnight and the crowing of the cock was the immediate payment of enormous sums as an initial bonus. According to early information, these payments would exceed $350 million.

In summary, this reprehensible deal using the non-renewable wealth of Venezuela was carried out under the following circumstances:

1. The contracts were signed in clear contradiction of the popular opinion of the country expressed when there had been freedom to do so; this opinion had acquired legal status when it was expressed in legislative form by the legitimate Congress of 1948.

2. These concessions were awarded by an usurping executive and a rubber stamp Congress, both results of disregard for the 1952 elections. This fact was published and commented upon by the leading newspapers in the countries from which the new investments came.

3. The people of Venezuela were kept completely in the dark on all phases of the process which culminated in these scandalous negotiations. Not a single article of adverse commentary published in Venezuela could be exhibited in the future as demonstration that there had been any discussion at all on a subject so vital to the nation.

The oil companies obtained their new concessions in 1956, but they had already, in 1950, attained one of their most desired goals in Venezuela—the return to the days of Gómez' tax policies. With the obvious complicity of the government, the oil cartel again converted Venezuela into its private fief, to be exploited and impoverished at a spectacular rate.

The Extortion of Venezuela by the Companies, in Figures

To back up the statement just made, statistics reveal the dramatic reality— figures that can be understood by anyone with a modest knowledge of economic and fiscal matters. The difference between the value of the oil that was exported from the country and the money that was paid or invested in the national economy will show which changes occurred. All of this information is available in Central Bank bulletins. All one has to do is make a comparison between what Venezuela got for its oil under AD and what it failed to get under the dictatorship to understand why the oil companies were increasing their dividends to stockholders and how the betrayal of those in the government had been paid for.

During the three years of AD government (1946–48), the value of oil exported from the country for each year was $648 million, $665 million, and

$1081 million. During these same years, bolivares purchased from the Central Bank were worth $301 million, $442.5 million, and $675 million. Thus, during three years, $1418.5 million were put back into the country while $2230.4 million were exported. In other words, 63.6 percent or $.63 of every oil dollar was returned to the country without taking into account salaries paid directly in dollars or the dollar value of merchandise imported by the industry.

During 1949, the first year of the dictatorship, the situation remained much the same. The companies carried out massive layoffs of workers but paid them indemnities. The memories left by the energetic Venezuelan policy of AD was very fresh. Both the companies and the government hesitated before returning to colonial methods. However, in following years, the big international oil consortium operated without restraint. Oil production records were broken in 1950. With exports reaching a value of $1217 million in that year alone, $522.3 million remained in the country—46 cents per barrel as compared to the 63 cents under AD. The following year, 1951, oil exports were $1418.4 million and the companies returned only $600 million to the country, only 43 cents per barrel.

Exports this year were 28 percent higher than in 1948, the last year of democratic government. Instead of receiving more income, the country received less—$608 million versus $675.2 million in 1948, or $67 million less. If the same conditions had prevailed as during the three years of 1945–48, the country would have received 66 percent of the total value of its oil exports, during the two year period of 1950–51.

In only two years (1950–51), did the excess earnings by the oil industry in Venezuela equal one year's national budget of the Venezuelan government and one-fourth of the total capital invested in the oil industry. Some ingenuous person might believe that the tolerance of this swindle of the nation was due to the lack of experience of the military junta in their early days. On the contrary, the impoverishment of the country continued to increase along with growth in earnings of the oil companies. No written agreement was needed between the companies and the government. It was a question of mutual convenience. The government had no support from the public and was impotent when confronting the aggressive international oil companies. The military and the police under control of a small group of cronies of the little despot could deprive the people of their rights but were helpless before the thievery of foreign companies. The country was offered as a propitiatory sacrifice. This is stated not with the bitterness of an antagonist, but simply because of what the figures show.

In 1954, oil production again broke all records in Venezuela: 1,895,000 barrels daily. This was 7 percent higher than in 1953 and 7.8 percent higher than in 1948. However, Venezuela's income did not increase proportionally with the amount of petroleum produced. In 1954, the companies left $800.6 million in the country, an increase of only 1.49 percent over the previous year, whereas production had increased 7 percent. The comparison is really disturbing, however, when it is taken back to 1948, the last year of democratic government. In that year, the companies contributed $708.8 million. If the 1954 contribution of $800.6 million is compared to 1948, the increase is only 11.45 percent; but the increase in production, as we have seen, was 70.82 percent.

Another factor helping to widen the gap between what we gave and what we received was the price of the oil taken from our country. In 1948, the average American oil price was $2.50 per barrel while the price in Venezuela was $2.30. In 1953, the American price had gone up to $2.85, a 10 percent increase; but the price in Venezuela did not even go up 2 percent. Using the international price of petroleum, the difference between this true value and the amount the Anglo-American companies actually left in the country increased steadily. This difference truly reflects the impoverishment the producing companies imposed on Venezuela during the days of the dictatorship.

Relation Between the Value of Oil Production and the Dollar Value the Companies Left in the Country

Year	Production Value		Dollar Value left in Venezuela	% Relation	Increase or Decrease
	Tax Value	True Value			
1948	$1,227,000	$1,227,000	$708,910	62.9	—
1953	$1,513,870	$1,610,500	$788,860	48.9	− 14 %
1954	$1,660,272	$1,798,628	$800,600	44.5	− 18.4%

The above chart show how the Big Seven of oil took advantage of the dictatorship. For each dollar's worth of oil taken from the nation, never to be replaced, they returned less than half the value. At the 1948 tax values, for oil worth $1799 million in 1954, the companies should have returned to the country $1132 million. Since they returned only $801 million, $331 million was lost to the nation through lack of interest by the government in watching over this national wealth.

The losses of Venezuela and the Venezuelans became the excess profits of international capital. On April 11, 1955, a United Press dispatch reported that 55 percent of the net foreign earnings of the Standard Oil Company (New Jersey) came from Latin America. More importantly, it was the Creole Petroleum Corporation, the Venezuelan affiliate of the company, which accounted for 42 percent of the total net earnings of Standard Oil.

In 1954, Creole net earnings were $240 million, of which $228 million provided income for the parent company whose total was $585 million for the year. In the first half of 1955, Creole earnings took off like a rocket. The nearly $118 million it made in the first quarter was among the highest figures in the history of the company. These incredible earnings of the "Venezuelan" affiliate of the worldwide empire of Standard Oil were based upon the lowest capital investment that can be imagined, as shown in the following chart:

Relation of Fixed Assets to Net Earnings

	Fixed Assets	Net Earnings	Relative Percentage
Standard Oil	$3375	$585	16 %
Creole Petroleum	$ 546	$228	42 %
Standard without Creole	$3029	$357	11.7%

These figures show that Standard Oil, with its investments in Creole of Venezuela, obtained nearly four times the earnings from its other investments in the entire world, including the United States. The Shell and Mene Grande Oil companies, the other two sides of the triangle which enjoyed a practical monopoly of Venezuelan oil production were in a similar situation. To these improper earnings were added those of subsidiary refineries and oil tanker companies belonging to the parent concerns outside Venezuela. The entire swindle brought absolutely no protest from the dictatorship.

In the six year period 1949–54, the oil companies exported oil worth $8876 million. They returned $4217 million to the country when, at 1948 tax rates, they should have returned $5538 million. In other words, the dictatorship accepted the loss in these six years of $1321 million—almost two years worth of the national budget.

Thus, in six years, the famous "50/50 agreement" which had revolutionized oil participation by countries in Latin America and the Middle East showed that it would not work unless it were under the care of a responsible and ethical government. The dictatorship would not have been capable of formulating the 50/50 arrangements, as did AD at the time when it governed; much less so was it capable of carrying out the agreement when there were higher production rates, higher prices, and lower labor costs.

The annual reports of the oil companies, insofar as they were published, bear out the contention that the companies were short-changing the nation. The London *Economist* published a long report on Shell on June 13, 1953, which showed that in the two years, 1951–52, with an average capital of £994.4 million, the company had net earnings of £496.4 million—or half the total amount of its capital. This profit was based upon an annual production of 597 million barrels of crude. Since its Venezuelan production was 200 million barrels without counting additional production (that it received from Mene Grande Oil), 40 percent of its production originated in Venezuela where, as is well known, profits are higher. Therefore we can say, even though the British Consortium does not publish its accounts, that its earnings ratio is very high.

Creole Petroleum does issue annual reports to its stockholders so its earnings can be accurately established. The 1952 annual report of the company showed that a dividend of $7 per share was paid, 15 percent more than 1951 and 100 percent more than 1948.

The total dividend of $181 million represented 35 percent of the net assets of the company. In 1948, the last year of AD government, Creole had earned $198 million and in 1951, it reported $202 million—a level of earnings more or less the same. In 1948, however, it had paid $93 million in dividends with $440 million in net assets, for an earning rate of 21 percent; but in 1951, it paid $149 million on a capital of $473 million for an earning rate of 34.4 percent—or half again as much as in 1948. The upward tendency continued in 1952 when $181 million were paid in dividends with a capital of $514 million, a return of 35.2 percent.

This company had been warned in 1948 that the rate of return on its capital investment that year would not be tolerated in the future. It was doubled in 1952, however, under the protection of a government which gave a free hand to the big companies. From the time of the November 1948 coup to 1955, the affiliates of Standard Oil and Shell had paid out more than half their total capital investment in Venezuela as dividends. On the other hand, the income of the government had risen from 27.2 percent in 1945, under the Medina government, to a high of 37.6 percent in 1948, the last year of AD government. Under the dictatorship, it fell rapidly to 30.8 percent in 1949 and 25.7 percent in 1950. It rose slightly above 30 percent for the next three years and fell to 27 percent in 1954. The average yearly government income under AD was 35.5 percent, while under six years of dictatorship, until 1954, it was 29.5 percent.

Comparison should also be made between what Venezuela provided in unjustified profits to the oil companies and those which North American investors received in other countries of Latin America, as shown by the 1954 publication of the United States Department of Commerce, *Direct Private Foreign Investment of the U.S.* The total investments of the North Americans in Latin America, excluding Venezuela, were $3742 million, which earned $421.7 million for a return of 11.2 percent. The oil companies in Venezuela, with an investment of $771 million, had net earnings after taxes of $200.3 million, a return of 25.6 percent. Non-oil companies of United States origin operating in Venezuela earned an average profit of 9.8 percent on their investments of $135.9 million.

On the other hand, United States investments in Brazil and Cuba, the two countries next in importance for American investment, showed a profit rate of only 12.7 percent. Thus, the oil companies were earning 2.6 times more than other American firms in Venezuela; 2.2 times more than that of American investments elsewhere in Latin America; and two times more than what was being earned by American firms in Brazil and Cuba.

Furthermore, it should be recalled that not all the profits from Venezuelan oil were accounted for in these figures. The oil companies tried to keep their mine of black gold out of sight in Venezuela; in this way they were aided by the indifference of the dictatorship to matters of nationalistic concern. Very near the Venezuelan coast, on the islands of the Dutch West Indies, the companies had constructed their largest refineries. There, with an investment of $296 million, they realized a profit in one single year (1950) of $103 million.

All of the above figures were easily available to the ordinary man. During its years of underground activity, AD hammered at these numbers to keep Venezuela and the international public informed about this incredibly unjust distribution of oil income. It was ingenuous to think the lackey government would do anything but try to twist facts and deceive the public, as was done in the annual report of the Ministry of Mines and Petroleum in the year 1955. The minister who made this report, Edmundo Luongo Cabello, spoke—not as if he were an employee of the government—but as if he still worked for the oil company on whose payroll he had been for many years. He gave a cent-by-cent estimate of how oil company income was distributed. The figures were just as false as those that this man had presented in 1943, trying to make out that the proposed oil law would assure the government a much greater income than that of the companies. Edmundo Luongo had then been an official of the ministry but he had been dismissed as soon as AD came to power. The companies at that time admitted the imbalance and agreed to return to the treasury that portion of their excess earnings which was considered unacceptable. The official who had been run out of the government in 1945 was now the minister of mines and petroleum for the dictatorship. He continued his familiar line. Without any apparent twinge of conscience, he propagated figures regarding oil income which the oil companies had prefabricated, and he concluded with this hardly patriotic benediction: "The government receives more than a quarter of each bolívar generated in tangible form while the benefits to the nation, including government income, amount to three-quarters of every bolívar."

The poor companies not only earned very little but were threatened with earning much less in their moving and generous efforts to sacrifice themselves for Venezuela, encouraged by such faithful friends as the minister of mines and petroleum. The 1955 annual report of the ministry statistically expresses the philanthropic conduct of the oil cartel: in 1953, its production was 2.42 percent less than in 1952; however, its cost rose 7.99 percent. The annual report implicitly suggested to the companies that they reduce their costly laying off of new lots of workers when it stated: "An increase in costs means a weakening of the competitive margin of the Venezuelan oil industry."

The minister, acting like a company lawyer seeking to defend his clients in the courts, reported as factual their false division of oil income between the investors and the state. The members of the oil fraternity, like ascetic monks, had been satisfied with receiving only Bs. 1261 million, while the super-favored national treasury had received Bs. 1568.05 million. This meant 55 percent for the government and 45 percent for the companies.

Despite the fact that the petroleum cartel had to suffer these presumed reductions in proportionate income, its spirit of sacrifice led to supernatural extremes. A good part of its slim earnings were reinvested in an industry from which it barely extracted a livelihood. In 1953, the companies earned Bs. 901 million, of which 75 percent was for production. The ministry rejoiced: "This reinvestment is a very good sign because it means that Venezuela continues to attract capital."

Finally, the annual report was enthusiastic about the total of the industry's assets, which had increased by 6.59 percent in the course of the year. The index of solvency brought forth the admiring cry of "magnificent" from the ministerial report. The oil industry in Venezuela ran no risk of bankruptcy despite its almost pathological tendency to earn such small profits in order to help the home country.

The companies knew perfectly well that many of these statistics had been so manipulated as to lack all truth. They were already preparing a new maneuver to avoid future claims that the national treasury might present regarding hidden earnings. The trick consisted of quoting lower prices for Venezuelan oil than those that existed on the international market. First the Creole Petroleum Corporation, then the other big producing companies, began to post prices for their crude available at Venezuelan high sea ports. In 1955, because of alleged pressure from competition, Shell announced that it was obliged to lower some of its prices by $.15 cents a barrel, at the same time as prices were tending to rise in consuming countries.

The United Nations Economic Commission for Latin America (ECLA) analyzed petroleum export prices under the dictatorship and concluded that the "average prices show fluctuations which are not apparent in international markets" (page 69, volume 54, 1953). I showed how in 1948—the last year of democratic government—Venezuelan prices were $15.61 per cubic meter, but had not returned to this level. They had gone down to $14.73 in 1950, and for 1953 were $15.25, despite the fact that world market prices had risen an average of 10 percent during the year and the proportion of higher priced refined products exported was greater than in 1948.

U.S. prices went up still more in 1955 and the general consensus in the industry was that prices should go up even more because of higher costs. The major U.S. companies, however, made their affiliates in Venezuela reduce prices there. The apparent paradox disappears if one remembers that a single gigantic cartel controls the international oil market.

The reduction in prices by their affiliates in Venezuela would be picked up by the companies of transportation, refining, and marketing, which also belonged to the cartel, so there would be only a paper loss. At this time, the exclusive club of the Big Seven did not fear that their maneuvers would be watched by the United States government because the Republican administration had buried the antitrust investigations that had been carried out in the days of Truman. Meanwhile, the submissive dictatorial clique governed in Venezuela and it was easy for the oil companies to place their candidates in the Ministry of Mines and Petroleum to facilitate their maneuvers.

There is an old saying that you cannot shut out the sun with a finger. The documented statistics that we have used here have fully demonstrated how the dividends distributed among the coupon-cutters were sharply increased while the income to our nation went down. Our government carefully watched the dividend payments in order to keep them at an equitable level. That is how we achieved what was considered to be a reasonable division of income between the nation and the concessionaires. This vigilance was abandoned, however, and in 1949, dividend payments again got out of control, in prejudice to the country and to the joy of the absentee stockholders. The changes which were made in the income tax law, for all the careful planning that was involved, would never be enough to restrain the clever maneuvers of international capital. This was even more true during the shady times of the dictatorship, when the government completely lacked any sense of ethics or national responsibility.

The Simpson Bill in the United States

It might be claimed that the semblance of outrage by the dictatorship at the time the Republican congressman Simpson presented a bill to the United States Congress, affecting oil imports from Venezuela, was a contradiction of what has been said about the colonial submissiveness of the Venezuelan military government. It will be easy to show that in this case, as in others, the government was acting simply as the spokesman for the oil cartel.

The Simpson Bill came up early in 1953. Tons of printers' ink were spilled thereafter in arguing the pros and cons of this legislation. First, it was claimed that it would undermine the commercial treaty with the United States signed by the Caracas dictatorship, wherein Venezuela made numerous tariff concessions to assure the entry of Venezuela oil into the United States. Second, Venezuela's capacity to import from the United States would be adversely affected. Venezuela bought about one billion dollars of American products annually, ranging from heavy machinery to eggs. Finally, it was urged that Latin America would react adversely to import restrictions as "bad neighbor" policy.

A curious common front was formed to fight against the restrictions. It included the Venezuelan government, the oil companies, the State Department, the chambers of commerce in both countries, and the big newspapers of New York and Caracas, as well as all those individuals or groups who had access to the press or radio. On the other side were the spokesmen for the independent producers of the United States and the workers and owners of the coal industry. Although unable to debate matters publicly, we of AD also took part in this discussion. But we defended the Venezuelan viewpoint from a different angle.

It should be recognized that the spontaneous reaction of Latin America against the Simpson Bill reflected the high degree of uncertainty on the continent regarding the future raw material market in the United States. Protectionist sentiment had been growing in the American Congress. There was a strong current contrary to world economic interdependence that favored the private interests of isolationist groups.

There had never been any real danger of a drastic restriction of Venezuelan oil imports into the American market. Both of the big political parties of that country were on record in support of the idea that United States domestic oil reserves should be conserved and oil reserves should be developed outside the country. The authoritative Paley report in 1950 had concluded that the United States should promote the importation of crude oil in view of future growing demand and limited supply.

Regardless of the Simpson Bill, however, other aspects of the question should be analyzed. Would it be convenient or not to reduce the astronomical volume of Venezuelan oil now being produced? Would Venezuelan tax income necessarily be drastically reduced by a prudent decrease in its oil production?

With regard to the first question, it must be stated that those of us who followed the Venezuelan economy with patriotic interest did not agree that Venezuelan production should continue in an uncontrolled manner. This conclusion had nothing to do with partisan politics or our feeling regarding the kind of government then ruling the country. The government was an impermanent accident. Venezuela and its economy, together with the destiny of its people, are permanent realities. Venezuelan oil exports during the five years of war, 1940–45, averaged a record 188.9 million barrels annually. In the following five years after the war, 1945–49, exports jumped to an average of 408.8 million barrels annually—an increase of more than 100 percent. During the time we governed, we agreed to this increase because it was needed for the reconstruction of a devastated Europe, not because we wanted it for the country, although we made every effort to efficiently use the additional income. On more than one occasion, it was stated that the AD regime thought that the limits of reasonable use of this income were being reached and that there was risk of wasting what should be considered to be national capital, not national income, since it came from a nonrenewable source.

The 1940 production level, justified only by the postwar transition, continued to grow, however, until it was completely out of proportion in the following years. By 1952, under a government devoid of any sense of national interest, the big companies were able to take out 627.1 million barrels of oil, which meant that Venezuela was exporting 333 percent more than it had during the war and 50 percent more than during the five postwar years. Production continued to spiral upward. In 1954, production was 691 million barrels and it went up 14 percent more in 1955. All of this meant that the companies were making exaggerated profits and depleting, at an accelerated rate, the natural resources of the country.

An oil policy of benefit to Venezuela did not always coincide with the short-term interest of the private companies whose principal motive was rapid gain. Venezuela wanted to have its millions and millions of hectares under concession to the companies explored, and for new oil fields to be found there. Certainly, it was not in the country's best interest to sell more and more oil from its wells and to spend the resulting income within a short period of time. The wealth of the natural resource did not belong to just a single generation, but also to those who would come later. Rather than receive an excessive amount of income now and waste it in unnecessary expenditures, it was preferable to conserve the oil wealth below the ground and not fight for additional markets.

This was a question that was important, not just to Venezuela, but to all of America. The oil fields of my country were the source of liquid fuel for the entire continent because of geographical reasons. The continued economic development of the three Americas and hemispheric security itself were directly related to a steady and dependable flow of Venezuelan oil.

Now let us discuss the other question regarding income. If Venezuela were to reduce its oil exports, could it maintain the same level of tax income and its ability to import from abroad? Obviously, an abrupt reduction of oil income would seriously affect life in the country. More than 70 percent of the national income came from oil, as well as 62 percent of the funds needed for the national budget. Almost all of the nation's foreign exchange—96 percent—came from oil. Truly, Venezuela is a word written in oil.

It would be possible, however, to reduce production and still maintain, or even increase, the income from the oil industry. All that would be needed would be the application of the system of state participation put into effect and proven during the three years of democratic government, but abandoned later by the dictatorship. It has already been explained how the average income of Venezuela under AD was 35.5 percent of the oil income, but this was reduced during the first six years of the dictatorship to 29.5 percent. It would have been enough, therefore, just to reestablish the fiscal policy of the last year of democratic government and not even take into account other changes occurring during these years which were adding to the income of producing countries. Thus production could have been regulated without affecting the income received by the country.

Let us take one year at random to show how the figures would work. In 1952, if the 1948 participation formula had been applied, oil production would have been valued at Bs. 4897 million. The government would have received Bs. 1841 million, Bs. 333 million more than the Bs. 1508 million it actually received. The 1948 formula wws used to show how there could be less production without any loss of income simply because that is one which is well-known and tested. However, the 50/50 formula should not be considered as sacred or unchangeable. In recent years, the principal oil exporting nations have been receiving more for their oil produced by foreign companies than has Venezuela. We established a new landmark with our 1948 formula of 50/50. This formula was extended later to the great oil producing zone of the Middle East, but afterward we lost ground. Official circles were no longer concerned about the basic national problems and the regime was more interested in repressing popular revolt and in satisfying foreign investors than in the defense of the national patrimony. The Middle Eastern countries continued to increase their take from oil, although ours was reduced. Thus, in

1952, Iraq got $5.85 per metric ton while the Venezuelan share was only $5.17. The case of Canada was even more dramatic. It received $8.70 per metric ton in 1953, despite the fact that production was much less than ours and productivity per well was also smaller.

These estimates show that it would have been perfectly possible to diminish our production but to increase our income. This could not be argued in Venezuela itself, however. The press was under censorship. The political parties were illegalized, and the government did nothing more than chorus the clever arguments developed by the companies interested in producing the greatest amount possible within the shortest period of time. This was not because they were managed by devils sent from hell, but because the dynamics of the capitalistic system is to produce benefits without limit in countries governed by oligarchies or dictators which do nothing to protect the national interest. In its desire to maximize the advantage of the defenseless country, the cartel at all times had the full cooperation of government officials.

The close identification of the dictatorship with the oil industry during the time of Juan Vicente Gómez was resurrected. One of the most comparable demonstrations of this occurred in connection with the alleged restriction of petroleum imports to the United States. Pérez Jiménez himself played an important role in this comedy that had aspects of tragedy for the nation. It was mounted by the big North American oil companies to counteract the plans of the independent oil producers and the coal industry of their country. To some degree, these plans coincided with what should have been the Venezuelan interest in limiting the exorbitant increase in oil production.

On January 30, 1955, the dictator had made an impulsive and foolish declaration—at the time of one of the recurrent national crises over Formosa and the adjoining islands—offering "the strategic resources of Venezuela, especially oil and iron, to the United States and its allies." A few months later, however, responding to the directives of those who managed the farce, he changed his tone and became ridiculously threatening. Early in May 1955, in presenting the budget, he referred to possible restrictions of oil export to the United States and said:

> Venezuela believes that its strategic materials should be administered by a unified concept. If one of them is affected, the policy regarding all will be changed. Thus a change in the situation of our oil in the United States market will immediately affect the export to the United States of our iron, for which we are the leading suppliers.

This ridiculous posture would provoke laughter if it were not for its tragic background. This was not the voice of Venezuela. The regime of those years had absolutely no control over the iron mines or the oil. It was the voice of U.S. Steel, of Bethlehem Steel, of Standard Oil, of Texaco—the true beneficiaries of the exaggerated production of Venezuelan iron and oil. If Venezuela had really been able to make itself heard, it would have demanded a larger share of the earnings and a smaller and more stable market for these nonrenewable resources.

In any case, the vainglorious declaration of man was completely anticlimactic. It came after there was plenty of evidence that the Simpson Bill on compulsory oil import restrictions did not stand a chance. On February 20, 1955, the report of President Eisenhower's Cabinet Committee on Energy Supply and Resources was released. It categorically rejected any legislative effort to establish mandatory restrictions for foreign oil imports. Later in March, Secretary of State John Foster Dulles warned the Senate Finance Committee that mandatory quotas "to restrict our Venezuelan imports would completely disrupt our global policy in Latin America."[1]

In fact, it was so clear that there would be no legislative restrictions that the statement by Pérez Jiménez must have some ulterior motive. Generally, people do not make themselves ridiculous for the pleasure of doing so. The Presidential Cabinet Committee Report in the United States recommended that imports be frozen at 1954 levels, although it vetoed any kind of mandatory restrictions. The 1954 imports had averaged 656,000 barrels of crude oil daily plus 333,000 barrels of heavy fuel oil. This was about 10 percent of domestic production. Most of these imports came from Venezuela—388,000 barrels of crude and 326,000 barrels of heavy fuel oil. The imports of other American countries were insignificant—7000 barrels from Canada and 37,000 barrels daily from Mexico. The remainder came from the Middle East—213,000 barrels, and the Far East—37,000 barrels.

The presidential cabinet committee had recommended imports be limited at 1954 levels "by the voluntary action by those who were or would be importers." The managers of the big oil companies apparently were ready to accept this recommendation. During the first week of April 1955, they hastened to make public their readiness, but they continued to secretly maneuver. Their moves to obtain more commercial gain were made both inside and outside the country. This explains the pompous and apparently incongruous declaration in May of Pérez Jiménez and perhaps provides the key for the final decision of the United States Office of Defense Mobilization. As explained by its director, Arthur Fleming, on November 2, 1955, its formula—worthy of Solomon—was to limit imports, but—in the name of Pan-Americanism and hemispheric friendship—give the green light to the cartel which was sucking oil from Venezuela at such a rapid rate without consideration for the depletion of its wells. The solution met everyone's needs except Venezuela's.

The Office of Defense Mobilization did establish a limit on imports and thus satisfied the independent procurers of the oil and coal industries. The limitation was not large, however, because Venezuela and Canada were excluded from its effects; thus it applied to less than half of the total imports. In effect, the only country whose oil production was left free of any restrictions to import was Venezuela which accounted for more than 50 percent of United States imports because those from Canada were insignificant. The exclusion of Venezuela and Canada from import limitations pleased the cartel in two respects: it was based on the convincing and honorable argument of geographic proximity and hemispheric economic solidarity, and it also permitted an increase in the already incredibly high level of Venezuelan exports to the United States, where they were classified as "cheap petroleum." In return for the depletion of its reserves, Venezuela was going to receive a reduced share of the total income but enough to finance the carnival of sumptuous public works, new military constructions, and the fabulous life styles of a few dozen Venezuelan families at the apex of power. As far as the people and future generations of Venezuela were concerned, they could go to hell.

It is not necessary to think long or hard to understand why the cartel preferred the Pan-American solution of importing more oil from Venezuela than from the Middle East. The fact is that we were receiving less for the oil at that time than various oriental rulers. Since 1953, the cartel had to pay $.786 per barrel in taxes to Iraq, with the average price per barrel $2.00. In Venezuela, it was only paying $.738 cents per barrel of oil, of which the average price was $2.25. This was a difference of only five cents in taxes but it was increased much more with a price difference of $.21 attributable to freight differentials.

Pérez Jiménez, in his peculiar message to Congress on April 21, 1956, said: "The charitable compassion which some countries have professed for us now has been converted into a poorly disguised dislike owing to the oil progress of the country." In other words, some nations—presumably Latin American, because they were then closest at hand to the miracle—envied Venezuela.

Neither Mexico or Canada showed any enthusiasm when they received this treatment from the Untied States with regard to oil exports. As a matter of fact, Canada imported more oil from the United States than it exported there, and it imported an even greater amount from Venezuela. The new discoveries of Canada in Alberta should be able, eventually, to satisfy the domestic demand of the country. The Canadian government has repeatedly stated, however, that it does not wish to see this oil produced rapidly but wants to conserve its reserves to meet the growth of domestic consumption. Mexico has followed a similar policy of limiting the export of its non-renewable resources. Antonio Bermúdez, the head of PEMEX, the state oil monopoly, has publicly stated that Mexican oil consumed within the country is much more valuable than that which is exported. Venezuela is already a large oil exporter. International demand, its own potential, and the decisive impact of oil production upon the national economy, require us to continue being a major producer. That is a different matter from allowing the oil cartel to export without any limit, or to allow the income from the oil trade to be unevenly distributed.

The dictatorship not only permitted our oil wells to be tapped as if they were inexhaustible; it also cooperated actively in the antilabor policies of the oil companies. The acquiescence in the exhaustion of the oil wells went hand in hand with toleration of depletion of the human resources of the country.

Shame and sorrow came from what is about to be related regarding one of the most outrageous aspects of the dictatorial regime—that of labor-company relationships in the oil field.

The Military Dictatorship: Instrument of the Companies to Repress the Union Movement

The largest and most combative sector of the Venezuelan proletariat was found in the oil camps. For obvious reasons, it had the best organization, the longest tradition of struggle, and the clearest understanding of the connections between union freedom and public freedom. That is why the oil unions, after 1936, had been on the front line of combat—not only to obtain worker benefits, but also to capture democratic liberty for all of the people.

There had been a singular development of the labor movement in the oil fields under the three years of democratic government, and the workers had obtained substantial economic and social benefits. Their unions had been legally recognized; the first collective contracts in the history of the industry had been signed. Wages and benefits had been raised by 84.2 percent. In summary, the oil workers had ceased to be pariahs and had assumed the role of producers in a community where the state, not the foreign investors, regulated labor relations. All of this had been achieved without the industry having become involved in a strike of any importance.

The coup of November 24, 1948, returned the workers to that state of total helplessness in which they lived during the first twenty years of the industry, during the times of Gómez. The repression of the workers began almost immediately. The ILO commission which visited Venezuela in 1949 reported on the police measures taken against the workers who went on various strikes to protest the fall of the government, and the dismissals of workers and union officials which took place immediately thereafter. The companies were terminating thousands of workers. Most of them were paid legal indemnities, but no complementary measures were taken by the companies to ameliorate the effects of this drastic and sudden reduction in labor force. The situation took on alarming dimensions. As unemployment spread throughout the producing zone, there was great unrest, reported by even the conservative press in Caracas. The oil unions which had survived the government offensive began to give signs of life. The collective contracts signed in 1948 were in effect. Under their terms, the classification tables of salaries and the commissary price list were to have been reviewed after two years—in 1950. The unions asked that this be done when the time limit had expired, but it was impossible to reach an agreement with the companies because of their intransigence. The workers then resorted to their legal right under the labor law to draw up a list of demands for discussion. Under the labor law, in case no agreement was reached within 120 hours, they had the right to strike. The list of demands was discreet and cautious. It asked for a salary increase in the light of the increase in the cost-of-living and the big increase in worker productivity. It also asked for government intervention in the problem of layoffs.

Representatives of fifty-one labor unions interviewed the minister of labor, the socialist, Rojas Contreras. He reluctantly accepted their list of demands but insisted upon some delay in applying the lapse of 120 hours. When time was running out, he issued a communiqué which stated that the workers had no legal right to introduce demands under current contract and that any strike or work stoppage would be illegal. The workers sensed the danger and retreated, falling back on their right to take their conflicts to a federal labor court, granted them under decree number 447 of the revolutionary junta. This judicial process dragged on while official repression against the workers increased in the oil camps. In view of official hostility, a strike broke out on May 3, and oil production was completely paralyzed throughout the country. The reaction of the dictatorship to this labor movement, whose character and content were strictly economic, was reported by two well-known United States labor leaders—Matthew Woll, vice-president of the American Federation of Labor and Jacob Potosky, president of the Congress of Industrial Organizations' Commission for Latin America—in an accusation against the Venezuelan government presented on January 15, 1952, before the Economic and Social Council of the United Nations. They reported: "The government took brutal measures to break the strike. It cut off the water, gas and electric current in all the workers' homes. The National Guard agents searched all the homes and took away the food kept by the workers' families. All grocery stores were closed by the police. Soldiers of the army tried to force the workers to go to work."

The heroic resistance of the workers lasted ten days. They were treated like the population of an occupied country by a force that was not the modern army of a civilized nation, but acted like medieval mercenary troops assulting a town with the purpose of sacking it. The military government, as usual, attributed the strike to political motives. It decreed the dissolution of forty-seven oil unions, closed all of their headquarters, and seized their bank deposits, which totaled Bs. 5 million. Two months after the end of the strike, there were still more than three thousand oil workers in jail.

A year later, the oil workers returned to the fight when the collective contract expired in November 1951. The workers who belonged to the unions dissolved the previous year delegated their representation to five leaders who formed the union's Committee for a Collective Contract (CosiPetrol). They urged all of the workers to form a movement, a united front to draw up a single draft contract. This was done and the draft was already under discussion with the oil companies when another outrage occurred, demonstrating the military government's partiality to the oil companies. A decree was issued on April 9, putting an end to the discussions and arbitrarily fixing working conditions. Among the arguments used to justify the decree, it was stated that the junta should be empowered "to determine the exact degree to which the demands for increase in salaries and benefits should be granted without provoking an excessive increase in the cost of production." This was to avoid the creation of "difficulties" for Venezuelan oil on the international market.

This was the same story the oil companies were putting out in the local press with the obstinacy of a hand-organ player, repeating the same tune over and over again: "Venezuela is about to lose its market because of the high cost of producing crude oil."

"Creole Petroleum," *El Universal* reported in February 1951, "has stated in a recent sensational publication that Venezuela has lost most of its European market due to the fact that we cannot compete successfully with oil in the Middle East. It is also stated that our costs are so high that our position is threatened even in this hemisphere and that it is necessary to reduce costs if we are to keep the markets which still belong to us."

Neither the companies nor the government, which supported their anti-worker conduct, were ignorant of two facts. First, reasonable increases in salaries and benefits did not substantially alter production costs. According to oil economist Paul Frankel, they only made up 10 to 15 percent of production cost. Second, as shown in figures of the Central Bank, the greatly increased oil production under the dictatorship had been accompanied by a drastic reduction in the number of workers in the industry and in the total labor costs. According to the bank's annual report for 1951, production in three years had increased 26.98 percent, but the number of Venezuelans had decreased by 30.41 percent during the first three years of the dictatorship. From 1948–52, production had increased three times, but the number of persons employed in the industry fell from 58,418 to 45,684.

In citing these figures, it is not my intention to oppose technological advances. This was not the factor operating in Venezuela at that time. Rather, there was an increase in the work load upon a smaller number of employees and workers who had no protection because their union rights had been suppressed by labor authorities acting in conjunction with the companies.

The situation continued to worsen and labor relations were governed by "the law of machete." The labor leaders who come to Caracas to discuss the new contract with the companies in May 1951, issued a mimeographed handout to protest the government's decision since they could not get space in the controlled press. They also tried to organize a new national federation of oil workers, but they were informed by the Labor Ministry that the government would not permit this. Later, in June, national security agents raided the CosiPetrol offices and arrested the officials there. Some were sent to the Guasina concentration camp. In August, the oil workers union at Punta Fijo in Falcon State was occupied by the police and the leader of this union, Andrés Hernández Vásquez, was also sent to Guasina.

The persecution continued in 1953. The government organized a collective contract with a union organization called the Independent Union Movement (MOSIT), created and directed by the security police. Most of the oil workers refused to sign this contract, so the dictatorship arrested the other CosiPetrol leaders. They paid for their rebellious attitude with long years in jail.

The Other Aspects of the Colonial Oil Policy Under the Dictatorship

The steps which the AD government took to conserve natural gas were not followed up with much interest. In 1952, only 4.2 million cubic meters of gas were recovered, while 17,445 meters were flared and burned—triple the entire oil production of the neighboring republic of Colombia, eliciting only a mild comment from the ministry: "The waste is still very high." Nothing about new programs or plans and study to end this criminal waste of an irreplaceable natural resource.

The dictatorship also terminated the practice, established by AD, of taking part of the royalty in crude for direct trading by the government, thus ending the possibility of Venezuela using its oil for bilaterial transactions with countries which did not want to use foreign exchange to buy fuel. These deals were not pleasing to the big companies. Anything which irritated the skin of the mammoths of international capital was fearfully rejected by those who governed Venezuela—at this dramatic hour of its history—with the subservient mentality of servants.

AD had clearly intended to undertake production of part of our national oil resources by state enterprise, or jointly with private capital. It had also planned to construct a national refinery. This was not just a vague idea; it was actually under study when our government was overthrown. Four years later, however, nothing had been done, nor will anything be done under a dictatorship which does not want to offend the oil companies. Pérez Jiménez, who fearlessly asserts his nationalism when it comes to sovereignty over rocky islands off our coast, humbly bows down in colonial submission before the altars of the foreign consortia of black gold.

Certainly the idea of having Venezuelans undertake part of the development of their petroleum resources for the benefit of the overall economy of the country should not cause hesitation. More than thirty years have passed since the blowout of the first commercial well in our nation Barroso number 2. At this time, we have become the world's first supplier of oil. It is high time for the Venezuelan to cease being merely a spectator of oil operations and to participate directly in them. There are reserves to be developed. There is money to put them into operation. There are Venezuelan engineers and workers with sufficient experience in all phases of the business. All that is required is to carry out what was planned by AD—to organize a state company which would immediately begin to drill for its own account to produce and refine petroleum. This method of direct operation could be combined with other possible systems which would be much more beneficial for the country than the colonial formula of long-term concessions.

There is a constant debate as to whether or not state enterprise has positive results in other economic areas. This is not true with petroleum. It lends itself to a "natural monopoly." It is universally admitted, in theory and in fact, that the state must actively intervene in its development—whether as a constant supervisor of private owners or as an operator itself.

The ideal for Venezuela—and the final goal for all patriotic Venezuelans—is the nationalization of the oil industry. Serious reasons militate against carrying out this objective under present national and international circumstances. These reasons will be set forth later in this book. Even if it is not possible for the nation to take over the entire industry in Venezuela now, however, it would be feasible for the state, through the proper agencies, to engage directly in the production, refining, and marketing of part of the oil produced in its territory. Both economic reasons and the national interest dictate this. A nation which does not manage, even partially, its own natural wealth—indefinitely allowing it to be developed by foreign capital and management—runs the risk of acquiring a distorted colonial mentality.

One does not have to look in theoretical revolutionary writings to find support for this idea, nor is it to be found only in countries which are opposed to private property and to "free enterprise." One can cite that capital of tradition, Great Britain and its Tory chieftain, Winston Churchill, in support of the idea of state oil administration. Winston Churchill, First Lord of the Admiralty in 1913 when the British government acquired majority interest in the Anglo-Persian Oil Company, ardently defended this government intervention before the House of Commons. He insisted that the admiralty must be independent both in time of war and in time of peace for its supply of oil as well as the price at which it could be acquired. And how fabulous the results were!! The British Crown, through its control of 52 percent of the stock of Anglo-Persian, later renamed Anglo-Iranian, acquired its greatest single source of government income. Although a sworn enemy of all kinds of nationalization, Churchill's frank defense of a government role in the oil business could not have been more explicit. It was enough to make the well-known oil professor Paul Frankel exclaim: "Since that time, all evolution of the international oil industry has tended to lose its private character."

In the United States itself, that bastion of "free enterprise," the government organized the Petroleum Reserve Corporation in 1943 to carry out oil operations in the Middle East. This was the idea of Harold Ickes, Roosevelt's Secretary of Interior; it was opposed so powerfully by the companies that it finally disappeared, but not before Ickes had replied to their criticism of state intervention by calling attention to the many inefficient and wasteful practices of the private oil industry.

In Russia, the oil industry was nationalized by the 1917 revolution. The petroleum trust under its aggressive European captain, Henry Deterding, was the architect of the so-called prophylactic belt around the Soviet Union by the western powers. Some members of the Labor party feel that this quarantine of Russia was responsible for its subsequent aggressive nationalism. If so, Deterding was largely responsible.

In any case, the plan had no positive result for the oil companies. The nationalized industry continued in the hands of the Russian state and became prosperous. Paul Frankel, whose liberal and democratic beliefs cannot be questioned, has written that the Soviet experience shows that an oil industry can function well in the hands of a state monopoly. The experiences of two countries of such different economic structures and ideologies as England and Russia show that the state can have success in managing the oil business. The experience has also been satisfactory in less developed countries, with oil fields, including those in Latin America—Mexico, Brazil, Argentina, Chile, and Bolivia. All of these countries have intervened to a greater or lesser degree in the production of petroleum with positive results.

Coming back to Venezuela, the state oil enterprise should also carry out work of exploration in areas where there are no concessions. The nation would then be able to arrange for contracts—with Venezuelan or foreign companies—with better knowledge of what lies underground, and could demand a greater share of the income since the element of risk cited by the companies to justify their high profits would be eliminated. In this connection, the recent case of the Neches oil field in the state of Texas may be cited. After public bidding, this area was assigned to the Humble Oil Refining Company, which made the extraordinary offer to pay the state 90.5 percent of the value of all the oil produced in the area, with amortization of capital investment and production cost for the company's account. This is the highest amount ever to be paid by a private company to the government.

Another significant case occurred recently when the Mares concession in Colombia reverted to the government. Another affiliate of the Standard Oil Company (New Jersey)—the International Petroleum Company—agreed to continue operating the old concessions on a cost-plus-commission basis under the general supervision of the Colombian state oil company.

In the Venezuela of the days of the National Welfare, however, such ideas had no place in government thinking. In Miraflores, all the talk was about how much money was received by this or that functionary from some recent clever deal; or the expertise of the political police was admired because they had been able to capture a number of members of the democratic resistance in a single raid. If the theme of petroleum came up, it was only as a result of someone's get-rich-quick scheme, not as a problem of national importance.

This explains why the plans for a national oil company were set aside, why the innovations in Texas and Colombia got no attention, and why nothing was done to satisfy the national wish for state refinery in Venezuela to manufacture all of the oil products needed for the domestic market. The country insists that the absurd situation be ended under which most of our crude oil is refined in the Dutch Antilles.

We had tried to do something about this when in power. It was under the

AD regime that the big refineries of Shell in Punto Cardon and of Creole at Amuay were begun. When finished, they provided a very substantial increase in the amount of crude oil refined in the country. Only 8.46 percent had been refined before the construction of these refineries. By 1952, when they were finished, 18.42 percent of the national production was refined in the country.

The military government has resorted to various publicity tricks in an attempt to silence public criticism for its lack of action in obtaining greater refining capacity for the country. One of these was to stage a great propaganda campaign when a government petrochemical industry was dedicated. It was reasonable enough that petroleum and gas be used for the manufacture of a series of industrial products, ranging from synthetic rubber to cosmetics and including agricultural fertilizers. It would have been much more logical, however, if one or more state oil refineries had been put into operation. Much was made of the role being played by the military general staff in the installation of the petrochemical industry as if this activity were considered preparation for war.

Probably the real reason was the desire to emulate what Perón had done during his triumphal years in Argentina using the wizardry of justiciability. There had been claims that Argentina, without uranium, had gone further than either the United States or Russia in thermonuclear experiments. Why should it be strange, then, to have the military thermochemists of Pérez Jiménez aspire to surprise the world one day by manufacturing an H-bomb out of natural gas from the wells of Caripito?

How the Factory Works

It has been repeated over and over again that Venezuela's economy has been dangerously distorted as a result of the oil boom. The nation and the government become more and more dependent upon a single source of income. Oil was such an extraordinary source of income even though it was nonrenewable. There was an added element of danger because foreign capital managed this production. This meant that the very structure of our ostentatious but vulnerable national economy was built on a shaky foundation. We were conscious of this dramatic reality and had tried—when we were in power—to do something about it. We wanted to end our condition as a semi-colony, as simply an oil factory. The two correctives we began to apply were: to increase the share of income for the country from the oil industry to a reasonable level, and to reinvest a good part of the oil income in the development of a diversified national economy and the education and welfare of our people. Our nationalistic policy was brought to a halt by the 1948 coup. The oil industry was again managed as though it were a colony while the government engaged in an orgy of ostentatious public works and encouraged private deals by favorites of the administration.

The complete dependence of the country on the oil industry, the early results of the effort to change this situation in 1945–48, and the catastrophic consequences after 1949 can be best understood by analyzing three aspects of the nation's economy: the national income in terms of oil value, foreign commerce, and the government's budget and the part played by oil taxes.

The National Income in Terms of Oil Value

The proportion of national income attributable to the oil industry and the value of oil production offer irrefutable indices of the national economy. In addition to the contribution directly made by oil production to national income, there are many other indirect contributions which cannot be computed. In estimating the direct contribution of oil, however, it can be observed that this factor tended to grow more and more, increasing the danger to the country. The following chart illustrates this:

Formation of National Income in the Years 1936–51				
	1936	1949	1950	1951
National Income (millions of Bs.)	1500	7080	7108	7195
Oil Salaries:	58	633	645	735
General Increase (without oil)	1442	6447	6463	6460
Value of Oil Production	532	3417	3957	4622
Ratio	2.71	1.88	1.63	1.39

These statistics show that our national income minus oil salaries was 2.71 times oil income in 1936. In 1951, it was only 1.15 times the value of oil production. The preponderant role of oil in national income is so overwhelming that it should have been reduced. The opposite occurred, even though the country had received less for the oil taken from its wells after the year 1949 and until 1958. Furthermore, what was received was poorly invested; as a result, the moment was approaching when the national income exclusive of oil would be less than the value of the oil production. This is the moment—to use an Anglo-Saxon expression—"when all the eggs will be in a single basket."

The disproportionate increase of oil production and the decreasing proportional share by the nation in the product of this national wealth were twin factors in bringing about this tragic tendency under the dictatorship. The critical nature of the trend is evidenced by the fact that while the total value of the petroleum taken from Venezuela increased by more than one-third, the real income per person diminished by 12 percent, as demonstrated in the following chart:

	1936	1949	1950	1951
National increase (millions of Bs.)	1500	7080	7108	7195
Index cost of living	74	136	138	148
Real cost of living index	2027	5206	5150	4861
Population inhabitants (millions of people)	3364	4787	4927	5070
Real increase per person (in Bs.)	602	1087	1045	949
Percentage increase or decrease		+80.5%	−3.8%	−8.3%

The above data are from studies made by the Central Bank of Venezuela. They demonstrate how the 80.5 percent increase in national income achieved by 1949 over the base of 1936—in good part due to the policy of the AD government—had been diminished by almost one-sixth by 1951, notwithstanding the fact that the value of oil increased by one-third over the three year period 1949–51.

Foreign Trade

Foreign trade is one of the most important aspects of modern economics and reveals the state of development and the economic stability of any country. We always stress the fact, both in and out of government, that the Venezuelan economy was in a dangerous situation because of the exaggerated importance of its foreign trade, above all because this trade was based overwhelmingly on just one product: petroleum. In 1947, petroleum made up 95.3 percent of Venezuela's exports. In 1949, there was a bad recession in Venezuela because of a decline in the total oil exports. The impact suffered that year led ECLA to warn that although Venezuela was one of the richest countries in Latin America, it was one that was most vulnerable to external factors.

The terms of trade improved for Latin America between 1947–52. In the case of Venezuela, the value of its second export, coffee, doubled. However, the preponderance of petroleum continued to increase in our foreign trade. In the UN report, *Commodity Trade and Economic Development*, which noted that

98 percent of Venezuela's exports were oil, Venezuela was designated as the Latin American country in greatest danger because of its mono-productivity. It was followed by Bolivia with 90 percent of tin and Chile with 80 percent of nitrate and copper.

The degree of our dependence upon oil and foreign trade emphasized, on the one hand, that the nation was receiving an inadequate income from what this resource produced; on the other hand, the unsatisfactory manner in which oil income was being reinvested was also highlighted.

The National Budget and the Share of Oil Income

The national budget is always important in the economic life of a nation. This was more true in Venezuela than elsewhere in America because the state received most of the income from the oil industry so that the role of the budget in the national economy was proportionately larger. After 1945, when the AD government obtained a larger share of oil income, oil tax receipts exceeded in the budget all other sources of income together. They came to represent 60 percent of the total budget under the dictatorship despite the fact that the real income which Venezuela got from oil diminished. The unprecedented increase in production papered over this declining share.

Both the oil companies and the colonial government tried to mask this reality. In printed propaganda and in documentaries shown on screens throughout the continent, Venezuela was portrayed as a country enjoying an exceptional economic bonanza or, as Senator Margaret Chase Smith said in the United States Congress on April 27, 1954: "It is a nation that has large gold reserves and seems to be making piles of money with its oil."

The truth was different. Venezuela was not receiving what it should have. Two-thirds of the budget was covered by oil income, but this was at the price of a rapid depletion of reserves. The decline in what it received per unit meant that Venezuela was getting less at this time for its oil than countries of tribal structure in the Middle East. National income, excepting oil, diminished from year to year and would soon reach the point where the total value of petroleum produced each year was superior to it. Foreign trade was overwhelmingly based on oil and per capita income was declining. The oil industry workers were no longer protected by unions and, just as in the times of Juan Vicente Gómez, the oil companies were the only law in the oil fields.

For all the fanfare of its big military parades and the spectacular celebration of the "Week of the Fatherland," Venezuela was returning to a situation similar to that in which it lived before 1810. It was rapidly becoming just an oil factory. National sovereignty is a juridical concept, a legal abstraction. For it to become reality, a country must be able to have a fair degree of control over its own economic destiny, but this cannot be true in a country where the big economic decisions are completely in the hands of a dozen or so North American and British oil company directors.

Short-Term Joy, Lasting Rancor

The total lack of responsibility of the dictatorial government toward Venezuela was translated into excessive earnings for the oil companies, harm to the Venezuelan economy, and the exploitation of oil industry workers. The executives of the oil companies exuded satisfaction and were as happy as fish in water under the dictatorship which was so implacable with the "natives" and responsive to the foreign investor. This joy had its counterpart, however, that rendered future relations between the nation and the foreign investor highly uncertain—the deep-seated ill will among the Venezuelan people who bitterly resented having their country treated as a factory.

Many newspapers in the United States and many U.S. government officials will resent the frank language I am using. At best they will consider it "nationalistic demagoguery." However, the public men of the United States themselves use rough language when they are defending national interests. President Harry Truman, for instance, expressed himself with unusual bluntness when he sought to protect the oil wealth of the United States against the trusts. Referring to the federal rights on the coastal title strip, he said in Washington on May 17, 1952: "If we back down on our determination to defend this common property, we will be robbing our people of their legitimate right. This is just what the petroleum clique wants. It wants us to turn over this enormous wealth to a few states so the powerful private oil companies may be able to develop it at will. This would be robbery on such a large scale that the Teapot Dome scandal would seem small by comparison." He added that the oil sought by the trusts was worth $40 to $100 billion and that federal title to his oil had been reaffirmed by the United States Supreme Court. Moreover, the American press continually denounced the schemes of the trust to gain control over this oil. The vehemence of the accusations is very similar to our nationalistic demagoguery in Latin America.

The foreigners living in Venezuela do not hide thier admiration for Pérez Jiménez and his methods of government. Those connected with the oil business are especially given to indiscreet loquacity. Robert H. Hallet, Latin American editor of the important newspaper, *The Christian Science Monitor*, described them in mid-1952, explaining that they included most of the North American colony in Caracas which felt that Venezuelan government had been "poorly interpreted and misunderstood." *Time* magazine also commented on the reasons the North American oil and iron concerns supported Pérez Jiménez:

> One place where U.S. businessmen abroad can still flourish in a climate of high-riding free enterprise is the oil-booming republic of Venezuela. . . . The gratified government has thrown the door wide open to foreign enterprise, and the biggest colony of U.S. businessmen overseas is happily at work making money in one of the world's most profitable markets.[2]

The writer did not ignore another aspect of the Venezuelan economic situation—the lack of well-being of the people:

Caracas prices average twice as high as Manhattan's, but oil keeps the money moving; the buying power of Customer Juan Bimba (Mr. Average Venezuelan) has risen 63% in eight years. The country is the U.S.'s fourth biggest cash customer (after Canada, Mexico, and Cuba), taking everything from steel beams to baked beans.[3]

Finally, the magazine reported about what these people who impoverished the country with official complicity thought about it:

> The majority of the 'misius' [foreigners in Venezuela] are not in the least concerned with local politics. Discussing the army dictatorship that has bossed Venezuela for the past five years, a banker explained recently: "You have freedom here to do what you want to do with your money, and to me, that is worth all the political freedom in the world."

"Go to Venezuela and Get Rich" is the title of an article in *Coronet* magazine, November 1953. It rings the bells to call all to the prodigious feast just five hours by plane from the Miami airport: ". . . 23,000 Americans are enjoying what Venezuela offers today. One hears them say that they have never worked so hard in their lives, but they say it with great pleasure and satisfaction. Listening to them, you get the impression that the American companies are doing the best business of their history."

One might think that this is the opinion of an unknown writer expressed with superficiality. It was confirmed, however, by the Bible of the world of high finance, that oracle for Wall Street, the magazine *Business Week*. Its issue of January 9, 1954, published a report entitled: "Venezuela Lives High." It emphasizes the unprecedented earnings of the investors as well as the problems of the average Venezuelan in getting enough to eat and a place to live:

> The Venezuelan boom, keyed to oil, continues to mushroom. Food prices and rents average one-third above the United States, taxes are low, local and foreign investors are having a field day. In 1952, U.S. direct investment in Venezuela, heaviest in Latin America, earned a huge $256 million net, more even than in Canada.[5]

The importance of the comparison with Canada will be appreciated more if it is recalled that United States investments in Canada totalled $5 billion while in Venezuela they totaled only $98 million dollars. Although investments were five times greater in Canada, earnings were less than in Venezuela.

In the days following December 2, 1953, many ceremonies were staged to commemorate the first anniversary of the coup by Pérez Jiménez and his praetorian guard, contrary to the will of the people expressed in the elections of November 30, 1952. Among these affairs, there was one given at the American Club in Caracas, whose membership included most of the United States businessmen who lived there. There were many toasts to the dictator whose hands were stained with the blood of Ruiz Pineda, Carnevali, Pinto Salinas, and so many others of those fallen for the liberty of my country. The reception was offered in the name of the honorary president of the Club, Fletcher Warren, ambassador of the United States to Venezuela.

Information About Latin America and Ignorance in the United States

There was full knowledge among the people of Latin America, but little public information in the United States about what was going on in Venezuela and how hatred was building up and nearly ready to burst out. This was true despite the fact that the largest number of American investments in Latin America were in Venezuela. This ignorance in North America was explained in a statement published by the powerful Oil Workers Federation, the United States affiliate of the CIO, in July 1952. After referring to the imprisonment and torture of the Venezuelans, the statement said: "These things are going on in a country which is almost next door in this age of aerial communication. It can almost be said, however, that a conspiracy of silence exists in the United States with respect to what the dictatorships are doing in Latin America. Almost all of the press has ignored the situation. The only newspaper that has published something is the *New York Times*. Apparently the press does not consider it prudent to mention the Venezuelan situation, although it devotes ample space to similar situations in the world."

The statement ingenuously suggested that the United States present the Venezuelan case to the United Nations. It took a more realistic attitude when it said: "If the United States were to intervene against the Venezuelan dictatorship, it would certainly have a battle on its hands with North American capitalism because Venezuela is one of the richest colonies of Wall Street."

The final statement was not mere rhetoric. It reflected the truth. When he spoke in Caracas on behalf of two hundred North American businessmen in Venezuela before the visiting Capehart committee of the United States Congress, Joseph Foss—president in Venezuela of the American Chamber of Commerce, was able to state that Venezuela contributed $1 billion annually to the United States economy—$500 million to pay for imports and $500 million in the form of earnings, insurance payments, and services. The ECLA 1951–52 report to the United Nations pointed out that the United States got 40 percent of its Latin American earnings from investments in Venezuela; it furnished other figures which explained why these investors eulogized the administrative capacity of the dictatorship. During the four year period, 1945–49, of which three years were under AD government, the average yearly earnings of United States investors was $150 million. After the 1948 coup, without significant new capital investment, these earnings shot up like a rocket and were more than $324 million in 1950 and $278 million in 1951.

Despite the fact that so little was written in the United States, except to show that Venezuela lived in the best of all possible worlds, the spokesman of U.S. labor continued to tell the truth about what was happening. Serafino Romualdi, leader of the AFL, spoke before the annual convention of this powerful worker group in St. Louis, Missouri, in September 1953, describing what had really happened in the Venezuelan elections:

After four years of dictatorial rule, the junta decided to risk elections after illegalizing the main political party. When the votes were counted, the government had been defeated by a two to one majority. Then at 3 a.m., all of the voting places were occupied, the ballot boxes seized, and strict censorship imposed while the principal opposition leaders were arrested. The votes were then recounted secretly and the government announced two days later that it had won. The electoral fraud was so obvious that no responsible observer could be deceived.

However, as Romualdi pointed out, this blatant robbery of the elections and his totalitarian system of government ceated no problem for Pérez Jiménez in his inter-American diplomatic relations, especially with the State Department. There, the same people who tore at their clothes and cried to heaven about the police crimes of Lavrenti Beria, shamelessly closed their eyes to the police crimes of Pedro Estrada. The assault upon liberty and human dignity was just as great in Latin America of the fifties, balkanized as it was by dictatorships, as those which were occurring in Russia and the so-called popular democracies of eastern Europe. Romualdi, who was speaking at the time before an audience which included the then vice-president Richard Nixon and the secretary of state, John Foster Dulles, concluded:

> This illegitimate government has been honored with the responsibility of organizing the Tenth Conference of the Organization of American States. Even though it seems incredible, one of the most brutal dictatorial overnments of Latin America will serve as host for a conference which has been called to strengthen the cause of democracy and liberty.

The union leader ended with a comment which explained everything: "Venezuela is rich in oil and iron, and powerful American interests have built up friendly and productive relationships there. Thus, its military regime has become untouchable and it is appeased and flattered in every way possible."

National resentment at this partnership of political repression and economic exploitation intensified in the country. The *New York Times* of June 27, 1952, reported on a poll carried out among oil company workers which showed that although 80 percent of the workers believed that Venezuela was obtaining an advantageous income from oil industry earnings, and a similar number were satisfied with the treatment given to Venezuelan workers by the companies, they still wanted Venezuelan oil to be nationalized. Even this negative attitude was used by the "intellectual" advisors of the dictator to gain support from abroad. They cynically warned the company managers and the United States and British embassies that the only way to maintain a containing wall against the dangerous risks in the future was to continue the kind of government existing in Venezuela—with its concentration camps, brutal tortures, assassinated leaders, and police terror. Sidney Gruson, correspondent of the *New York Times*, wrote from Caracas on December 18, 1953, about how the government was trying to convince people that the reconquest of Venezuela by a democratic regime would mean a takeover by the Communist party:

> With so much dependence on oil, it was inevitable that it would become a political issue in one way or another. The oil companies steer as far away from politics as

possible. But the government of Colonel Marcos Pérez Jiménez has convinced itself that its political opposition would destroy the industry by nationalization and the government uses this as a pretext for its continued suppression of the opposition.

The opposition Acción Democrática party held the presidency of the country for ten months in 1948. There was no move to nationalize then and there is nothing on record to show that its leaders advocate nationalization now. However, government spokesmen insist that the communists so thoroughly infiltrated Acción Democrática since 1948 that they would call the tune in the oil fields if Acción Democrática were to return to power. . . . American observers in Venezuela do not agree with the government on the extent of communist penetration of Acción Democrática. . . .[6]

The political position of AD, with its own ideology and its irreconcilable doctrinal and tactical differences and its communists, was so obvious that the agents of the dictatorship could not do more than denounce nonexistent "infiltrations" in our ranks. The communists, for their part, were not under any illusion. They well knew that AD had never served them and never would serve them as an aircraft carrier. For this reason they constantly hurled insults at us in their sixth national conference in June 1951. They even engaged in autocriticism—that fawning concession to Russian psychology—for their "serious weaknesses" with regard to us. They pleaded that they had been insufficiently energetic in "mobilizing masses to defeat the AD policy of surrender to imperialism, of capitulation and division."

The Unknown Future

The concerned Venezuelan must seriously reflect on the preponderant role which the oil industry has in his country. Its uncontrolled growth and its role in the national economy has tended to make it a state within a state. Its antidemocratic influence on the political direction of the country in favor of authoritarian regimes is felt in different ways, some more ostensible than others. The character of the material produced—of prime strategic importance for both peace and war, especially the latter—gives these foreign influences on our national political life a particularly dangerous aspect. The negative influence of the big private concerns influences not only the policy of our government but also the diplomacy of the countries from which these companies come. In view of the explosive mixture of oil and diplomacy, the most favorable solution for a country such as ours would be to nationalize the industry. Let the state take control of oil production after indemnifying the concessionaires, thus freeing the country from the presence of these aggressive economic and political forces from abroad.

From the viewpoint of modern international law, there is no reason why this cannot be done. In its famous resolution number 6, overwhelmingly approved by a majority, the United Nations in 1953 established the right of all people to dispose freely of their raw materials. The same world organization and the International Court at the Hague admitted the right of the Iranians to nationalize their oil industry. In Latin America, the cases of Mexico and Bolivia in nationalizing their oil production provide a solid precedent. Notwithstanding these reasons, the AD party which has governed in Venezuela and which will govern again, has never argued for the complete nationalization of the oil industry. Our position is a reasonable one, based on a serious and realistic anlaysis of our situation.

Countries such as ours—producers of a raw material indispensable for human progress—should not take an isolationist view. They have primary responsibility to defend and use this wealth for the well-being of their own people; they must also be conscious of their duty with regard to other countries. The truth is that much of the western world, including the United States, fuels much of its industry with oil from Venezuela. Furthermore, it would be frivolous were we to insist that Venezuela presently can, by itself, efficiently maintain oil production that had reached two million barrels daily by 1956.

There is another reason that should be fully understood. Should the industry be fully nationalized, it would be shut down for an unpredictable length of time. Producing oil is easy. To refine, transport, and market oil, however, is most difficult, especially when it is produced on the scale reached in Venezuela. It would be ingenuous to think that the international oil cartel would accept nationalization of oil by the world's first supplier without a long and bitter fight. It has many resources since it controls the largest volume of oil production, refineries, and means of transport in the non-Soviet world. The United States Senate report under Truman showed how this cartel of seven big companies—five American and two English—controlled 55 percent of the world tanker fleet. The same report told how 99 percent of Venezuelan production belonged to three companies of the cartel.[7]

Previous experience would indicate that this gigantic international consortium would boycott the nationalized oil of Venezuela, as was done earlier in Iraq and Iran, while production would be increased in other areas to cover the deficit. Arguments should not be needed, after what has been analyzed in previous pages, regarding the importance of oil income to the Venezuelan economy, or to understand what a negative repercussion would result from a prolonged production stoppage.

The diplomatic complications which would result also cannot be ignored. Petroleum is not like bananas, coffee, or lumber. It is rightly considered as a basic element of western security. This is especially true in the case of Venezuela because of its large volume. All people want peace. They prefer coexistence to co-destruction, but the threat of war will hang over the modern world as long as Russia and the United States continue to store atom bombs and mutually accuse each other of the worst intentions. This somber but predictable prospect puts Venezuela in a unique position because its oil fields are one of the key elements in the security of the non-Soviet world. It must be recognized that the Middle East—the oil supplier of Western Europe, a good part of Asia and principal source for the countries making up the North

Atlantic alliance—is a zone which is militarily indefensible. Its production, which in 1955 was two million barrels of oil daily, is essential for that part of Europe outside the Soviet zone for the Far East and India. If the suicidal stupidity of the big powers brings on a new war in which Russia is involved, the Soviet military will descend without difficulty through the Caucasian passes, occupying or neutralizing the oil fields of the coveted triangle where three continents meet and the globe divides between east and west. Even without war, even if humanity achieves its age-old desire of lasting peace, this great oil zone will continue to be a powder keg.

Under the present historical conditions, a defiant gesture by Venezuela in nationalizing its petroleum, together with its sequel of international commotion, would elicit the most eulogistic commentaries from *Pravda* and the euphoric and noisy support of communist parties. However, the truly responsible leaders of the national liberation movements in Latin America are concerned with the welfare of the people. They are not interested in having the agents of Russian propaganda or the more aggressive wielders of the big stick in the United States use their countries as pawns in the big power game.

One must then ask: if AD does not propose to fully nationalize the oil industry under present international circumstances, must it admit that powerful foreign influences inevitably continue to influence the political destiny and the economic development of the country? The answer is: no, definitely not. This party has already governed from 1945–48. Its conduct with regard to the oil companies and the big countries from whence they came is well-known. By our actions, we made the companies understand that a government ruled in Venezuela whose officials could not be bribed and who were fully aware of their responsibilities. The foreign offices of the big powers—the United States and England—also had to admit that a political party ruled in Venezuela which could not be intimidated and which had a real sense of dignity and independence, as well as full respect for its legitimate obligations. From the time we left the government until now—1955—a series of national and international events have occurred which have not only confirmed our original experience in the administration, but have also given it historical perspective.

From 1948 to the present, oil companies in Venezuela did not hesitate to take advantage of the venality and cowardice of the government to bring back their colonial methods of exploitation used during the time of Gómez. On the world scene, we have witnessed the instructive Iranian crisis, the changes in the relationship between the oil companies and the other oil producers in the Middle East; the inclusion of Canada, an industrial nation with adult attitudes as an important petroleum producer; the historical event whereby the United States federal government published the facts of the oil cartel down to the last detail. Furthermore, in recent years, the Middle East—the major competitor of Venezuelan oil—has become the most unstable, disorganized, and anarchic zone in the world, and the most receptive to Russian political and diplomatic maneuvers. That means that this vast oil basin can no longer be used to scare the Venezuelans out of their legitimate claim to obtain the greatest share possible of their oil wealth. Finally, another favorable development of the postwar years should be mentioned—the climax of the powerful anticolonial movement in Asia and Africa. Entire nations and many millions of men have reclaimed their right to self-government and to a just share of their national wealth.

It is generally admitted now by influential political leaders in English speaking nations that it was not Russian intrigue, but basically a deep-seated desire for freedom which has led these peoples to demand an end to imperialism. A similar movement has agitated the people of Latin America.

The concurrence of all these factors makes it possible for Venezuela to achieve efficient control of its oil industry without need of a nationalization law or decree. A popular government in the future will have plenty of arguments with which to justify the intervention of the state to determine—along with the industry, but in a position of pre-eminence—the norms of production. These arguments are found by the dozens in the report of the United States government on oil cartel, where it is shown how the Big Seven decide years in advance how much oil will be produced in each operating area, the refining volume of each country, and the common stand which they will take with the officials and the workers in the countries where they operate. They also determine, in general, the market prices of oil.

In this connection, two observations should be made. First, the existence of the cartel as an international regulator of production and marketing would seem, under the present circumstances, to be the only obstacle to a bloody price war among governments to rationalize production on all the continents of a raw material of such exceptional importance. Second, although this cartelization of the oil industry is the result of a highly developed economic process, it is completely unacceptable that this giant financial complex function be a conspiracy of the Big Seven. It is inadmissible, to say the least, that the governments of nations that are the owners of oil fields produced under the concession system have no say when long-term production plans are drawn up, as they are now, in the closed meetings of concession-company directors. The representatives of the producing nations should have seat, voice, and vote at these planning sessions of the industry.

We state this thesis with utter frankness in regard to Venezuela. In the arrangement made in July, 1954, with Iran, there were aspects which may help to provide a formula for this result.*

---

*Only the cathedral bells were lacking to ring out the "hallelujah" when an oil agreement was signed with Iran on August 5, 1954. President Eisenhower, Prime Minister Eden, and John Foster Dulles all made enthusiastic statements. In Moscow, *Pravda* editorially denounced the deal; the United States press and Europe commented favorably. The architect of the agreement was the same Herbert Hoover, Jr., who had structured the oil reform in Venezuela in 1943. This time he crossed the Atlantic seven times and made five trips to Teheran, bringing home the deal signed with the dictatorship of General Zahedi. On the last trip, he was promptly named under-secretary of state in his own country. Thus the president of Union Oil Company, according to columnist Drew Pearson, took over the second most important post in the foreign office of

Nobody can object that the Venezuelan share of oil income be carried to its maximum possible level, when the conditions are recalled under which concessions are being worked in Canada and in one recently obtained from the state of Texas by the Humble Oil Company. Neither should there be serious objections to having the Venezuelan government produce, refine, and market part of its oil; reserve the domestic market for itself; and make barter deals with other countries. Neither should there be objections if not another inch more of the republic's subsoil is handed over in colonial-type concessions, or that concessions given by the dictatorship after 1948 may be questioned.

Should the government punish any oil company interference in its international politics, it would have the decided support from the people of Latin America and other continents, as well as from the liberal political sectors and England and the United States. Even more sweeping measures could be taken if the oil industry as a whole took an intransigent position, forgetting that our country now has a clear idea of what its oil fields are worth. If it ever became necessary for the state to take an extreme position against the cartel in case it tried to unilaterally impose its will upon the government, nobody should doubt that the people of Venezuela would accept any kind of sacrifice needed for the sovereignty and dignity of their nation. Venezuela will be in a strong position to take action if its government is strong because it has the support of the people who know it to be honest in administration and sincere in its democratic beliefs. There will be no danger of internal subversion because the feudal and military groups which have always supported the dictatorial regimes will have been eliminated. Venezuela would then be able to obtain all of the benefits and advantages of nationalization through a system of mixed enterprises, of joint ventures with private companies under direct state supervision. In addition, part of the oil industry would be directly operated by the state. It is obvious, however, that such a vast program can only be carried out under present or foreseeable international conditions by a government with a well-defined foreign policy. In this respect, AD will not need to take an opportunistic path, as it has always maintained a clear-cut line of conduct.

AD has always followed a careful and responsible policy with regard to the United States. We have recognized our political and economic ties with the

---

the Potomac, the Iranian deal having earned him the assignment. It is a complicated arrangement. The *Washington Post* reported that it truly enabled Iran to emerge from colonial status and ended the state-within-a-state status formerly held by the Anglo-Iranian Company. The *Christian Science Monitor* was less enthusiastic, pointing out that the British had offered Mossadegh more attractive terms than now given to Iran. The deal, in summary: maintains the principle of nationalization, but turns operations of the company over to a consortium of seven international oil companies; two of the seven directors of the new consortium are named by Iran; Iran gets a royalty estimated at $400 million on a production of 500 million barrels during the next three years, quite a bit less than the $ .70 per barrel estimated by *Le Monde* of Paris; a contract for twenty-five years, renewable for fifteen more; and, the National Iranian Oil Company will manage several oil fields directly and has a monopoly on marketing oil products in the domestic market. This, plus the presence of two Iranian directors on the board, are the most interesting provisions of the deal for Venezuela.

only big power of the American continent. Economy and geography have brought about a close relationship—not only between the United States and Venezuela—but between both Americas, since there are only differences of style between our situation and the other nations of the continent. This inter-American relationship—for those of us who speak Spanish, Portuguese, or French—should not take form either as colonial submission or as aggressive verbal provocation. The colonial attitude is only taken by those who deny the heritage of our economic and political independence. The dogmatic anti-Yankee position is characteristic of noisy minorities, the communists, or those who mimic thier strategy—in any case, by political movements which have no true possibility of success. A different attitude is taken by the popular movement which has a solid root in the collective faith of our people, as is the case of AD in Venezuela.

These parties called to face up to the responsibility of guiding their countries cannot be, and should not be, either lackeys to the Yankees, or anti-Yankees. This is not a weak position of compromise, the product of opportunism. AD has experience with this middle way and no motive to repent. That is the attitude we took when in government and the one we will take when we return.

The attitude which Venezuela takes toward the Soviet Union should also be discussed here. We have no reason to hide what we think. We have never been admirers of the Soviets and AD criticized the brutal methods of the Stalinist dictatorship at least fourteen years before Nikita Khrushchev denounced them at the twentieth congress of the Bolshevik party. We have always rejected the popular front propositions made to us by the small group of Venezuelans organized in the Communist party. It would be stupid to follow the Russian diplomatic strategy when we are so distant—both in geography and tactics—from the zone of influence of the Soviet Union. Neither would it be responsible to form a common front with a group so lacking in strength or reputation as the Communist party of Venezuela. We are neither stupid nor irresponsible. The AD leadership had never had any intention of flirting with the Russian government or of making any kind of alliance—permanent or temporary—with the communist groups in our country. On the contrary, we have maintained, and continue to maintain, a constant ideological fight with them. We believe that the communists have never truly carried out a revolutionary program—Venezuelan and constructive in nature; rather thay have introduced harmful foreign ways into our country.

It would be ingenuous, on the other hand, to believe it easy to carry out the plans I have outlined. Political movements which seek to change the direction of a country's history are not destined to travel over asphalt highways. Internal obstacles and lack of international comprehension will have to be faced by the government which gives a permanent solution to the oil problem. We are encouraged by the political maturity of the Venezuelan people, however, and by the growing influence of progressive forces. We have no doubts regarding the future. It will be possible for Venezuela to progressively acquire control of the oil industry and its own destiny without resorting to bitter struggles with the oil companies and the governments behind them.

There is an additional obstacle not to be forgotten in discussin the difficulties of an oil policy in the post-dictatorial period, especially if it is hoped to combine a nationalistic outlook with flexible realism. There undoubtedly will be an angry public reaction to the close association and visible complicity between the oil companies and the despotism now affecting the country. (I wrote this page in 1956.—R.B.). Our public sees this close alliance between the foreign companies and the Venezuelan reactionary military clique as one of the fundamental supports for a regime opposed by most Venezuelans. The companies' disdain for workers' rights—now that they do not have freedom to organize—is also sowing seeds of mistrust.

There is a marked similarity between the conduct of the oil companies and that of the governments of their countries of origin: the United States, England, and Holland. The State Department, so eager to defend human rights in eastern Europe and the Asiatic regions under communist control, has had no interest whatsoever and has even sought to block the effort in 1949 by some Latin American governments, especially that of Uruguay, to obtain international condemnation of similar outrages committed in Venezuela against human rights. In November, 1954, the head of the Caracas political police, Pedro Estrada, visited Washington as the guest of the government. This was the individual who boasted publicly of having personally shot handcuffed political prisoners in their cells. It was he who gave the order to liquidate Leonardo Ruiz Pineda, Antonio Pinto Salinas, Captain Wilfredo Omaña, and dozens of other democratic fighters for liberty. He was the same person whose activities in the Caribbean in the years 1945–48—as he traveled under false names with a Dominican diplomatic passport as a secret agent of the dictator Rafael Leonidas Trujillo—were regularly reported by North American police to their Venezuelan colleagues. Now he was received in official circles of Washington with the utmost cordiality. This cheap copy of a Himmler or Beria, a stowaway who doubled as a hangman, was eulogized by the New York *Herald Tribune* as the one who liquidated the alleged communist threat in Venezuela and formed a police network of outstanding efficiency throughout the Caribbean.

The government which is supposed to exercise leadership of the free world against the totalitarian challenge went even further in its complicity with the petroleum based despotism of Caracas. In 1954, the United States government decorated Pérez Jiménez with its highest honor—the Order of Merit, rank of commander-in-chief. The United States press frankly admitted the connection between this honor and the petroleum policy followed by Venezuela. Of course, these decorations merit little credit. People look upon them with a high degree of skepticism. They see them as a gift of glass beads to flatter vain and ignorant persons. In this specific case, however, the medal for which space could hardly be found on the multidecorated chest of the megalomaniac, was accompanied by a citation which did little credit to the government of a democratic nation. The president of the United States seemed to forget, when he signed it, that a chief of state whose office was a result of a majority vote ought always to be free of the suspicion of acting under the influence of unscrupulous millionaires who do not represent the people.

The sentiments of the American common man were set forth by Robert Alexander, an economics professor of Rutgers University, whose letter to the *New York Times* was published November 2, 1954:

> Our government seems eager to recommend democracy to the Asians but to care very little about it in our own hemisphere. Recently, President Eisenhower warned South Vietnam that unless it established a more democratic government, it could not expect more aid from the United States.

On almost the same day, President Eisenhower conferred the Legion of Merit decoration on one of the worst dictators of Latin America, President Marcos Pérez Jiménez of Venezuela. Alexander's letter got a reply from one of the lackeys of the dictator, Dr. César Gonzáles, ambassador in Washington. He did not deny any of the concrete charges made in his letter to the *New York Times* and the newspaper itself replied to the dictator's diplomat in an editorial entitled "The Americans," November 28, 1954. It declared: "One of the most effective criticisms coming from Latin America is that Washington supports and is ostentatiously rewarding the military dictatorships because they are anti-communist. The most recent example was the decoration of Col. Pérez Jiménez of Venezuela with the Legion of Merit."

Of course, political crimes and denial of human rights could not be the justification for such an honor. There was another aspect worthy of exultation by the president of the United States, however: the regime's enthusiastic support of foreign capital with special solicitude for investors from the United States. "Just listen to the drum," as the natives of my home region of Barlovento would maliciously say:

> His excellency, Colonel Marcos Pérez Jiménez, both as president of Venezuela and before, has given special emphasis to the spirit of cooperation and friendship with the United States. His intelligent policy in economic and financial matters has facilitated the increase in foreign investment, enabling his administration to make great contributions to the welfare of the country and the development of its immense natural resources.

This was the citation of the president of the United States for the man who had intensified the subjection of his country to the oil industry, and who had made Venezuela a source of scandalous enrichment to the coupon-cutters, most of whom lived in the United States.

The accommodation of the Republican administration of the United States with the Venezuelan dicatorship went hand-in-hand with that of two other governments, from whose countries came other companies feeding upon the petroleum manna of our country—England and Holland. Traditionally, the

English island of Trinidad and the Dutch possession of Curaçao had offered asylum to Venezuelan political exiles. In the time of Pérez Jiménez, however, they cooperated slavishly with the despot's police. The universal rules of political asylum were constantly violated and the Venezuelan exiles were continually persecuted.

Article 14 of the Universal Declaration of the Rights of Man approved by the General Assembly of the United Nations on December 10, 1948, reads: "In case of political persecution, anyone has the right to seek asylum in any country." This principal of international law with a long tradition behind it was repeatedly violated by the Tory government of Great Britain as an accommodation to a regime which allowed Royal Dutch Shell to obtain profits in Venezuela similar to those that the Anglo-Iranian company once got in Persia. In 1954, the *Trinidad Guardian* admitted that "the officials of Caracas were giving the English orders on how to treat political refugees," including the constant threat of deportation from the island.

These were the factors which have contributed to the animosity felt by Venezuelans toward the foreign oil companies in our country. The popular parties in Venezuela that profess a militant faith in political democracy and economic nationalism, especially AD, view the future with alarm because of this widespread animadversion among our people. We are fighting with earnest perseverance to solve the dramatic political-social crisis of our country. If the solutions are delayed, if the antagonism growing among our people is not checked, then these problems are likely to receive a more radical solution than prudence would dictate.

Our position regarding the principal problem—that of petroleum—has been defined by the leadership of AD and summarized in the preceding pages. We continue to believe in the suitability of a policy similar to that followed in the three years of 1945–48, adjusted to new conditions which have subsequently arisen.

23

Summmary and Forecast

Venezuelan history for the last one hundred and fifty years—with all of its greatness and misery, its long dark periods and its brighter interludes—has been summarized in these pages. The villain of the piece is that great god of the mechanical age, petroleum. The tormented and passionate history of Venezuela, however, began centuries before the NorthAmericans took asphalt from Guanoco or the English drilled their first oil well in Zulia. What happened then has done much to determine contemporary events, just the same as negative realities of today affect our possibilities of progress for tomorrow. Thus we must once again review the fascinating drama of yesterday before making a final interpretation of our present life and attempting to look into the future.

The Colonial Background

Ovidio y Baños, one of the historians of the Spanish conquest, wrote: "this province was inhabited by people of many tribes, none of whom recognized a single monarch. Each tribe owed allegiance to its own chief." The Spanish conqueror in Venezuela did not find a highly developed indigenous population like the Aztecs of Mexico or the Quéchua or the Aymara of the Peruvian and Bolivian highlands. There were numerous tribes such as the Caribe, the Caquetios, and the Jirajara—all poor and backward—that were the Indian element in the mixture which made up our national mestizo identity. There was not much left of the original population because it had been decimated

368

by the firearms, horses, and dogs of the conquerors in hand-to-hand warfare in defense of its homeland. The remaining Indians not subject to forced labor in fields or mines continued to fight fiercely in unequal combat. To justify the drastic punitive measures taken against them, nearly resulting in annihilation, they were accused of cannibalism.

The foreign elements came with the Spaniard and also with the Negro, brought in iniquitous slave ships to work in the cocoa plantations of Barlovento and in the mine shafts of the Andes. We Venezuelans all have some Indian, Negro, and white in the pigmentation of our skin and in our psychological reactions. Vallenilla Lanz, that cynical but intelligent theoretician of the Gómez regime, used to say: "In Venezuela we are all 'coffee with milk' *(café con leche)*." Out of the melting pot, there came a typical man with certain typical characteristics. Europeans who visited the country during the eighteenth century, such as Alexander von Humboldt, describe the Venezuelan and his behavior. He was a restless type, lively but punctilious; he was an avid reader of the subversive ideas expressed by the philosophers of the Encyclopedia; he was inclined to be pugnacious with the Spanish authorities and began to evidence a thirst for independence after the pacification of the Indian tribes was accomplished by their virtual extermination.

Various circumstances have tended to mold the Venezuelan character since the days of the colony, providing the particularly mysterious soul which seems to give each people its own national identity. The geographical location of the country in the northernmost part of South America and the extensive coast line facilitated the coming of people and ideas from overseas. The galleons of the Guipuzcoana Company made relatively regular runs between Venezuelan and Spanish ports. They brought, as contraband—earlier perhaps than to other American people—the books in which the prophets of the Encyclopedia denounced the myth of the divine right of kings. Venezuelan society was permeated by ideological novelties and a strong conservative force did not prevail there as it did in other regions where the vice-royal administrations, the royal audiences, and the pontifical universalities molded a Creole caste of obstinate fidelity to the absolutist monarchy and the scholastic philosophy.

These antecedents helped to explain why the Venezuelan Francisco de Miranda was the first South American international personality of the eighteenth century, why this land produced Simón Bolívar, and also why, despite the fact that Venezuela was the Spanish colony with the smallest population and least natural resources, it was among the first to participate in the emancipation of South America.

Simón Bolívar was the leader of that stupendous American independence movement of 1810 and had the most truly continental vision. "Only the unity of all of the people of Latin America will make us great and respected by other nations," was the phrase stating his thought. As a man of action, he put these words into effect. He led his people in a liberation crusade, our most beautiful national adventure. They fought against the armies of the Spanish king and contributed to the independence of people throughout South America. The disinterested enterprise of a people which, for fifteen years, fought over half a continent, traveling from one end to the other on foot and horseback without any thought of conquest, was possible because of the close identity of the leader with his people. The multitude which followed Bolívar when he crossed the Andes, from the plains of the Apure in Venezuela to the Bolivian highlands, was just as visionary as he was and just as impassioned by liberty.

Some superficial observers, noting the years of autocracy in Venezuela during the nineteenth and twentieth centuries, have concluded that the birth of Bolívar must have been an aberration in a country which gave rise to so many despots. They see the Liberator as alien to the social environment in which he was born. Our historian, Enrique Bernardo Nuñez, however, has properly called this a superficial judgment. He wrote: "From whence came these half-clothed soldiers, barefoot, unpaid, sleeping in the open during the interminable campaigns? Who are the ones who accompanied the Liberator to the islands, to the congresses, to the council meetings? Who were these men and women who showed such faithfulness under adversity, such willingness to sacrifice? Anyone who stops to think must realize that an entire nation followed Bolívar."

Venezuela sacrificed half its population during the fifteen year war. There were little more than half a million people when independence was finally won. Some time back, I surprised my audience when I was able to demonstrate, at a university roundtable discussion in New York City, that my country had suffered greater human loss in its fight for independence than did the United States in two recent wars—World War II and the Korean War. When there were no adults left to fight, the adolescents who studied in the Tridentine Seminary of Caracas were recruited by an order given by Bolívar in 1813. Some months later, out of the eighty-five students who marched off to fight, only one remained.

The republic was begun in a country that had few people and much land. The lack of people was matched by another adverse inheritance left by the group of famous Venezuelan generals. Their victories in the twenty-four great battles of the war against Spain in Colombia, Ecuador, Peru, Bolivia, and Venezuela produced an abundant crop of heroes who, on more than one occasion, were a serious hindrance to the normal political evolution of the republic because of their exaggerated desire for personal power. The Mexican historian, Carlos Pereira, has noted that the principal problem of Venezuela after 1830 was to liberate itself from its liberators. After the deaths of Bolívar, Sucre, and Urdaneta—the greatest military leaders, the other survivors did not live up to their glories. Páez, Mariño, and the Monagas brothers were among those who became chiefs of rival factions in the civil wars which ravaged the country. During the years that followed, there were always people ready to take up arms in the hope of finally realizing what had been promised in the War of Independence. On the other hand, many educated Venezuelans began to take refuge in the heroic past and to live immersed in history rather than trying to make history. They sought to escape from the miseries of heroic romanticism. Symptomatic of this narcissistic preoccupation with the past, the writing of history has always been the most popular literary form in Venezuela. Many intellectuals have avoided a response to the shameful facts of contemporary life by writing about the grandeur of the past.

The Republic of the General-Presidents

The economic backwardness of the country and the tremendous loss of life and wealth as a result of the struggle for independence were obstacles to the formation of a middle class. The war had almost annihilated the urban and rural property-holders who could have and should have taken power. Weak and insecure, they abdicated their political independence. They accepted a secondary role, leaving power to those who, as Bolívar once said, "demand credit with their lances." The warriors became government leaders and served as an arm of the landowners and businessmen. Once Bolívar was gone, his revolutionary ideas were either lost in the Constitutions and codes or ignored in practice. Under an aristocratic election system, the vote was given only to land-holders or those who possessed university degrees.

In 1835, the educated class with economic power sought to reduce the control which General José Antonio Paez had exercised over the country, and elected Dr. José Maria Vargas as president. This interlude of civil government did not last long. It was soon ended by a military coup. One can say, years later, that the failure of the first civilian government in Venezuela may have been partly due to the unfortunate selection of the candidate. Vargas was an illustrious scientist and a citizen of great civic virtue, but he lacked political ability. He accepted the presidency with great unwillingness and soon afterwards threatened to resign over a minor difference with the Congress. His state of mind made him incapable of facing the military uprising.

After the failure of Vargas, the propertied class preferred to maneuver behind military presidents, maintaining the unjust economic social system handed down from the colony. This was a shortsighted and suicidal policy on the part of the educated and economically powerful sectors and produced two negative results. First, the country would very slowly integrate itself as a nation under a rule of law because arbitrary war chieftains were almost always in control of the government. Second, a feeling of hatred and a desire for revenge grew among the lower classes because they had been denied social justice and political participation.

The hate exploded with terrible violence in the Federal War (1859–64), using as an example the Paris uprising of 1848 and the preaching of the Utopian socialists who, at that time, were inflaming the European workers. The Venezuelan leader who advanced these ideas was an extraordinary demagogue, Antonio Leocadio Guzmán. His liberal ideas aroused the poor of the country and the people generously poured out their blood in the fight against conservative rule until a government came to office pledged to his messianic faith. This Long War, as it is known in our national history, eliminated practically all that remained of the conservative oligarchy. Its leaders defrauded the popular hope, however, and became the chiefs of a new oligarchy. There were a few favorable results, however: the breakup of the social caste system, consolidation of freedom for the slaves, and a variety of new civil laws.

The new liberal oligarchy also governed through a series of military chieftains. There were two brief periods of civilian government in the second half of the nineteenth century under Rojas Paúl and Andueza Palacios. However, the Monagas brothers—Falcón, Guzmán Blanco, Crespo, and others were all products of military life, and governed in typically caudillo fashion during the years preceding the culmination of autocratic government in the country with the two dictatorships of Cipriano Castro and Juan Vicente Gómez.

The negative factors hindering the political and social progress of the nation also helped bring foreign intervention to the country. Venezuela more than most Latin American countries, suffered from the progressive pressure of the big powers. In 1858, various European nations, headed by England and France, in support for the overthrown dictator, José Tadeo Monagas, blockaded our ports. Later, in 1895, England threatened to land marines on our coast because of the dispute over the boundary with British Guyana. President Cleveland of the United States, invoking the Monroe Doctrine, intervened to prevent this. The unfair arbitration which followed, however, turned over to the British Empire a vast portion of our national territory. With its Victorian arrogance of the mid-nineteenth century, England refused to accept arbitration, the solution proposed by Venezuelan governments to settle a dispute involving 50,000 square miles of land along the Orinoco. Venezuela had a perfect right to this territory, but Albion claimed it as part of British Guyana. When the British refused arbitration, President Cleveland in January 1896, named a commission of North American jurists to study the controversial matter. England then gave way, as it was sure that this investigation would be unfavorable to its claims. An international tribunal was formed, made up of five judges selected by the two parties: Russell and Collins, who were English judges; the chief justice of the United States Supreme Court, Fuller; and another judge of the court, Brewer. De Martens, a Russian expert in international law, presided over the tribunal which gave its decision without an opinion on October 4, 1899. It was notoriously partial to the British claims and gave British Guyana 90 percent of the territory in dispute. Venezuela got to keep only 5000 square miles southeast of the Orinoco mouth and control over the various channels whereby this river entered the sea.

Venezuela protested the unjust decision but only recently have the facts of what went on behind the scenes become known. In July 1949, the American Journal of International Law published a posthumous memorandum of the

American jurist, Mallet-Prevost, who was one of the American lawyers representing Venezuela in the arbitration. He explained that the panel's decision was not based upon law or justice, but was the result of a deal made between the Russian judge and the two English magistrates, the product of a diplomatic agreement between the foreign offices of London and Moscow. The two North American judges either had to sign the decree as it came out, or let the English obtain control of the Orinoco mouth. Mallet-Prevost wrote how the former American president, Harrison, another of the lawyers representing Venezuela, expressed himself in the crude language of the frontier when he was advised of what had been decided. He added that both of the lawyers for Venezuela and the two American judges decided to accept the formula of the Anglo-Russian trio as the lesser of two evils. In the light of these facts, the attitude of the Venezuelans down through the years regarding the usurpation of their territory is understandable. We have not made restitution of these lands an immediate demand because there has been a consensus that other national problems have priority. The problem, however, does exist and in the long run must be given a just solution.

Finally, petroleum appeared. This unexpected source of wealth provided financial backing and international support to military regimes. It poured money into the treasury and underwrote the increasing costs of army and police. Tacit agreements of mutual convenience existed between the Venezuelan autocrats and the international oil cartel. The new mineral wealth caused additional damage to the country. Easy wealth corroded the austere concept of life in many social circles. The unrestrained desire to make a fortune substituted for the traditional sobriety of the Venezuelan. To obtain wealth, people were willing to work either for abirtrary and venal officials or as representatives of the oil companies, forgetting the true interest of the country. Those with the best education, the most obliged to concern themselves with public questions, selfishly followed their personal interests. The religion of success—the possession of luxurious mansions, automobiles in the garage, and a big bank account—had a wide and devoted following. Few lawyers in the middle and working classes were immune to the contagion of a grossly materialistic life. The scramble for new riches and ostentatious living led many to forget their civic duty.

The Other Side of the Coin

So far only one side of Venezuela has been under scrutiny. It is dramatic and sad. It has given rise to a cult of pessimism and despair among men who have ignored the existence of more affirmative and promising elements that exist side by side with those that have slowed the harmonious development of our national personality. The first and most powerful of these is the passion for liberty among our people. The military caudillos and the imperious autocrats could never govern peacefully. A spirit of democratic resistance flourished among thousands of dissidents who faced persecution, jail, and exile, or who often perished in armed struggle. The civil tradition of Venezuela contains names which symbolize militant loyalty to democratic ideas. Their books and activities have influenced Latin American liberal thought, often going beyond our country's frontiers. The writings of Juan Germán Roscio on the conflict between liberty and despotism, had a decisive influence on the political behavior of Benito Juárez. Andrés Bello was one of the founders of the legal system and democratic institutions of Chile. Miguel José Saenz, teacher of Bolívar, who fell on the battle field during the wars of independence, was a pioneer in modern concepts of mass education, Fermín Toro, in the middle of the past century, formulated criticisms of economic liberalism and political autocracy with unusual dialectic ability. José Martí found in Cecilio Acosta a kindred spirit in his devotion to liberty and humanistic culture. In our own time, this tradition of civilian opposition to autocratic barbarity has continued. Arévalo González, a fearless newspapermen, wore leg irons in the jails of Juán Vicente Gómez for more than fifteen years. Pio Gil, the writer of combative, biting prose, gave his life to a pamphlet war against the misgovernment of Castro and Gómez. Jacinto López for many years edited a New York magazine against the Gómez and other dictatorships in Latin America, and criticized the North American policy of the "big stick" in the days of the first Roosevelt, Harding, and Coolidge. Rómulo Gallegos wrote some of his best books during his first exile in the thirties, after having rejected the corrupting offers of the Gómez dictatorship. Andrés Eloy Blanco, our greatest national poet and an amazing lyric voice for America, also wore leg irons under Gómez and died in exile. Antonio Arráiz also wrote of his experiences as a political prisoner. Armando Zulcaga Blanco left behind his promising studies in the Sorbonne to give his life for the struggle against dictatorship. Alberto Adriani and Mariano Picón Salas, two brilliant representatives of Venezuelan twentieth century thought, acquired much of their culture during prolonged exile. Enrique Bernardo Nuñez refused the temptations of his surroundings to exalt the highest values of our nationality. Rafael Blanco Fombona and José Rafael Pocaterra, in their best years, represented this tradition of dignity and intelligence, even though their will to fight declined in later years.

The tradition continued during the hard days of the Pérez Jiménez dictatorship and the torch passed from one hand to another. Leonardo Ruiz Pineda and Valmore Rodríguez, Andrés Eloy Blanco and Alberto Carnevali, Antonio Pinto Salinas and Luis Troconis Guerrero, and many others who died in jail or in exile due to their unremitting struggle to free Venezuela, are examples of the continuing barbarism which still plagues the nation.

There have also been military men who sought to install the personal rule of law at the service of the people: Carlos Soublette, a general in the Independence Wars, was one of the leaders most respectful of human rights. Rafael Urdaneta, another of Bolívar's lieutenants, was austere in his civic conduct. Ezequiel Zamora, the self-taught strategist of the Federal War, was a dedicated revolutionary. José Manuel Fernández, the romantic crusader for popular suffrage, spent his life in jail, exile, and armed uprisings. Antonio Paredes, another self-taught military figure who fought the despotism of Cipriano Castro, before being shot wrote books in prison extolling liberty. There were other generals who gave their lives in the fight against the barbarism of Gómez: Moracio Ducharne, Ramón Delgado Chalbaud, Rafael María Carabaño, Juán Pablo Peñaloza, Doroteo Flores, Bartolome Ferrer, as well as military men such as the Alvarado and Parra Entrena brothers. In our own days we had the examples of Mario Ricardo Vargas, who died in exile, and Captains Juan Bautista Rojas, Wilfredo Omaña, and Lieutenant Droz Blanco—who were assassinated. These civilians and military men were all moved to oppose arbitrary government by their latent rebellion and desire for democratic life which has always been present in our people. It is this deep-seated feeling which caused Guzmán Blanco to utter: "Venezuela is like a piece of dry leather. When one side is trod upon, it rises up by the other."

In addition to their passion for liberty, the Venezuelan people have another very defined characteristic—the rapidity with which they asssimilate new information. They have an agile and creative intellect and are surprisingly receptive to new social ideas. This quality could be particularly noted in the years following the death of Gómez. After such a long period of oppression, it was to be expected that the people would be mentally impoverished. Quite the contrary was true. Political parties, unions, professional and student organizations developed more rapidly than in other Latin American countries that had an historical evolution less turbulent than ours. When the people were offered the chance to vote after the 1945 revolution, they did so as a nation "long accustomed to the ways of civil society," to use Bolívar's phrase. The poverty-stricken rural workers consistently voted against candidates favored by the landholders who had exploited them. The great mass of workers voted likewise for men and programs representing principles and social justice in political democracy.

The Venezuelan people loyally defended the democratic regime which lasted from 1945 to 1948. They restrained their impatience and confidently waited for the programs underway to better their depressed living standards. There were no anarchistic uprisings of infuriated mobs. When the constitutional government was overthrown, the people gave their determined help to the underground resistance led by AD. After four years of military dictatorship in 1952, the people again clearly showed their political maturity by voting for the only two legal opposition parties, URD and Copei. They defeated a regime that had used all those resources of power and the techniques that had been so useful to totalitarian governments in other Latin American countries: police threats, demagogical propaganda using the most modern publicity methods, millions of bolívares spent by official agents in a useless effort to buy voters. The result is now known: a decisive defeat for the dictatorship such as has never been known in the political annals of Latin America.

This fact is sufficient to invalidate the thesis, repeated so often by a sector of the press in the United States, which attributes to the people of Latin America an almost congenital incapacity to govern themselves. They are considered incapable of exercising and enjoying representative government. The truth is quite different. It has been the alliance of authoritatian sectors of the military with civilian reactionary groups and foreign corporations which has interfered with the desire of the people to have a government of law. In the specific case of Venezuela, those who have read this book should harbor few doubts regarding the role of foreign oil capital in promoting and supporting dictatorial government.

It must be asked why Venezuela has not yet acquired a representative stable political regime despite the decided democratic tendencies of its people (this was written in 1956—R.B.). In attempting to answer this question, we must analyze briefly the role of the military in contemporary society. We shall see that they do not inevitably support despots and dictators in the countries of Latin America.

The Army Before the Nation

Karl Mannheim, the great sociologist, has accurately defined the role in the political conflicts of our time played by "the concentration of the instruments of military power." The technological advances in modern arms have given organized armies a great repressive force. A company of shock-troops with armored cars, hand grenades, and machine guns is as powerful as an entire battalion used to be. That is why Mannheim says that "the concentration of military arms diminishes the chances of any kind of insurrection or revolution, or any kind of popular decision." He adds that the secret of democratization during the eighteenth and nineteenth centuries was the power of a single man with a rifle, or of a thousand men with a thousand rifles. Today, however, resistance is not measured by individual rifles but by the number of people who can be killed by a single bomb. Thus, he concludes, a socially isolated military force can always be used against the people.[1]

Nehru, who governed India, confirmed Mannheim's thesis when he noted how the 1952 popular uprising in India failed because the organized military force was on the other side. He said, "No matter how numerous the multitude is, it cannot impose itself by force on the armed forces unless the armed forces join with it." Lenin and Mussolini, ideologues of radically different doctrines, concur in admitting that it is impossible in our day for an insurrection without arms to triumph over military power. Lenin said it was impossible to have a revolution without the help of at least part of the army that defended the old regime. The creator of fascism coined the graphic phrase: "A revolution can be made with the army or without the army, but not against the army." These are undeniable truths. Not to admit them would be senseless. A political leader who sends defenseless masses into action against regular military forces would be irresponsible.

If a desperate uprising is collective suicide and if the "action of the masses," about which the communists talk so much, is an adventure condemned beforehand to fail, neither is passive resistance to dictatorship a sufficient response on the part of popular political parties and the men who direct them.

Between one position and the other—between an epileptic lunge or rheumatic inertia, both of which are unacceptable—there is to be found a third and correct position: a strategy of orienting and leading positive action by the people for the recapturing of their fundamental rights. An important factor in this strategy is attracting to democracy at least a part of the military force which supports the dictatorship.

Two Sides of the Venezuelan Political Situation

Venezuela and the Dominican Republic enjoy the unfortunate reputation of being "the two countries of the western hemisphere still under bloody, absolute dictatorships, where no kind of liberty is permitted," to use the words of the executive council of the AFL-CIO in its declaration of June 7, 1956.

Four years after the second coup d'état of December, 1952, in disregard of the overwhelming election defeat of the dictatorship, the complete denial of public liberties continued along with assassinations, arbitrary and rigid censorship of the press, and other forms of repression.

On February 3, 1956, it seemed that the situation might be favorably modified. It was announced from Caracas that there would be a general amnesty for prisoners in exile. In practice, however, this led to the return of only some fifty of the thousands of expatriate Venezuelans, and freedom for a few dozen out of the hundreds of political prisoners. Then, just a few weeks later, a massacre of students occurred in the streets of Caracas.

Pérez Jiménez did not even mention in his message to the puppet Congress on April 21, 1956, this latter occurrence which so outraged opinion within Venezuela and abroad. Instead, he defiantly ratified the intention of his government to continue its arbitrary and repressive policy. He confirmed that people had been jailed or deported without legal defense "whenever the circumstances required,"—always, of course, "in defense of the community and to preserve the peace and climate of liberty in the best sense of the word." He went on to describe how, at the end of the previous year, his government had authorized the return of persons outside the country and the liberty of others, and concluded with an arrogant statement worthy of a regime that openly practices the law of the jungle in this age of UN's and OAS's and International Commissions of Human Rights: "This should not be understood as amnesty. There is no intention to pardon the guilty or to conciliate supposed enemies. Neither has there been clemency or even desire to rectify possible errors."

A few weeks later, there was another demonstration of the lack of "desire to rectify possible errors." On August 10, 1956, the national security police announced the discovery of a vast terrorist plot to assassinate the chief of the regime. The author of this book was accused of being responsible for the supposed plot and a group of industrialists, businessmen, intellectuals, workers, and professors were its presumed financiers and agents. This prefabricated plot by the political police—the classical trick of Fouché inherited by Himmler, Beria, and their tropical American imitators—was the pretext for a new wave of persecution which again filled the jails of the country. One of the imprisoned—the industrialist, Mario Pérez Pisanti—perished in jail under circumstances that were never clarified. Again, none of the accused were given an opportunity to appear in court. Hitler permitted those accused of the Reichstag fire to defend themselves judicially; Stalin, before one of his political purges, staged a spectacle in which the accused publicly confessed their guilt after being broken by physical torture. In Venezuela, the opponents of the regime were jailed, tortured, and killed without the pretense of a trial.

It might be thought under these circumstances that the reestablishment of a civilized government is impossible. Oil continues to flow without interruption, bringing financial resources and international support to the dictatorship. Such a conclusion is the result of superficial analysis. The people, encouraged by the organized political forces, are determined to recoup liberty. History proves that whenever there are large sectors of the population with superior moral and intellectual resources who persevere in resisting a totalitarian force, a rule of democracy will eventually prevail. Andrés Eloy Blanco, a great poet, said it beautifully with his political intuition in a last speech and testament a few hours before his death in Mexico:

> Economic factors should be given their importance, but let us also remember the reality of our people, a people of a backward economy but of a splendid heroism— underdeveloped people economically, but millionaires in their humanity; small in population but great in heroes. Among our people the emotional factor, the human factor, is basic. Our first resource, our primary source of wealth, is human.

There are other viewpoints with a more optimistic slant on the future of Venezuelan politics. Some relate to national reality; others derive from recent historical facts, in America and in the world. As far as Venezuela goes, clearly the regime which had imposed itself upon the country is an historical anachronism inappropriate to the degree of development of the nation. Its empirical methods, its disdain for any rule of good government, and its political methods make it completely unsuitable to modern society as well as hateful to the people. Venezuela today is not the Venezuela of Castro and Gómez—with scarcely two million people, rural and backward, without industry, isolated from the world in an epoch of difficult communication, suffering from malaria, and with little culture. Today we are a modern nation incorporated in the industrial revolution of the twentieth century. Our territory has been cleansed in good part of tropical diseases and there is now a population of more than five million with a half a million workers in industry. Many of the population are educated and well-informed. There is a large middle class. The country is no longer an isolated island; on the contrary due to its geographical location and its economic potential, it is a key point of aerial and maritime communication. The radio has broken down the isolation which those who govern would like to impose upon us, like the Paraguay of Rodríguez Francia in the nineteenth century. All this explains why a great majority of Venezuelans, no matter what their political belief or social position, find the present political situation completely unacceptable.

The present country is different from that which existed in the time of Gómez and the same is true of the present army. It is certainly not the same horde as that commanded by ignorant machete-swingers. The needs of national development and the technological complexity of modern arms have given groups of highly educated officials to some branches of the armed forces, in particular the navy and air force.

It has been the educated officials of the military who, in some countries of Latin America, have contributed to the change in antidemocratic political situations. Such events have confirmed another of Mannheim's concepts regarding the support of the military for the dictatorships of our time: "The subjugated elements of society learned to adapt their tactics to all kinds of threats, including the military." Recent experiences in Latin American politics bear out this judgment.

Peru, Bolivia, and Argentina Show the Way

Two recent political developments—those of Bolivia and Argentina—have been examples of the violent ending to political crises for which there was no peaceful solution. Also, there are the interesting developments in Peru which may well be applicable to other countries. Peru had a dictatorship, supported by the military, which looked like it would last much longer. It was defeated at the polls, however, by an overwhelming majority of Peruvians on June 15, 1956, ending the role of the dictator Odría. The people, by an avalanche of votes, showed that they wanted a civilian, democratic government. General Odría and his military cabinet accepted this verdict, not only because of the intensity of civilian opposition but because there were many officers in the armed forces who did not wish to continue underwriting a government which denied liberty to the people.

Two other events occurred earlier, but were of equal importance on the Latin American political scene. The people, aided by sectors of the military, threw out authoritarian regimes. The 1952 popular insurrection took place in Bolivia with the help of the armed police *(Carabineros)*, who had been convinced by the leaders of the National Revolutionary Movement (NMR) of their patriotic obligation to eradicate the land-holding and tin mining oligarchy. After four years under the government of Victor Estensoro, the Bolivian people on June 7, 1956, ratified with their votes what had been won by bullets. Hernán Siles Suazo was elected president in the first universal secret vote ever held in the country.

In September 1955, the totalitarian regime of Juán Domingo Perón in Argentina was overthrown by sectors of the armed forces, especially the navy. General Eduardo Leonardi, one of the leaders of the revolution and provisional president, revealed that the strategy of the military conspirators was to obtain the cooperation of civilian sectors. The events of Argentina helped clarify the problem presented to those military men giving support to what is nothing more than old-fashioned Latin American dictatorships, no matter what kind of military philosophical sauce it is cooked in. These governments do not even have the prestige attached to the old caudillos. Certainly, those military sectors really concerned about the future of the armed forces in their countries should be interested in finding a solution to the crisis caused by the ambition and avarice of some of their leaders. These military groups often fully understand their inexorable dilemma: either the truly professional sectors of the military rise up shoulder-to-shoulder with the people against the military dictatorships, or the moment will come—maybe not for years, but it will come—when a revolutionary tidal wave will wipe out both the dictatorship and the armed forces which give it support.

With this in mind, the events in Argentina, especially the developments after the military had given a final push to the dictatorship typical of military neofascism, have extraordinary significance for the rest of the continent. General Leonardi was replaced by a military junta, which announced that it would rule only until elections could be held in 1957. Furthermore, it specified that no member of the military government could run for office. This clearly left the field open for the normal process of political parties running candidates in a democratic manner.

At the moment that this is being written, the immediate political future in Argentina cannot be predicted. If the process develops in the direction indicated by those who have overthrown Perón, it can be concluded that the first dictatorship of Latin America which spoke and acted in the name of the armed forces was overthrown by the military itself, to defend the moral and material heritage of the nation and its own prestige. Ten years of experience convinced an important sector of the Argentine military that the so-called regime of the armed forces in reality only represented the dictator and his clique. To avoid a similar situation in the future, the armed forces are trying to develop legal formulas which will make it more difficult for any military official to be tempted to believe that he has been called by providence "to save the country" and to install an autocratic government in the name of the armed forces. If Argentina continues on its present course, the result will have tremendous importance for the stability and development of democracy in Latin America.

The soldier has the same right as anybody else to run for office; however, he should then take his place as a civilian in the area where the parties are carrying out their ideological struggle and not seek to use the armed forces as a "springboard to power." The military institution does not belong to any man or any group of men, but is a public agency subordinate to the state.

The Peruvian, Bolivian, and Argentine developments have encouraged all those who are fighting against despotic governments. What is more, there are new situations developing on a world scale that also enable the Venezuelans to look forward to the immediate future of their country with considerable confidence.

The détente between the two major world powers and the growing belief that a third world war is unthinkable tends to remove one of the most solid supports of the Latin American dictatorships in an era of peaceful coexistence. The military will no longer influence the formulation of foreign policy as allies of the western powers. It is to be hoped the competition between Russia and the United States will progressively become more a matter of ideas than of arms. In this respect, the Soviets will have a marked advantage if the western camp, at the same time as they publish the speeches of Khrushchev to demonstrate Stalin's criminal conduct, continue giving support to Latin American governments whose methods are similar to those of Stalin. This basic foreign policy flaw of the United States has been repeatedly criticized by important sectors there, especially by the unified labor movement and by influential newspapers and public personalities. It is quite possible that this criticism will bring about a change in American foreign policy within a relatively short time. Such a change, of course, would have an impact upon the European countries of the Atlantic community. With these favorable prospects, we have great faith that our country will soon have a stable government that respects public liberties, especially the right to vote; which is concerned about solving community problems by modern methods; which is honorable in its management of public money; and which will make foreign investors understand that this is a country for legitimate business but not for the abusive exploitation of its natural resources and its working class. In other words, governments capable of staging a national democratic revolution are a historical necessity for our country.

A Free Venezuela Within a Just America

The sociopolitical process of Venezuela must be seen within the framework of what is going on everywhere in Latin America, which "has entered into revolution," to use Marti's phrase. There is a great wave of popular rebellion from one end of the continent to the other, similar to what is going on in Asia and Africa or in other areas which have been under prolonged domination of antinational oligarchies or the big powers. A powerful revolt has extended from Cape Horn to the Mexican–United States boundary. We seek an organic Latin American integration which would help stabilize the representative, democratic system of government without interfering in the sovereignty of each nation. A front of this nature would be supported by public opinion in Latin America and would have the sympathy of those in the United States who profess to liberal democratic beliefs. The relations between the two Americas will be more normal, less characterized by resentment and jealousy, when a greater equilibrium of forces exists between the two portions of the hemisphere. We have many good reasons of historical coincidence to work out a good understanding, despite the differences of our culture, economic development, and life style.

Venezuela should have an important role in achieving regional Latin American integration. It has been blessed with great natural resources, some of which—like oil—obtain a stable income. This has allowed the country not only to develop its own economy, but also to aid in the development of other peoples with whom we have a common destiny. The Venezuelan public has a long tradition of cooperating with sister countries without desire of self-aggrandizement.

Like any nation which has had the opportunity to make history, Venezuela is capable of large and generous undertakings. Isolationism and chauvinism do not go with the psychology of our people. There is a line in our national anthem which expresses the true feeling of our people: "All America exists as a single nation."

If Venezuela is to realize its own destiny and contribute to the integration of Latin America, however, it must achieve political stability under democratic government. In 1945–48, we demonstrated that the country need not fall into the extremes of either permanent disorder or imposed authority. Spurious sociologists supporting the dictatorships have talked a great deal about the alleged swing of the pendulum between authoritative order and anarchic disorder, but this has not been true in our recent national life. The rule of law substitutes for the whim of the dictator. The practice of democracy at all levels of public administration and respect for human rights have produced harmonious and creative community activity.

Our recent dramatic experiences should keep us from falling again into absolutist forms of government. Even those who have habitually kept clear of civic activity understand today that "eternal vigilance is the price of liberty." A national conscience has been created, determined to end once and for all the sequence of autocratic arbitrary governments that has so held back the evolution of our country.

As Aldous Huxley has written, there is a tendency toward oversimplification when we seek to determine the cause of complex historical events. Are we then condemned never to understand our history or to learn from what has happened? Even though our understanding will probably never be complete, he wrote, we can at least understand enough for practical purposes. "For example, we can learn enough from our recent catastrophes to carry out a political policy—if we so desire—which at least will be less suicidal than that which we have followed in the past."

Huxley's thesis is very applicable to the Venezuelan case. We are convinced that we can have government by law in our country, elected freely by the people, if the political parties (Acción Democrática, Unión Republicana Democrática, Copei, and others that may be founded in the future), as well as other organized groups of the community, follow a policy less suicidal than in the past. As far as AD is concerned, we have tried to analyze our own errors, as well as those of others. We trust that we will not repeat them. The "entente" established among the political parties and other organized groups to confront the situation brought upon the country with the coup d'état of November 24, 1948, should be continued in the future. Its continuation would guarantee a less hazardous future for the nation. Our rich natural resources will facilitate accelerated progress of the country under orderly, responsible government. At the same time, however, this exposes us to the ambitions of powerful national and foreign interests.

We must clearly understand these future risks and possibilities if we are to avoid the kind of intemperate interparty discord which would again open the way in the future for the same coalition of reactionary forces that frustrated the democratic experience of 1945–48, and which plunged the country into a long period of political, economic, and social stagnation.

We are firmly convinced that the political parties and the uncorrupted sectors of the armed forces will be guided by this patriotic concern. The country has matured and learned its lesson in the school of adversity. That is why I can declare here, as the final summary of this lengthy book: in the immediate future, Venezuela will again have a democratic government. In the international field, our nation will undertake the glorious task of trying to assist this vast archipelago of dispersed, deprived, and despised republics— the Latin America of our days—with efficient organized action.

Washington, Havana, San José de Costa Rica, and San Juán de Puerto Rico 1951–1956

Epilogue

The Nationalistic Petroleum Policy
Following the Dictatorship (1958–67)

A nationalistic oil policy was proposed by the author when he became a candidate for the presidency of the republic. A summary of accomplishments during the period from 1959–67 includes: a) the fight against United States import restrictions; b) increase of government income from oil; c) creation of the state oil company, The Corporación Venezolana del Petróleo (CVP); d) reaffirmation of the "no more concessions" policy and general discussions of the advisability of a new formula: "service contracts"; e) establishment of an international agency for the defense of the small oil-producing nations—the OPEC (Organization of Oil Producing States); and f) substantial increases in wages, salaries and benefits for the workers, employees, and technicians working in the industry. The Arab-Israeli war confirmed the wisdom, firmness, and patriotic foresight of the democratic government after the dictatorship.

Summary of the Venezuelan Government's Oil Policy Beginning in 1958

The dictatorship's submissive policy of allowing Venezuela to be converted into an oil factory changed after the overthrow of this regime, which had always followed a policy so contrary to the best interests of the nation.

It would take too much space in this book were the post-dictatorship oil policy to be set forth in detail. A future book of mine—*De las Promesas a los Hechos (From Promises to Deeds)*—will have a thorough analysis of the policy followed by the democratic governments beginning in 1959. The former minister of mines and petroleum under my administration, Juan Pablo Pérez Alfonzo, published in 1967 a fine study of the subject entitled *El Pentágono Petróleo* (*The Petroleum Pentagon*).

During my campaigns of 1958 throughout the length and breadth of Venezuela, I continually explained the oil policy my government would follow if I were elected. This industry is—and will continue for a long time to be—the mainspring of the economic and fiscal life of the nation. I believed it necessary that Venezuelans everywhere be informed regarding the oil problem to assure that it be viewed from a truly nationalist perspective. Thus I discussed oil issues before the most diverse audiences. I even spoke before simple farm laborers in small rural villages about the matter, using simple language which any Venezuelan could understand.

Venezuela, as a nation and as a state, is dependent and will continue to be almost absolutely dependent on a single product—petroleum. The nation must create a more permanent economic base because oil is a non-renewable resource and it can be foreseen that within a few decades all that will remain will be some rusty oil derricks and the empty holes from which the oil has been extracted. The whole-hearted support of the entire population was needed for my government to develop a new oil policy far different from the subservient and compliant attitude of the dictatorship with the oil cartel. Our policy would follow the lines laid down by Acción Democrática. My innumerable speeches in public plazas were not recorded, but a series of speeches I made before managerial groups and the full text of the speech made to close my campaign on December 5, 1958, were taken down and published in the book *Posición y Doctrina* (*Position and Doctrine*). Most of the ideas voiced in these speeches were put into effect when my government took office.

I stressed that it was absolutely necessary to "modify the fiscal relationship between the state and the oil companies" and added, "In 1948 when we were in the government, the oil companies admitted that the 22 percent net profit they made then was exaggerated because the oil industry is similar to a public service. Now, in 1958, they are making a 32 percent profit. This cannot be accepted by the Venezuelan government. The oil companies must pay higher taxes."

At the same time, however, I made it absolutely clear that if it fell to me as the elected head of the new government to achieve this objective I would do so with the instruments at hand and without demagoguery in the public plaza. My statements could not be misunderstood. For instance, it was stated:

I repeat that which I have stated on other occasions: to increase oil taxes it will not be necessary to call you out to big public meetings. The government will solve this problem in a simple way. Since it is a government problem, it will be handled by means the government has at its disposal. The one who makes daily denunciations of Wall Street is not more of an anti-imperialist than the one who takes effective government action. Venezuela is now an adult country. It no longer suffers from a depressed, semi-colonial mentality. We only need to act to obtain greater benefits for the country from our increasingly valuable oil.

I ended with a paragraph which constituted a promise to the nation, which was largely carried out during my mandate and the following one of President Leoni. This paragraph said:

> We will not limit ourselves to obtaining a greater income from the oil companies. We will also create a national oil fleet. The remaining national oil reserves will be turned over to a national oil company and not a single centimeter more of national territory will be awarded as concessions. A state oil refinery—either forming part of an enlarged petrochemical industry or a new one to be built—will refine oil and gas products and these will be marketed by the national oil company. After thirty years of development in Venezuela we cannot continue as a passive spectator, with crossed arms, with regard to the production, refining, and marketing of Venezuelan oil.

A climate of opinion was created in the country conducive to obtaining a higher income from the oil companies, no doubt due to my reasoned arguments as Acción Democrática's candidate during the presidential campaign. After I had been elected, and during the period which intervened before I was inaugurated as president, the provisional government issued a decree changing the income tax law and increasing oil industry taxes.

The analysis which the provisional government had made of the oil industry demonstrated the accuracy of the data regarding its excess profits which I had published in my first edition of *Venezuela: Oil and Politics* (1956), and which I thereafter used repeatedly in public discussions. This data stated that in 1957, with an average capital investment of Bs. 8690 million, the companies obtained net earnings of Bs. 2738 million—or a return of 31.5 percent.

This is not the place to go into the rather unusual way that the decree was rushed out, with an elected president waiting in the wings. I will do this in my autobiography. The fact is that I put aside considerations of personal pride and supported the measure as favorable to Venezuelan national interests. I confirmed this in my inaugural address to Congress on February 13, 1959, when I said: "The income tax law reform by the provisional government, which I do not propose to alter with further tax increases under present economic conditions, will keep the treasury deficit from becoming alarming. We have a tight financial situation, it is true, because of the wasteful use of those public funds which were not stolen by the officials of the dictatorship."

Oil Panorama in 1959 and Fight Against United States Oil Restrictions

The situation of the oil industry was one of the gravest problems which confronted the government which took over on February 13, 1959. The oil hunger affecting consumer markets during and after the Suez Canal closure of 1956 now was past. The big consumer countries of western Europe and the United States joined their efforts to achieve a reduction in the price of oil. In 1958, the constant increase in production of the previous decade had diminished and production from Venezuelan wells was below that of 1957. The time of the "years of plenty," which the dictatorship neither wished to nor could take advantage of, was over. The dictatorship had not demanded more from the oil companies because it wanted to keep the good will of these powerful interests and, of course, of the governments backing them. It lacked the audacity to obtain a larger share of the excess earnings of the oil companies. Only a government which was fearless under pressure and sure of the support—rather than the repudiation—of Venezuelan public opinion, could do this.

As if the new government did not have enough problems, there now arose the obligatory restrictions of oil imports inaugurated by the United States government. This decision directly affected Venezuela, whose principal market for its petroleum exports was the United States. We pointed this out in categorical and energetic terms to the Eisenhower government. The Council of Ministers approved the text of a memorandum delivered to the Department of State on April 24, 1959. Two of its paragraphs will reveal the tone of its justified protest:

> The Venezuelan government is especially taken aback by the policy of the United States government which discriminates against imports of Venezuelan oil on the basis of United States national security. This policy seems to imply that Venezuela is being ignored and its oil production not considered, as formerly, essential to United States security. . . . The Venezuelan government seriously resents any discriminatory measure under the mandatory oil import program in favor of one or two countries—on the basis of national security—when it excludes other countries of the western hemisphere. Any exceptions made for oil imports from Canada and Mexico without the immediate security that these exceptions will be applied to Venezuela as well, will undoubtedly provoke an adverse reaction in Venezuelan public opinion and will assuredly promote hostile feeling towards the United States.

What we foresaw and feared happened an April 30, 1959. By proclamation of the president of the United States, crude oil and oil products imports were excluded from restriction if they arrived "by pipeline, motor, tank, truck, or railroad tank car from the producing country." That meant oil imports from Mexico—which hardly had any exports to the U.S.—and from Canada, a big exporter to the U.S.—were not restricted.

The note presented to the State Department served notice to the United States government that we would not take a fearful or passive attitude before a situation of such evident injustice to our national economy. President Eisenhower wrote me a letter attempting to explain the attitude of his government, using the dubious argument that oil entering the United States by land required a special guarantee in view of its secure supply during times of emergency. Reference was also made to a statement on March 10, 1959, by a

White House spokesman describing the mutual interests of the United States and the other oil producers of the continent "within the security zone of the free world" and added: "In recognition of this fact, conversations will continue with Venezuela and other nations of the western hemisphere to reach a coordinated solution to the oil problem, since it is related to defense considerations and the interests of oil-producing countries."

We did more than ratify our protest at the damage to our economy in our reply to the letter from the United States president. We warned that if the United States could adopt unilateral measures in limiting our exports there, we would take the same unilateral action with respect to imports from the United States. This was ratified by the Minister of Mines and Petroleum, José Antonio Mayobre, when he told the national Congress on May 31, 1967, that if quotas were placed on most of the articles listed under the trade agreement with the United States, they would provide protection for the development of a national industry. "For us, national security consists in our own economic development and we are applying our security clause."

The Venezuelan government continued to press firmly its arguments with the United States. We acknowledged that the exceptions accorded to Mexico and Canada were just and only asked that identical advantage be extended to Venezuelan oil imports. Washington recognized that our request was fair and used it to resist the pressure to apply the restrictions immediately, which came from the independent United States oil producers who were strictly regulated and could only produce from their wells a few days each month.

We discarded from the start any idea of demagogically blaming these measures on the ill will of the Republican administration of President Eisenhower, formerly so friendly to the dictatorship, towards the newly installed democratic government of Caracas. It was true that the overthrown dictator had displayed among his array of decorations the Order of Merit—awarded by the same administration of mandatory restrictions—but the whole restrictions matter had been planned by the powerful lobbies of the independent producers for years. In 1949 and again in 1950, delegations of businessmen went from Venezuela to Washington to talk with the State Department, congressmen, and exporters to Venezuela about the threatened restrictions. The official promulgation of such a measure had seemed imminent for some time.

When Kennedy was installed in the White House, we continued to fight for justice for Venezuelan oil. Various emissaries of his came to Caracas, even before his inauguration, to interview me. Some of them were personal friends whom I had known during my years of exile in the United States. We always talked about the restrictions and Pérez Alfonzo—whom I had selected to be my minister of mines and petroleum and who served with such efficiency and total devotion to the country during the 1945–48 period—spent hours methodically demonstrating and documenting the justice of our claims. The new president in Washington let me know that he wanted to repair this and other unfair aspects of the commercial relations between the two Americas.

The idea was proposed that our government would be consulted before any change was effected in the amount of oil import quotas assigned to Venezuela.

The system of consultation gave rise to an interesting episode. During 1960, the United States government advised us that President Kennedy was interested in installing a direct telephone line so that the two of us could converse without any delay at any time. I agreed and the necessary lines were installed in my Miraflores office and in my bedroom at the "Los Nuñez" residence. This gave rise to certain joking among my friends and I used to say: "These phones are minor offspring of the 'hot line' between the Kremlin and the White House. I think they will rust for lack of use!" But the forecast was not fulfilled. Within a month after the phones were installed, I was using them. We had been consulted by the United States government with just a few days of advance notice regarding a "proclamation" which President Kennedy planned to issue on import quotas. The proclamation brought little important change to Venezuela but the short time we were given to reply was, for us, inadmissible. I called the White House and the connection was made with the Florida beach house where the president was on Christmas vacation. My daugher, Virginia, was on the auxiliary line to act as translator. I was very upset and used some strong language which Virginia, in translating, softened up considerably. I insisted that she translate just the way I was saying things. Anyhow, President Kennedy immediately cabled me, asking if I would object to receiving a personal emissary of his during the holidays together with an expert on oil matters from the Department of Interior. I immediately replied that I would be glad to see them. When they came, my ministers of mines and treasury and I met at length with them in Miraflores palace. While we argued vehemently in defense of our nation's interests, we could hear outside the joyful sounds of the Caracas populace who especially delight in celebrating the Christmas and New Year holidays. President Kennedy, it should be added, had understood perfectly the counterpoint between my daughter and myself when she had tried to soften my remarks over the phone. The three of us recalled the incident with great amusement later when he visited Venezuela.

In interviews of the president of the United States with myself and my collaborators during his brief stay in Caracas, the principal theme was that of oil restrictions. In the joint declaration which President Kennedy and I signed in Miraflores on December 17, 1961, it was implicitly stated—I might say almost explicitly—what it was that Venezuela was asking from the United States with regard to petroleum. The sixth point of this statement made concrete reference to the discrimination against our oil, even though it was wrapped with the transparent cellophane of diplomatic language. This text says, "The two presidents expressed their belief that significant effort in social areas, in accord with the principles of the Alliance for Progress, must be closely linked with economic development. *The prices of basic raw materials and the commercial policies of importing countries should take into effective considera-*

tion the dependence of Latin America upon its exports. Recognition of this reality is vital for the life, both in letter and spirit, of the Charter of Punta del Este." (Italics by R. B.)

When I accepted the invitation from President Kennedy to make an official visit to his country, it was not to be superficially flattered—something always contrary to my temperament—or in order to have the Venezuelan national anthem played at the doors to the residence of the most powerful chief of state of the world. Rather, I went to continue my arguments—with tenacity and without pause or hesitation—on behalf of my insistent demand for just treatment of our petroleum sales to the United States.

Oil was the theme of discussion lasting for more than four hours in the White House between President Kennedy and myself with our respective advisors. After my presentation, Kennedy made his own—very extensive and with the aid of figures provided by his collaborators. I then whispered a question to the Venezuelan Minister of Treasury, Dr. Andrés Bermán Otero: "Do you have sufficient data at hand to dispute the figures of the president?" He replied with tranquil assurance: "I don't have numbers in writing but I know them by memory." And in his customary phlegmatic manner—more characteristic of an Englishman than someone from the tropics—he set about disputing one by one the figures used by the president with those put together by our ministeries of mines and treasury. The meeting ended with an agreement to set up a joint technical commission to make recommendations and to put an end to the controversy through a bilateral agreement. That same night the Kennedys offered us a reception and I had the satisfaction of having the president tell me: "I must congratulate you for the frankness with which you spoke and the precision of your treasury minister in his use of figures. I've checked the figures given to me and I'm convinced that those of your minister were the correct ones." I called Otero so that he himself might hear directly from our host the praise his fine presentation had merited.

With regard to my "frankness," I'd spoken without inhibition. I had asked that part of our interview be alone, without the help of any interpreter. My English was precarious but acquired greater fluency when I had some real reason to make myself understood. I stated that the imposition of oil import quotas on Venezuela and not on Mexico and Canada had not only been an unjust discrimination but also was a cover up for a racket—"a dirty business"—were the exact words which I used. There was a traffic—a speculation—in the permits given small refineries to import Venezuelan oil. The *Oil and Gas Journal* had editorialized: "The object is to distribute widely the profits to be made from low-cost foreign crude. The refineries have discovered that an import quota is like money in the bank. They can sell them and receive approximately $ .50 a barrel."

I concluded by telling him that the Alliance for Progress would not make sense—and would even seem to be nothing but demagoguery—as long as such patent injustice was unresolved. Here was an underdeveloped country—badly in need of making up for lost time and badly in need of development and material and cultural necessities for its people—from whose pockets $1 billion had been taken with all the skill of a professional pickpocket—to enrich a multimillionaire nation. As long as Venezuela was not paid in the same manner as Canada; as long as the speculation in import permits went on for the private benefit of a few hundred people in exchange for a few votes, Venezuela would be plundered by the United States. I made my case with some difficulty in words but with passion. President Kennedy looked at me with a penetrating gaze, listening attentively, one eye half-closed in a characteristic manner, and with a kind of humility that bespoke self-confidence and real greatness. I cannot recall his exact words but he said, in effect, that there was "an unholy combination of private interests" involved in the problem and that he was confident a solution would be found favorable to the interests of Venezuela before either of us had finished our respective terms in office.

I returned jubilantly to my country. The optimistic declaration I made to my countrymen at the airport of Maiquetia on arriving reflected this explicit promise of the American president. Then came the tragedy of Dallas. President Kennedy was assassinated before he could carry out the promise he had made to me. My presidency came to an end, but the sustained effort to obtain justice for Venezuela continued.

The restrictions issue was the principal theme discussed by President Leoni in his talks with President Johnson at the Punta del Este meeting. And recently, in November 1967, there was virtually a national mobilization of opinion against the threat that the United States Congress might pass legislation which would have indefinitely perpetuated the restrictions and the quota systems for Venezuelan oil. The unjust situation continues and the united purpose of the Venezuelan government and people is to fight incessantly against a state of affairs so unfavorable to us in our trade relations with the United States.

Those of us who have governed since 1959 have never made a big public issue of this tenacious defense of our national rights. There are two different ways of behaving in commercial relations with the powerful industrial states when you are responsible for the affairs of a small country which happens to be rich because it has a lot of that most sought after raw material of our age—oil. One can posture demagogically in public meetings; or one can persistently and without fanfare undertake action designed to achieve justice. The noisy hotheads of the extreme left reject this latter attitude. They should read the book, *The Gear*, by their admired Jean-Paul Sartre. The main character of this theatrical work is Jean Aguerre, a revolutionary who defends the oil interests of his small nation. He prevents his companions from bringing disaster to their country through radical measures against the foreign companies and the heavily armed nations from which they come. To govern with energetic but thoughtful nationalistic zeal in a small country with a limited capacity for self-defense—without falling over the edge of the abyss and breaking your neck—is quite a different thing from making fiery speeches in public or Congress with a wordy radicalism that is completely irresponsible.

A Reasonable Share of the Oil Income and Increased Wages and Social Benefits for the Oil Workers

The democratic government did a lot more with regard to the petroleum than engage in disputes with the United States over import restrictions. We acted according to the well-known maxim—but with a significant variation—"While you are asking something from God, keep using the hammer."

By resolution of the Ministry of Mines and Petroleum, the Coordinating Commission for Oil Conservation and Trade was established. The government thus had an agency—making use of the best available professional talent with ample powers to intervene in the operations of the private companies—to supervise the production and marketing of oil and oil products. It was not difficult for this commission to provide us with data which showed that the nation—despite the damage sustained in our oil trade with the United States—was receiving a high per barrel income from petroleum, while the unacceptable profit margins of the companies had fallen off considerably. Also, the freedom of the oil workers' union to bargain with the oil companies had resulted in substantial increases in wages and benefits—higher than those achieved at that time in any other part of the world.

In 1966, under the subsequent administration, another collective contract was signed bringing even more benefits to our oil workers. Their leader, Luis Tovar, is one of the most capable labor union figures of the country, and merited international recognition for his ability. He is presently president of the World Federation of Oil Workers, which includes millions of oil workers.

Our official policy of stimulating, not only allowing, unionization of oil workers, and not concealing the sympathy we felt for them in their drive for greater benefits through their collective contracts produced three results, all of great significance. It not only brought justice to the oil workers but it also increased their purchasing power to the benefit of our agricultural and industrial production; it guaranteed labor peace and the uninterrupted flow of oil; and it meant the eradication of communist infiltration of the unions, reducing it to only a minor influence in some of the smaller labor groups.

In 1967, the Mines and Petroleum Minister, Mayobre, could tell the Venezuelan Congress something that nobody could deny, because it was based on fact: "Venezuela has oil laws which give it the highest income in the world with relation to what is produced. In 1956, as is well know, the share of the state's income from oil was 52 percent, in comparison to the 48 percent taken by the companies. In 1966, the state received 65 percent, the companies 35 percent. The tax income went up from Bs. 3.39 per barrel in 1956 to Bs. 4.06 in 1966."

Former Minister Pérez Alfonzo takes the view that it would now be more logical and beneficial for the country to base the tax system on the net profits of the companies, establishing an excess profits tax above a fixed level so that those with more productive wells would have to pay more to the nation. This viewpoint merits attention since it is true that efficiency and management play a secondary role compared to the luck involved in finding a highly productive oil field. This idea should be seriously studied by those now responsible for running the government. Venezuelan tax policy must not become frozen but should remain dynamic in exploring all possible routes whereby the nation may receive the greatest possible benefit from its privileged position as the world's leading supplier of this highly prized source of energy. In any case, what has been achieved by democratic governments from 1958 to 1967 has enabled Venezuela to obtain an oil income much higher than that of any other producing nation within the capitalist system and world market economy.

This strongly nationalistic policy, however, did not prevent us from recognizing the right of the oil companies to make a legitimate profit. We were not impractical romantics in Miraflores and in the ministries. It would have been an act of stupidity to push the companies—capitalist enterprises dedicated to making profits—into a corner. We were not given to irresponsible demagoguery. We demonstrated this in 1960–61 when the nation and the treasury faced a grave recession. The hurried and indiscriminate payment by the provisional government of the enormous and often questionable floating debt left behind by the dictatorship—estimated at some billion bolívars—exhausted the national treasury. The dubious Emergency Plan—which remunerated idleness—used by the provisional government to deal with unemployment, cost more than Bs. 600 million. My own government made the error of increasing the national budget for the year 1960–61 at a time when our limited fiscal reserves were not enough to pay for the deficit that the high volume of state expenditures made inevitable. However, we were completely responsible and loyal to the program of Acción Democrática. In these years of serious economic and fiscal crisis, we never once thought of resorting to the easy way of overcoming our problems through the sale of new oil concessions or by increasing the taxes on the oil companies. It was preferable for the government to tighten its belt and spend less, appealing to the country to contribute more in taxes and spend less on luxury goods. It responded in splendid fashion to this patriotic appeal.

At this time, a law was passed which the communists immediately termed "the law of hunger." It was a very concrete demonstration that we did not seek to strangle the oil companies operating in our country. Defying the strident outbursts of the communists—who were now delirious in their praise of Fidel Castro of Cuba—and of other individuals who echoed them, we affirmed that this was not the time to increase oil taxes because the companies were receiving a much lower income. It was explicit in my message to Congress on May 4, 1961: "The present company earnings of 11 percent are low because they do not provide the necessary attractive margin to maintain investments abroad when the same level of profit can be made from investing in the home market. We are not willing to reduce our share in the income from oil. The problem lies in the low prices being received and our only hope for increased income from the oil income must be that prices will soon increase."

The then Minister of Mines and Petroleum, Dr. Pérez Alfonzo, amplified this stand and documented it when he spent a full day replying to congressional questioning. Oil company earnings had fallen vertically to 12.87 percent in 1959 and 13.12 percent in 1960. We knew that these profits would rise again in the future but at this time they were below the danger line. To increase taxes at this particular time would have been to invite the companies to close their wells in Venezuela and open new ones in the Middle East. Despite these solid arguments, Congress—with the support of the AD and Copei members—included the oil companies among those which should pay a tax on dividends, giving the president discretionary power to put this tax into effect. We decided not to apply the tax at all to anyone since we did not want to single out the oil companies for special treatment and were convinced that it should not apply to them at this time.

Eventually we were proven to be correct in our firm but responsible stand. Oil company profits increased again in later years and it was possible and justifiable for the Leoni government to increase their income tax, to reach an agreement with them regarding the settlement of back tax claims, and to negotiate a system of reference prices which stabilized the prices to be used in calculating the taxes paid for our oil.

The No Concessions Policy, the Creation of the CVP, and OPEC

Since its first time in government (1945–48), the Acción Democrática party had established a vigorous oil policy in defense of national interests. The foundation was laid then for an integrated and coherent policy intended to "Venezuelanize" the basic industry of the country.

One of the pillars of this policy was defined by the phrase: "no more concessions." We have recounted earlier how an enormous portion of national territory had been put under concession to foreign companies by a colonial-type system. The governments which had granted these were supine, inept, and careless of the public interest. We were going to be different. The oil industry had been in the country for fifty years and a passive attitude by the state could no longer be justified. It could no longer just collect taxes from those who produced the oil wealth. It was imperative that a national state oil company be established in Venezuela, as in other countries of Latin America and the Middle East.

The state oil company should participate directly in the oil business— exploring, producing, and marketing crude and products. It should be assigned the reserve areas—above all those in productive zones—and operate them itself or in conjunction with private concerns, not as concessions, but under a more flexible system which would give greater benefits to the country than service contracts. To carry out this policy, the Venezuelan Petroleum Corporation (CVP) was created by presidential decree on April 19, 1960. The historic date of our first political declaration of independence was deliberately selected, as we wished to stress that the national oil company would be used to achieve our economic independence.

The CVP was organized in a careful manner. It was not to be just another bureaucratic agency, overstaffed with incompetent people. It was not conceived to give only paper competition to the gigantic private companies operating in the country. Six years after its founding, the CVP had successfully drilled many wells and was in full production. It was marketing 16 percent of the gasoline used in the nation and struggling to reach the 33 percent assigned to it by executive decree. It was supplying more than 50 percent of the gas in metropolitan areas and was operating a refinery at Moron. It its oil fields it had an initial production of 20,000 barrels daily, scheduled to increase to 70,000 barrels daily by 1968. Its capital was approximately Bs. 400 million and it was paying the nation Bs. 72 million annually in various taxes. Most of the private companies were reluctant to cooperate with the CVP at the start, but soon began to accept the existence of the state company as irreversible, recognizing it as the reflection of profound Venezuelan feelings. A symptom of this change was the fact that fourteen companies signed up to have the CVP carry out a seismographic exploration of the Gulf of Venezuela, and are discussing another agreement to obtain geophysical data compiled by the CVP in Lake Maracaibo.

Another of the pillars of our nationalistic oil policy begun in 1959 was to form with the governments of the Middle East the Organization of Oil Producing Countries (OPEC). The Pact of Baghdad founding the OPEC was made public on September 24, 1960. Four countries—Venezuela, Iraq, Kuwait, and Saudi Arabia—were the founding members. Other producing countries joined later. It is a united front of oil nations to promote high prices for the crude oil being produced by the international oil cartel from wells in our countries. Another goal is to combine efforts to obtain the greatest share possible of the income from oil. The strategy of OPEC is to unite the developing countries in defense of their rights, which have been denied by the big industrial powers and the international monopolies. As was the case in other recent organizations of this type, the task has not been easy and there have been great obstacles. OPEC was received with scarcely disguised hostility by the big oil companies. United States and British displomacy sought to undermine the organization in the Middle East, trying to convince governments on which they could exert influence to abandon OPEC. There have been fights and internal rivalries within the organization and there will undoubtedly be more in the future. However, the survival of OPEC during the six years since its establishment show how these few countries which are oil producers—Venezuela and those of the Middle East and North Africa—

clearly understand the value of their oil wealth and that they can obtain a fair share of it only through coordinated defensive action.

The oil policy of our democratic Venezuelan governments since 1959 has been bitterly opposed by various groups, individuals, and periodicals. It has been attacked with aggressive intemperance by sectors ranging from the communists to the most stubborn reactionaries. The pupils of Moscow, under the tutelage of Fidel Castro for a number of years, accused us of following a "surrender" policy. The reactionaries—some just to fight against us, and others because of their more or less hidden connection with the oil companies—fired at us from different angles. They claim that we were guilty of almost anti-patriotic crime in raising the oil taxes; in founding the state company, the CVP; in joining with the Arabs to form the defensive bastion of the OPEC; in refusing to continue the sale of what remained of the oil lands in the country by the colonialist concession system. The companies, these horrified Cassandras clamored in prophetic tones, were going to leave Venezuela, pack up their baggage, and install themselves in more peaceful areas rich in oil where foreign capital was welcomed without any demands—the Arab and North African states.

The artifical structure of this argument collapsed dramatically on June 5, 1967, when the Arab-Israeli war broke out. This conflict demonstrated the risky nature of oil production in the Middle East and North Africa. Venezuela continued to be the basic supplier for the west and offered the most stable conditions. A brief recital of what happened before, during, and after the Six Day War, and a summary of the role that oil played and continues to play in the ongoing crisis of the Middle East, will confirm the assertion just made.

Petroleum: Hero and Villain of the Arab-Israeli War

On May 27, 1967, Egyptian troops closed the Straits of Teheran and blocked Israeli shipping from the Gulf of Aqaba and use of the port of Elath. Israel brought in oil supplies through this port for its industry, mechanized agriculture, and domestic consumption. Its foreign trade passed through the Gulf of Aqaba to reach the Red Sea. The Israeli government stated officially that this was an act of war. There was a brief period of negotiation and hope that these efforts would fail. Israel attacked the Egyptian and Syrian-Jordanian fronts simultaneously on June 5, with the results that everyone knows.

Petroleum—whether god or devil—then made its appearance. It had been an underlying factor in previous conflicts in the Middle East; now it was clearly involved. The Arabs who possessed enormous reservoirs of this precious natural resource made use of it for the first time as a weapon against the Israelis, striking with it against the United States and England, those countries considered the best allies of the enemy. The importance of this strategy will be appreciated if it is understood to what degree Middle East and African oil supplied the powerful industrial and war machines of western Europe. These countries consume 8.5 million barrels of oil daily. More than half of this comes from the Arab and North African countries. Great Britain is even more dependent, since it gets 66 percent of the oil it needs from them. Understanding this, the Arab governments decided that a boycott of oil shipments to the United States and England would be one of their best ways to get back at the Anglo-Saxons for the aid which they claimed had been given to Israel during the "lightning war."

In addition to this measure, there was the belligerent attitude taken toward the Anglo-Americans by two other Arab countries of the north of Africa—Algeria and Libya. The Algerians were producing 33.8 million tons of oil per year and Libya 72.3 million tons. These two North African Arab countires joined with their brothers of blood and religion in a holy war against the so-called tripartite aggressors: Israel, the United States, and Britain.

Another problem that faced the oil companies who supplied liquid fuels to western Europe was the explosive internal situation in Nigeria. This country shipped 20.7 million tons of oil annually to Europe. It was now engulfed in a furious civil war. The zone of this country where the most important oil fields and refineries were located had declared itself independent of the federal government and called itself the Republic of Biafra. This dissident regime insisted that taxes on the oil produced within its territory be paid to it rather than to the federal government, putting the companies and the governments which protected them in a most difficult situation.

The industrial nations of western Europe were thus gravely concerned when the war broke out in 1967. England had reserves for some five months, if rationing were applied; a similar situation or worse existed in other European states. The United States was confronted with the reduction of the 100,000 barrels of oil it had been buying daily in Saudi Arabia which it needed for the new war in Vietnam. Substitute oil could only be supplied by long costly maritime routes.

It was felt that despite the hate revealed in their denunciations, the Arabs would not be able to maintain the boycott against the Anglo-Americans for very long, nor would Egypt be able to keep the Suez Canal closed. Actually, by December 1967, oil production had been renewed, but the Suez Canal continues to be closed. Egypt received Bs. 1 billion yearly for transit rights from the canal and continues to sacrifice this income. Iraq received half of its budgetary needs from oil; Saudi Arabia, 88 percent, Kuwait, 92 percent. They are countries that hang by a single thread—petroleum—insofar as income is concerned. These countries recevied Bs. 11.5 billion in oil taxes in 1966. Without this income the desert would take over again in this inhospitable region in which water and natural resources other than oil are so scarce. Algeria and Libya have a similar dependence upon petroleum, although the Algerians do have other export products. In the case of Nigeria, the cruel civil war there gave rise to little optimism regarding its ability at any time in the future to maintain, let alone raise, its oil production. This helps to explain why oil operations were begun again in Egypt, Kuwait, and Saudi Arabia.

The tense relations between the state and the companies in the Middle East and North Africa were underlined again on June 18, 1967, when the foreign ministers of the Arab League met in Kuwait. Egypt, Syria, Algeria, and the Sudan all urged a total boycott of oil shipments to the West. They argued that the boycott against the United States, Great Britain, and Israel alone was an incomplete measure and it would not be possible to control the final destination of the product. Saudi Arabia was bitterly criticized for having allowed the Aramco Company to begin its operations again. There were other divergencies but the common agreement to retaliate against the Anglo-Americans and to use the oil companies which originated in these countries as hostages was renewed.

The perspectives for the big international oil companies, therefore, were not very tranquil nor comforting in this part of the world. In the west, there was speculation as to whether the claim made by President Nasser and King Hussein that United States and British military planes had cooperated in the bombardment of Egypt and Jordan was true or false. The Arabs did not doubt the truth of this statement. On May 26, 1967, the Arab Oil Workers' International urged: "When the battle begins, all oil wells and all oil installations should be destroyed." This radical threat was not carried out, but the situation of the oil companies during the days of the Arab-Israeli War was very difficult and the future was highly uncertain for them.

The authoritative, well-informed newspaper, *The Times* of London, in an editorial of June 9, 1967, recounted the anxiety caused among the oil companies and the governments of the United States and England. The violent riots in Syria obliged the companies to evacuate most of their personnel. The Saudi Arabian refinery and terminal at Ras Tanura were closed by the workers. The Kuwait government sent troops to protect the installations of the Kuwait Oil Company even before hostilities broke out. Infuriated mobs sacked the installations of Aramco in Saudi Arabia. Iraq stopped its production, not only as a retaliation against the West, but also because Syria had closed the pipeline carrying the oil through its territory, just as it did during the Suez crisis of 1956. Lebanon closed the pipelines crossing its country also. Weeks after the war was over, Arab nationalists dynamited and destroyed two giant tankers of Standard Oil in Aden, destroying their cargos of crude oil.

The influential London newspaper cited above predicted that the oil companies were going to face some very difficult times in the Arab countries following Israeli military victory. They would have to face greatly magnified public resentment and their dealings with the government would be much more difficult. There would be even greater difficulties with future governments, because those of Iraq, Kuwait, Libya, and, to a lesser extent Saudi Arabia, might possibly be overthrown. "Under the circumstances," wrote *The Times*, "the classical political expedient is to demonstrate true Arab virtue by throwing out the western oil companies."

The London organ warned that one of the first consequences for the companies of the war would be an increase in pressure to give their host countries a greater share of their income. Such a process might even go so far, it added, as it did in Egypt where all the oil companies in the country were expropriated in 1956 after the Suez crisis. Thereafter, the Nasser government signed service contracts with Phillips and Pan-American Oil. It was foreseen that Iraq would implement the so-called Law 80, which provides for the expropriation of 50 percent of the concessions belonging to the Iraq Petroleum Company. *The Times* concluded by affirming that "it will be very difficult for American or British companies to obtain future oil concessions in the Arab world."

Anticipating this, countries with sufficiently strong economies and technical expertise are getting ready to pour money and experts into the oil camps of the Middle East and North Africa. Italy, Germany, Japan, France, and even Spain are savoring the possibilities which may open up to them in the future. This may help to explain the "hands-off" policy taken by France during the recent Arab-Israeli war despite the phrase of General De Gaulle: "Israel, our friend and our ally," or the very visible polarization of French public opinion in favor of Israel. The motive for this enthusiastic "Arabism" of the French president became clear before the end of 1967. On November 23, amid an atmosphere of mystery, a Franco-Iraqi oil agreement was signed. When the fact became known, Iraq insisted repeatedly that it was a service contract, not a concession, because the latter was "colonial" in nature. Thus the very words and ideas of Venezuelan nationalists were echoed thousands of miles away!

The French state-controlled ELF group signed the agreement with the Iraqi government. Its terms are worth noting because they reveal that goals such as those of our own CVP can be achieved on the basis of service contracts. It was stipulated that ELF would carry out exploration in potential oil zones where no oil had yet been found in the name of the Iraqi state company. The exploratory work would go on until 1973—six years—when ELF would return the areas to Iraqi operation. If oil was found, ELF would produce it for a twenty year period, giving half the crude to Iraq. Five years after the beginning of production, the actual operation would be put completely in Iraqi hands, with the French acting as advisors. ELF paid Iraq Fr. 75 million for initial exploratory rights.

This agreement stunned the international oil world. Shell, British Petroleum, and the North American Esso-Mobil group, which together with ELF formed the Iraq Petroleum Company, accused their French partner of unfair procedures because they had not been included in the accord. The moral for Venezuela: service contracts—with special advantages for the producing nations—are not only acceptable to the big oil companies but they will compete for them.

Another determining and very important factor in Middle Eastern instability is the policy of Soviet Russia, which actively engages in maneuvers there to promote conflicts and stimulate chaos. In this respect, Joseph Stalin and those who succeeded him in the Kremlin took over the oil policy of the czars lock, stock, and barrel—considering the Middle East a "natural" zone for Russian expansion.

The Russians are playing various games in the area. On the one hand, they seek to discredit North Americans and the English even more than they have already been hurt by their own conduct in the area. Then, in competition with their Arab "allies," they aggressively seek to sell Soviet gas and oil in western European markets. They are not fully successful in this because their own needs are great and they must also supply the needs of the so-called popular democracies of eastern Europe.

On June 16, 1967, the *Financial Times* of London reported that the Soviet Union was aggressively trying to sell oil in western Europe, seeking to take advantage of the Arab oil embargo. It mentioned that various European importers, including the British, had received quotations, even though Great Britain had traditionally refused oil trade with Russia. Now, however, the big English industrialists were urging the government to change its policy and the newspaper said the Labor government of Harold Wilson had an "open mind" on the subject. If the British were doing business with Cuba despite the boycott imposed by the Organization of American States, why not buy oil from Russia? "Business is business."

Russia had also been discussing the sale of large amounts of natural gas to Italy. It was to be brought in a projected pipeline to be constructed from the Urals to Trieste on the Adriatic. Austria and France were to get supplies from branches of this line. Switzerland and other European countries also received Russian offers and there was a report published by the semiofficial Spanish news agency, although later denied by *Izvestia* in Moscow, that the Spanish official oil monopoly had received offers of Russian oil for a large part of Franco Spain's necessities.

Even though the Spanish story was denied by the Russian press—still under rigid censorship fifty years after the Soviet regime was established—it is a fact that Russian oil had been reaching Spain. CIFRA, the Spanish news agency, reported the arrival of specific tankers bringing Russian oil to Spanish ports and there is no reason to doubt that 500,000 tons of Black Sea oil was shipped annually as the agency originally reported. "La Pasionaria," the Spanish communist heroine in Moscow, and the rest of the Hispanic old red guard, can pontificate all they want to against Franco from the Russian or Czech radio; the Spanish government's firing squads can riddle the body of Grimau, the underground communist leader in that country, but meanwhile, diplomatic soundings between Moscow and Madrid multiply and the renewal of formal relations between the two countries is imminent and Russian oil is supplying Spanish state refineries. The Russians are rushing through the breach opened by the Arab oil embargo to pull a commercial coup. This is all for their own nationalistic political-economic interest—not just to weaken the international oil companies, as a French commentator suggested in *Le Monde*.

When its double game was discovered—professing love for the Arab cause and at the same time sabotaging the oil boycott against the West—the Russian government pulled back; on June 21, 1967, the Russian press reported that the offers of oil to England, Belgium, Norway, and Switzerland had been withdrawn for the time being. This was just a pause in the Soviet oil offensive to save face with the Arabs. Actually, Russian oil exports increased by 13.7 percent in 1966, reaching some 50 million tons. About 17 percent of this went to western countries.

Turmoil in the Arab World Has Been Favorable for Venezuelan Oil

The name of Venezuela was very prominent in the headlines as a result of the Arab-Israeli conflict—both before, during, and after the Six Day War. As an oil source, it became of prime importance to modern industrial production. With Arab and North African crude excluded from the west for a time, the major military powers turned to the 16.2 billion barrels of proved reserves in Venezuela. Actually, there is much more. The companies, in evaluating their oil reserves, used the most conservative geophysical methods to calculate them. Drilling can now be undertaken, reaching to the deepest zones, and the hundreds of thousands of idle hectares under concession to the companies must be explored.

It was predicted that Venezuelan production would increase in 1967 by 6 percent, a reasonable figure. We did not repeat the costly error of the tremendous jumps in production that took place at the time of the first Suez crisis in 1956 and the following years. This was avoided because the big oil company headquarters in New York and London no longer made such decisions by themselves. Since 1959 Venezuela had something to say about production policy and made its voice heard.

Venezuelan production increased before the Six Day War, during it, and later. These changes are shown in the following table:

Increases in Venezuelan Oil Production Because of the
Arab-Israeli Conflict
(Barrels per Day)

a) May 27–June 5, 1967	3,364,844
b) June 6–June 15, 1967	3,529,167
Increase:	
Absolute (in bbls.)	164,323
Percentage	4.9
a) June 1–June 15, 1967	3,462,971
b) June 1–June 15, 1966	3,293,427
Increase:	
Absolute (in bbls.)	169,544
Percentage	5.1

By December 1967, production reached the high figures of 3,800,000 barrels daily. All of this confirmed what U.S. Defense Secretary McNamara had said—that the crisis could be overcome if production was increased by the United States, Canada, and Venezuela. Nobody talked any longer about Caribbean oil reserves. The only country of the Caribbean—or of all of Latin America—where sizable spare capacity existed was Venezuela. Possible production increases in Canada and the United States are conditioned by three factors: the very high rate of demand in both countries; their high production costs—double those of Venezuela and triple those of the Middle East; and the conservation policies of both Canada and the United States, which make them reluctant to increase production. There is no need to consider Mexico, as it consumes all the oil it can produce. What is the lesson of all this? *As a new demonstration it was used to the utmost by Venezuela to support its campaign against the offensive restrictions on imports of our oil—that Venezuela is the only nation which can assure a continued secure supply of liquid fuel to the United States and western Europe both in peacetime and in war.*

The great importance of the Middle East and North Africa as large oil exporters, however, had also been made clear. The Venezuelan strategy of getting together with them (to structure OPEC and our global strategy to defend the prices of our basic export product) had been fully justified. The OPEC example was followed by others. In June 1967, four major copper producers met at Lusaka, the capital of Zambia. Chile, Peru, Zambia, and the Congo produce 2.5 million tons annually—three-fourths of the copper consumed in the western world. The idea was to organize an international group similar to OPEC to stabilize prices and regulate the production of copper.

The Arab-Israeli war also served to demonstrate that it was sheer nonsense —put out by those trying to intimidate our country—to believe that the oil companies would leave Venezuela if the government did not give up its nationalistic oil policy. Not only were their investments far too large for them to pull out, but they also knew that they had a hot potato on their hands in the Middle East. It burned their hands then, but ultimately it could burn their oil wells and refineries. *Venezuela was the only producing country—and the leading oil exporter—where conditions of real political stability and social peace, guaranteeing continuity and security in oil supply, existed.*

The greatest lesson we derived from the Arab-Israeli confrontation was that *the difficulties faced by the oil companies in the Middle East give greater value and justification to the patriotic decisions of our democratic governments after 1959 not to offer new concessions and to establish the Venezuelan Oil Corporation (CVP).* As a result of these events, nearly any newspaper reader or television viewer became aware of the strategic value of Venezuelan oil. If we had given out new oil concessions at bargain prices, we would have killed—or at least left with very little life—the promising gosling hatched from "the goose that lays the golden eggs," to use the suggestive language of Senator Arturo Uslar Pietri. Now we had additional evidence at hand to support our claim that

Venezuela—by the formula of service contracts—could obtain much more income for the country than was possible under the concession system. Today and tomorrow, we could not only get a higher financial return but we also—and this is of greater importance—share responsibility in planning the work program and general policy of the oil companies with regard to their unexplored and unproduced concessions. The CVP has already initiated active state participation in exploration, production, and marketing of crude oil and various oil products. Another very important role awaited it—that of representing the state in the novel mechanism established to administer service contracts.

To recapitulate and summarize, three conlusions can be drawn with respect to Venezuela from the lamentable armed struggle between Israelis and Arabs—so costly in lives and human suffering. These are:

1) Venezuelan oil is a key factor in assuring western industrial production and military security;

2) This event provided the Venezuelan government with new negotiating strength in its trade relations with the United States and the oil consortia established in their country;

3) The facts, the very stubborn facts, as the British would say, demonstrate that Venezuela's oil policy after 1959 was neither capricious nor inconsistent, but was realistically planned and applied in a flexible but irreversible manner, and followed patriotic and nationalistic principles.

Berne, Switzerland, December, 1967.

References

PROLOGUE TO THE SECOND EDITION

1 *Venezuela Independiente, 1810–1960*, Fundación Eugenio Mendoza, n. 275.

CHAPTER ONE

1 *L'Economie Pétrolière*, p. 144.
2 *America Conquers Britain*, p. 259.
3 *Fortune*, February 1949, p. 178.
4 *Petroleum in Venezuela: A History*, Berkeley, Calif.: University of California Press, 1954, p. 20.
5 *Petroleum in Venezuela*, p. 22.
6 Ibid.
7 *Recopilación de Sentencias del Tribunal de Responsabilidad Civil y Administrativa*, Imprenta Nacional, 1946, Vol. II, p. 184.
8 *Petroleum in Venezuela.*
9 *Recopilación de Sentencias . . .*, Vol. I, pp. 250–56.
10 Ibid., pp. 103–06.
11 Ibid., pp. 144–45.
12 *Petroleum in Venezuela*, p. 36.
13 *Recopilación de Sentencias*, Vol. III, pp. 270 ff.
14 *Petroleum in Venezuela*, p. 38.
15 "Dirección Administrativa y de Comercio del Ministerio de Fomento," Oficio No. 610, Boletín del Ministerio de Fomento, No. 6, p. 548.
16 MacDermond, *Who's Who in Venezuela*, p. 127.
17 *We Fight for Oil*, p. 116.
18 *The Secret War: The War for Oil*, London, 1927.
19 *We Fight for Oil*, p. 114.
20 Memoria del Ministerio de Agricultura y Cría al Congreso Nacional de Venezuela, 1936.

CHAPTER TWO

1 *El Universal*, Caracas, March 2, 1936.
2 *Fortune*, March, 1939.
3 *Latin American Politics and Government*, New York: Thomas Y. Crowell Company, 1949, p. 418.

CHAPTER THREE

1 *Acción Democrática*, no. 14, April 19, 1942.
2 *Aquí Está*, June 2, 1943.
3 *Acción Democrática*, no. 15, April 25, 1942.
4 *Acción Democrática*, no. 38, October 3, 1942.
5 *Acción Democrática*, no. 130, October 20, 1944.
6 *Acción Democrática*, no. 54, January 30, 1943.
7 *Acción Democrática*, no. 50, December 23, 1942.
8 *Acción Democrática*, no. 57, February 20, 1943.
9 *Petroleum in Venezuela*, p. 94.
10 *The Memoirs of Cordell Hull*, New York: Macmillan, 1948, Vol. II, p. 1511.
11 *Petroleum in Venezuela*, p. 96.
12 *Annual Report*, 1945, pp. 51 and 77–78.
13 *Acción Democrática*, no. 78, July 24, 1944.
14 *Annual Report of the Ministry of Production*, 1942, Director of Industry and Commerce, p. 104.
15 *El País*, November 1943.
16 *El País*, January 29, 1944.
17 *Latin American Politics and Government*, p. 42.
18 *La Verdad Inedita*, p. 50.
19 Ibid., pp. 127 and 152.
20 Ibid., p. 132.
21 *Trayectoria Democrática de Una Revolución*, Imprenta Nacional, Caracas, 1948, p. 324.
22 *Latin American Politics and Government*, p. 142.
23 "Roots of the Revolution in Latin America," in *Foreign Affairs*, January 1949, p. 281.
24 *La Verdad Inedita*, p. 146.
25 *The States of Latin America*, New York: Alfred A. Knopf, 1952, p. 101.
26 *Hombres y Sucesos de Venezuela*, p. 36.
27 *El País*, Caracas, January 12, 1946.
28 *El Gráfico*, Caracas, October 18, 1948.

CHAPTER FOUR

1 *Trayectoria Democrática de Una Revolución*, Imprenta Nacional, p. 335.
2 *Latin American Politics and Government*, p. 430.
3 *Trayectoria Democrática de Una Revolución*, p. 289.
4 *Washington Post*, December 17, 1947.

CHAPTER FIVE

1 *Fortune*, March 1939.

2 *Venezuela Vista por Ojos Extranjeros*, Report of the Fox Technical Mission, with a Critical Prologue by Rómulo Betancourt, Editorial Magisterio, Caracas 1942.
3 *El País*, Caracas, January 25, 1944.
4 *Petroleum Production Economics*, New York: McGraw-Hill Book Company.
5 "Informe de la Comisión de Fomento al Congreso Nacional," *Gaceta del Congreso de los Estados Unidos de Venezuela*, no. 18, Caracas, October 29, 1948, p. 986.
6 *Gaceta del Congreso de los Estados Unidos de Venezuela*, p. 1035.
7 *Petroleum in Venezuela*, p. 103.
8 *Foreign Oil and the Free World*. New York: McGraw-Hill Book Company, 1954.
9 *Hechos y Tendencias Pecientes de la Económica Venezolana*, 1950.
10 *Gaceta del Congreso de los Estados Unidos de Venezuela*, no. 18, October 1948, p. 1078.
11 *El País*, Caracas, April 8, 1947.
12 *El País*, Caracas, February 7, 1948.

CHAPTER SEVEN

1 *Trayectoria Democrática de Una Revolución*, p. 112.

CHAPTER NINE

1 Laureano Vallenilla Lanz, *Cesarismo Democrático*, Caracas, 1929, p. 158.
2 Institute of Inter-American Affairs, *Agricultura Development in Venezuela*, Washington, 1948, p. 8.

CHAPTER TEN

1 *Trayectoria Democrática de Una Revolución*, Vol. 2, p. 202.

CHAPTER SIXTEEN

1 Article 25 of the "American Declaration on the Rights and Duties of Man," approved at the Ninth Inter-American Conference at Bogotá, 1948.
2 *Time*, February 28, 1955.
3 *Sumario del Juicio Seguido a las Personas Indiciadas de Haber Cometido el Asesianto del Coronel Carlos Delgado Chalbaud, Presidente de la Junta Militar de Gobierno*, Official edition of the Office of National Publications of the Ministry of Interior, Caracas, 1951.

CHAPTER SEVENTEEN

1 Statement of Pérez Jiménez, *Time*, February 28, 1955.

CHAPTER TWENTY

1 *The Economist*, London, December 11, 1952.
2 *New York Times*, December 4, 1952.
3 *New York Times*, October 12, 1955.
4 *Venezuela: Oil Transforms a Nation*, Office of Public Affairs, Department of State, February, 1953.

CHAPTER TWENTY-ONE

1 *Time*, December 13, 1954.

CHAPTER TWENTY-TWO

1 *Washington Post* and *Times Herald*, March 24, 1955.
2 *Time*, September 21, 1953, p. 44.
3 Op. cit.
4 Op. cit.
5 *Business Week*, January 9, 1954, p. 116.
6 *New York Times*, December 18, 1953.
7 *The International Petroleum Cartel*, Washington, D.C., 1952, p. 167.

CHAPTER TWENTY-THREE

1 Karl Mannheim, *Liberty and Social Planning*, pp. 52–53.

Index